SENATOR LEAHY

SENATOR LEAHY

A LIFE IN SCENES **PHILIP BARUTH**

UNIVERSITY PRESS OF NEW ENGLAND   *Hanover and London*

University Press of New England

www.upne.com

© 2017 Philip Baruth

All rights reserved

Manufactured in the United States of America

Designed by Richard Hendel

Typeset in Utopia, Klavika, and Industry types
by Passumpsic Publishing

For permission to reproduce any of the material in
this book, contact Permissions, University Press of
New England, One Court Street, Suite 250, Lebanon NH
03766; or visit www.upne.com

Library of Congress Cataloging-in-Publication Data
NAMES: Baruth, Philip E. (Philip Edward), author.
TITLE: Senator Leahy: a life in scenes / Philip Baruth.
DESCRIPTION: Hanover: University Press of New England,
    2017. | Includes bibliographical references and index.
IDENTIFIERS: LCCN 2016038489 (print) | LCCN 2016047574
    (ebook) | ISBN 9781512600568 (cloth: alk. paper) |
    ISBN 9781512600575 (epub, mobi & pdf)
SUBJECTS: LCSH: Leahy, Patrick J. | Legislators—United
    States—Biography. | United States. Congress. Senate
    —Biography. | United States—Politics and government
    —1989- | United States—Politics and government—1945-
    1989. | Vermont—Biography.
CLASSIFICATION: LCC E840.8.L365 B37 2017 (print) |
    LCC E840.8.L365 (ebook) | DC 328.73/092 [B]—dc23
LC record available at https://lccn.loc.gov/2016038489

5 4 3 2 1

This book is dedicated to Beau

CONTENTS

ACKNOWLEDGMENTS

Among the many people who contributed to this biography, let me first list my wife, Annika, who gave me Sunday mornings free and clear to write—and who bought me the miniature recorder I used over the last five years to interview a host of Vermonters with intimate knowledge of Leahy's career. All those interview subjects deserve thanks, but particularly Senator Pat Leahy and his wife Marcelle, the late Marselis Parsons, Chris Graff, Carolyn Dwyer, Toby Knox and Brian Harwood, David Schaefer, Paul Bruhn, Ed Pagano, Garrison Nelson, Luke Albee, Mary Leahy, Chief Judge Beryl Howell, US Marshal David Demag, Governor Phil Hoff, Candace Page, Senator Gary Hart, and filmmaker Dorothy Tod.

One interviewee I feel I should mention even though our meeting never actually occurred. Richard Mallary, Leahy's opponent in the watershed Senate election of 1974, died just days before our scheduled interview—but we spoke by phone for thirty minutes or so, and I immediately understood him to be as gracious as my research had indicated.

And one photographer must be thanked in a paragraph of his own. The 1974 race really came alive for me when I discovered that Sandy Milens, Leahy's campaign photographer back then, lived just a few blocks from my home—and that he still had in his possession hundreds of photos from the period. This book showcases only a few of the most dramatic and illustrative, but looking through his complete archive was one of the most delightful moments of my research. And Sandy could not have been more generous in sharing his work with me, and you the reader.

David Carle and John Goodrow were of great help in providing information and background from Leahy's Senate offices. Julian Smith, a promising filmmaker and my project intern for several years, contributed greatly to the chapter involving Leahy's work with 1970s murder cases.

The exceptional research librarians at UVM's Bailey/Howe Library provided countless hours of assistance, as I combed through microfilm and Special Collections archives. The Vermont State Library and Saint Michael's College Library both deserve mention as well.

I owe large institutional debts to my college and to my department at the University of Vermont. From the dean of arts and sciences I received both sabbatical time to write and funds to help defray photo permission costs; my chair, Professor Val Rohy, helped in a hundred small ways to allow the writing to go forward. My friend Tony Magistrale provided in-dispensable wisdom, as always.

Finally, my thanks to my editor, Richard Pult, for green-lighting this book and for being the sort of editor who can lose himself with equal ease in political discussion or comic book trivia. And to my copy editor, Glenn Novak, for his sharp and careful eye.

Thank you all.

PROLOGUE

It is Monday, October 15, 2001, just after ten o'clock in the morning. Outside the tall office windows, it's a clear day and only comparatively cool after a broiling summer in the nation's capital. Fall sunlight pours into the air-conditioned suite. Off to one side of a large polished conference table, a young woman sits carefully in a chair. Rather than simply poised, she seems deliberately frozen, actively working to avoid motion.

The young woman wears a dark gray skirt and smart black shoes, the sort of stylish yet sober outfit a new intern might wear in order to err just slightly on the side of formality. In this, she looks not unlike a thousand other twenty-something newcomers to the administrative corridors of Washington, DC, interns who form the largest and outermost of several concentric rings around those in positions of authentic power. An intelligent air, square chin, pretty shoulder-length brown hair carefully highlighted and brushed. Presentable, determined, capable.[1]

Yet she is locked now in an undeniably strange attitude: bent over a stack of assorted mail balanced in her lap, holding a short envelope in both hands down near the black shoes, arms fully outstretched. Looking very closely, an observer might see that in addition to merely holding the envelope, she is also pinching shut a slit in its flap.

The intern's name is Grant Leslie, and she is clearly making an effort to breathe shallowly, taking only small necessary sips of air, her hazel eyes wide.

The chair is located on the sixth floor of the Hart Senate Office Building, in a work space deeded to Majority Leader Tom Daschle. At the center of the space is the long conference table heaped with envelopes; a terrorism false alarm the previous Friday has Daschle's in-house operation hopelessly backed up, so much so that several of the interns tasked with sorting can't fit around the table and have been working from their laps in chairs a few feet away.

Scattered across Leslie's lap and shoes—and standing out vividly against the dark colors there—is an extremely fine powder. Light enough for a trace to seem white, the powder has a uniformly tan caste where more of it remains pooled together. Leslie's first thought upon seeing it was that it must be baby powder, but it is clearly of another order altogether. When she cut an inch or so into the taped envelope containing it, just a moment ago, the powder seemed almost to rush out into the room, as though under its own motive force.

The powder has climbed into the air above her as well, where enough of it now hangs to be dimly visible, like a thin white smoke in the last stages of dissipation. But it doesn't actually dissipate; the constituent particles, having sought the air, hold it. If anything, they seem still to be climbing slightly rather than descending. It is as if the particles themselves have acquired the power of flight.

The well-cleaned conference room has now taken on a distinct musty scent, a nose-crinkling tang of mold and mildew.

Leslie has been told repeatedly not to move and not to worry by those who have gone for help. And she well knows from her staffer training that this powder dusting her lap is in all likelihood a hoax, as are the vast majority of such letters. But there are pressing causes for worry, as well. The room in which Leslie sits is just a scant few miles across the Potomac from the Pentagon, itself devastated by the terrorist crash of a Boeing 757 just over a month ago, on September 11.

Just ten days previously, a photo editor for the Florida-based supermarket tabloid the *Sun*, a man named Robert Stevens, died from inhalational anthrax. Originally and inaccurately attributed to infected drinking water, Stevens's death has within the last forty-eight hours begun to be linked with a series of other far-flung anthrax incidents at media outlets in Florida and New York as one of the "hallmarks of a terrorist attack."

And yesterday, the *Guardian*'s Sunday edition didn't stop at reporting the Boca Raton and New York incidents as terrorism—it revealed that the Bush administration has already leapt far, far down the road to a more or less inevitable conclusion: "American investigators probing anthrax outbreaks in Florida and New York believe they have all the hallmarks of a terrorist attack—and have named Iraq as prime suspect as the source of the deadly spores. . . . Contact has already been made with an Iraqi opposition group based in London with a view to installing its members as a future government in Baghdad."[2]

In another moment, a knot of four policemen will enter the room and ask Leslie to place the letter on the floor where some of the powder has settled. She will immediately do everything they ask: allow herself to be placed in a holding room separate from the other interns; permit doctors to swab the remote reaches of her nasal cavity; give up the carefully selected outfit she wore to work that day for laboratory analysis. But even as she does so, even as she remains remarkably calm to observers, there is a part of her that knows something is wildly wrong.

"I didn't really have that much faith in what was going on," she will later say of the procedures undertaken and the assurances offered by the Capitol Police and physicians. "Everything was so frantic when it happened. I sort of felt like nothing during the entire process was really under control."[3]

For one thing, none of the four Capitol Police officers who finally enter the room are wearing protective gear of any sort; only later will a team in hazmat suits continue the analysis. For another, that hazmat team's instincts will run counter to Leslie's—they will entirely unseal the letter Leslie has been desperately pinching shut, further contaminating the Senate majority leader's work space, and unfold a photocopied letter found within.[4]

They will then read the letter aloud, loud enough for Leslie to hear in the isolated office to which she has been relegated: "YOU CAN NOT STOP US. WE HAVE THIS ANTHRAX. YOU DIE NOW. ARE YOU AFRAID? DEATH TO AMERICA. DEATH TO ISRAEL. ALLAH IS GREAT."

★ ★ ★

The truth is that federal authorities would severely underestimate the power of the Daschle anthrax at every turn. Officials first thought that sealing off Daschle's office would be sufficient; when testing showed that the spores had spread far beyond that limit, they would expand the protective bubble first to the sixth floor, then to the southeastern quadrant of the Hart Building, before eventually shutting down all of Hart—and then, in rapid succession, the Rayburn, Longworth, and Cannon Buildings. Finally, the House of Representatives itself was closed at the order of Speaker Dennis Hastert for three days of environmental scanning.

For that reason and others, the FBI's "Amerithrax" investigation would stretch on for nearly a decade, and in so doing it would only extend a long, twisting series of miscalculations and underassessments tracing back to the very moment that Leslie Grant picked up her letter opener, expecting a whimsical note from the fourth graders at the Greendale School in Franklin Park, New Jersey.

But one call the investigators got absolutely right.

The CDC determined, by studying patterns of infection and tracing potential maps of cross-contamination in the government mail system, that there might well be at least one more anthrax letter mailed to Capitol

Hill in addition to the Daschle letter. All government mail had been impounded in the forty-eight hours following the attack on Daschle's office, and workers in protective suits had spent weeks sifting through 280 fifty-five-gallon barrels of it in a remote location.

In mid-November, they finally turned up precisely what they were looking for: a still-sealed second letter, this one addressed to Senate Judiciary Committee chairman Patrick Leahy of Vermont, containing approximately 0.85 grams of the same powder Grant Leslie had discovered.

The Leahy letter was every bit as inscrutable—the same cryptic message, the same false return address. But about one thing there was no mistake. The anthrax in the Leahy letter could also fly, under what amounted to its own surreal power, and it was every bit as deadly.

★ ★ ★

It is Friday, November 16, 2001, a little before six in the evening. Pat Leahy pulls his cell phone from his shirt pocket to see his caller identified as Robert Mueller, director of the FBI. He blinks at it, then lifts an eyebrow.

His brow furrows as he scrutinizes the screen, but he is not immediately concerned; as chair of Senate Judiciary, he checks in with Mueller on a fairly regular basis. He punches the call-back button.

At age sixty-one, the chairman from Vermont stands an even six-four, broad-shouldered and fit enough to fill out the dark power-suits he prefers; the bald head is large and undeniably magisterial, lent additional force by snowy eyebrows that tend to tilt up slightly, skeptically at the edges. The quirk of nature that left Patrick Leahy legally blind in one eye has caused him also to squint a good deal through his rimless eyeglasses —especially in the bright lights that mark television studios and Senate committee rooms—and that squint is easily mistaken for severity, displeasure, gathering wrath.

This squint of concentration marks his face now, but almost immediately it deepens into genuine worry as Mueller comes straight to the point—a letter almost identical to the Daschle letter has been discovered in one of the barrels of confiscated mail, this one addressed in childlike block letters to Leahy. It appears as though the letter never crossed the threshold of Leahy's Senate offices because of an apparent misreading of the zip code, but the investigators can't be certain.

And so they'll be closing the Russell Building at 4 p.m. the next day.

And Leahy will be assigned a twenty-four-hour Secret Service detail for the foreseeable future.

Although Leahy seems genetically designed to fill out the imposing public profile of Senate Judiciary chairman, he never fails to strike strangers as sunnier and more prone to edgy humor than his physical appearance would otherwise indicate. He is a man of continually surprising and only seemingly contradictory dimensions: one of the longest-serving members of the Senate, an acknowledged powerhouse as chair of Judiciary and a member of Appropriations, a hardened criminal prosecutor, and yet a lifelong fan of the Grateful Dead and the most sensational comic books, with impressive credits acting and narrating in various iterations of the Batman franchise.

It is the gallows humor that surfaces now, as Mueller pauses carefully to see how the news is being digested. "Bob," Leahy rasps finally, "you know I'm always happy to take your calls, but could you try to find something a little more cheerful to call about next time?"[5]

Mueller laughs, then dives back into the inevitable details.

Leahy is now pacing the floor, and while a part of his mind is stunned at having been personally targeted, this isn't the first time, of course. As a state's attorney during the late '60s and early '70s—a period that saw a pronounced spike in murders and violent crime in Chittenden County, Vermont—Leahy received more than one death threat, and from individuals later freed from custody. In the late '90s he was prominently listed in blood-red letters on a radical antiabortion website called Christiangallery, a site that crossed off the names of listees once they had been assassinated (the abortion provider Dr. Barnett Slepian met precisely that fate in 1998). Leahy has lived most of his adult life with the knowledge that a disturbed individual could fixate on him, seek him out in public, appear out of nowhere.

Still, this is the first such credible threat for some years, and this one is backed with an honest-to-God weapon, an unprecedented weapon now undeniably at work in the world outside his home and office. An invisible breathable microscopic spore that might yet lead to the death of innocent staff or workers who cross paths with it. Or to Leahy's own death, for that matter.

"Chilling" and "haunting" are the words Leahy will use to describe the feeling later to reporters, but he pushes those feelings away as Mueller runs through the points he needs to make.

Still, as he listens, Leahy's mind can't help processing deeper logistical implications. This call means a return to the rootless wandering days of the previous month, when the Daschle letter briefly closed the Russell Building along with the Hart and others, and Senate staffers worked from closets and nearby Starbucks outlets for weeks. That was in fact where they had written most of the final version of the Patriot Act—in hide-aways and borrowed offices and alcoves in the Capitol.

And of course, this call means a stunning loss of privacy for Leahy and the members of his family, at least for the immediate future. As his family comes fully to mind, Leahy realizes with an additional jolt that he'll have to miss Thanksgiving at his family farm in Middlesex, Vermont—a place he and his wife have long called Drawbridge Farm, for its peacefulness and sense of sanctuary. Given the need to monitor and assist the investigation in DC, in fact, he'll be lucky to make it home for Christmas.

But there's not a thing to be done about it.

And so, when he and Mueller have said their good-byes and planned a face-to-face meeting the next day, Leahy sits down at his couch and proceeds in a first-things-first fashion: he calls each member of his family, his wife Marcelle first.

Marcelle's voice is immediately suffused with fear, and Leahy tells her not to worry, knowing that his own voice is not entirely free from it. Their marriage and political partnership have been extraordinarily tight, even in a world where spouses often work as teams. The phrase "Marcelle and I" is so common in Leahy's speech that for Vermonters of a certain age, the couple has come over the decades to seem a joint personality. He delivers the news about the twenty-four-hour security detail—bad news in the long run, but comforting just now—and they say a quick good-bye.

As during the September 11 attacks just weeks ago, Marcelle agrees to stay at their McLean residence and handle the phones once the news hits and the frantic calls from family and Vermont friends begin.

After his family, Leahy begins to run down through the members of his staff, top to bottom, so that they will hear the news from him personally. One of those first calls goes through to his chief of staff, Luke Albee. It is quick, with a promise to check in more fully later.

"There's an anthrax letter addressed to me," Leahy says by way of introduction. "It's going to be on the news in ten minutes. But I wanted you to hear it from me."

★ ★ ★

Albee hangs up with the feeling that the other shoe has finally dropped. He has had a lingering, disquieting intuition of threat for months now, even prior to the discovery of the Daschle letter, and this inkling has now been entirely borne out. Albee has both engineered and applauded his boss's emergence as the top Democratic antagonist of the new Bush administration, but even as Leahy has engaged the neoconservatives in the White House on issue after issue, his chief of staff has also felt something like a distant car alarm sounding at the very edge of his consciousness.

Interviewed about the incident more than a decade after the fact, Albee is still occasionally at a loss for words about that feeling. "In my head it was—Senator Leahy was a *target*. He was a target then, for the political opposition, because he was already in the bull's-eye due to the judge stuff [opposition to Bush's conservative judicial nominees]. Then he was saying slow down, we're not going to throw two hundred years of liberty out the window in a heartbeat [in writing the USA Patriot Act]. Leahy had a national profile before that, but now he had a very *particular* national profile.

"I thought it was a right-wing extremist doing this. And right-wing commentators had really noticed Leahy for the first time. Leahy had really became a target then for the opposition."

He runs his hands through the silver hair at his temples and searches for the proper metaphor, and then suddenly he has it. "He was on their *screen*."[6]

Introduction

LEAHY, MEDIA, ANTHRAX, BATMAN

If—as Euclidean geometry maintains—just two points determine a unique line, then the discovery of a second anthrax target highly placed in the US government should have provided key information about the anonymous attacker's motivations or frame of reference. And the discovery of the Leahy letter did touch off a frenzy of activity within the FBI, with agents attempting to trace individuals who might have specific reason to hold grudges against both senators simultaneously.

But while the Leahy letter gave rise to a certain amount of speculation in the public sphere, it was of a curiously muddled and muted sort. Commentators in the mainstream media did not seem willing to look beyond the obvious fact that both men were highly placed senators, noting only in passing that both were Democrats.

After observing a week of such cautious coverage, *Salon*'s Anthony York charged that the media as a whole were tiptoeing around the obvious—"the fact that the anthrax letters were sent to Democratic leaders and the media, groups that right-wing extremists tend to have a grudge against."[1]

York's deduction wasn't unique—Washington and media insiders had immediately reached similar provisional theories—but it was uniquely audible. Given the sharply polarized nature of American political discourse, it was difficult to avoid the conclusion that the mailer saw him- or herself on the other end of the spectrum from Daschle and Leahy (and the putatively liberal media)—a conservative red stater attacking liberal blue staters, to reduce the equation to its lowest common denominator.

But beyond that elemental theory, the twisted logic behind Leahy's targeting remained elusive. Patrick Leahy was not, after all, second to Tom Daschle in Senate leadership, a position then held by Harry Reid of Nevada. He was not in leadership at all. Nor was he the most outspokenly liberal member of the body—Russ Feingold actually recorded the only Senate vote against the Patriot Act, for instance. Ted Kennedy had long been considered the liberal lion of the Senate, but Kennedy himself was not targeted.[2] Leahy was a powerful committee chairman, true, but only one of many such (Robert Byrd, at eighty-three, was both chair of Appropriations and the Senate president pro tem, and therefore third in line for the presidency).

Time magazine finally puzzled it out this way, five days after York threw down his gauntlet: "While Daschle, the Senate majority leader, could have been chosen as a representative of all Democrats or of the entire Senate, Leahy is a less obvious choice, most likely targeted for a specific reason. . . . Targeting Leahy seems to give more credence to the theory that the anthrax culprit is a domestic terrorist with personal grudges."[3]

A "specific reason," a "personal grudge"—fair enough, but that line of thinking left one with less in the way of results, really, than the countervailing assumption that Leahy was simply another representatively powerful senator.

But when looked at from a certain angle, Senator Patrick Leahy presented as clear and tempting a target as the institution's most powerful member. Leahy had been a Washington power player for decades, wielding great influence through the Judiciary, Appropriations, and Agriculture committees. In 2001, he was the Senate's third-most-senior member, having served Vermont since 1974. As the chair of Senate Judiciary, he was the gatekeeper for high-profile judicial nominations, up to and including the Supreme Court; he was the go-to senator as well for changes, large and small, in the federal criminal justice system, particularly when it came to enhancing or curtailing the government's power to conduct surveillance over its citizens.

In this last regard, Leahy had loomed particularly large since September 11, as the Bush administration attempted not simply to fast-track but to openly rush the gargantuan Patriot Act through Congress. In the aftermath of 9/11, Leahy was just reaching the apex of his fabulously long congressional career, inarguably high-profile, powerful across a broad spectrum of the Senate's activities, and an increasingly regular fixture on the Sunday morning political shows.

More to the point, Leahy was one of very few powerful Democrats willing to directly oppose what would come to be called the War on Terror, as it rapidly came together in the confused days following the attacks on New York and the Pentagon. If the attacker had been seeking the Democrat just below Daschle in collective senatorial power at that precise moment, Leahy made a certain solid intuitive sense.

To Chief of Staff Luke Albee, in fact, Leahy made even *more* sense as a target than the Senate majority leader, because Leahy was "public enemy number one" in the right-wing talk radio world, partly because "Daschle hadn't quite emerged yet."[4] Leahy *had* emerged, Albee suggests, and it is the nature of that emergence that promises the most insight into the mystery.

The question bluntly posed in the title of York's *Salon* piece — "Why Daschle and Leahy?" — broke down almost immediately into a follow-on question even more intricate and opaque: Why, when it came right down to it, Patrick Joseph Leahy?

It was not the first time the conjoined political and media worlds had asked this particular question, and it would not be the last. It was first posed in 1974, when Leahy, then a thirty-three-year-old state's attorney and a relative unknown statewide, announced that he would challenge Vermont's incumbent Republican congressman for an open Senate seat that had been firmly in the GOP's grasp for the last 118 years.

It would be asked again, more urgently, when the dust settled, with Leahy miraculously holding on to a 4,406-vote lead over the anointed Republican.

And the media would ask it again in 2008, curiously enough, when Warner Bros. suddenly announced a Leahy cameo — not merely a walk-on but a speaking appearance — in the next installment of director Christopher Nolan's acclaimed *Dark Knight* trilogy.

New York magazine immediately demanded to know, "What Is Senator Patrick Leahy Doing in 'The Dark Knight'?" For its part, Warner Bros. offered no particularly enlightening answer: "Other than the fact that Leahy's apparently a comic-book fan . . . Warner Bros. publicity representatives had no knowledge of any special connections between director Christopher Nolan and the current chairman of the Senate Judiciary Committee, though maybe they're just playing their cards close to the vest."[5]

Three distinct moments in time, three distinctly puzzling questions.

Why was Pat Leahy the first — and still technically the only — Democrat ever elected to the Senate from the state of Vermont? Why was he specifically targeted in 2001 with the most lethal bioweapon ever detected? And why would Leahy appear in not one, but a string of Batman films, recordings, and comic books, over a span of some two decades?

All three questions present themselves as more or less rhetorical and unanswerable, but each is clearly susceptible to solution, given information enough and time. And while recognizing the radically differing levels of urgency attaching to each, it will be my contention throughout this book that each of these questions ultimately brushes up against the others. Their answers are not and cannot be the same, of course, but in some surprising ways they are part of the same broad, thematic discussion.

How and why does Pat Leahy *emerge*, to borrow Albee's phrase, and what are the implications of that emergence within a post-9/11 environment grown increasingly, relentlessly, bitterly partisan?

It is the purpose of this biography to unfold that discussion, even as it documents the life and work of the gravel-voiced chairman whose forty-plus years in Washington have helped reshape and redefine the modern United States Senate, a man until recently just third in the line of succession to the presidency itself.[6]

There is a productive connection to be made between Leahy, media, anthrax, and Batman, that is to say, if we are willing to take what seems a very modest leap of late-postmodern faith: accepting that the media and political worlds are not now and never have been entirely distinct entities, and that the lurid DC and Marvel comic book universes are finally indivisible from our own.

A modest leap, indeed.

Of course, given the astonishing capabilities of the bioweapon with which Leahy was targeted in 2001 — a weapon that seemed to have aerosolized directly off the pages of a graphic novel — we actually have very little choice in the matter.

★ ★ ★

Leahy's immersion in popular culture, particularly the Batman franchise, has been much trumpeted by the media, but very little analyzed and even less understood. Every new Batman role has ignited a sunburst of whimsical publicity, almost all of it in the form of puns and puffs couched tediously in Robin-speak. (In 2008, the *New York Times* ran with "Holy Cameo, Batman! It's a Senator!" while Vermont's *Rutland Herald*, thesaurus at the ready, slugged its own puff piece "Holy Solon, Batman!"[7])

Inevitably, Leahy's bit parts are portrayed as a joyful sort of dilettantism, a harmless sentimentality for the comic books of his youth, and this determined (lack of) interpretation Leahy himself has encouraged by pairing the film openings with readings for children at Montpelier's Kellogg-Hubbard Library, where Leahy read as a kid, and to which he now generously donates all appearance fees and royalties from the films.

And of course Leahy's delight in the world of the Hollywood blockbuster *does* derive in part from sentimentality, and it *is* a relic of his Rockwell-ready childhood spent reading Batman comics in Montpelier, at least on one level.

But to see Leahy's durable presence in the Batman narrative as the result of *only* these elements—as accidental or beside the political point—is to fail to grasp one of the most basic principles by which Patrick Leahy functions, and has always functioned, ever since his quixotic 1974 challenge of an incumbent Republican congressman for a Senate seat that had never once in history gone Democratic.

Leahy's entire career has been painstakingly built around not simply the crucial daily work of the prosecutor and the Judiciary Committee chairman, but also and always the accompanying trope of the crime fighter, the powerful crusader for order and public safety—what Paul Bruhn, manager of the '74 Senate campaign, would eventually come to call the Top Cop image.

As a Chittenden County state's attorney, Leahy had learned the ins and outs of prosecuting the worst that the state's most populous county had to offer; as a dark-horse candidate for the US Senate eight years later, he managed, with the help of a savvy young campaign team, to diffuse that Top Cop image throughout the totality of Vermont's truncated media landscape, in ways that confounded his opponents and radically distended the technological boundaries of the moment.

But more than any other single element, it would be a professional campaign film that would finally put Leahy over the top in '74—a thirty-minute documentary that showcased the young state's attorney and his Vermont roots, all the while drawing subtly on the popular crime dramas of the day.

Director Dorothy Tod called it "the Leahy Walton film," an affectionate comparison to CBS's long-running family drama *The Waltons*—and an acknowledgment of its careful yet lavish deployment of sentimentality. Leahy himself would inevitably refer to the film project as "the blockbuster," and he counted on it as his final firewall in an election he seemed doomed, even in the final days, to lose.

In a very real sense, Tod's "blockbuster" helped make Pat Leahy the powerful Washington icon he is today.

That other blockbusters of varied genre might later enhance that stature Leahy seems to have guessed at very early on; but that a specific connection to the Batman narrative could dramatically ink and color the outlines of his prosecutor's image—that popular culture could in fact undergird and drive political culture—Leahy recognized immediately as a self-evident sociological fact. Leahy was the first Democrat ever elected to the US Senate from Vermont, in other words, not solely because he was a skilled professional with a very strong track record in criminal justice, although that he absolutely was, but also because he was more than willing to be actively constructed as a hero—to be the top cop not merely in the street-level reality of Chittenden County, but also in the greater evolving imaginary of post-Watergate Vermont.

The Batman credits and pop cultural cred are not and never have been merely a lark, or a whimsical overlay to an otherwise very serious career. Rather, these elements—from the Batman cameos to the high-profile Senate hearings to the walk-on appearances at Grateful Dead shows to the Sunday morning show ubiquity—have always been tangible, active components of a highly successful political image drawn simultaneously from high, low, and popular cultures. This confluence Leahy achieves half-consciously, as has been his wont from the beginning; but when one looks at his life in totality, the signature approach is impossible to miss, especially in contrast to politicians more traditional, less adaptable.

Dick Mallary, his front-running GOP opponent in 1974, was clearly stunned by Leahy's deft and aggressive media push. But more generally, Mallary was put off by the increasingly intimate reach of campaign coverage itself, and by the power of the media to drive campaigns, rather than vice versa. "It was clear that the kind of campaign evolving in Vermont —that was so media-heavy—was not a place where Dick Mallary was at ease," says Candace Page, a senior *Burlington Free Press* reporter who covered Vermont's first post-Watergate election.[8]

Not so for the dark horse who surged past him in the final days of the race. Even in the early 1970s, Leahy knew deep down that this coming new world was undeniably for him, this intensely public sparring and self-fashioning, this immersion in and dispersal through media. Evolution is only achieved by mutation, and in this case it was as though Leahy had been born with an uncanny, prehensile grip on broadcast technologies that most politicians still handled only clumsily and occasionally.

While no one has ever accused Pat Leahy of Kennedy-style looks, the truth is that—in terms of sheer media savvy—Leahy brought Kennedy-style politics to Vermont.[9] And not surprisingly, it was in part a stunning televised debate that would help Leahy eventually loosen the GOP's stranglehold on Vermont's US Senate seats.

Political scientist Garrison Nelson sees it as no accident that Leahy was "the first politician post–World War II to win statewide office without going through Montpelier" or climbing the traditional statewide ladder. "Patrick grasped the role of media before anyone," Nelson says. "Print journalism in Vermont focused heavily on lawmakers in Montpelier. But he knew that Channel 3 could beam him statewide every night, and in the competition between print journalism and broadcast, who wins? Broadcast wins."[10]

Leahy's nickname for the '74 campaign film captures at once his politician's shrewd grasp of the "box office" power there, but also his utterly ingenuous love of the medium itself, of the movies and the heroes that animate them. It was (and remains today) a uniquely populist and anti-elitist ethic. Leahy has always evinced a characteristically postmodern joy in transgressing and obliterating such boundaries.

For Leahy, then, as early as 1974, it was not simply that the medium was the message, but that *all* mediums—all genres, all multifarious forms of the same crime-fighting leitmotif—were the message. And this force-multiplication has helped to make him one of the most popular senators in the country, and arguably the most powerful lawmaker Vermonters have ever sent to Washington.[11]

It is a lifelong approach that has enabled Leahy to adapt smoothly over the decades, to ride out Vermont's own relatively rapid transformation from quintessential red state to swing state to its position currently among the most consistently Democratic of the blue states (Vermont was called for Obama seventeen minutes after the polls closed in 2008, and just four minutes after in 2012[12]). And it helped to position Leahy, in the aftermath of 9/11 and the all-but-unprecedented political and policy overreach of the Bush administration, as a de facto alternative to the tough-talking Texan in the White House. This biography centers quite purposefully on those years, when the small rural state of Vermont suddenly emerged as the home of something like a shadow administration, and arguably the wintertime refuge of civil liberties in the United States of America.

It's worth noting that 9/11 marks a dramatic turn in American box office as well. The year 2001—when novelist Michael Chabon won a Pulitzer Prize for his comic-themed *Amazing Adventures of Kavalier and Klay*—signals the triumph of the comic-book adaptation in Hollywood.

Of the twenty-five all-time top-grossing comic adaptations, twenty-four have been released post-9/11, and all but one feature superheroes battling supervillains for twenty-first-century America.[13]

That the Global War on Terror would be prosecuted alongside DC and Marvel's wars on everything else isn't so surprising; comic book superheroes were originally born in the angst of World Wars I and II, and they have always provided the clarity and psychic release that goes missing in a real world involved in real wars.

Given that synergy, it's also not surprising that the political and comic book worlds would occasionally cross-pollinate. For Pat Leahy to face down the Joker in 2008's runaway blockbuster smash, even momentarily, makes excellent sense for Pat Leahy the politician, as suggested earlier.

His single line of bravado in *The Dark Knight* (2008) reached an estimated one hundred million people worldwide, and it was a line that campaign manager Paul Bruhn would have killed for during the 1974 Senate campaign: "We're not intimidated by *thugs*."

But of course, the benefits did not all accrue to Leahy. There was a potent narrative symbiosis at work. Leahy's cameo lent the film something undeniably powerful that it would otherwise have lacked — a touchstone to an *actual* crazed domestic terrorist still very much at large, the man the FBI had taken to calling the Amerithrax killer.

Leahy was the perfect person for his role, in short, because he was the one actor available who had actually been targeted by an actual supervillain — and emerged unscathed.

★ ★ ★

Of course, no politician, no matter how prodigious, comes to master forces on so titanic a scale without incident — and here Disney's *Fantasia* (1940) might be the better touchstone. If Leahy's intuitive grasp of media has made him the vastly powerful figure he is today, it is also telling that his most damaging political missteps have stemmed from failed attempts to manipulate or control the flow of those same media. Vermont's senior senator, like Goethe's sorcerer's apprentice, has suffered the most painfully over the years from spells of his own casting.[14]

Far and away the most damaging of these incidents involves the leaking of a Senate Intelligence Committee draft report in 1987. The report concerned the byzantine Iran-Contra weapons deal, and the committee had narrowly voted against releasing it. But the report surfaced anyway in a series of NBC News stories, all citing a "reliable, confidential source."

Speculation as to why the report was leaked ran rampant. Some thought that a Republican source had put it out, in the belief that the draft exonerated President Reagan; others found the early version of the report devastating for the administration, and thought a Democrat must be behind the leak.[15]

But eventually Patrick Leahy was more or less definitively fingered. (It turned out that the copy of the report used by NBC had the word "declassified" written in the corner of the title page—and "when copies of the report were recalled after the panel voted not to release it, Leahy's was the one with that word on it."[16]) Faced with the prospect of being publicly outed, Leahy privately agreed to resign from the Senate Intelligence Committee six months before he was already scheduled to do so.

Six months later, though, under pressure from a new CBS investigation into the private resignation and a still-confidential ethics finding, Leahy offered a carefully tailored admission: that he had "carelessly" left the report on a desk where a reporter in the room might see it, and he had resigned because "nobody is more annoyed at me than me."[17]

A statement from Leahy's office took this positioning one puzzling step further, indicating that he had resigned because it was an apt expression of his own "anger"—allowing Leahy to share somehow in the general anger at the act to which he himself was now admitting. The national press thought the move too cute by half, and then some.[18]

The Vermont press in particular was outraged by what it saw as tap-dancing around questions of basic honesty and accountability. Chris Graff, then Vermont bureau chief for the Associated Press, describes the growing backlash in his own news-themed memoir, *Dateline Vermont*: "At first, for example, in an interview with me he admitted only that he had shown the reporter 'a couple of unclassified pages' to prove that the committee wasn't holding back the report for political reasons. . . . But Leahy conceded later that he had allowed the reporter to take the report from the building for several hours without putting any restrictions on use."[19]

On the heels of these continuing revelations, the late summer of 1987 was a scorcher for Leahy back home. A week after the first national news reports, he held a press conference on the leaked intelligence document that may well have been the most brutal of any in his long career. The Vermont reporters felt triply burned—that they had been first kept in the dark and then scooped by the Washington media, and that they were still being fed half-truths even at that late date.

Finally, Leahy bowed to the onslaught, but still noticeably clinging to the caveat that the leak was accidental: "I was incredibly careless, and I apologize for that," he said at a tense Burlington news conference in which reporters heatedly questioned his version of events. "I have paid a high price," he said. "It is very embarrassing. It has been of concern to me and my family, and I am sorry for them. That is a price, and it bothers me very much."[20]

The timing of the incident was fortuitous in just one way—Leahy had won reelection the previous November and now had five long years before he would face the voters again. He had time to absorb the bitter lessons and to apply them resolutely thereafter. But the moment would leave a scar across Leahy's long-standing relationships with the members of the Vermont press corps. Worse, it would provide an easy, mocking handle for increasingly influential right-wing talk-radio personalities like Rush Limbaugh, who would refer to Vermont's Democratic senator as "Leaky Leahy" forever after.

And Limbaugh's burgeoning red-state radio audience—listeners who styled themselves "dittoheads" for their reflexive agreement with the host's outspoken views—gleefully followed suit.

★ ★ ★

In *Nixonland* (2008), biographer Rick Perlstein captures a certain signature schizophrenia that has characterized America since the early 1970s, a condition that Richard Nixon did not himself cause but certainly exacerbated and exploited:

> It is the America where two separate and irreconcilable sets of apocalyptic fears coexist in the minds of two separate and irreconcilable groups of Americans. The first group, enemies of Richard Nixon, are the spiritual heirs of [Adlai] Stevenson and [John Kenneth] Galbraith. They take it as an axiom that if Richard Nixon and the values associated with him triumph, America itself might *end*. The second group is made up of the people who wrote those telegrams begging Dwight D. Eisenhower to keep their hero on the 1952 Republican ticket. They believe, as did Nixon, that if the *enemies* of Richard Nixon triumph— the Alger Hisses and Helen Gahagan Douglases, the Herblocks and hippies, the George McGoverns and all the rest—America might end. . . . "Nixonland" is what happens when these two groups try to occupy a country together.[21]

If Perlstein is correct, we should expect that what we now know as the red and blue Americas would continue to clarify their stances politically, post-Watergate, and that eventually the opposed sides would simply *stop* trying to occupy a country together—and move slowly but spectacularly to war with one another. A post-9/11 Nixonland, as adapted for the screen by Marvel Comics.

Certainly the opening years of the twenty-first century provide a wealth of supporting evidence. As Limbaugh's audience was growing and purifying itself ideologically, so too was Vermont becoming bluer and bluer. In point of fact, the George W. Bush years see a certain style of sustained critique-and-response from Vermont that might best be thought of as a shadow administration, so outsize was its effect and so far-ranging and sustained its critique.

Consider that it is Vermont senator Jim Jeffords who single-handedly wrests control of the Senate from the GOP and delivers it into the hands of Tom Daschle in May 2001. It's difficult at this remove to re-create the electrical charge with which that event crackled, but it was as though America's bicameral political brain had suffered *petit mal*.

Trent Lott angrily dubbed it a "coup of one." Leahy's office, almost immediately the office of the chair of Senate Judiciary, printed up cheeky bumper stickers reading, "Don't Mess with Vermont."[22]

Jeffords saw the political phenomenon at hand with perfect clarity, as the final pages of his *My Declaration of Independence* make clear: "The two political parties are undergoing an ideological purification," he laments, "which I regret having contributed to. It has been under way for decades, at least since the Johnson Administration in the 1960's. The ranks of moderate Republicans have shrunk bit by bit, almost to a last redoubt in New England."[23]

Of course, neither Jeffords nor Leahy was the state's most outspoken and aggressive critic of George W. Bush. That distinction belongs to Vermont governor Howard Dean, whose breakthrough line—"I'm Howard Dean, and I'm here to represent the Democratic wing of the Democratic Party!"—also typifies the state's movement from a mere tint of blue to what was then the nation's deepest shade of that color.

Dean rode his sharp critique of Bush's adventurism in the Middle East to front-runner status in the 2004 Democratic primaries, before seeing his campaign derail spectacularly following his third-place finish in Iowa. But the former governor's unexpected surge—particularly the way in which his campaign demonstrated that the Internet and small donors could directly power a liberal response to administration policy—continued to focus the eyes of the nation on Vermont.[24] (And of course that gaze would return almost compulsively, midway through the following decade, with the stunning outsider presidential campaign of Senator Bernie Sanders, whose critique of Wall Street and *Citizens United* took him much further than Dean, though not quite as far as the White House itself.)

For much of the first decades of the twenty-first century, then, Vermont stood in equipoise with George W. Bush's red Texas as the de facto capital of blue America.[25]

And the president of the United States acted accordingly. Suffice it to note that George W. Bush methodically visited forty-nine of the fifty states over the course of his two terms as president, and just as methodically left office without once setting foot in the Green Mountain State. (Which was just as well: Vermont was the one state of fifty in which local voters had formally called for issuing a warrant for Bush's arrest, "for crimes against our Constitution."[26])

And while no single act of Leahy's has yet produced a media shock wave to rival Jeffords's "short walk across the aisle" or Dean's foundational fund-raising miracle, it was Leahy who provided the most consistent, productive, long-term counterbalance to Bush administration overreach.

It's interesting that two successive chiefs of staff to Leahy now independently reach for remarkably similar metaphors in describing their principal's position with regard to the conservative establishment and press: he was "on their screen," in Luke Albee's phrase, and "in their viewfinder," as Ed Pagano remembers it.[27] Both metaphors implicitly acknowledge Leahy's deft, sustained use of media, as well as the danger that can come with sitting exposed, and occasionally alone, in the spotlight. In addition to his powerful chairmanship, then, Leahy had his own Senate-size bully pulpit, and during the first years of this century he used it to outsize effect.

Long after Americans had forgotten the Jeffords switch or the Dean scream, it was Pat Leahy they saw lighting into the president and his people on the Sunday morning political shows, Pat Leahy whose high-profile Judiciary Committee hearings would eventually force the resignation of Bush's attorney general, Alberto Gonzales. Pat Leahy whom Vice President Cheney would infamously and revealingly F-bomb on the floor of the United States Senate.

Cheney's open vulgarity in 2004 was revealing not because he would later double down when asked if he regretted cursing in the Senate chamber, where the vice president is technically the presiding officer. No, the moment was revealing because for all its initial shock value, it had a surprisingly predictable quality. What else was America expecting, really? In the relentlessly binary politics of a twenty-first-century Nixonland, the Top Cop of blue America automatically becomes public enemy number one of its red antagonist, and vice versa. Cable news stokes and balances this antagonism in real time, moment to moment, on a twenty-four-hour basis. Is it any wonder, then, that Bush White House insiders would come to refer to Vermont's senior senator, in the us-versus-them days following 9/11, as "Osama Bin Leahy"?[28]

Only in the Marvel and DC Comics universes—where the advent of any powerful new hero acts to call forth a perfectly matched supervillain —do we see anything even remotely similar.

★ ★ ★

The subtitle of this book, "A Life in Scenes," bears a moment's explanation. As much as anything, the phrase is meant to reference Leahy's media-savvy positioning over the course of his impressive Senate career; beyond that, it suggests for me the multiple ways in which Leahy has actively sought to blend Hollywood convention (and American popular culture more generally) with his own emerging political myth.

Finally, the phrase should also suggest a certain dramatic concision. Leahy's Senate career now verges on five decades, and if any reader comes to this biography in search of a comprehensive history of his important committee work or votes cast, he or she will be bitterly disappointed. On that score, a much better book than mine remains to be written. Instead, I have contented myself here with telling a sequence of targeted stories, a chronological selection meant to capture most of the eventful life of my subject, but also to cast light on a larger argument about the America we inhabit now, more than half a century after the rise of Perlstein's Nixonland.

For that reason, this volume leans heavily on Leahy's response to the presidency of George W. Bush, at the expense of his years as a less influential journeyman senator. No offense intended to quiet committee rooms or arcane amendments—I myself have spent a good deal of time in the former trying diligently to pass the latter. But the life of Patrick Leahy is replete with powerful, dramatic, sensational moments—and I have allowed myself the luxury throughout of simply jump-cutting from one to the next.

I find it hard to believe that the average reader—or the myth-making subject of this biography himself—would have it any other way.

Leahy Begins

The Origin Story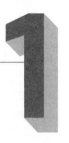

In one very literal sense, Patrick Joseph Leahy had a Norman Rockwell Vermont childhood. In the early summer of 1940—the very year of Leahy's Montpelier birth—the famed illustrator Norman Rockwell abruptly relocated his small family from New Rochelle, New York, to the smaller, sleepier community of Arlington, Vermont. New Rochelle had been rocked by the high-profile kidnapping and beheading of a twelve-year-old boy, son of a prominent Manhattan attorney, and the unbelievable viciousness of the act helped spur the Rockwells to finally make their Vermont summer home a permanent residence.

"The Rockwells felt that their sons would receive the bucolic, innocent childhood Rockwell himself idolized as every boy's ideal," writes biographer Laura Claridge, "and the personalities of the Vermonters lent themselves, the artist believed, to opening a whole new panoply of models to him."[1]

Rockwell saw 1940s Vermont as most closely approximating the idealized world that had become his own signature, and in that unusual sense, he quite deliberately selected the boyhood that lay ahead of Pat Leahy for his own three sons. It's worth noting, too, as Claridge does, that the artist came seeking not only the reality of Vermont's innocence, but a steady stream of models with which to more elaborately (and lucratively) construct the national myth of it.

Very much like Rockwell's, Leahy's story would increasingly intermingle the real-life savor of small-town Vermont with a celebrity dependent on conjuring the vivid impression of that sweetness in the minds of others. From the very beginning of Patrick Leahy's long and productive political life, then, Vermont myth and reality would never truly be in competition, but rather in something much richer and more complex, something that can finally only be called *cahoots*.

★ ★ ★

Consider, for instance, what the boy saw looming directly across Montpelier's State Street each morning, when he left for his early paper route. It was then and remains now the most distinctive single postcard image in Vermont: the golden dome, one of the nation's oldest continually functioning statehouses, the dome covering its impressive rotunda gleaming with twenty-three-karat gold leaf. It would be enough to rivet the ambition of any child, but particularly one whose parents talked politics relentlessly at the supper table each and every night.

And in the autumn especially, with a boa of red and orange maples strung lavishly about it, the Statehouse was not simply the seat of state power, and the family business's bread and butter—it was also heartbreakingly beautiful, civic devotion made a lovely, solid, permanent thing.

Now consider that view from Leahy's side of State Street, and close one eye. The left one.

Always tall and gangly for his age, Pat Leahy had more than the one good reason to be physically awkward: he was also born legally blind in his left eye, a fact that he has managed to keep relatively quiet over the bulk of his political life. The diagnosis was congenital toxoplasmosis, an infection produced by the *Toxoplasma gondii* parasite and passed unknowingly from his mother at birth.[2] The parasite reproduces only in cats (with litter boxes being the most common site of infection), and Alba Leahy—like many of those afflicted—apparently experienced no symptoms.

But although Leahy's sight was severely affected, doctors considered the family fortunate that both eyes were not compromised. Still, the boy's monocular field of vision was from the outset significantly smaller than normal, and almost entirely lacking in stereopsis, the perception of depth. Leahy has little to no peripheral vision to this day, but he compensated as he grew by swiveling his head more from side to side to increase that visual field. The tilting, rolling mannerism carried just a trace of bashfulness, and with his thick glasses and unusual early height, it all combined for the pleasant impression of a gentle giant.

But these same factors also made it very easy to stumble, growing up, and very hard to coordinate hand to eye. Leahy became a physically deliberate boy, slower in his walk than most kids his age, careful on stairs or a bicycle. He was told, many times and in many different ways over the years, that one injury to his good eye could leave him truly blind. So it was a workable handicap, but it cost him in myriad ways.

Sports—at least the popular team sports—were out.

Mary Leahy singles out the high school basketball team as something that her older brother wanted very badly, and was denied. "Saint Michael's was a tiny, tiny little school, and it had a tiny, tiny little basketball team, and because he was so tall, that would have been something he'd have loved—but he couldn't, because he just had no peripheral vision or depth vision, so a ball could come at him. So what he did was become the manager of the team, and he was very involved with that. But I always kind of felt that he wished mightily that he could be out there playing."[3]

It was a sense of rejection that would be compounded, later on, when Leahy failed a military physical and was prevented from enlisting in the armed forces. That stung him painfully, and even today—more than fifty years later—Leahy can't help but bring it up in an initial casual interview about his upbringing, can't help but re-litigate the unfairness of it all.

But of course any good origin story begins in deprivation and unfolds by way of extraordinary overcompensation. More than a few robust presidents were especially sickly children (the bull-necked Theodore Roosevelt, to name the best-known example), and more than a few superheroes began by suffering the loss of their parents, or their planets.

In the young Patrick Leahy's case the absence was visual, and the overcompensation nearly immediate. Pore over his college yearbook, Saint Michael's College's *The Shield*, and the defiant pattern almost immediately leaps out: Leahy more or less limits his activities to politics, and extracurriculars that demand exceptional eyesight. Far from avoiding the visual challenge, he made it his undergraduate calling card.

His early handiness with a gun, for instance, Leahy quickly leveraged into a spot on the varsity rifle team, where he eventually became one of the team's top sharpshooters (a fact he would later point out to the military recruiters, with no luck). And on the staff of *The Shield* itself, Leahy immediately went all in for photography, climbing the ranks to become one of the yearbook's several photography editors. He insisted on belonging—to the club or the group or the team—*because* of his sight rather than in spite of it.

Leahy's lifelong obsession with the camera, his own impressive semi-professional career in photography, properly begins here: a young kid bent on proving himself visually, who discovers that as long as he picks a game where everyone else has to close one eye too, he cannot only compete but dominate.[4]

The most famous photos taken *of* Patrick Leahy, in a career full of them, are most probably presidential bill-signing photos — Leahy standing just behind Bill Clinton or George W. Bush or Barack Obama, as they sign landmark legislation, like the Lilly Ledbetter Act or the Patriot Act. And the reason Leahy stands out in those historic photos is that he himself is usually holding a camera, focused intently down on the presidential hand moving the pen.

It's a jarring visual detail in these photos, something that somehow shouldn't be. But it's a license that successive presidents have allowed him, and with that license no one has "more blurred the line between photographer and subject," according to the *New York Times*'s admiring photography blogger James Estrin. Leahy being photographed as he himself photographs history in the making — no image could make clearer the way that Leahy has insisted on being seen as a preeminently *visual* being, one for whom sight and witness are continually offered as self-definitional.

"I'm happiest when I have my camera with me," Leahy says. "I feel something lacking when I don't."[5] And it's that lack that is most intriguing.

Over the years, Leahy has attempted to draw a bright line between himself and the more publicity-hungry breed of senator. "We have some members who would do anything to get in a picture," as he likes to put it. "I'd rather take them."[6] But the truth is richer. Leahy *knows* the eye is drawn to the man holding a camera *behind* the president, rather than those merely being beheld by the camera. He knows his hobby makes excellent newspaper copy. It has been a staple of his office's public relations for decades.

But more to the point and at the deepest level — because this is an origin story, after all — there is the lack.

And so when Leahy stands behind President Bush or President Obama, staring down through the lens of a Nikon D300, it is not simply because he's intent on capturing history, and it's not simply that he needs, as a working politician, to be seen capturing history — although both those things are true. It's also that there is still a very important part of Patrick Leahy that needs, even after all these decades, to be seen *seeing*, and seeing well.

★ ★ ★

Truth be told, the mythic overtones of Leahy's 1950s childhood are every bit as much Benjamin Franklin as Norman Rockwell. The family home, purchased in 1925, was simultaneously the family printing business — the Leahy Press occupied the entire rear section of the boxy Italianate Victorian at 136 State Street, and the Leahy boys worked most every stage of the process.

"You walked through the kitchen door and into the Leahy Press," as Leahy recounts it. "I remember coming home from school, finishing my homework and going out to the kitchen to help collate. I would run the presses. I learned to proofread."[7]

As much as anything, he seems now to remember the transition itself, that charged liminal point at which his home gave way to the foundry of the printed word: "I remember, as a little child, walking through the kitchen door to the sounds, smells, and amazing actions of a printing plant."[8]

Before his death, Leahy's father liked to say that his middle child had printer's ink in his veins, and certainly the boy came by that professional compliment honestly. It was the pre–offset printing era, with everything still done by letterpress.

And Leahy handled every machine his father had on site, from "the Chandler & Price and the Little Giant to the more sophisticated Heidelbergs." He learned the hard way to be careful with the Ludlow Typograph press because if mishandled it could actually squirt hot lead alloy directly onto a pressman, or his teenaged printer's devil. Especially tricky work, of course, for the son with only one good eye and real challenges with hand-to-eye coordination.[9]

Almost from the time they could toddle, all the Leahy children delivered print jobs to the Statehouse, where they were known and generally doted upon. In 1953, someone gave the family a barrel-chested long-haired German shepherd with the improbable name of Hans Gustav Von Lindenwald III — a dog that lived for his new thirteen-year-old master. It was not unknown for the dog to stroll blithely down the road and into the Statehouse, poking its snout into the powerful committee rooms off the central corridor. Leahy would come running behind to collect the animal, apologizing profusely, impressing lawmakers and staff with his contrition, his manners, and his prematurely adult demeanor.

Nearly every strand of Leahy's early life finally wound its way into Vermont's granite seat of state government. Teaching his younger sister to ride a bike, for instance, was an undertaking that began in the vast parking lots behind the new state office buildings, Mary Leahy recalls, before finally transforming into a giddy steeplechase through the Statehouse itself.

> We would go out in back of the state office building, which was very new, and behind it were the parking lots, so he would bring me to practice, and bring me and bring me. This was before the days of training wheels—and he'd let me go, and I'd flop right over. But then the day I could finally do it, it was just so *remarkable*, and then we both went flying up through—in those days there was this area behind the Statehouse, like a little tunnel, with legislative counsel crammed into this little building, joined by a walkway overhead, and it formed a little tunnel back there. . . . But anyway, flying through that tunnel when I could finally ride my bike, and a band would play a concert on the Statehouse lawn every week during the summer, and the whole idea was just to fly around it all as fast as you could. It was *wonderful*.[10]

And in addition to the Leahy clan invading the Statehouse, the Statehouse eventually returned the favor. Always on the edge financially, and looking to maximize the potential of their combined home-and-business, the family began the practice of renting out a room to legislators—Pat's room, to be precise.

It was a part-time arrangement, given that the Vermont legislature meets most years from early January to mid-May; but while the session lasted, Pat slept downstairs on a sofa substantially shorter than himself. He did it more or less uncomplainingly, though, his long legs hanging over the edge, and Hans the shepherd curled up protectively where his dangling arm met the hardwood floor.

It was a family in which everyone made real sacrifices to make ends meet, and occasionally those sacrifices involved more than just simple inconvenience. Hans would pine for Pat when he was away at school, and the dog defended the house against all comers—including, unfortunately, customers stopping by to pick up their print jobs from the Leahy Press. It was a tension Pat initially tried to calm by taking the dog to weekly obedience classes, but when Pat left the house for school each day, so did the dog's memory of having been trained.

The final straw came when the big animal actually lunged at a customer, right through the thin screen of the door leading to the press—and within days Hans was gone, to a nice farm out in the country, according to Howard and Alba, although Pat suspected the worst and "just became very grim."[11]

There was only one force, in fact, that rivaled state government in the Leahy household, and that was the Catholic Church. In 1974, when Leahy won his quixotic bid for the Senate from Vermont—as a thirty-four-year-old Catholic Democrat—it was a feat that appeared effectively impossible. Neither Democrats nor Catholics were elected to statewide or national office in Vermont, and certainly not a candidate unrealistic and imprudent enough to be both.

Yet the fact is that the Leahy family stood out as extraordinarily and unabashedly devout, in both its piety and in its politics. Even today, Pat Leahy relishes his late parents' iconoclasm: "The joke used to be, 'That's where Howard and Alba Leahy live. You know them. They're Montpelier's Democrats.'"

But it wasn't entirely a joke, of course, which is part of the reason why Leahy's relish persists to this day. Montpelier was the center of stalwart Protestant Republicanism, and a company town, with state government the singular business of that company. Howard Leahy's leanings were more than a bit problematic, given that he had opened his printing press catty-corner to the golden dome and had quickly become a consistent low bidder for Statehouse printing jobs. Even ballots used in the primary and general elections were increasingly issuing from Howard Leahy's presses.

From the establishment point of view, it was a lot of money to funnel to someone who clearly backed the wrong teams. A paradox for the 1950s: the Leahy Press was too useful to be ignored, and too much like a Democratic beachhead to be encouraged. And while these soft bigotries ordinarily ran well below a layer of small-town pleasantry, it is true that Leahy's father was visited at least once by a self-appointed delegation of townsmen with advice about his livelihood.

"I remember my father telling me," Mary is willing to say now, "and he only told it once, but it made a profound impression on me. . . . My father was a gentle, shy man, great sense of humor, but when he began his business a group of Montpelier businessmen came to see him. And they told him—they didn't do this with violence, they actually did it with a spirit of helpfulness, I think—they said, if you're ever going to succeed in business, in this city, you need to either change your political affiliation—he was probably the only Dem in the state of Vermont, he and my mother—or change your religious affiliation, and preferably both.

"And my father, with his quiet sweet smile, said, 'Well, I'll do neither. Thank you.'"[12]

★ ★ ★

But it was Alba Leahy, born in America to Italian parents, who knotted tight the family's ties with the Catholic Church. Alba would walk to Mass each morning, often in "the early morning freezing cold"—the car mostly reserved for Leahy Press deliveries and special occasions—and as often as not her boys John and Patrick would serve the Mass. She cooked for the priests in town on a regular basis.

"My mother was always making food and saying, *Mangia, mangia,*" as Mary remembers it. "She was always convinced they weren't eating well." When a group of young novitiates from Boston moved to Bradford, Vermont, to make headway for the church in the Connecticut River Valley, Alba sent them money as well as food. "And we didn't have a lot of money," Mary makes clear.[13]

The children were sent, of course, to the Catholic "graded school," on East State Street, at the time a more or less derelict building that the church leased from the city for a dollar a year. Given the paucity of Catholics in town, it was bare-bones arrangement. "The chunks of plaster would fall, and the nuns would have us get up and say a prayer of thanksgiving for our lives being spared again."

But derelict building or no, there was no questioning of the nuns who ran the school, ever. Mary Leahy has very clear memories of both her older brothers coming home "with torn shirts and broken glasses because the nuns, who had no restrictions on them as far as corporal punishment, would take the boys out of class—these were just little kids—and bang them against the walls of the cloakroom, where we'd hang our coats.

"You could come home bruised and battered by the nuns, and of course my parents would never go to bat for the kids . . . and they'd say, 'Well, you must have deserved it.' They weren't distant parents, and it wasn't okay with them, but they weren't going to take your side against the nuns."

It would be hard to overstate the influence that the priesthood and the sisters had on Leahy's early life. When the nuns recommended that the eldest Leahy boy, John, skip a grade, Alba immediately sought the advice of Monsignor Crosby, for whom John had served Mass on those many cold early mornings.

"No, that's not in God's plan," the Monsignor quietly ruled, and Alba

Leahy did not complain but took the verdict as a settled matter. John remained unchallenged and bored, and his behavioral problems multiplied accordingly.

When the nuns later recommended that Patrick skip the fourth grade, though, Alba experienced "an amazing bit of dissonance"—and quickly advanced her youngest boy without bothering the Monsignor with the matter. It would become something of a settled pattern in Leahy's life: charmed, rapid movement through institutions that halted or impeded others.

Without a doubt, Leahy's own connection to Catholicism has been lifelong—of the three Leahy children, Pat is now the only practicing Catholic. But his relationship with the church, so strong so early on, has had its share of late turbulence. His staunch and outspoken pro-choice tendencies have rankled successive priests and bishops, including some who took their case (and their castigation) directly to Alba.

When Leahy had married and moved out of the Montpelier house at 136 State Street, Alba took one of the town's young priests under her wing, feeding him and offering him Pat's room in the Legislature's off-season. But a few years after Leahy's election to the Senate as a pro-choice Democrat, this particular novitiate and his bishop took the liberty of writing directly to the new senator's mother, "telling her how her boy was going to go to hell because of his pro-choice beliefs."[14]

It was a disillusioning experience for Alba, one that left her "short-circuited and intensely sad." But for Leahy himself—always a ferocious defender of family, but particularly of his mother—the priest's letter was more or less a declaration of war. And once he'd seen his way clear of his first reelection to the Senate, Leahy would take that bruising fight straight to the op-ed pages of the *Washington Post*, pushing back against the early muscle-flexing of the Reagan-era Moral Majority.

Maybe only a former altar boy, a young Catholic who had attended one Saint Michael's for high school and another Saint Michael's for college, could confront the church so directly. Readers of the *Post* the morning of March 8, 1981, could not have missed the sharp note of personal injury and outrage: "During the past two years, the Catholic Church in the United States and extremely conservative Christian evangelical groups like the Moral Majority have formed a de facto political alliance. That alliance will ultimately benefit right-wing goals while diminishing many of the positive gains in justice, compassion and human dignity made with the help of the Catholic Church during the past few decades. Many of the

Catholic laity—myself included—are increasingly concerned that the church we love is being used in a dangerous way."[15]

★ ★ ★

It's not that there weren't opportunities to deviate from the straight and narrow, even in a town the size of Montpelier, with just over eighty-five hundred souls throughout the 1950s. Trouble lives in every town, large or small, and in this case it was readily available just a long stone's throw from the rear door of the Leahy house. The Winooski River meandered quietly around a long bend back there, spanned by several iron bridges, and one of those bridges in particular sheltered a hobo jungle peopled by the poor and the transient, some of whom rode in on the slow-moving cars of the Central Vermont Railway.

The Leahy kids were sternly warned away from the encampment on the other side of the river, but it held a particular sort of fascination for Pat's older brother John. Curious and exceptionally mechanically minded, John was always looking for secondhand motors and machines to repair, which he kept under his bed by day, and one way or another the men living beneath the bridge could usually put their hands on workable castoffs.

But Pat had his eyes always on a different and far more tangible prize. When he wasn't in school, or managing the basketball team, or dutifully spelling his father at the Leahy Press, he was generally holed up in a silent basement corner of the Kellogg-Hubbard Library on Main Street. There, when his schoolwork was done, he read voraciously. It was a habit developed early on—by the time he had finished third grade, he had finished the works of Robert Louis Stevenson and most of Dickens.

And, not incidentally, he had also become powerfully hooked on DC Comics, picking up the latest exploits of Superman and Batman at Donnelly's Variety on the corner of State Street for a dime an issue. The white-haired children's librarian, Mrs. Holbrook, enforced no distinctions in reading material—to *read* was the thing, and Leahy's eclectic and (now much-publicized) popular tastes developed with her blessing.[16]

And it was a crucial blessing. Montpelier had little if any television reception in the 1950s, and children gravitated perforce to the radio (the *Lone Ranger* and *Inner Sanctum*) and to fourteen-cent Saturday matinees at the Strand Theatre on Main Street (Hopalong Cassidy, Tarzan, Flash Gordon, Jungle Jim, and Batman). But the library was free, it was welcoming, and Leahy was content to move from school each day almost directly back into the embrace of another local institution that no doubt felt like a continuation of school to a majority of his classmates.

It wasn't that Pat didn't share John's restlessness, his powerful, inchoate desire to burst the bonds of State Street. On the contrary, John's younger brother was motivated by much the same impulses, and in increasingly refined ways. The difference was that, from childhood, Pat trusted the institutions in which he found himself—the church, the library, his parochial high school, government—to perform as advertised, with respect and hard work leading to steady advancement. And in his case, for the most part, reality mirrored expectation.

Pat had decided very early on that schooling itself (both institutional and autodidactic) was his ticket to a larger place in the world. He was aiming from the start for law school, because he knew one thing for certain, after years of roaming the Statehouse: a law degree was a likely skeleton key to any and all of the offices in that golden-domed temple across the street, if not the US Capitol itself.

And, of course, schooling amounted to making grades, and grades came down finally to reading, the visual, the (good) eye on the page for more hours than the next guy. That sort of contest Leahy was psychologically calibrated to win, and he well knew it. Drive and single-mindedness brought him the grades to enter Saint Michael's College, a highly ranked Catholic school in Colchester, Vermont. There he was put on the dean's list and secured his acceptance to Georgetown University Law Center, where he earned his law degree at the tender age of twenty-four, along with a prestigious fellowship offer (graciously declined). He was appointed the youngest state's attorney in Chittenden County history at age twenty-six, for essentially the same reasons that the sisters at Saint Michael's had allowed him to skip the fourth grade years before.

The Patrick Leahy who found himself fantastically and unexpectedly a US senator at age thirty-four, then, had every reason to cherish the institutions that had shaped and advanced him, because they had done so with an almost miraculous celerity.[17]

And if anything, love itself—young love, true love, love-at-first-sight love—came even more quickly. Leahy was nineteen and a junior at Saint Michael's when he and his family attended a party thrown by Dana Haskins, a family friend who also happened to be intimate with the Pomerleau family, a name increasingly prominent in Vermont real estate and development circles. It was interesting timing—the Leahys had just returned from the wedding of Leahy's older brother John. Whether watching John take his vows had predisposed Patrick to think in matrimonial terms isn't clear, but what is certain—and well-documented—is that Leahy and Marcelle "happened to be there and they happened to look at one another. And that was *it*."[18]

Marcelle was just seventeen, soft-spoken but energetic, in the first year of a three-year nursing program. And she was strikingly, even a little overwhelmingly beautiful as well: big soulful eyes beneath thin arching brows, and the facial structure for a career in modeling. But she was approachable, and quick to laugh. She found Leahy "very good looking" in his own way, but beyond the physical she was powerfully attracted to his manner, the gentleness one could immediately sense in the towering young man. "He was a very kind person," she remembers. "He was always gentle, and cognizant of other people's feelings. And I think that attracted me to him an awful lot."

Ernie Pomerleau, Marcelle's cousin, liked Patrick from the first. "He became family very early on. And the two families were always close."[19]

It would be two years before they married, but the Haskinses' party more or less decided things. Leahy's ambition and momentum were infectious; starting a family seemed the natural next step. "I think we decided almost immediately we were going to get married," as Leahy puts it. If Leahy was a man in a hurry, he had found someone who could more than match his long stride.

It would turn out to be one of the most famous matches in Vermont history. And certainly the most public: less than fifteen years later, the two would be describing this very meeting at Dana Haskins's party in a Senate campaign film designed to reach every home in Vermont, in prime time, just as the good people of the state were sitting down to dessert and a little bit of television.

And their marriage, their partnership, their affectionate voices and images, would be front and center in every campaign Leahy would ever run. Far from being put off by the intense public exposure that characterized the political approach her husband would introduce to Vermont, Marcelle found it all enlivening, exhilarating. In that crucial way, as in many others, she was truly Patrick Leahy's soul mate.

★ ★ ★

Only once as a young man did Leahy find himself on the wrong side of the law. As an upperclassman, he was arrested for hitchhiking his way from the Saint Michael's campus to Burlington's livelier downtown, and although it was a common infraction, he was finally brought before Judge Edward J. Costello at the District Court on a misdemeanor charge. Costello was famous for running a briskly efficient docket, and as the defendant was contrite, he quickly disposed of the trifling case.

But all was not quite forgotten. When Leahy was unexpectedly appointed Chittenden County state's attorney by Governor Phil Hoff in mid-1966, he arrived at the ceremony only to realize that he was to be sworn in by Judge Costello himself, who sized him up mock-sternly before proceeding.[20]

"Nice to see you on the other side of the bench for a change, Mr. Leahy," the judge finally remarked. And since it was clear that a joke was being made, the room immediately filled with polite laughter. But other than the crimson-faced new state's attorney, no one really had the slightest idea what Costello was talking about.

That night there was a double celebration at a local restaurant, honoring the outgoing state's attorney John Fitzpatrick and welcoming the new man to what everyone knew to be a drudging, thankless job.

In black-and-white photographs of the event, Leahy is seated next to Judge Costello, who contentedly chomps a cigar. Leahy looks wide-eyed, ebullient; Fitzpatrick, on the other hand, wears a shrewd, slightly jaded expression, as though he knows the punch line to a joke his replacement has yet to hear. Their long table is wreathed in cigarette and cigar smoke; highball glasses and Schlitz bottles litter the cloth.

Judge Costello's son Paul says today, looking at the faded pictures of the event, "I can't help but see this picture as a reflection of the time when the Irish came into their own in Burlington." True enough, historically speaking. Certainly it was Patrick Leahy's own coming of political age.

But it wasn't his first real trial under fire. That would come just two short months later, with the brutal murder of Robert Freeman Bishop II, a two-year-old Essex child known to the neighbors mostly by his family nickname, Beau.

The Accidental State's Attorney

One of the things you notice immediately about Leahy's inner circle is the generally impressive scale of the inhabitants. Whether by design or happenstance or both, the eight-term senator has surrounded himself with aides and staffers who mirror his own height and physical command. In fact, in any hall packed with Vermont political types, you can ordinarily pick out the Leahy people simply by glancing over the heads of the rest of the crowd.

The Leahyites have come, over time, to have the feel of a distinct evolutionary strand: uniformly fresh-faced, whip smart, and well in excess of average height, the men and the women alike. This effect is only enhanced in Leahy's downtown Burlington offices. Access is tightly controlled, and the well-appointed hallways are populated almost exclusively with Vermonters who bow their heads slightly as they move through doorways.

Leahy manages to dominate the space, even so.

And when I sit down with him for the first of many interviews for this book, in mid-August of 2011, Leahy's casual charm is on full display. He offers local cookies, and pinpoints Burlington landmarks from the large windows that overlook Lake Champlain. He shows off a striking series of photographs he took on a fact-finding mission to Tibet during the late 1980s — one of a sad young Tibetan who had secretly begged Leahy to snap his picture, only to open his coat and reveal his own secret snapshot of the Dalai Lama just before the flash.

Each story leads naturally to another: Leahy returned to his Tibetan hotel to learn that the room below his own was actually occupied by Chinese agents monitoring listening equipment; he managed to warn the rest of the traveling delegation by writing "The room is bugged" on an itinerary he passed around the next morning; and finally, when Leahy invited the Dalai Lama to his Washington offices years later, and gave him the framed original of the photo, the man wept openly.

All these stories are moving and illuminating, but they are also well rehearsed, with the layers of emotional polish that any talented politician applies over time to good raw material. So I decide to take the conversation somewhere unexpected, further back into the past, to see what surprise and spontaneity will produce.

"You were the Chittenden County state's attorney for eight years," I begin, "before the run for the Senate in 1974. What's the case that you remember most powerfully after all this time?"

Leahy stops, a bit surprised, and the white brows slowly knit. He laces his fingers carefully together, leans back in his armchair. It would be easy to mistake the concentration, the slight squint, for gathering anger. "Most powerful memory," he repeats, deliberately.

"The case that you can't help thinking back on, even at this point," I offer.

The pale blue eyes close altogether. When it comes, the deep voice is gravelly, but there is no mistaking the certainty there. "Trivento," Leahy says distinctly, eyes still shut.

★ ★ ★

It was just after 11:30 a.m., on July 11, 1966. In the otherwise vacant cytoscopy room of the Fanny Allen Hospital in Colchester, Vermont, the boy-child lay on a stretcher, covered by only a thin hospital sheet. The full name on the certificate of death would read Robert Freeman Bishop II, but police would soon learn that to his distraught mother and older brother the child had always been known simply as Beau.

Just two years old, Beau had arrived at the emergency room moments before—seemingly deceased—in the arms of his stunned babysitter, producing a small but immediate swirl of action. Patricia Flaherty, a surgical technician, was the first to sound the alarm: "I ran into the operating room and told our sister, Sister Mary Magdeline [sic], that there was a child out here and I thought the child was dead, so I ran out and she told me to get a doctor. So I ran into the doctor's room and—well, I just hollered in that I thought one of the doctors should come. There was a child that they should look at."[1]

The babysitter, a clearly panicked young man in his late twenties, in bare feet and with his shirt entirely unbuttoned, told the nurses that the child had fallen from the top bunk in the room he shared with his brother. Georgiana Adam, an operating-room technician, noted that the young man "seemed quite concerned," and that after pacing anxiously for five or ten minutes outside the examining room, "he started going down the corridor and I told him that he had better stay around the hospital so that we could get his name and everything to go on our records." With that, Adam returned to assist the examination.[2]

Within the next twenty minutes, three nurses and three doctors would all scrutinize the tiny corpse, and for very good reason. When the doctors removed the child's T-shirt and underpants—all he was wearing upon arrival—they found that the body, in addition to being "cold to the touch," was also badly bruised, from rings around the eyes to "a large black and blue area over the upper front of the body" and "a black and blue marking on the skin of the penis."

There were also deep, prominent bruises on the boy's back, including "one very close to and just above the boy's anus." Perhaps as disturbing, the examination found "tiny cuts on each eyelid."[3]

At this point the two MDs in the room—Doctors Fitzgerald and Thabault—believed they knew what they were looking at, and they called in the on-site deputy state pathologist, a Dr. Shaw. Shaw concurred almost immediately. Convinced that there was undeniable evidence of "some sort of sexual activity involved," Shaw placed a call at 11:50 a.m. to the Essex Police Department.

It was then that the doctors thought to turn their attention to the babysitter, only to find that he had disappeared from the hospital moments earlier, telling one of the nurses he needed to check on the deceased child's older brother. Unfortunately, although several hospital personnel had asked the young man for his name, no one could remember it when questioned.

And so, when the two Essex police officers arrived at the hospital some twenty minutes later, they listened to Dr. Shaw's opinion and then, sensing the gathering implications of the case, immediately placed a call to the still largely unknown Chittenden County state's attorney, Patrick Leahy.

Leahy, of course, was just twenty-six years old that July. He'd had only one class in criminal law, two years before, at Georgetown University. And he had been running the state's attorney's office for all of two months.[4]

★ ★ ★

Only a year out of Georgetown Law, Leahy had returned to Vermont in 1965 to find himself easily the "youngest lawyer in the state," due to having skipped a year in grade school.[5] He'd been the youngest in his law school class as well, but his height, his intellect, and polite demeanor — and of course his prematurely thinning hair — helped Leahy more than pass muster in legal circles.

And for an utter novice to the profession, he wasn't doing badly for himself: he had accepted a clerkship at the governor's own law firm, Black, Wilson & Hoff, making between sixty-five and seventy dollars a week. Furthermore, the senior partner was convalescing after a serious heart attack, which meant substantially more actual trial work for the newcomer to the office.

And that sort of luck, such as it was, would only intensify. In May of 1966, the sitting state's attorney for Chittenden County — a well-connected trial lawyer named Fitzpatrick — announced that he would be stepping down midterm. The state's attorney's office was more or less a one-person, part-time office at that point; the holder of the seat paid his own expenses and salaried his own secretary, if he chose to employ one. Rather than a plum, it was seen as something of a curse — a great deal of work and responsibility for very little reward or recognition.

Whatever it might be today, the office then was no stepping-stone to higher office — quite nearly the reverse, in fact. The governor would need to appoint a successor to Fitzpatrick, but it was even money that the most credible prospects would beg off.

And so when Governor Phil Hoff looked around him, his eye landed very naturally on the one young Burlington lawyer who could not reasonably say no — his own junior-most clerk. Hoff makes it clear today that the appointment also had as much to do with Leahy's parents, diehard party Democrats in a state still overwhelmingly Republican, as it did with Leahy's own qualifications: "Keep in mind that I knew his parents — he had two of the most wonderful parents. His father was a lifelong Democrat, his mother was one of the most gracious, lovable people you can imagine, and I had come to know them, so I just appointed Pat. And because I thought he was an ideal candidate, and townsperson."[6]

Of course, Hoff made then and makes no bones now about the fact that he thought he was merely hiring a caretaker, someone to hold down the fort in Chittenden County prior to the November elections. "I'm going to name you state's attorney on Monday," Hoff told a startled Leahy over the phone one weekend that May. He stressed that he wanted Leahy to clear up the backlog of cases and put out political fires. "Clean up the mess. I'm up for reelection in the fall, and I don't want people saying look at this mess in Chittenden County."

As offers go, it couldn't have been more pressing—the call was not just from the governor, but Leahy's own boss as well. Still, standing in his small Burlington apartment, Leahy felt himself hesitating. The fact of the matter was that he had almost no experience with criminal law. In fact, he had turned down a prestigious fellowship at Georgetown, one designed to make students master of the criminal courtroom, because he was certain he wouldn't need the credential in Vermont.

But Hoff didn't become the first Democratic Vermont governor in over a century by failing to appreciate a pregnant pause following a job offer, and he smoothly sweetened the deal. "Do it for a year," Hoff soothed, "and then we'd love to have you come back to the office and become a partner." Thinking back on it today, Leahy gives a sly smile and admits, "I don't know if I actually said the word 'Sweet!' but that's what I was thinking."

Still, he felt obligated to make clear that he didn't feel qualified when it came to criminal law. He protested just a bit more: "But I've been doing civil, not criminal law."

Hoff laughed and waved off the concerns, sensing that he had the candidate in the bag. "Well," he joked, "you'd better bone up on your criminal law over the weekend. Because it's a *real* mess here in Chittenden."[7]

Once duly appointed, Leahy set about modernizing and expanding the state's attorney's office. He duly worked through the backlog of cases, in court all day and then working late into the night at the State Library in Montpelier, to which he had his own key. Leahy says of these early days in the office, "I'd sit [in the State Library] and write my briefs for the Supreme Court at two or three in the morning, drive back to Burlington, get two or three hours of sleep" before waking up to try another case at eight the next morning.

It was grueling work, in relative obscurity, and Leahy had actually taken a pay cut for the honor of doing it. He won his first few cases, which gave him increasing confidence in the role of state's attorney, but niggling at him always in those first months was his relative inexperience in the criminal law. It's fair to say that he badly overworked himself as a result, checking and double-checking his approach and his work, and in that way made himself a truly superior criminal lawyer over time. But mid-1966 was a time for the occasional private doubt.

And in the summer of that year, Leahy had a strong additional reason to worry about bobbling a case: on June 13, the US Supreme Court handed down a 5–4 decision in *Miranda v. Arizona*, the landmark case that would transform the nation's arrest and interrogation practices and immortalize the phrase "*Miranda* rights."

Miranda immediately enshrined an interlocking series of suspect rights, but it would also unleash a peculiar sort of angst within the nation's law enforcement community, as officers struggled to understand the new restrictions — mishandling of which might mean, in practice, the summary overturning of their cases.

From J. Edgar Hoover on down, American law enforcement officials at all levels were just beginning what would become a years-long struggle to clarify the ruling's effects on their own internal practices. Studies conducted in the immediate aftermath of *Miranda* showed widespread confusion about the subtler implications of the requirements. "Another casualty of *Miranda* was a certain procedural orderliness in the station house which almost immediately on publication of the decision gave way to confusion. What, police asked themselves, *could* they do under *Miranda*?"[8]

One bedrock certainty was that many law enforcement officials nationwide felt that they *themselves* had been targeted by the Court, and that the decision represented at once a rebuke and a distinct threat to the average beat cop. Within weeks, anti-*Miranda* horror stories were swirling: "Stories circulated describing extreme adaptations to the *Miranda* ruling: the policeman who looked the other way when a crime was being committed, unsure of his authority now and fearful that if he made a mistake, he, rather than the suspect, would end up on trial."

Such myths began to circulate freely, station house to station house, and more studies were quickly conducted to determine whether in fact the decision actually hindered the capture, arrest, and trial of criminals. The findings of a 1966 Yale University study provided a fairly typical answer: "They reported that *Miranda*, in fact, had had little immediate impact on police practices, that law enforcement was carrying on business very much as usual."[9]

In other words, while often changing their daily practices disturbingly little, most law enforcement officials were worrying about the potential for radical change very, very much, and in the general confusion, insubstantial myths were hardening quickly into articles of faith.

For his part, Pat Leahy determined immediately that the officers in his county would fully implement *Miranda* and that he would combat misinformation directly, and personally. It would be hard to overstate Leahy's own concern with proper handling of the new procedures, once they were in place, but it bordered on the obsessive.

At his own expense, Leahy had small white cards printed up, designed to slip into an officer's wallet, outlining precise wording and order of the warnings. The idea was not an original one—other police districts were doing the same nationwide—but in other states, chiefs of police were handling the information campaign. Leahy made a point of taking matters into his own hands (or rather into his father's—the Leahy Press handled the print job for the Chittenden state's attorney). In addition to distributing *Miranda* cards, Leahy took it upon himself to lecture at local gatherings on the new procedures, speaking every few weeks to groups of law enforcement officials. The first of these events took place just a month after the Supreme Court's June ruling, on July 15, 1966. Slugged "Law Officers Hear Leahy," a tiny squib in the *Burlington Free Press* gets at the style of the meetings: "Recent US Supreme Court rulings and changes in procedure were discussed by State's Atty. Patrick J. Leahy before 40 law enforcement officers Tuesday night in Essex Junction."[10]

At these public briefings, Leahy would make a point of insisting that officers call him directly—no matter the time, day or night—when confronted by a serious criminal act, but especially in the event of violent assault or murder. "I told the officers I'd rather they got me out of bed than mishandle what evidence could be gathered and what couldn't."[11]

In this case, the timing and the placement of the previously scheduled *Miranda* briefing for Essex Junction could not have been more perfect: Leahy had in fact been called to the Junction to investigate the strange death of two-year-old Beau Bishop just four days previously. Suddenly the twenty-six-year-old was able to speak about violent death—and the need for extreme care in evidence gathering—from fresh, graphic, first-hand experience.

★ ★ ★

Leahy arrived at Fanny Allen Hospital on July 11 at just after 12:30 p.m., roughly thirty minutes after receiving the call from the Essex police—no small feat, given that the family sedan was in for repairs and he'd had to search a little frantically among his neighbors for a car to borrow.

But once on the scene, Leahy was confronted immediately with a delicate situation: Beau's mother, Pearl Bishop, was waiting outside the examination room, in a predictably distraught emotional state. It fell to Leahy to ask her to view and identify her youngest son's body, and he accompanied her into the room, then quietly questioned her about the bruises and cuts.

Mrs. Bishop was stunned but clear about one thing: "The only markings on the boy's body at the time she left to go to work that morning had been the large bruise on his chest and upper abdomen."[12] Leahy himself found the viewing of the little body even more emotionally jarring than he had expected. His breath caught in his throat. Beau was just a few months younger than Leahy's own two-year-old son, Kevin, and he found himself struggling with disgust and real anger as the doctors relayed their collective suspicions.

Leahy wanted to see the Bishop residence as soon as possible—it was already, in the young state's attorney's mind, a potential murder scene—and within minutes, he and the Essex officers were escorting Mrs. Bishop out of the hospital. But just as quickly, the five-minute car ride became considerably more complex from a procedural standpoint, when Mrs. Bishop spotted her boyfriend and Beau's babysitter, Eddie Trivento, now sitting on the front steps of the hospital.

Even sitting and smoking quietly out of the noontime sun, Edward Louis Trivento would have given the officers pause. A rangy figure at six feet tall and twenty-eight years of age, Trivento had once been a marine for just over three months before being discharged.[13] Yet in that small window, he'd had himself tattooed as completely as any twenty-year veteran, with "USMC" running up his right arm and a heart surrounding his own nickname "Eddie" running down the left.

He had worked a disjointed series of short-term jobs—traveling circus roustabout, truck dispatcher, liquor deliveryman, janitor—before being fired abruptly from each. While his brown hair was short and worn neat to his head, the hazel eyes were agitated and intense beneath sharp, straight brows.

At some point after leaving the hospital, Trivento had clearly managed to neaten his appearance. He was now wearing shoes; his shirt was buttoned, and he'd combed his hair smoothly into place.

Two elements mark the official record from this point forward: Leahy's instinctive and increasingly aggressive impulse to tighten control over Trivento as a suspect, and the correspondingly deep deference that he and the officers under his direction gave to both the spirit and the letter of the *Miranda* decision. Leahy's dogged insistence upon informed consent became increasingly noticeable as the party moved to the Bishop household.

Having suddenly acquired Trivento by accident, for instance—a man he could only regard as the chief suspect in a highly suspicious death—Leahy clearly had no intention of letting him go, not even for the duration of the ride back into the village proper. Captain Douglas Fortune's report neatly captures the way Leahy squared this particular circle: "Officer Moquin went over to the subject, confirmed his identy [*sic*] and stated that we were all going to the Bishop home if he would like a ride up. At this time we distributed ourselves, the writer and the State's Attorney bringing Mrs. Bishop's Volkswagen to her residence (at her request). Officer Moquin drove the cruiser and Mrs. Bishop and Mr. Trivento were in the rear of the cruiser and all five persons went to the Bishop household at 217 Pearl Street."

Initially and importantly, Eddie Trivento was asked if he would like to go back to the Bishop residence, and he willingly assented. But it stands out here that neither Mrs. Bishop nor her boyfriend would drive her Volkswagen, given how close they were to home. It stands out as well that she would turn the keys over to the state's attorney and choose to ride in the rear of the police cruiser. After all, if she was too distraught at that moment, her boyfriend could certainly have driven; the police reports make it clear that he had a license, and borrowed her car frequently.

And it's a fair assumption that Trivento himself had absolutely no desire to ride with law enforcement. But the situation was handled in such a way that Mrs. Bishop offered her consent to the "distribution," and Trivento found himself with no option but to duck his own head into the back of the police car.

The actual search of the house betrayed much the same double impulse, to prosecute aggressively even as consent—deliberate, redundant consent—was secured at every stage. "Upon arriving at the Bishop residence, the State's Attorney asked Mrs. Bishop if it was all right to check the house over." When stains were discovered on the sheets of Beau's unmade bunk bed, Leahy asked for consent to remove the sheets for further examination; he repeated the request in the master bedroom, when similar stains were discovered. "Mrs. Bishop again answered in the affirmative."

As with the delicate maneuvering around transportation to the house, Leahy now moved to secure his suspect, but again entirely within the framework of consent and concern for the mother of the deceased: "At this time it was suggested that in an effort to spare the mother of the VICTIM any unnecessary grief that we remove ourselves to the police department there to continued [*sic*] the investigation. The State's Attorney asked Mr. Trivento if he would care to accompany us to the police station. Mr. Trivento readily accented [*sic*] to this."

The change is unavoidable once Mrs. Bishop and Eddie Trivento enter Captain Fortune's highly detailed report—it becomes less generally descriptive, and more a long list of requests for permission, assent, voluntary consent to every motion of the investigators. For a state's attorney still very much wet behind the ears, the need to prevent his first high-profile murder case from being fouled by bungled procedure was paramount. Given that Leahy and Fortune rode to the Bishop house together, it's a decent assumption that they discussed post-*Miranda* procedure during those moments in private. Certainly when the time came to take Trivento's statement at the Essex Police Station, Fortune left nothing to chance, but elaborated each of the Supreme Court's warnings individually: "At this time State's Attorney Leahy informed Mr. Trivento that any statements made by him could and would be used against him in a court of law. Mr. Leahy stated to Mr. Trivento that he could be represented by an attorney at this time. He also stated that if Mr. Trivento could not afford an attorney that the State would appoint one for him. Mr. Trivento indicated at this time that he did not want an attorney and that he was quite willing to answer any questions."

When it came, Trivento's story was a smoothly elaborated version of that he had told in the hospital. As usual, he told the officers, he had given Beau breakfast about an hour after his mother left for work; then the child had gone back to bed, while Trivento himself relaxed in the master bedroom listening to the radio; hearing a loud thump, Trivento feared the worst—that Beau had fallen from the top bunk—and came running out of the bedroom in time to see Beau heading unsteadily to his potty chair and then collapsing suddenly beside it. That was when he had wrapped the unconscious child in a housecoat and rushed him to the hospital.

It was a story that might have held water for anyone who hadn't carefully examined the boy's body, and Trivento seemed genuinely in turmoil about the death. But clearly Trivento's account was at odds with both the state of the corpse and the preliminary results of the investigation at the residence. The stains on Beau's bed, for instance, had also been found in the master bedroom — yet Trivento's story offered no reason as to why that might be the case. And there were the clear signs of violence, some of it sexual in nature, on the corpse.

All the officers in Captain Fortune's office were in silent agreement: Trivento's story had to be challenged, but delicately, and within the rapidly emerging context of *Miranda*.

It was at this point that Detective Irvin Maranville asked Leahy to step out into the hall.[14] In hushed tones, Maranville made a quick but impassioned case for a polygraph test. It was a way of deepening the interrogation without the need for direct confrontation, and Maranville firmly believed that the device could locate holes in Trivento's testimony that could later be exploited in court.

Leahy considered it briefly. Maranville had far more experience, and yet the consequences of the decision would ultimately come to rest with the young state's attorney. And there was a good deal to consider. The use of polygraph machines, while it would be firmly checked by Congress in the late 1980s, was undergoing a boom in America, with many private firms screening employees and applicants, even as more law enforcement units opted for the promise of a more scientific interrogation method. Courts had it within their discretion to accept the results and expert witnesses to explain them, but there was no certainty at the end of the day.

And the nearest polygraph machine and operator were both in Montpelier, the state's capital, a good forty-five minutes away from Essex.

After a minute or two of thought, Leahy chose to gamble. There was no telling how strong a circumstantial case he would finally be able to build, and a fall from a high bunk might explain many of the injuries to the body, if not all. He also knew that in the best-case scenario, even if the polygraph found dramatic holes in Trivento's story, a good attorney would likely challenge not only the machine itself, but the manner in which Trivento had been induced to submit to it.

And so again, as was rapidly becoming his signature approach, Leahy agreed to a polygraph but only in the context of more elaborate and redundant demonstrations of consent. Having already read Trivento his rights once, Leahy and Maranville reentered Fortune's office and read them again: "In the presence of the writer, Capt. Fortune and Officer Moquin, the State's Attorney informed Mr. Trivento that he could remain silent, that he did not have to answer any questions . . . that he could be represented by an attorney at this time if he so desired."

This time, though, Eddie hesitated, and then told Leahy that he couldn't afford an attorney. Leahy's response is nuanced, and telling: "Mr. Leahy told Mr. Trivento that . . . in the event that he desired an attorney and yet could not afford one, the State would appoint one if he were found to be indigent or without funds. Mr. Trivento was silent for a few moments and then stated that he had no desire to be represented by an attorney." Leahy very carefully does *not* assume, when Trivento says he has no money for a lawyer, that the suspect in fact *desires* a lawyer. Rather, he reiterates that *if* Trivento wants a lawyer, one will be provided—very much within the letter and the spirit of *Miranda*, but still holding open the possibility that the suspect will choose to be directly interrogated without one.

And so it was: "Mr. Trivento stated willingness to go to Montpelier to have this [interrogation] conducted."

★ ★ ★

In the summer of 1966, only about a third of Vermont's Interstate 89 had been completed, but the segment between the state's capital and its largest city had been a priority and was newly open to traffic. But the scenic high-speed route to Montpelier must still have seemed novel as Leahy, Fortune, and Trivento made their way there at about 2:15 in the summer afternoon. Talk was purposefully limited. Leahy insisted that the conversation in the car include no reference to the earlier events of the day; he was already sparring mentally with a future defense attorney over factors that might be used to negate the polygraph result.

Still, Leahy makes it clear in interviews today that he found various ways to impress upon Trivento the consequences for lying to investigators, a seed he thought couldn't do any harm if planted.

As it turned out, that seed had a good amount of time to germinate. In addition to the longish car ride, they arrived in Montpelier to find that the only polygraph operator was busy with another case, and so the party of three cooled their heels for another hour and a half. And once the test proper began for Trivento, it was no in-and-out affair—"the polygraph test commenced approximately 1630 hrs. [4:30 p.m.] and to the best of recollection of the writer ended at approximately 2015 hours [8:15 p.m.]."

In other words, Trivento had some six hours to think through the connections between his story and the emerging evidence, the last four of which involved focused questions covering every aspect of the account he had given earlier in the day.

The result was better than Leahy had any right to hope: the door finally opened, and the polygraph operator, a Corporal Ryan, "indicated that Eddie had something that he wished to tell . . . relative to the case in question."

Leahy's heart jumped, but even then he stopped Trivento before he could speak, to reissue him his *Miranda* warnings.

And then Eddie Trivento proceeded to pour out a much different account, a disturbing but also protective new narrative: "Mr. Trivento stated at this time that he had engaged in sex play with the VICTIM." It was a powerful admission, but with its own new contradictions and paradoxes.

In sometimes halting phrases, Trivento now admitted to a single instance of forcible sodomy with Beau—but a month previously—and a single instance of forcible oral copulation the previous day, but then maintained firmly that "that is the extent of the sex play he had with the victim." To explain the deep bruising on the stomach and back, Trivento told the investigators that the previous day he had been lying on his back and twirling Beau on his feet, to give him the sensation of flying, but he had stopped when he noticed the boy was bruising. And he stood by his earlier statements about Beau's fall from the top bunk.

In short, Trivento had incriminated himself well beyond recovery now but had also made it amply clear to his questioners that he wouldn't admit to the actual events that resulted in Beau's death.

Leahy was stunned. He realized—assuming the physical evidence bore out his early assumptions—that he had managed to crack his first real murder case in just shy of nine hours. But he could already intuit a vast web of legal subtleties expanding outward from the polygraph facility, any single strand of which might entangle the mounting case against Trivento in later difficulties. Clearly there would be pressing questions of competency now, in addition to those surrounding the polygraph and the resulting confession.

And so Leahy did what he could to whistle past that particular graveyard: he asked Eddie Trivento not simply to listen to his *Miranda* rights for a fourth time that day, but then to actually write them out longhand, along with his partial confession, on statement paper that would yield three copies—white, yellow, and pink—each featuring the babysitter's own version of what was quickly becoming something like a charm repeatedly invoked against procedural mishaps: "I been told that I do not have to say anything that I may keep silent that anything I say can and will be used against me and that I have a right to a lawyer and if I can't afford one the State will provide one free. Knowing this I freely make this statement without any threats or promises."[15]

In all, there were five complete Miranda warnings associated with the first day's testimony of Edward Trivento on July 11, 1966. Trivento himself was given the pink copy to keep, before being transported back to Essex for immediate booking.

It's fair to say that the new state's attorney was taking no chances.

★ ★ ★

A reader of the *Burlington Free Press* could be excused for missing the Trivento story entirely when it eventually ran two days later, on July 13. Chicago was dominating the news that week, with dueling blockbuster stories: Watts-style riots had broken out on the city's West Side, and a single deranged man with a knife had bound and gagged eight student nurses in their dormitory, calmly murdered them one after the other, and then vanished almost without a trace. Police were left with only the single survivor's composite sketch, and her traumatized assertion that the killer's hair color was somewhere "between black and blond."[16]

But there were other more specific reasons to miss the killing of Beau Bishop—neither of the two references to it in the paper that day mentioned a murder at all. The child's very brief obituary, which ran on page 17, tactfully avoided the actual cause of death: "Roger F. Bishop, Jr., 2, of 217 Pearl St., Essex Junction, died at his home Monday." And the short ninety-word account of Trivento's arrest and booking—buried on page 26—ran under the accurate but misleading headline "Milton Man Pleads Insanity in Morals Case": "A Milton babysitter, Edward L. Trivento, 28, was committed to the Vermont State Hospital Tuesday after pleading not guilty and not guilty by reason of insanity to a charge of lewd and lascivious conduct involving a 2-year-old boy."

In the obituary there was no mention of foul play; in the arrest article there was no mention that the "lewd and lascivious conduct" had terminated in a gruesome death. And as a result, no one outside a small circle knew that Beau Bishop had died at the hands of a very disturbed and very persistently violent local assailant—a fact that Leahy was quickly and methodically seeking to document for a potential grand jury.

The misdirection was unintentional, then, but unavoidable. Leahy had opted to charge Trivento under a more straightforward morals charge to give him time to prove what he now strongly suspected—that Eddie Trivento was a compulsive sexual psychopath, defined under Vermont law as a person who "by a habitual course of misconduct in sexual matters has evidenced an utter lack of power to control their sexual impulse and who, as a result, are likely to attack or otherwise inflict injury, loss, pain, or other evil on the object of their uncontrolled desire."[17]

The first step in this process was having Trivento evaluated by the psychiatric staff at the Waterbury State Hospital, and ultimately the case would turn on that testimony. But standard police work was also quickly turning up a wealth of disturbing details about Trivento's characteristics and movements in the preceding years.

Some of the most bizarre yet convincing testimony came from Trivento's ex-wife, Theresa Cadieux—it turned out Eddie had been briefly married the previous year, before his new bride had quickly sought an annulment. The reasons for the marriage's failure after just six weeks were strange and unsettling, but precisely in line with Leahy's intuitions. Cadieux told investigators that almost immediately following their marriage, Eddie had been fired from his job at a local beer distributor and then "made it quite plain to her that it was his expectation that she work and that he would stay home and babysit. Mrs. Cadieux stated that she was not inclined to go along with this arrangement," as his behavior had quickly become "moody and erratic."[18]

Theresa Cadieux had four young daughters—ages sixteen, fifteen, thirteen, and six—and she was understandably protective of them, especially as Trivento had frequent fits of temper, during which he might slap his new wife or any of the girls present.

More than anything else, it was Trivento's overt attempt to force his way into the role of babysitter that piqued investigators' interest, given the direct parallels to the situation at the Bishop household almost exactly one year later. Another close friend of Trivento, Roland Lamore, told investigators that during an even earlier stint in Massachusetts, Eddie had found still a third very similar situation, moving in for seven months or so with another single mother, one of whose three daughters was handicapped and needed extra care.[19]

The pattern was sharp, distinct, and too pronounced for coincidence.

But there was a great deal of other, more general material to work with in building a case that Trivento's sexual proclivities were violent, and compulsively repetitive. The annulment, it turned out, was eventually secured with the classical excuse, but in this instance it seems to have been quite literally true: the marriage had never once been consummated. Although they had had sex "five or six times" before the marriage—and "on none of these occasions did [Trivento] show any signs of enjoying it"—afterward Cadieux had no sexual relations with him "of any type."

Trivento slapped Theresa once, in fact, for daring to touch his "private parts . . . and informed her that she was never to do that again."[20]

And there seemed to be a general sense, wherever Eddie Trivento went, that his behavior to children was abnormal, frightening, alarming. On her wedding day, Cadieux was confronted by her own aunt, who had known Trivento for years and told her in no uncertain terms that "her new husband was 'queer' and that if he ever touched one of [Theresa's] kids, she would kill him." Roland Lamore's wife recounted that Trivento would "holler or shout" at Beau, who would inevitably "shiver and shake and appear to be very frightened."

Even David Bishop, Beau's six-year-old brother, told police that he had walked into the Bishop house once to find Trivento undressed in the master bed with Beau, only to be sternly ordered back outside.[21]

The testimony from family and neighbors and friends was all entirely of a piece. Trivento was unpredictable and unquestionably violent, and he seemed to use women mostly for money, shelter, and access to their young children. Clearly, he sought only secretive, compulsive sexual satisfactions. And given the distinct pattern of moving from one "babysitting" situation to the next, always with single mothers of several young children, it was an odds-on assumption that Beau would not have been the only child to fall victim to Trivento over time.

The twenty-six-year-old state's attorney hadn't simply unmasked his first murderer, the mounting evidence suggested. It seemed at least a decent assumption that Leahy had arrested an incipient serial predator as well.

★ ★ ★

By late September Leahy had impaneled a grand jury and issued subpoenas to seven key witnesses, to bolster the extensive file produced by the Essex police. And that grand jury would give the prosecutor what he sought: a charge of first-degree murder.

Leahy approached this new grand jury gingerly. Only a few months earlier he had sought an indictment of Robert C. Gold, an air force sergeant who had inexplicably emptied a Beretta pistol into his wife and two small sons. That grand jury, Leahy's first, had voted *not* to indict, on the reasoning that Gold was clearly criminally insane. The experience would shape Leahy's final approach to the Trivento case—he would play his cards more cautiously, and closer to the vest.[22]

But the secret proceedings, following the crime itself, were unavoidably graphic in nature. Among other exhibits, Leahy showed the jurors a sequence of color photographs of Beau's body, as it was photographed on the day of the murder. Color photography was still mostly the province of filmmakers and artistes; color film and color prints were available, but came at a price that kept them mostly out of the hands of amateurs and workaday law enforcement.

So while the more elaborate color process had been used at least once before in a Vermont legal case, it was still painfully new in this context. Leahy felt the new technology to be absolutely necessary, given that he needed to match multicolored bite marks and bruises on the boy's body to the dental records of the assailant.

Like the use of the polygraph, it was a bold move, and one that would eventually help to usher in the near-exclusive use of color photography in Vermont criminal cases. Still, in spite of Leahy's several warnings, one juror nearly fainted when presented with the graphic exhibit, forcing Leahy to take an unscheduled break in the testimony. Trivento's attorney would later argue—unsuccessfully—that the "inflammatory" color medium in and of itself had tainted the grand jury.[23]

It would be midway through the following year before Trivento would be brought to trial, and if the headlines had been largely nonexistent or misleading in the immediate wake of the murder, they were large and brutal now. "Trivento Pleads Insanity to First-Degree Murder Charge," the *Free Press* offered its readers, along with not one but two large photos and a side story of Trivento confronting the assigned photographer. "I hope the [expletive] thing breaks," Trivento was reported to have snapped outside the courthouse, after Leahy requested (successfully) that bail be set at a record $75,000.

After a full year of work on the case, most of it in relative obscurity, Patrick Leahy now emerged into the spotlight in the role of hard-nosed prosecutor. "The allegation is very, very serious; one of the most serious ever brought in this court or that can be brought," Leahy told reporters, with just that hint of hyperbole that would eventually make his statements so quotable to the local—and later to the national—media.

As Leahy had long suspected, Trivento was prepared to fight the premeditated murder charge with everything he had; the insanity defense promised a long, bruising battle that could easily end with the suspect committed to Waterbury, the same outcome Leahy could expect from a lesser charge of manslaughter. In either case, psychiatrists were ready to present compelling evidence that Trivento was indeed a sexual psychopath, who would inflict uncontrollable "evil on the object of his desires."

And so after long consultations with the attorney general, James Oakes, Leahy finally reduced the charge to manslaughter, and on May 12, almost exactly a year from the date of the murder itself, Trivento pleaded guilty to manslaughter.

"In this case," Leahy told reporters, further explaining the reduced sentence, "we feel he will never be cured and will be committed indefinitely."[24]

★ ★ ★

It was an overly optimistic read on the situation, as it turned out. After just four years and eleven months in the Windsor State Prison, Eddie Trivento was judged to be no longer a psychopathic personality, and he was then sentenced on the separate manslaughter charge.

By the mid-1980s Trivento was free and had migrated west, to Las Vegas. Details of his later life are all but nonexistent.

Trivento's obituary in the May 2, 2005, edition of the *Las Vegas Sun*—not unlike Beau Bishop's thirty-nine years earlier—is very short and perhaps equally misleading. "Ed Trivento, 67, of Henderson died Saturday in a local care center. He was born Nov. 25, 1937, in Vermont. A resident for 17 years, he was a retired supervisor in the gaming industry."

For his part, Leahy had taken himself through every step of a long, byzantine, and often excruciating murder case. To make up for his relative lack of experience, he had worked twice as hard at every turn, and along the way he had developed a signature belt-suspenders-and-Super-Glue approach to formal procedure. He made it clear that he was willing to cover every necessary step three times, if that was what it took to ward off error or procedural mishap.

It was a work ethic, and a painfully deliberate caution, that earned him immediate respect from the officers with whom he found himself working. And Leahy had come to appreciate something else as well. The public not only liked a tough-talking prosecutor—they clearly had an open, visceral need for one. Violent crime was there in the daily news, and in fact it would partially account for the final rise of Richard Nixon in just a few short years. Even in a rural state like Vermont, with relatively low crime statistics, public safety was a real and increasingly pressing concern.

Pat Leahy had learned—each in its turn—how to catch a murderer, how to hold and convict one, and how to let the public know that the job was well and properly done. The governor might have appointed him with the idea that he would prove an adequate and quiet caretaker for the position, but Leahy was discovering that the job had a way of taking sudden hold of the news cycle. He had no way to know it in 1967, but murder—and his style of handling it—would cement the public's long-term impression of him.

Because as the 1960s came slowly to a close, homicide in Chittenden County, Vermont's most populous and fastest growing, was about to spike in a way that no one to this day has been able to properly explain or understand.

★ ★ ★

Memories tend to vary, of course, but in the case of Leahy's years as state's attorney they don't vary all that much: most Chittenden County residents of a certain age remember the '60s and '70s as a time when they couldn't seem to pick up their morning paper or turn on the evening news without seeing Patrick Leahy pointing at a corpse.

The impression remains widespread today, nearly half a century later. And over the years, it has directly fueled a secondary impression—that Leahy, in addition to becoming an able and effective prosecutor, must continually have sought the spotlight, manipulated the media. He was "blatant," in the succinct opinion of Brian Harwood and Toby Knox, his opponent's managers in the 1974 Senate campaign.

Longtime Vermont Associated Press reporter Chris Graff reluctantly goes in the same direction: "Nobody would probably disagree with this, and it's not real nice to say, but he was a shameless promoter. You know, he took the office of Chittenden County state's attorney that no one knew anything about, and . . . he was on WCAX all the time."[25]

And certainly there is real evidence that Leahy wanted his office's exploits broadcast as widely and as advantageously as possible. Reporters from the period all nod vigorously when asked whether Leahy ever called to arrange coverage before a bust or a trip to a crime scene. "He was a good judge of a slow news day," says retired news anchor Marselis "Div" Parsons carefully, before sidestepping "a forty-year-old confidence" and relating a story about Leahy's office alerting him to a public corruption bust just in time for the eleven o'clock news.[26]

Clearly the public side of the job was a top priority from the first. If Leahy hoped to increase funding for his new and relatively obscure office, he needed first to remove it from obscurity—and the same, of course, might be said of his own political ambitions.

Leahy well knew that his ill-paid position was also a potentially brilliant showcase for a smart, competent prosecutor. And so when news broke, the new state's attorney always made time for the cameras; when news didn't, he offered reporters the next best things—access, alcohol, and inside information. Parsons remembers the routine well: "He would say, 'Div, come on over to my house. I'll give you a gin and tonic, and we'll talk about *Miranda*.' . . . When you couldn't get anyone else to comment, I'd call up Leahy."

Yet there were significantly larger factors at play as well, factors at societal scale.

During the entire decade of the 1950s, Chittenden County saw just one homicide—that in 1953 of a man named Oscar Clark, ascribed in police reports simply to "an altercation." It wasn't as though murder didn't exist in the first half of the twentieth century, but it was so fantastically rare in Vermont that each and every instance burned itself indelibly and individually into the public mind.[27]

The 1960s, predictably only in hindsight, were radically different.

Those years of marked cultural and demographic change saw eight homicides, the bulk of them in the second half of the decade. For a mostly quiet and rural county, eight homicides—four of those in one year, 1966, Leahy's first as state's attorney—was a sea change in violence. By the 1970s that historically high number had nearly quintupled, to thirty-eight, and it was still heading skyward.

Mercifully, the trend peaked in the '80s at forty-two homicides before finally subsiding measurably in the '90s and the first decade of the twenty-first century. But the swift change made for a stunning, palpable rent in the fabric of daily life.

Mathematically speaking, if you wanted to insert a rookie prosecutor into the state's attorney's office just when the incidence of murder was running up at a genuinely historic rate, you would pick the late 1960s and the early 1970s, a period that tracks precisely with Leahy's eight years as state's attorney. The collective memory that you couldn't seem to pick up the paper during the '60s and '70s without seeing Pat Leahy pointing at a corpse is more or less accurate, then, but only as far as it goes. It's better reworded to place it in context and in proportion: actually, during those turbulent years, you couldn't seem to pick up a newspaper without seeing a *corpse*—full stop.

The evening news, like *Dragnet* or any popular cop show, had a new murder mystery almost every time you turned around.

Where his predecessors had dealt with perhaps one or two homicides in an entire career, Leahy would investigate twenty-two cases during his eight years as state's attorney. He was an ambitious prosecutor, yes, but the truth is that *anyone* who stepped into the office when Leahy did—no matter how self-effacing—would have seemed suddenly ubiquitous to the public. Leahy of necessity rode, rather than ever drove, that larger story. His attempts to publicize the work of his office were a factor, but a contributing factor beside the looming reality—that American society itself seemed to be coming unceremoniously (yet photogenically) un-glued. The timing of the 1966 *Miranda* decision—and Leahy's ensuing determination that he would rather be called out of bed in the middle of the night than risk a bungled investigation—only intensified the need for a hands-on, highly public prosecutor.

It so happened that Governor Hoff had unwittingly installed a novice criminal prosecutor at perhaps the worst possible time and place in Vermont's history. But Hoff, whatever his reasons, had also clearly chosen particularly well. As the Trivento case and others demonstrate, Leahy was a supremely quick study, and he grew rapidly into the expanding needs of the job.

It is no exaggeration to say that the violence, particularly the violence he saw visited upon women, would change him forever. The majority of the homicides Leahy would investigate were gun crimes, and male-on-male in nature; "gunshot to the head" appears most frequently in the police records, closely followed by "gunshot wound to the abdomen." But the killings of women were always somehow harder to take, partly because they were generally more graphic and brutal, more clearly the result of premeditated violent impulses.

There was Rita Curran, to take one lone, heartbreaking, unsolved example. Curran was a twenty-four-year-old Milton elementary school teacher living on the south side of Burlington; she moonlighted as a chambermaid at the Colonial Motor Inn. An attractive but quiet young woman, she was given to referring to herself at work as "an ugly duckling." On the night of July 19, 1971, she attended practice with her barbershop quartet until ten o'clock. Shortly after 1 a.m., her roommates discovered her body in their street-level apartment—she had been bludgeoned, strangled, and sexually assaulted. Apparently the assailant had watched her through the curtains and attacked while she was alone. Curran's face in particular had been pummeled bloody, and the coroner believed this had been done with bare fists. Blood was everywhere. The killer had apparently fled covered in it.

Leahy found himself staggered by the open viciousness of the act. "An extremely brutal homicide," he finally managed to tell waiting reporters. "Certainly the most brutal I've seen in my years as State's Attorney."[28]

As was now his trademark, Leahy had been called to the scene in the small hours the night of the murder; the rest of the week, he worked the case until two or three in the morning. It was a level of scrutiny and social anxiety he had never seen before. There was a sharp spike in Peeping Tom reports; the entire city seemed leery of any movement at a window. Within days, the spotlight on the murder grew so bright, so hot, and so potentially disruptive to the investigation that Leahy made the decision to impose a virtual gag order on the proceedings. The rest of the case, he explained to an almost immediately skeptical press, would be "handled in secrecy."

He had never felt the public's eye so unwaveringly upon him during his years as state's attorney, and denying the media information produced an almost immediate chill in Leahy's relations with them. The *Free Press* was suddenly curt: "No definite reasons for the news shutdown were given."[29]

But unlike the Trivento case, the Curran killing grew only murkier, and more insidious. There were no incriminating prints, no helpful sightings by neighbors, no telling forensic evidence. A weeklong shakedown of the city's usual suspects—individuals with sex offenses on their records—produced absolutely nothing. The killer had been either extraordinarily careful or preternaturally lucky, or both.

Some years later, after the Florida arrest and trial of serial killer Ted Bundy, crime writer Ann Rule would make a case that the Curran slaying fit Bundy's early modus operandi all but exactly, and that there were other outstanding reasons for suspicion—Bundy had in fact been born in Burlington in 1946, at the Elizabeth Lund Home for Unwed Mothers, next door to the motel where Curran worked as a chambermaid.[30] But the detectives in Burlington, after a few hopeful communications with law enforcement in Florida, determined that the Bundy theory didn't hold water—or not enough to allow any serious legal action, at least.

Leahy worked every lead he could turn up. It was as though he had taken on an extra third-shift job, so reliably did his work marathons stretch into the early morning. But here was another bracing lesson for the young state's attorney: not every criminal can or will be caught. Officially, the Curran case went unsolved. It remains cold today.

Still, like Wanda Horne—killed that same year by repeated "blunt impact to abdomen . . . ruptured duodenum"—Rita Curran would stay with Patrick Leahy. In a very real and persistent way, these women would drive his legislative agenda for decades after, leading finally to Leahy's expansive reauthorization of the Violence Against Women Act in 2013. (The chair of Senate Judiciary didn't mention Curran explicitly in his official remarks upon passage, but he might as well have: "I will never forget going as a young prosecutor to crime scenes at two in the morning and seeing the victims of these awful crimes.")

But for the most part, in spite of the blood-soaked crime scenes and the debilitating hours, Leahy made it all look easy on television.

Chris Graff marvels now at what those years of investigations and prosecutions and courthouse pronouncements produced by way of public perception: "He went everywhere . . . jacket flung over the back, really came across in a charismatic way as a fighter, and that was his image—this Chittenden County prosecutor, this fighter."

★ ★ ★

Of course the job wasn't all murder. There was skinny-dipping, too.

Although New England still shows its Puritan influences, it's fair to say that nude swimming has been a part of Vermont life since the sun has been hot in the summertime. That historical tension has made skinny-dipping—along with nudity in general—a perennial headache for local authorities over the years.

Very occasionally, that headache becomes a migraine. During the summer of 1971, with student unrest a top concern across the nation, two seemingly unrelated trends began cropping up in the local coverage of the *Burlington Free Press*: the first was an "epidemic" of venereal disease, and the second was an epidemic of nude swimming.

For weeks, through June and into July, *Free Press* readers were treated to evidence of the horrors of VD, to studies, to firsthand accounts, to doctor's opinions and warnings. And at more or less the same time, a run of articles in the same pages noted a worrisome upswing in skinny-dipping around the state—and not just skinny-dipping, but the accidental flashing of outraged Vermonters who happened to surprise those same scofflaws in the act. Letters to the editor began to crop up, both for and against the practice.

In hindsight, it's hard to avoid the conclusion that one trend was feeding the other, that a good deal of the hysteria suddenly surrounding nude swimming was concern repurposed from the VD debate, which was itself being fueled by anxiety repurposed from the larger cultural debates around student protests, unrest, and free love.

Still, the papers and the courts were treating the skinny-dipping phenomenon as worthy of real attention, and so it was. At the end of June, an eighteen-year-old Warren boy named Walter Whetstone was arrested for swimming "in the altogether at the Thayer's Dam site" and sentenced to a full twenty days in jail after pleading guilty. And although that sentence was almost immediately overturned when the judge realized Whetstone had had no idea that jail time might be involved with his guilty plea, it put the state on notice that skinny-dippers were potentially subject to arrest.

Yet within a week, three more cases would surface, under the cheeky headline "More Nudes Swim into Court," these charges brought by a scandalized fisherman: "Three Bridport students, Robert D. McClaren, 20; Jane Sexton, 22; and Carol P. Smith, 19, are free on $300 bail each after pleading innocent late Monday to charges of breaching the peace by nude swimming."[31]

In short, the skinny-dipping issue was statewide, it involved prickly issues of local control, and it was nothing that the Chittenden County state's attorney needed to confront.

But the temptation was too much. And over an uncharacteristically leisurely ten-day July stretch at the family farm in Middlesex, Leahy couldn't resist taking the plunge. Over the course of those days, he penned a very sly, tongue-in-cheek skinny-dipping advisory to county law enforcement, then released those guidelines publicly.

It was a small masterpiece of tone, designed to provide actual, workable advice, yet all the while mocking the righteous tone of those reporting and prosecuting the swimmers. Other than the actual advice on prosecution (which consisted almost entirely of police politely asking the nude swimmers to dress and arresting them only if they refused), the bulk of the piece consists of an account of Leahy's "research" into the issue.[32]

"I began," Leahy wrote, "by reviewing the old Norman Rockwell paintings, thoughtfully resurrected by the ACLU, showing such activities taking place allegedly in Vermont." As an opening it was a twofer — an approving reference to the famed Arlington painter and cover artist, and a reminder that the ACLU was even then threatening to intervene on behalf of the swimmer's constitutional rights. But Leahy went further in linking the practice to sacred Vermont icons: "I was unable to either confirm or refute the persistent rumor that Vermont's number one politician, Calvin Coolidge, had also engaged in such activity within the borders of this state while subject to Vermont laws."

To make sure that no one could miss the indictment of moralism and hypocrisy, the state's attorney closed with a reference to the obvious — that the state was not a moral universe unto itself, but part of a larger culture that was experiencing a healthy revolution in mores and attitudes. "Today such things are apparently allowable in most movies, on Canadian television, in the *National Geographic* and *Life Magazine* but by no means in the pristine streams and rivers of Vermont." The memo was a dose of adult leadership on an entirely overblown issue, and in its very straight legal context, it was also wickedly funny.

Leahy had a sharp nose for populist issues, but the reaction surprised even him. Almost immediately the story was picked up not only by the state's major dailies, but carried on the Associated Press and United Press International wires; three weeks later *Time* magazine ran a piece about the advisory, accompanied by a reproduction of Rockwell's 1921 *Saturday Evening Post* cover, *No Swimming*.

Leahy was deluged with mail, both from within and without the borders of the state. Probably no other single act in the state's attorney's office earned him as much pure, unalloyed affection from Vermonters.

★ ★ ★

Leahy was on call, to put it simply, during the sixties, and all his chief concerns as state's attorney — drugs, rising murder rates, even escalating public nudity — stemmed from that sudden national re-litigation of most basic American social mores. Vermont and Pat Leahy came of age together, in that way. Again and again, he would be called on to fashion innovative solutions to problems that had only just popped into existence.

And for every one of the eight years he spent as Chittenden County's top prosecutor, the war in Southeast Asia made its particular brooding presence felt.

Ask Leahy today about the epic, failed conflict in Vietnam, and his answer is unhesitating and unequivocal: "I was strongly opposed to the war."[33] It is also true — Leahy *was* opposed to the war, and that opposition did form a significant part of his campaign strategy in the post-Watergate Senate election of 1974. But Leahy's now-standard response also loses more than a bit of nuance in chronological translation.

The richer truth is that by the early 1970s, Vermonters were extraordinarily divided on the war, and from the first Leahy instinctively sought ways to turn the focus to areas of broader agreement. Rather than rail openly against the president and his excursions in Cambodia, for instance, Senate candidate Leahy was far more likely to reference the Congress's vote to fund a nerve-gas facility in Arkansas — a way of suggesting the brutal excesses of the war without alienating patriotic (and still predominantly GOP) Vermont voters.

But it is Leahy's nimble reaction to the Kent State shootings a few years earlier that provides the most lucid example of his style in avoiding a "Which side are you on?" dichotomy.

At just after noon on Monday, May 4, 1970, Ohio National Guard troops were attempting to disperse a large group of student antiwar demonstrators when the troops suddenly opened fire, without warning, killing four and wounding ten.[34] Graphic images of the dead and wounded seared themselves immediately into the American consciousness. Many of the nation's campuses, already increasingly tense as the bombing in Southeast Asia intensified, broke into open violence. Governor Warren Knowles called up Wisconsin's Guard after a night of rioting left buildings smoldering on the U of W campus in Madison.

All across the country, tens of thousands of students were suddenly staging sit-ins, die-ins, throwing rocks and bottles, carrying black coffins through the streets. If the revelations of a secret bombing campaign in Cambodia had poured gasoline on the Vietnam issue, the Kent State shootings struck the match.[35]

The University of Vermont in Burlington was no different. As word of Kent State spread, spontaneous gatherings took place across campus, impromptu organizing sessions awash in anger and grief. Governor Deane Davis placed the Vermont National Guard on standby but agreed to make any deployment at the university contingent on a request by the school's president.[36]

By late Monday night, a student committee had formed to stage a week of memorial events and protests — the Total Involvement Committee — and just a few hours before midnight the first of those events came all but spontaneously together: a candlelight parade of between a thousand and fifteen hundred students, marching across the UVM campus to the white bell tower at the Ira Allen Chapel. The late spring evening crackled with energy.[37]

There's no way to know how Leahy's predecessors would have handled such a charged moment. But it's fair to say that the Chittenden County state's attorney needn't have involved himself at all—law enforcement was well represented by the state police, Burlington's chief of police and a squad of his men, as well as the university's own sturdy police force.

And earlier state's attorneys, underpaid and overworked as they were, had seen no need to take on duties outside their required scope. It wasn't done. But Leahy didn't operate that way. Far from it, in fact: "I practically lived on campus" during the seven days of Kent State protests, Leahy now says with a laugh.

In fact, he went a good deal further. Once word began to spread of the midnight candlelight parade, Leahy decided on the fly that he actually wanted to march with the students himself.

But first he took very careful steps to de-escalate the situation. To the Burlington police chief who swore he wouldn't allow students to take to the streets and would arrest them if they tried, Leahy posed a reasonable question: "Yeah, well, who's going to prosecute them? 'Course they can march."

In fact, most of Leahy's efforts in the hours before the vigil involved de-fanging over-the-top *counter*protesters. Fraternity brothers brandishing hunting rifles from their porches, vets threatening to beat up the demonstrators—Leahy had a small contingent of sympathetic policemen talk each group down, in part by letting them know that Leahy himself would be marching. "State's attorney's marching with them, you go home. We don't want any trouble. You been drinking now, you go home."[38]

With those potential flashpoints addressed, Leahy handed his radio to his deputy state's attorney and joined the somber flow of young people, candles flickering in their hands. And the truth is that—putting aside his tie and collared shirt—the gangly thirty-year-old in the thick-framed glasses could easily have passed for a graduate student himself.

In that particular moment, it was an act of some courage. The *Burlington Free Press*, still the state's go-to opinion maker, had immediately launched an editorial campaign demonizing the student activists, routinely accusing them of "intellectual perversion and moral cowardice," of trading "academic freedom for academic anarchy." Leahy was up for reelection in November and risked being labeled a feckless panderer or worse, especially by the *Free Press*'s staunchly pro-Nixon editorialist, Franklin Smith.[39]

By Wednesday of "Education Week," the students had taken over the Federal Building in downtown Burlington. Again, Leahy was not only present, but front and center. The front page of the *Burlington Free Press* for Thursday, May 7, 1970, shows Leahy standing next to US attorney George Cook, arms crossed and looking sternly down on a group of students occupying the building's lobby. "Although the affair was outside Leahy's jurisdiction," the *Free Press* blandly noted, "he appeared 'as a courtesy to the U.S. Attorney.'"

Leahy, of course, had been determined from the first to see the Kent State repercussions through to the end; the thinking on the US attorney's part seems to have been that the young state's attorney, given the connections he had formed with the students, just might be able to dislodge them from the lobby peacefully. And Leahy seems to have managed just that. When it became clear that not all the demonstrators were going to leave by 5 p.m., Leahy told them, "You're blowing it all.

"You have made one of the best impressions ever on the people of Burlington," he said. "People who weren't willing to enter into meaningful dialogue before are now willing, as a result of what you did yesterday." Referring to the large, peaceful demonstration on the University of Vermont green Tuesday, Leahy said, "You made a point, and you made it peacefully." However, he cautioned, "In the eyes of the community, you people here are the same people as the 1,500 who held the demonstration yesterday. Now you are running the risk of blowing the whole thing."[40]

By 8 p.m., the demonstrators—just seconds in advance of the US attorney's final warning—responded to Leahy's pleas by leaving the premises. He had again managed, mostly through force of personality, to exert a calming influence on the week's potentially volatile proceedings. And his own personal sympathies—against the war and with the student demonstrators—had been on public display.

Neither a sharp-tongued opponent of the war, nor a defender of the president, Leahy emerged from Education Week something else altogether: the county's acknowledged top cop—fair, active, Johnny-on-the-spot, a tireless crusader for public safety. The write-up of the week's events in the UVM student newspaper, penned by university president Edward Andrews himself, Leahy must have found particularly satisfying: "State's Attorney Leahy particularly distinguished himself as a compassionate but firm guardian of public order and as a persuasive participant in a continuing dialogue with the students."[41]

Leahy's instincts had always leaned institutionalist rather than revolutionist, and he was committed to the belief that opponents of the war —himself included—could finally end it through the lawful workings of

American democracy. Which meant sending people to Washington, DC, who would vote to shut the whole far-flung military mess down.

People, that is, like Patrick Leahy.

★ ★ ★

The final year of Leahy's term as state's attorney would coincide with his all-consuming, hopelessly underdog campaign for the US Senate. And in large part, Leahy insisted upon and achieved a working compart-mentalization between his campaign and his day job.[42] But there were moments when his work as the county's top prosecutor would suddenly rise up and seize his complete attention and refuse to let it go.

On June 22, 1974, just as his campaign message was beginning to find unexpectedly fertile ground in the southern and northeastern parts of the state, just as Leahy was finding a rhythm between his days in court and nights on the campaign trail, he managed to squeeze in a meeting with Richard Beaulieu of the Burlington Police Department. Dick Beau-lieu was a good friend, as well as the captain of the Detective Bureau; in 1970, he and Leahy had together assembled a drug task force within the bureau, a team now composed of three promising young officers — Harry Miles, Kevin Bradley, and Dave Demag.

The idea was that the task force would interface with the federal Drug Enforcement Administration in Boston and constitute an experienced and specialized unit within a unit, the go-to outlet for quick, reliable prosecution of drug-dealing offenses.[43] Murder was not the only sort of crime to expand dramatically in the late '60s and early '70s. Drug dealing had come to top the agenda for most state and municipal police forces, and the clamor from the public for tough prosecution had grown louder with each passing year.

Leahy had seen such task forces succeed elsewhere, and he had quickly imported the working concept to Chittenden County. But there were two pressing problems in the unit, Beaulieu told Leahy once they had closed Leahy's office door.

First, the Burlington task force was having real problems making drug buys. Miles, Bradley, and Demag were diligent and making all the right moves — but the drugs seemed not to be there for the undercover buying. In hindsight, this first revelation by Beaulieu seems an indication that the drug problem had been hyped beyond the actual threat level; but at the time it had the captain worried that his young trio of officers might need to train with a more experienced agent.

And that was the second problem Beaulieu needed to report: in the last several weeks, they had imported an undercover narcotics agent from Franklin County named Paul Lawrence. And now there was real trouble with Lawrence.

Leahy almost couldn't believe his ears.

Lawrence was a breezy, fast-talking undercover agent with the St. Albans Police Department who had been credited with hundreds of drug-dealing arrests across the state—but also accused of the worst sorts of malfeasance. He had worked in Brattleboro as well as St. Albans, and in both cities his record had been first spectacular and then, finally, checkered. Jerome Diamond, Windham County state's attorney, had finally refused to prosecute any more of Lawrence's cases, given the high rate of discrepancies in his court testimony and his clear penchant for violence and controversy.[44] Leahy felt much the same way and had said so plainly and publicly.[45]

And yet here was Dick Beaulieu, telling him that while Lawrence might not have lucked into the top job on some fancy new metropolitan strike force, he had managed to worm his way into Leahy's very own personally structured drug unit here in Burlington.

Leahy could barely contain himself. What in the *hell* was Lawrence doing in Burlington? How had he managed to make his way onto the task force, dragging as much baggage as he did? Hadn't Leahy himself been clear about his opinion of Lawrence's character?

Beaulieu was sheepish but explained as best he could: he and Miles had concluded that their own three officers were "burned," too well known in town to conduct effective undercover operations, and they had managed a trade with St. Albans, so each city could begin work with experienced but still unknown officers. Lawrence had been available, and he did hold the record for the most drug busts in the state.[46]

Leahy just shook his head. So what's the problem then? he finally asked Beaulieu.

If possible, the captain looked even more uncomfortable. Finally he repeated what he had told Leahy's deputy earlier: I think Lawrence is bad. My men suspect him of framing people.[47]

Leahy couldn't believe it. Or rather, while he could believe that Lawrence was an apple rotted entirely through, he couldn't believe and for a moment couldn't accept that in spite of swearing off Lawrence's cases entirely and publicly, he had somehow wound up with him as a Burlington drug officer. Worse, he was now Leahy's own very personal problem, a problem that looked likely to metastasize, whatever the Chittenden County state's attorney decided to do about it.

Beaulieu had already green-lighted some early attempts to put Lawrence under surveillance, but he now wanted permission for something much larger and much riskier: a full-blown sting, with a hired decoy, maybe two, and false drug-dealer identities propagated within the Detective Bureau.

Leahy said nothing, his mind working.

He now summarizes the dilemma in simple terms: "I actually thought it might cost me the election, because this guy Lawrence was very popular. But it was my job, and I had to get him, so I did."[48] In the moment, though, it was a dark set of options, and a damned-if-you-do, damned-if-you-don't choice between them. If he did nothing, he could be accused of complicity or protecting his Senate ambitions; if the sting were botched, he could be accused of incompetence or a grudge; and even if the sting were perfectly successful, the end result would be a nightmare of convictions challenged and overturned retroactively. The courts might work for years to clear away the vast tangle of tainted prosecutions Lawrence had rapidly woven.

But there was also a very basic, gut level to Leahy's response, and in that way it was never actually a choice. He had sensed from the first that this was a dirty cop—period. And to his credit Captain Beaulieu had come forward with a very workable strategy to trap him.

Do it, Leahy said, and any help you need from this office, you've got.

He instructed Beaulieu to continue working with his deputy, Frank Murray, who would update Leahy as he shuttled relentlessly between his Burlington office and as many campaign events as he and Marcelle could shoehorn into their evening hours. Beaulieu seemed relieved.

But for Leahy, an internal corruption probe conducted in near-complete secrecy was an unlucky break wrapped in ongoing misfortune. He was running hard, right this moment, on the success of his aid to law enforcement and, among other things, on his creation of the Burlington drug task force.

The investigation of Lawrence had the power to sink him, he realized when he looked at it in a cold light. And an elaborate, long-planned campaign swing through the difficult southern tier of the state would have to be canceled.[49] No way around it: Leahy had to be in the city while the investigation heated up.

An unlucky break wrapped in ongoing misfortune, and then wrapped one last time—for good measure—in a nightmare.[50]

★ ★ ★

Serving as the top prosecutor in the state's most populous county and running a suddenly tightening race for the US Senate gave Leahy the occasionally vertiginous sense of inhabiting two worlds. But there was actually a third, of course: the secret sting investigation of Paul Lawrence. Only he and a small handful of agents in the Detective Bureau knew about the ongoing attempt to catch Lawrence in the act, fabricating drug sales to boost his own arrest record.

Captain Beaulieu would come to Leahy every few days with status updates, or when the investigators at the task force were at a loss for how to proceed. Only Frank Murray in Leahy's office knew anything about the closed-door discussions.

At the first of these reviews, Beaulieu told Leahy that they had set up a decoy—actually Officer Harry Miles's seventeen-year-old nephew from Colchester—with a fake identity and arrest record, and then passed that record and photo on to Lawrence. The response had been amazingly fast: less than eight hours later, Lawrence reported buying twenty-five dollars' worth of speed from the decoy, and yet according to Miles's nephew, Lawrence had never even approached him in Burlington's City Hall Park.[51]

The outcome shocked even the most jaded members of the task force. The crooked undercover cop in their midst wasn't even dealing in half-truths; apparently he was making his arrests up out of whole cloth.

Still, Beaulieu thought that using a decoy related to one of his officers might present a problem at trial, and he wanted Leahy's help getting a more professional decoy. Leahy thought a minute and then told Beaulieu to call Eugene Gold, the district attorney in Brooklyn, New York. Gold and Leahy knew each other from the National District Attorney's Association, and Leahy was sure Gold would have a man free. Better to have not only a professional drug decoy, but one from as far out of town as possible.

The drug decoy provided by Leahy's friend Eugene Gold turned out to be a short, balding cop from Brooklyn named Mike Schwartz.[52] Schwartz wore his hair short, surprisingly enough, and his clothes leaned to the expensive side—not your typical 1970s undercover agent. The task force officers worried that he would stick out in Burlington's counterculture, which leaned to the cheap and dirty. But the task force duly created a drug-world identity for their second decoy—"the Rabbi" was the street name they settled on—with careful documentation and mug shots to match. Schwartz wore a wire, and he would be observed by task force agents positioned in an upper floor of the nearby Huntington Hotel.

As the morning of July 11 wore on, the faked records were casually passed to Lawrence, along with a hot tip: the Rabbi was back in Burlington, after a year's absence, and he was almost certainly there to deal heroin for the next several days. Lawrence took charge of the folder and studied the mug shot intently.

As it turned out, Beaulieu and Demag and the others needn't have worried about the undercover decoy's appearance. Schwartz had hardly begun to warm his bench in City Hall Park before Lawrence burst triumphantly back into the station. "I just made a heroin buy from the Rabbi in the park," he bragged to the office. "Got a spoon of heroin from him. Thirty bucks." For good measure, Lawrence even added a second buy, some speed from an anonymous motorcycle rider.

Anyone who didn't know for a fact that Schwartz was a double undercover agent would have thought it was Lawrence's best day yet in Burlington. And for the rest of the afternoon, he continued to trumpet the buys to any officer who walked through the door.

Schwartz, of course, had never even been approached, although he had seen Lawrence's blue Mustang circling the park.

The task force now had a case against Lawrence, but that case was still maddeningly thin in spots. The first decoy was related to one of their agents; a smart defense attorney might be able to get a jury to discount those two fabricated buys. And the buy with the Rabbi — since it involved nothing on the wire — might be presented as a case of mistaken identity. Beaulieu decided to try just one more Rabbi buy the next day.

But the morning of July 12 brought a host of niggling doubts: Div Parsons called out of the blue, trolling hard for information about a possible arrest of a suspect named "P.L.," and Lawrence himself had come into work seemingly out of sorts, edgy, saying he would like the day off to go swimming. Maybe it was nerves, but the captain had the feeling that someone had slipped, or deliberately tipped Lawrence to the impending arrest.

And so Beaulieu took the problem to Leahy, who immediately cleared his office but for Frank Murray, and the three men quietly hashed it out.

By this point, although still in his mid-thirties, Leahy was an undeniably seasoned prosecutor. He had prosecuted more murder cases than any state's attorney in modern times, perhaps in the county's history, and he had worked extensively with drug cases at every level. He had developed a gut feeling for the aggregate required to secure conviction, but that instinct was not entirely unreasoning—it was more the instantaneous sifting of the myriad facts of the case, set against a thousand remembered inclinations of Chittenden juries and judges.[53]

In this case, he felt that what they had as of today on Lawrence was a solid minimum—enough, although he would dearly love a little cushion, another arrest, or some solid physical evidence, though that might well come with a search of Lawrence's apartment. But secrecy was clearly collapsing. If Div Parsons had the identity of their suspect, then that knowledge was almost certainly going to find its way into the hands of someone who felt Lawrence deserved to be forewarned. If not this morning, then tonight.

It was time to close the trap.

Again, if his call was wrong—if the case blew up, if Schwartz turned out to be a poor witness, if the antidrug community rallied strongly behind Lawrence, who had been their supercop for several years running, after all—if any of a thousand things, they'd be letting the only truly dirty cop that Leahy had ever met simply go about his business, perhaps even sue for wrongful arrest.

And, not incidentally, Leahy himself would almost certainly be crucified on the campaign trail for incompetence, or even political grandstanding.

But there it was, and no going around it.

★ ★ ★

Paul Lawrence was brought into custody later that day, July 12, 1974. Although there were problems with the initial conviction—and although Lawrence's appeal was once upheld by the Vermont Supreme Court—Lawrence would ultimately plead guilty to the charge of false swearing in the Rabbi case. As part of the deal, he was sentenced to a term between three and eight years in prison, although eligible for parole six months earlier than he would otherwise merit.

Demag sees it clearly enough now: "You know, I think—looking back on the whole thing—I think Paul was kind of a sociopath kind of guy. I mean, just—the things he would do, that everybody found him attractive for doing them, you know?"[54]

A particularly dangerous and corrupt cop was off the street, although not for as long as Leahy or Beaulieu might have liked. The wave of prosecutions Lawrence had put together—some 120 or more drug busts in total—could now be looked at and in some cases properly reevaluated.[55]

And for the Democratic US Senate candidate, the headlines turned out to be mostly dream rather than nightmare. Kim Cheney, the Republican attorney general whom Leahy had aggressively waved off the case when it threatened to disrupt his own probe, had no alternative but to tell the press that Leahy and the Burlington task force "had done an excellent job" and that their policing proved "the law enforcement community ultimately can be trusted." Leahy and Beaulieu's monthlong probe won plaudits across the state.[56]

And eventually Cheney would be forced to accede to calls for a special panel to oversee the handling of the Lawrence affair, one appointed by the governor and widely seen as a vote of no confidence in Cheney himself.[57]

Leahy hadn't gone looking for the Lawrence case, but when it found him, he hadn't shirked or slow-tracked. Yes, he'd had a bit of the luck of the Irish, but he had also prosecuted aggressively and efficiently, and within the very task force that he himself had worked to create. The message was there for voters, as they watched the case unfold in the pages of their daily papers: Leahy wasn't afraid to prosecute corruption wherever he found it, and he got clear results.

Leahy's campaign manager Paul Bruhn was beside himself with joy. The Top Cop image he'd spent the last year painstakingly building for his candidate had suddenly materialized in three dimensions, battling real, palpable corruption, and not a moment too soon.

Best of all, from Bruhn's point of view? Leahy's opponent, Congressman Dick Mallary, had spent weeks putting together a four-step plan to fight inflation, by some accounts the top concern on the minds of voters. The congressman had then duly introduced the plan at an event in Randolph on July 12, the day Lawrence was being quietly handcuffed in Shelburne.

And on July 13, with Leahy's eight counts against Lawrence featured on the front page of the *Burlington Free Press*, the Mallary-whips-inflation story was unceremoniously kicked to the back pages.[58]

But Bruhn wasn't kidding himself. He had long ago calculated the basic odds of Vermont electing a thirty-four-year-old Catholic Democrat to the US Senate in 1974, and those odds hadn't been changed significantly: a snowball's chance in the hotter side of hell, more or less.

And quite possibly less.

The Children's Crusade

THE SENATE RACE OF 1974

Let's be precise: it was not, technically speaking, impossible for Patrick Leahy to be elected over Richard Walker Mallary to the United States Senate from the state of Vermont in the year 1974.

But the fact of its eventual narrow possibility has come over the decades to almost entirely obscure the outcome's complete and utter implausibility. That is to say, Pat Leahy should *not* have been elected to the Senate in 1974, by any realistic reading of the challenges he faced. His contemporaries can certainly be excused for having laughed at his chances, because in point of fact those chances were laughable.

And laugh they did. Brian Harwood, one of Mallary's campaign managers, sums up the prevailing wisdom with a fairly intimate moment from a key campaign strategy session at a restaurant in central Vermont: "I'm standing in the men's room at this place down in Quechee, next to Al [Moulton, then a top GOP strategist], and we're there at the urinals, and Al said, 'So what do you think about Leahy?' and I just laughed and said, 'Ah, pay no attention, pay no attention at all. Nobody knows him outside of Chittenden County. *Forget* about it.'"[1]

There were a host of reasons to forget about it, of course, but among these were three paramount handicaps, any of which alone would have been enough to doom Leahy's candidacy. Taken together, they were clearly an electoral death sentence, and a sentence stronger than the sum of its parts at that, because each unelectable trait seemed only to leverage the next.

In ascending order of unacceptability, then: Leahy was very young, very much a Catholic, and—worst of all, from a historical perspective —he was a Democrat.

When he announced his candidacy on March 1, 1974, Leahy was just thirty-three years old, a relative political novice. Vermonters preferred their senators a good bit longer in the tooth—no one under fifty had ever represented the state in that capacity. And the smart money on both sides suspected that Leahy knew that as well as anyone: more than a few insiders saw this 1974 run as broadly sacrificial, merely designed to build name recognition for a later, more serious run at attorney general or governor, or even US senator again in 1976, when Bob Stafford's seat would be in play.

Yes, with his height, gruff baritone, and purely symbolic comb-over, Leahy seemed a good deal older than his thirty-three years. Dick Mallary, Leahy's GOP opponent, was himself a bit young by historical standards, at just forty-five. By even his own campaign's admission, Mallary was never truly comfortable in campaign mode. "Mallary was the quintessential New Englander," says *Free Press* reporter Candace Page, "rock-ribbed, Protestant, hill-town New Englander—stoic, and a little prim. He came across as almost a New England preacher."[2]

But of course Mallary had a proven and impressive record at the ballot box, and he was currently Vermont's lone US representative, having won a special election during the previous cycle. Whatever his personal quirks, Mallary was a genuine and respected statewide personality, with near-universal name recognition and ready access to the front pages of the daily papers.

And it's an unvarnished historical fact that Vermonters as a whole also still preferred that their elected officials be Protestant. In fact former governor Phil Hoff, who snapped a 108-year losing streak for Democrats when he scored a stunning upset in the gubernatorial race of 1962, was himself chosen by party elders partially with an eye toward reassuring conservative Protestant voters wary of his Democratic affiliation. "Jack Spencer [chairman of the Democratic Party] had a very firm idea of the kind of person he thought could win," Hoff noted. "He recruited me because he wanted a person who was progressive, enthusiastic—and Protestant."[3]

If JFK had broken the Catholic barrier in national politics for well and for good—and certainly his aura had helped pull Hoff into the governor's office in '62—that ceiling was still mostly intact over the Green Mountains.

Most to the point, though, and least to his advantage at the ballot box, Leahy was an outspoken Democrat, and Vermonters sent Republicans to the Senate—and only Republicans. Since 1866, when Congress had mandated that state legislatures elect senators by an absolute majority, those majorities had stood rock-solid with the GOP. In 1974, Vermont was still one of the most reliably Republican states in the Union; Richard Nixon, as he anxiously counted votes in the run-up to a possible impeachment trial, would certainly have seen the state as some of the sturdiest masonry in his firewall.

As former governor Hoff succinctly put it, "Starting not too long after the Civil War, Democrats marched to the polls, and got murdered every time. Just murdered."[4]

Mallary had the comfort of a full 108 years of pro-Republican history on his side, and even with a deeply troubled president and the unsettling metastasis of Watergate, no one with an eye on Vermont politics expected that history to change anytime soon.

And as though that weren't quite enough in the way of insurmountable obstacles, Leahy would also eventually face a spirited long-shot challenge from the Left, in the form of one Bernard Sanders, the Liberty Union Party's highly outspoken thirty-two-year-old nominee.

While Liberty Union—forerunner to the state's Progressive Party— had over the years proven chronically unable to crack the 5 percent mark, Sanders himself had recently had a great deal of success in challenging an eye-popping 38 percent rate increase by New England Telephone. It was a particular triumph, for which he had been lauded by a number of major papers in the state. On the heels of that success, and banking on his already well-known ability to question closely and speak unflinchingly, the Liberty Union's standard-bearer was intent on reaching 10 percent of the vote in the November elections.

Sanders—who "speaks with somewhat of a Brooklyn accent," the *Free Press* politely noted—had a penchant for attacking not merely the Rockefellers and corporate titans, but both the Democratic and Republican parties for what he saw as complicity in "socialism for the rich."[5]

So here was the last of the rapids Leahy would have to run. Liberty Union would be targeting antiwar liberals and other long-standing Democratic constituencies; it was an excellent assumption that a corrupt White House might make it a growth year for a reformist third party as well. Asked in 2011 if there was any attempt on the part of the Leahy campaign to persuade Sanders to forgo a run and unify the Left behind a Democrat, Paul Bruhn allows himself a very small smile and demurs: "As Bernie is today, so was he then."[6]

All of which left Republican congressman Dick Mallary very much in the catbird seat. And from that controlling position atop those many stacked advantages, Mallary made one decision that, more than any other, would help to create the basic dynamic of the race. Rather than match Leahy's early start, Mallary would very deliberately go the other way: he would make a point of staying down in Washington, DC, and legislating, as the voters had elected him to do, and come home only on weekends to campaign.

It was the right thing to do, Mallary declared, and that was that.

Needless to say it was a decision that gave his campaign strategists serious pause, as Leahy was nothing if not hungry, and having the state's tiny retail political events more or less to himself for seven months would give the Democrat plenty of room to make his case. Yet Mallary's decision was "principled," they felt, in keeping with both the reality and the campaign's preferred image of the congressman.[7]

But as it happened, there were extraordinary factors about Patrick Leahy that Mallary and his small inner circle did not, and could not, take into account. It's fair to say they had never seen anything like Leahy's particular sort of hunger before — a fire in the belly that could only be called incandescent — and they didn't at first fully appreciate the demographic and ideological forces already rising up to feed it.

Leahy's intuitive grasp of the synergy between media and politics had led him very early to what seems now an inevitable postmodern conclusion: rather than continually dunning the media for coverage, it made far more sense to set up the campaign as a media arm in and of itself, engaged independently and from the start not simply with selling a winning image but *producing* that image for wholesale consumption.

As Leahy's media strategist David Schaefer sums it up in hindsight, "A lot of this stuff was brand new, the television thing and the rest — all of these were bunnies coming out of the hat that no one around here had ever seen before."[8]

DEEP ORIGINS OF THE LEAHYITES

Like all political stories, the Leahy story is actually one of social networks; like all stories of remarkable political success, it is one of extraordinarily close and talented social networks.

It began unspectacularly, with a start-up.

In 1969, twenty-two-year-old Burlington native Paul Bruhn — after an admittedly checkered academic career at both Fairleigh Dickinson University and the University of Vermont — decided to launch a magazine. He had been working for a community newspaper called the *Suburban*

List, selling ads and eventually working as a reporter at twenty-five dollars a week, but Bruhn had bigger ideas. He had the sense that there was a niche in the market for a city-themed magazine like those then popping up in, and named for, cities like Boston, New York, and Philadelphia.

Bruhn pushed ahead, with the strong financial backing of his ex-bosses, the owners of the *Suburban List*, Ruth and Proctor Page. And he staffed it with close, trusted friends from around the city, young, energetic, irreverent types like himself. It was the sort of creative urban venture that shines very brightly and looms large locally for a handful of years, before subsiding and disappearing utterly—in this case, the magazine was shuttered just four years later.

But during those four years, *Chittenden Magazine* became the meeting place and the proving ground for an impressively talented staff. In fleshing out his stable of writers, Bruhn hired a tall, urbane young reporter at the *Burlington Free Press* named David Schaefer, and eventually Schaefer's wife Jane, as well as another reporter for local television station WCAX, Donald Steffens, and then Donald's wife Gael. Rounding out the talent pool were a gifted freelance photographer, Sandy Milens—still a noted Vermont photographer today—and a wickedly satirical cartoonist, Jane Brown, who died in 2009.

It was Brown, of course, who first thought of depicting the ever-watchful state's attorney as a badger. And after a series of similar cartoons, the name stuck inside the magazine.

"We always called him the Badger, you know," Bruhn remembers, a little sheepishly. "The cartoons were really fun. They spoofed him a little bit, because when he was state's attorney, he was just kind of *everywhere*. He really paid attention to the job, and he worked about ninety hours a week. I think about badgers being very intent, and wide-eyed and watching everything. That was Patrick."[9]

Was Leahy offended by the cartoons showing him continually digging (literally) into this and that controversy around the county? Quite the contrary. He liked the magazine's coverage very much indeed, and said so. And over the next several years that occasional coverage of Leahy continued.

Soon the Leahys were socializing with the *Chittenden Magazine* staff after hours as well. The group had begun regular monthly "international dinners," with the location moving from house to house, mostly in the Burlington area. Schaefer and his wife would make Scandinavian dishes, Donald Steffens and his wife would prepare Thai food, and eventually—

choosing carefully between Patrick's twin ethnic heritages—the Leahys would offer Italian. The group also included others from the magazine, and eventually Charlie Tetzlaff, a young energetic deputy state's attorney from Leahy's office.

It was good food, and it was good fun, but there was much more to it than that. Pat Leahy was a gregarious type and loved a party, but he was also a highly ambitious politician with a sharp intuitive feel for talent. Sitting in Schaefer's living room in the early '70s, swapping stories and eating Swedish meatballs and gravlax, Leahy clearly realized the political potential in the group seated on the couches and chairs around him, plates balanced haphazardly on their knees.

He and Bruhn were *simpatico* from the first. Although Leahy would announce as a candidate for the Senate quite early, "we had been talking long before," Bruhn says, making it clear that even that is something of an understatement.

And so, rather than waste time leavening a traditional political staff with a media-savvy type here or there, the two men adopted a far more elegant solution: when the *Chittenden Magazine* folded in 1973, Leahy and Bruhn waited a decent interval and then simply renamed it the Leahy for Senate Campaign of 1974.

Eventually, there would be another, less formal name for that campaign —"the Children's Crusade." Where it originated is a matter of speculation at this point; the *Free Press* casually reports the nickname in mid-September of 1971 and attributes it only to "one staffer."[10] But whether that staffer worked for Mallary or Leahy—whether the nickname was a taunt or a self-effacing rallying cry—is impossible to determine.

Whether barb or badge of honor, though, both parts of the phrase reflected more than a bit of truth. The Leahy campaign, and its candidate, were extremely young and notably lacking in hard-core statewide campaign experience. And like the actual Crusades, this one had no one structure, no real top-down apparatus, but more a directed and slowly growing stream of like-minded warriors moving toward the same general goal. It was "less an organization than a network of contacts that can be tapped to help out with scheduling when Leahy is in a given area."[11]

The Vermont Education Association, to take the most powerful example, broke with tradition to publicly endorse Leahy, and created a separate fund-raising vehicle, VOTE (Voice of Teachers of Education), to aid in the Senate campaign.[12]

But while the additional funding was more than welcome, it would eventually be labor's manpower that would significantly tilt the scales. In addition to phone-banking, labor volunteers helped the Leahy campaign staff massive tabloid drops around the state—one topping one hundred thousand copies, where the opposition was managing ten thousand—tabloids blandly labeled "What Is the Difference between Pat Leahy and Richard Mallary?" but filled with carefully wrought comparisons on key issues.

"They went literally door to door," Toby Knox says, shaking his head at the memory. "I don't think they, obviously, hit every door—but they had a massive street sweep."[13] A very young Doug Racine, later state senator and lieutenant governor, acted as the campaign's organizational link to these tabloid-wielding troops.

But it goes without saying that this "ride to the sound of the guns" strategy can only work if the candidate is himself or herself an extraordinary retail campaigner, not just shaking hands but changing hearts and minds everywhere at once. And in this regard, Leahy had not just himself to fall back on, but his wife Marcelle as well. They could have been a duo sent from central casting—although central casting Montpelier, rather than Hollywood.

In 1974, Leahy was six feet, four inches and two hundred pounds, the deep-voiced top cop in the state's fastest-growing region, a thirty-four-year-old who looked reassuringly older; his shirts, jackets, and ties were respectable but far from showy—workaday prosecutor's garb. His smile was not perfect, but by its imperfections it was rendered perfectly disarming, and Leahy had a way of growling a private word or two down into the ear of a much shorter voter that made the two of them seem joined, briefly, in a joking conspiracy against the rich and powerful.

Marcelle, by contrast, was a strikingly beautiful woman who seemed too young for her three children and her ready grasp of the mechanics of statewide campaigning. Always impeccably dressed—one reporter was taken with her "blue suit . . . paisley scarf, black low-heeled pumps and a navy coat with white trim"—Marcelle made "a picture" in the endless gritty locations to which the campaign took her.[14]

Ultimately the newspapers would refer to her as the Senate campaign's "potent secret weapon," and it was true in more ways than one. If Leahy had a minor celebrity, in the *Free Press*'s phrase, together they seemed an authentically dashing pair. But there was also the French effect.

To recount the combative histories of the French and the English in Vermont, and of French and English in Vermont, would require a volume far larger than this. Suffice it to say that French speakers in the state had been so long and so long-sufferingly in the minority—especially those who were also Catholic—that they rarely figured in anyone's electoral calculations, except as reliable Republican voters mostly lodged in the state's Northeast Kingdom.

But the conventional wisdom didn't factor in several new elements. First, Marcelle (maiden name Pomerleau) had grown up in an actively bilingual household, one where even the smallest Pomerleau child knew to respond in French when asked a question in French, or be thought "very rude." And second, Pat Leahy had decent reason to believe that his French-speaking wife might make a difference in French-speaking areas, and he had zero qualms about deploying her in that targeted capacity.

And thus was born a truly trilingual arm of the 1974 campaign: Leahy here, there, and everywhere in his own gruff, locally accented English; Marcelle working not just the Northeast Kingdom but urban pockets like Winooski and Bennington in French; and, not incidentally, Leahy's mother Alba—the southern European fork of his parental ancestry—giving interviews in Italian, aimed primarily at the immigrant Italian craftsmen who had come to dominate the stoneworking industry over the decades.

For more than a few women, Marcelle's presence on the trail reinforced not simply the fact that a wife could matter, but that grassroots democracy itself mattered. "I haven't voted since Kennedy ran," Mrs. Lois Hammond of Newport Center shyly confessed to a reporter. "He got killed so I thought I'd better stop."[15]

Together and apart, Patrick and Marcelle campaigned over the months from town to town, in the time-honored tradition: diners, factories, street corners, chicken suppers, and church groups, one after the other after the other. "The *Free Press* thought Dick Mallary hadn't been supportive enough of Nixon, so probably he's gonna win easily anyway," Leahy sums it up in hindsight. "So we had nobody. Marcelle was helping to drive, and we had three young kids. Our car was falling apart."

They would eventually put over thirty thousand miles on that ailing sedan, most of it on small lonely roads, winding into tucked-away villages. Driving home late at night, with her exhausted husband napping beside her, Marcelle would sing pop tunes—Diana Ross, Helen Reddy, Elton John—to keep herself awake. And then she would spot a small crowd collected outside a high school or a movie theater, and she'd nose the sedan into the parking lot, shake Leahy awake, and they would gamely try to shake twenty more hands between them before calling it a day.

"His name recognition was zippo outside of Chittenden and Washington Counties, but in those counties his favorability was way, way high," Bruhn says now, shaking his head. "So our job was to introduce Patrick and help people get to know him the same way that people in Chittenden and Washington knew him."

And the numbers did climb, slowly but surely, each and every poll, while Mallary's remained almost preternaturally static.[16]

But even though Leahy's numbers were on the rise throughout the spring and summer, the Mallary campaign seemed unflappable. Maybe more than unflappable. "They were pretty cocky," Schaefer says, narrowing an eye, even today.

FORCE MULTIPLIERS: TECHNOLOGY AND MEDIA

Although Leahy and Marcelle were slowly winning hearts and minds across the state, it was the fact that these far-flung efforts meshed so neatly with Bruhn and Schaefer's relentless image making that rendered them ultimately so powerful. More to the point, it was the Leahy campaign's several technological advantages that enabled this often remarkably deft, deadline-making coordination.

Whether Marcelle was accompanying her husband on the road or not, Leahy was never quite alone. In his car were not one but two Dictaphones—one dedicated to campaign business, and another deeded to work from the state's attorney's office—and a police radio with a telephone handset that allowed Leahy to be contacted anywhere within the state that its signal could reach. When taken together with the sedan's siren—which Leahy was occasionally known to activate just for the sheer sweet forbidden pleasure of it on a dark country road[17]—there was more than a hint of Batmobile to the whole setup.

Granted, the police radio-phone was designed for official business related to the prosecutor's office, and Leahy was generally very scrupulous about that distinction. But with reporters, the car-phone principle was neither black nor white, but a more changeable shade of gray: the state's television and print reporters had long had both Leahy's unlisted home number and his car radio number, and they would occasionally use either or both to confirm breaking information.[18] That had been true of stories when he had been exclusively the state's attorney, and it continued to be true now that he was also running hard for the Senate.

Yet the GOP campaign's link with their candidate was never entirely reliable, which made for a certain inevitable frustration. Mallary had made the decision to focus on legislating, and that put him often in long meetings from which he could not be roused. "There would be times when Dick just wouldn't be accessible . . . there was always a delay getting things back from Washington." This lag, along with Mallary's insistence that each major campaign decision have his personal okay, made for a stop-and-start feel to decision making, even at moments where the pace of the campaign had accelerated dramatically.

"I can't remember anything we ever did, really, that didn't have his stamp on it," Knox says, and then asks Harwood, "Can you?" Harwood cannot.[19]

Leahy's technological edge wasn't limited to a superior and faster-moving communications network. He and Schaefer worked out a means for the candidate to speak to breaking issues even while he was pumping hands in another part of the state entirely: the "radio actuality."

Says Schaefer, "When there was a hot story [taking hold in the press], it was a way to get his voice on the radio. Patrick would record it, and then we'd call up the radio stations and play this thing throughout the day, and it was a little attack or a response, going through all the radio stations. It was so primitive, when you think of the Internet now and all the stuff that can be done."[20]

But the radio actualities, like the radio car-phone, were delightfully novel at the time, and they took the campaign's production of image to a slightly higher level. Rather than only prepping the candidate to field queries by editors and producers, Bruhn and Schaefer also offered up prerecorded sound bites shaped to provide answers on a range of pressing issues — but answers cut at a certain angle, to fill holes in later stories that the "responses" would themselves suggest.

And thereby, one might argue, the team had moved very subtly and almost invisibly into reverse-engineering the media's questions themselves.

Reporter Candace Page, looking back on the relationship between Leahy and the press, describes a natural rapport based on youth and personality: "I can't emphasize enough: the demeanor was everything. . . . Leahy was a young, energetic, not stodgy guy, and political reporters tend to be young, energetic, and not stodgy. So we sort of spoke the same language in a way that Dick Mallary did not."[21]

The harsh truth of the camera is that when it's pointed in one direction, it is not — by definition — pointed in another. For the Mallary campaign, the media's acquired taste for their opponent's crime stories and tough talk generated endless frustration and *agita*. To counter the Top Cop image inside their own headquarters, Mallary's staff eventually adopted a mocking nickname for Leahy: "Clarabell," the bald, horn-honking clown from the old *Howdy Doody* show.

Their candidate might be occasionally unreachable in Washington, and he might be visibly uncomfortable on the campaign trail, but at least Congressman Richard Mallary wasn't out there every night blowing his own damn horn on Channel 22.

THE "LONG DARK SHADOW" OF NIXON

Of course, one key player in the Senate election was some 450 miles away to the south, holed up in the White House and plotting an endgame to a presidency that had begun to unravel years before. Richard Milhous Nixon was driving many races around the country in the year 1974, not the least among them Bill Clinton's original failed run for Congress in Arkansas. Incumbent House Republicans in particular were engaged in a brilliant display of nuancing and political fan dancing on the issue, trying desperately to suggest outrage, loyalty, independence, and ardent love of the Constitution all at the precise same instant.

The national picture suggested the tentative feel of a wave election, although no one could be sure: the nation was in almost entirely unexplored territory.

The *Burlington Free Press* had taken to strongly downplaying Watergate's impact. It wouldn't have been unusual, even in the midst of the country's pronounced Watergate backlash, for a Republican voter to catch a glimpse of a reassuring headline in another man's paper at a lunch counter: "Presidency Not Expected to Affect Vermont Campaigns."

For his part, Toby Knox calls Nixon "the long dark shadow" who influenced, and rendered far less effective, every step they took. Mallary "was kind of tiptoeing around" on Watergate, Knox adds, "and I think a lot of Republicans were not happy with Dick because he was not a stalwart backer of Richard Nixon."

It was a sick-making dynamic for incumbent House GOP members. It was no accident, then, that Mallary's campaign buttons read, pointedly, "I Say What I Think."

Still, Nixon was certainly not a slam-dunk issue for many Democrats, particularly those from more conservative states. A pro-Nixon sympathy backlash was a recognized, and very real, possibility. With Vermonters such a traditionally conservative voting bloc—and with part of his overall strategy being to narrow differences with Republicans on crime, public safety, and other select issues—Leahy didn't want to risk igniting sympathy for the president, or prompt a backlash against himself as a traditional liberal.

Hence the nerve-gas strategy.

Like most outsider candidates, Leahy was determined to pore over and dissect his opponent's incumbent voting record (and in so doing turn his own disadvantage into a tactical edge). And since a good proportion of the votes taken in either the House or the Senate consist of a thousand issues wrapped in a single bill, outsiders usually find exquisite pickings. Nowhere was the Leahy camp more effective than in the way it drove the coverage of the Senate campaign with near-daily attacks on Mallary's congressional voting record.

A trio of headlines from October gives a sense of the strength and pace of those broadsides: "Leahy Says Mallary Altered Position on Profits Taxation" (October 10); "Leahy Continues to Hit Mallary on Foreign Policy" (October 19); "Leahy: Mallary Oil 'Proposal' Could Cost Consumers Billions" (October 31). The *Burlington Free Press*, although a ready customer for such pugilism, couldn't resist tweaking the Leahy folk with another attack-filled headline during this late-October stretch: "Leahy Attacks Mallary for Running Ads Which Attack Leahy."[22]

Looking back on the result today, and in light of the history written about the Watergate wave, Brian Harwood now calls what his campaign was experiencing "the perfect storm," but it is clear that part of the reason that storm so effectively inundated the Mallary campaign was that the congressman himself refused, on principle, to batten down the hatches.[23]

And amid all the other useful issues that Leahy's operatives found buried in Mallary's record was a vote taken in August of that same year, an appropriation that included, tumbled in with other unrelated items, a nerve-gas factory. Or as Leahy would eventually frame it: "He has on several occasions voted for amendments that weaken social legislation, but on August 6 he voted to keep intact a $5.8 million appropriation to build a new nerve-gas factory in Arkansas."[24]

It was not a project that Bill Clinton could rail against down in Arkansas, of course—even nerve-gas factories bring jobs—but it was absolutely custom-designed for Leahy's purposes. No one in Vermont could hear the words "nerve gas" without thinking of Vietnam and the horrors being visited on that country from the air.

The *Free Press* captured Leahy's well-honed rhetorical singsong: "He tells voters that Mallary is for money for limousines for public officials, but against money for transportation for the handicapped; for money to build a nerve-gas factory but against money to combat child abuse."[25]

For his part, Mallary staunchly attributed the nerve-gas vote to legitimate concerns about storage safety. "Binary" nerve gas was shorthand for a weapons system that held the various lethal ingredients in isolation until the missile exploded and mixed them on impact; proponents in the White House and in Congress argued that if the country was going to use nerve gas, here was a safer means of storage until it was needed.[26]

In that way, the Arkansas nerve-gas factory became a very reliable scrap of shorthand for Leahy—Nixon *sans* Nixon—and he deployed it often, particularly in highly public situations where he also needed to speak candidly about Vietnam. Case in point: the public debates between the candidates, none more climactic or consequential than the last and final match-up, just two weeks before Election Day.

THE FINAL DEBATE: A TECHNICAL KNOCKOUT

By mid-October, Dick Mallary had satisfied his scruples and, not incidentally, seen that his Rose Garden strategy was disastrously ineffective with someone as aggressive and media savvy as Leahy. He was more than ready to come back from Washington and fight for the Senate seat. And in spite of a long-standing tradition for candidates to limit television advertising to the final two weeks of the fall campaign, Mallary green-lighted a three-and-a-half-week television campaign, and managed in that way to be up on the air before his rival.

For the small political chattering class, it was an eyebrow-raising move, essentially a 50 percent increase in the expected ad buy. Leahy was gaining, there was no question, and Mallary had finally shucked off the last of his reluctance to engage.

For the coup de grâce, Mallary's team had hired a media consultant out of Boston named Sam Miller. Miller was known for sharp, gut-level spots, and for Mallary he had put together something equally earthy—an ad attacking Leahy's support from organized labor. The spot showed overweight, shirtsleeved men passing money back and forth over a backroom table: "You couldn't see any faces, just big hands, big cigars, big money, big ashtrays; and it was all no people, just hands and money and cigars."[27]

The spot crystallized a line of attack that Mallary and national Republicans had been pursuing for months, that Democrats were in the pocket

of thuggish union bosses. Leahy had, in fact, accepted substantial contributions from labor, some of it from out of state, and made no bones
about it (the *Free Press* put that total at $30,000, including the primary
spending).[28] It represented the support of very hardworking men and
women, he said. And Leahy defended himself on the issue by pointing
out that he had turned down certain contributions from unions he did
regard as suspect. But Mallary thought he had a winning issue — one that
tarnished Leahy's reformist, crusading prosecutor image — and he drove
it home with an unusually large ad buy.

Suddenly, Leahy, so long the aggressor in the race, found himself relentlessly on the receiving end. And in the debates — which had finally
begun to draw real voter interest — Mallary's attacks now left Leahy vulnerable to sniping from the Left as well. During a candidates' forum at
Johnson State College in mid-October, Leahy called Mallary's ads "slan-
derous" and demanded, "Are you saying that I can be bought?" Mallary
shook his head at the direct language: "I never said you can be bought."

Leahy, having come prepared for the denial, then actually held up the
text of the ad to the audience. "Dick Mallary says that he never meant to
imply I accept money from bankers and tycoons; well, listen to the ad
itself," Leahy said, before reading the text aloud to the audience, which
burst into laughter and applause.

"There was even louder applause, however," the *Free Press* observed,
"when the Liberty Union candidate for Senate Bernard Sanders told the
students, 'The real answer is that they can *both* be bought . . . for the
next 10 debates now this is going to be a real circus, with Pat Leahy asking, "Are you saying I can be bought?" and Dick Mallary saying "I never
said that!"'"[29]

It was a dangerous situation in which to find himself, and Leahy's first
impulse, predictably enough, was anger — and media-ready outrage.

"Richard Mallary has launched the most expensive, most personal advertising attack on an opponent in the *history* of Vermont politics," Leahy
thundered. "I wish Dick Mallary had the courage to stand face to face
with me in our next public confrontation and say what he thinks. Is he
saying the people of Vermont can be bought? I want to hold Mr. Mallary
accountable for those ads."[30]

But his second reaction, suddenly and humanly enough, was confusion and self-doubt. To David Schaefer, who was also driving Leahy
during that stretch, Leahy seemed suddenly plagued with anxiety about
the race: "I think he had lost his balance for a little while."

Tuesday, October 22, turned up cold and wet and miserable, calling-in-sick-to-work weather. Rain turned to snow and back again as the day wore on, and the wind gusted against the doors of the sedan, but Leahy and Schaefer doggedly kept to the campaign schedule. As they drove, Schaefer did his best to prep Leahy for the debate, but he could see that the candidate's heart wasn't truly in it. Neither addressed the mood, but it was clearly the moment where losing candidates and their campaigns both first begin to feel the chill come killing into their marrow.

And then, out of nowhere, came what can only be described as a miracle: Leahy's car phone rang.

The phone call was from a United Press International reporter, Floyd Norris, looking for a response to a story only just at that moment moving over the wire. As Leahy knew, Mallary had accepted a $20,000 contribution from the Republican Boosters Club, a Washington-based organization set up to fund local races around the nation—but the new information was that apparently $7,500 of that bloc donation had come from the Seafarers Union, a national labor organization then lobbying aggressively for a bill requiring that a higher percentage of imported oil be handled by American shippers.

It was a trifecta: out-of-state contributions that were also union contributions that were also arguably an attempt to influence the congressman on prospective legislation.

Both Leahy and Schaefer realized what they had in this breaking information, but by the time they reached the WCAX television station for the debate that evening, Leahy was still nervous, uncertain whether the untested story line might not blow up in his face. And they had no way of knowing, of course, whether the Mallary campaign had received the same heads-up, and if so, how they might be prepared to react.

The two tall men sat in the sedan for a minute in the parking lot, just to walk through it one more time in the quiet. Schaefer shakes his head and laughs quietly at the memory: "Patrick was *really* nervous going through that—for a guy who was a prosecutor, he was really sweating that. You know, when you've been to brutal murder scenes, in politics there isn't much that will scare you, but he was scared at that moment. And I remember saying to him, 'Well, Patrick, just remember who you are,' and that seemed for some reason to turn him around." Leahy patted Schaefer's shoulder, and they ran through the drizzle to the studio.

Once inside, Leahy went immediately to speak with Charlie Lewis, the moderator, and Schaefer joined some other Leahy staffers—and a few from the Mallary campaign—in a small, second-floor viewing room overlooking the studio. It wasn't the most comfortable grouping; the two sides had been going at it hammer and tongs for months now. Small-talk was limited, and limited to one's own team.

But eventually 8 p.m. came, the klieg lights went up, the program went live, the viewing room hushed. Leahy's angry challenge of the week before—that Mallary stand face to face with him and repeat his union attacks in person—hadn't been forgotten by anyone present, campaign operative or journalist.

And for the first few moments the debate bumped along like any other, with a few inconsequential exchanges and both the candidates rehearsing lines from their stump speeches one more time. The candidates fenced, but warily, each unwilling to close with the other on anything controversial.

But then, in complete keeping with his campaign's long-standing playbook, Mallary took what seemed like a casual opportunity to again reference Leahy's out-of-state contributions, during the course of which he uttered the word "unions."

In the observation room above, Schaefer froze in his chair.

There's an old saying among prosecutors that if you want a jury to convict, you have to be willing to point directly at the accused. Leahy didn't go that far, but he turned directly to face Mallary, and no one could miss the directness of the charge, or the heat of the indignation: "I'm surprised to hear you say that sort of thing, Congressman, because we've just now learned, today, that your campaign is taking out-of-state money from another union, the Seafarers Union."

And as Leahy filled in the implications of the new information—the strong suggestion of hypocrisy, the fact that the Seafarers were in fact currently seeking preferential legislation—the live studio cameras caught the unguarded process of the congressman's face sliding into open disbelief. Only British slang manages to capture the particular posture and expression: Mallary just stood behind his podium, gobsmacked.

There was no doubt whatsoever, on either side, that this was a watershed moment. Schaefer, now leaning out to touch the glass in the overhead observation room, notes that "there was like a collective gasp in that room I was in, because it turned out [Mallary's people] had no idea this was coming. No idea at all. Mallary was just stunned; he probably didn't even know there was money from the Seafarers Union in the campaign coffers. It was the major 'aha' moment of the campaign."[31]

Brian Harwood, in front of his television screen at home, half an hour away in Moretown, watched in horror as his candidate struggled: "His face fell. And he was literally just speechless. I mean, I think he mumbled and fumbled a little bit—because he didn't know it. I mean, he had no idea that this had happened." Like Schaefer, Harwood knew immediately that here was the next day's headline, if not a game-changing theme for the final two weeks of the campaign. "That was a real moment for me of 'Holy crap.'"[32]

What Mallary eventually was quoted as saying looks composed enough on paper: "I am frankly unaware of the funds which Mr. Leahy is referring to." But for anyone watching the broadcast, the way the words actually came together was unforgettable, and all but devastating. Mallary tried to pivot away from the damaging new information with a reference to his success among small donors, pointing out that his average contribution had been just twenty-two dollars. But Leahy attacked again, pointing out that the Seafarers contribution was thousands of dollars, from an out-of-state union with a very particular agenda, just the sort of contribution Mallary had denounced for weeks.

Again, Mallary struggled.[33]

The defenses came up again quickly enough, though. Mallary worked his way through the remainder of the debate, although for good measure Leahy grilled him on his support for the Arkansas binary nerve-gas factory when allowed a direct question. ("Clearly," Mallary shot back, "I do not like germ warfare. I do not like nuclear warfare. I do not like any kind of warfare.") And by the next day Mallary's campaign had a very plausible spin for the new information: the congressman in fact opposed the oil shipping set-aside that the Seafarers were seeking, as did Leahy, because it could potentially raise gas prices in New England.

But of course the damage had already been done. What mattered most was what had happened personally between the two men. Vermonters had seen their one-term congressman genuinely staggered on live television, seen it with their own eyes; they'd seen Leahy in sharp command of the same exchange, and it was an impression that couldn't help but linger.

Then, in an embarrassment of riches, came the capper for the Leahy-ites: a late-breaking poll commissioned by the *Vermont Times* showed that Leahy had actually closed to within 4 percentage points of Mallary. It was a head-turning result, made even better by the Democratic candidate's own invariably sunny math: "Figuring the error factor, we're ahead."

Leahy, who had been working brutal eighteen-hour days, now found that even five hours of sleep was no longer possible. The excitement was simply too much, and wherever he was in the state he was up before the sun. Suddenly, the momentum was entirely with the Children's Crusade.

Until October 31, Halloween Day, that is, when Congressman Dick Mallary received a miracle of his own.

THE NARAMORE POLL

The Halloween miracle was a front-page *Rutland Herald* headline, there to be perused over morning coffee by all the southern Vermonters the Democratic Senate campaign had spent the last six months so desperately courting: "Polls Bolster Mallary." It must have been Congressman Mallary's favorite headline of the campaign to date, but by the next day the *Herald* had found a way to boil it down into something far sweeter, a headline for the ages: "Chittenden Poll Dooms Leahy."[34]

The poll in question, conducted for radio station wvmt by perhaps the state's best-known and savviest pollster, Saint Michael's College professor Vincent Naramore, showed Mallary suddenly breaking the race wide open, leading Leahy 53 percent to 40 percent. Equally stunning were the geographical breakdowns: out of eight geographical regions, Leahy led only in his two home counties, Chittenden and Washington, and even there only relatively weakly so. The *Free Press* headline was far less sensational but equally devastating to the hopes of a campaign that had just declared the race a toss-up: "Mallary Leading Leahy by 13 Points, Says Poll."

Leahy's team was not entirely blindsided. Schaefer had gotten wind of the result the previous day, and then — terrified that the candidate would be confronted publicly with the news and photographed looking as though he'd been sucker-punched — he had driven the two hours to Rutland to warn Leahy, as the radio-phone was off-limits to the campaign team. So Leahy had had a chance to compose himself, at the very least, and to prepare a response before the results hit the presses.

Still, doom it was. Yes, it was a poll like any other, in most regards no different from the encouraging *Vermont Times* poll of the previous week, but the reception of the two samplings was day and night — a very sunny day versus a very inky night.

The Naramore poll (as it was almost instantly known, although co-conducted with Dr. Frederick Maher of Saint Michael's College) would be the last major poll before Election Day; at a stroke, therefore, it seemed to counter and turn back Leahy's new fifteen-hundred-vote-margin line.

If Naramore's numbers were to be believed—and his past polling both statewide and in his hometown of Salisbury had been highly accurate —then the margin in the race was closer to twenty-five thousand, a gap that simply couldn't be closed by the challenger in the space of a week.

But worse still, the Naramore poll was very deliberately released in dribs and drabs over an extended period in that last week. "The poll was publicly released in two sections, to allow a couple of radio stations that paid for the work to broadcast 'new' results every hour" over the course of two days.[35] The conservative *Herald*, for its part, massaged the material into three full days of headlines—announcing the buzz about the poll on Wednesday, the verified results on Thursday, and then delivering the actual sentence of "doom" on Friday, making it almost the sole topic of discussion during the final weekend before Election Day. Suddenly, savvy insiders—who had taken to hedging their bets over the last two weeks—saw how foolish they had been to believe that 1974 would see a Democrat sent to Washington. Even former governor Hoff, now the Democratic state chairman, admitted that his faith in Leahy's chances had been badly "shaken."[36]

Within seventy-two hours, the two rival Senate campaigns had neatly exchanged emotional places.

Harwood and Knox were now ecstatic; every factor they had believed to be underlying the race had been finally borne out, and without a moment to spare; even Mallary's maddening unwillingness to actively campaign until mid-October, even this now seemed like the admirably cool play of a man who had known all along that his hand was pat. The endgame looked like a matter of simply staying the course. "We thought everything was going to go pretty well from that point on," Harwood says, nodding, summing up the reaction. "I don't remember we adjusted much of anything after that. I think—given the cushion we thought we had—I think we basically kept everything as it was."

For the Leahyites, "dispirited" was the adjective that the papers would eventually settle upon, but it wouldn't be overstating the case to say that they were devastated, to a person, even despite the fact that the Naramore poll had been taken before that crucial final debate with Mallary. "The campaign was working, and it was slowly growing, gaining," Paul Bruhn remembers, recounting the methodical trends they had been tracking in the polling data, "and then there was the Naramore poll. And that just had an incredibly deflating effect on all of us—including Patrick—and on the voters."[37]

Gallows humor quickly became the order of the day. The campaign had a *Hagar the Horrible* cartoon tacked up, showing Hagar and his few men utterly surrounded by an army brandishing spears and swords, with Hagar shouting, "Take no prisoners!" It tickled Leahy and Schaefer particularly, and when Leahy would head out to an event, Schaefer would shout behind him, "Take no prisoners!"[38]

But Leahy himself had one last scrap of hope to offer doomsaying reporters and the generally dispirited, the small remaining scrap he had himself been feeding on since Halloween and which had the potential to be the Senate campaign's boldest innovation to date. It was what Leahy himself would eventually come to call the "blockbuster": the thirty-minute, prime-time, game-changing, every-single-last-rabbit-out-of-the-hat campaign film.

THE "LEAHY WALTON FILM"

For all their various tones and shapes and sizes, there are only two sorts of candidates when all is said and done—those who campaign as though it's a fact of political life, and those who campaign as though their lives depend upon it. Loss is a very real sort of emotional death to this second sort, and for that reason it's impossible to miss them in a crowded field of candidates. Not only do they outwork their opponents on a day-to-day basis, not only do they project a more coherent path to victory—or more often several paths—but they simultaneously and secretly reverse-engineer a series of powerful defensive bulwarks against defeat.

In a word, they firewall. And Leahy was no exception. Rather, his 1974 firewall would thereafter determine the outermost limits of the rule.

Leahy's get-out-the-vote operation was superior to any the state had seen since 1962, when the Kennedy wave had brought young volunteers flocking to the Hoff campaign, and that was some real comfort. But as Leahy drove the state's highways and back roads in those final days of the Senate campaign, he could also tell himself with some grim satisfaction that he hadn't waited for disaster to strike in the final week of the campaign. He had imagined that disaster clearly months before, and taken steps to construct a highly elaborate firewall: a thirty-minute prime-time campaign film, produced for television entirely by the campaign team itself, and designed to boost Leahy's poll numbers radically in the final week of the campaign.

The idea was to introduce the candidate, to show him among his family and in friendly settings, to control the media frame entirely for the space of thirty minutes — and then, of course, to repeat those same thirty minutes six or seven times to saturate the target audience. It was a bold concept, though not entirely original; this particular political art form had been pioneered and developed by filmmaker Charles Guggenheim, among others. Guggenheim made similar films for Senator Howard Metzenbaum and eventually presidential candidate George McGovern, with budgets as much as $100,000 to operate within.[39]

But when consultant Joe Rothstein suggested a half-hour film to the Leahy operation, it was clear that it would need to be done on a relative shoestring. Of the $13,500 eventually spent on producing and airing the film, only about half the amount actually went into production of the film itself: Warren-based documentary filmmaker Dorothy Tod eventually made what she still calls "the Leahy Walton film" on sixteen-millimeter stock for just $7,000.

Still, the overall economics of the thirty-minute chunk of airtime were compelling. wcax, for instance, was charging the Leahy campaign $1,973 for nine thirty-second spots and six sixty-second spots, but by contrast the station was willing to part with an entire half-hour block in prime time for just $854, less than half the price.[40]

Tod had bought a house in Warren in 1970 and was, in her own words, "pretty new to Vermont — I would say stupid. Or impressionable or whatever." But not inexperienced: she had been working in the New York cinema verité world for years, and had only recently finished working with *Sesame Street*, where she had created very brief live-action animal films to provide transitions between Jim Henson's Muppet sequences.

Helping to launch *Sesame Street* had been exciting, but Tod was frankly disillusioned — the clipped, occasionally hyperactive editing of the children's program struck her as a bad road to travel down, developmentally speaking. So she "wandered up to Vermont, résumé in hand," telling herself, "I have to find a way to start making something longer."[41]

The assignment for the Leahy film — arranged through Rothstein and the ad firm Reed-Worthley — came just in the nick of time, financially speaking (Tod still says wryly of her operation, "There's a thread of poverty that goes through the program here"). Once she had gotten the bare bones of a script, mostly in the form of a list of short interviews between Leahy and representative constituents, Tod was free to work as she saw fit. And she saw fit to use very little in the way of scripting. She wanted to move around with the camera, follow Leahy and capture intimate moments, and she found a cameraman to match her style, Adam Gifford.

For months, the two had followed Leahy up and down the state, Tod taking sound and Gifford with camera at the ready. But while Leahy gave her unlimited access, and had been a solid booster of the film idea from the first, he wasn't a natural in front of the camera. Leahy's hundreds of hours speaking to the lens had all been done in highly scripted formats: television news hours, on-camera interviews at crime scenes, debates with rigid rules and time limits and choreography.

Tod's approach was more or less the reverse, however, and at first it was an awkward fit. "He was, I'd say, a little uncomfortable [on camera] . . . he needed a prop. Dave Schaefer was a good prop, he could play off Dave, or Marcelle — or he needed his camera as a prop. That way he could go in and take still pictures and be present [but not the focus]. To me he's a somewhat removed character on film."

And so, partially via inspiration and partially via necessity, Tod hit upon the film's disarmingly casual structuring device: Leahy, driving his battered sedan down a long Vermont road, speaking softly to the camera positioned in the passenger seat. Other than an occasional glance at the camera, the candidate of course had to keep his eyes on the road; the steering wheel and oncoming traffic thus became his props. Best of all, the set-up allowed Leahy's conversational style the time and space it needed to come through to listeners, as it invariably did in personal appearances.

(And it's worth noting that for the sedan itself — Leahy's own battered yet technologically enhanced Batmobile — this was a quantum leap. In addition to its two Dictaphones and two-way radio handset, the car was now, quite literally, a fully operational film set as well, capable of producing images wherever it traveled or en route with equal ease. It was the apex for a campaign that had thus far managed to co-opt or bypass much of the traditional media apparatus. Only the lack of a suitable antenna and a broadcaster's license prevented the Leahyites from dispensing with that apparatus altogether.)

To watch the opening to Tod's film today is to realize immediately why so many Vermonters would be engaged by it in the final days of the race — it functions almost precisely like the opening of a thirty-minute detective drama, a cop show like *Dragnet* or *Adam-12*, the sort of show that might have been in reruns during the 7 p.m. slot the Leahyites had their eye on for broadcast.

When the film's title comes up in white below Leahy's face — *Senate '74: Choosing a New Leader for Vermont* — it might as well be the title sequence of a Jack Webb crime drama, an effect heightened by David Schaefer's sober narration: "This year we will choose a new senator for Vermont. . . . This is the story of the 1974 Senate campaign, Vermont's people and their problems, and one candidate, Patrick Leahy." Like *Dragnet*'s tag, "The story you are about to see is true," Schaefer's words framed the film as a true story, but more primarily as a *story*—as entertainment, of the sort that viewers were accustomed to enjoying in the hour following their local news.

During the course of these thirty-minute segments—the film would eventually run in prime time on five separate television stations—Pat Leahy became not simply a character with whom viewers were familiar, but a de facto hero in a real-world drama, one that featured their own trials and troubles as well. And predictably it was this highly effective narrative stitching, the segments with Leahy chatting behind the wheel, that elicited the most derision from the Mallary camp.

"It was highly unusual. Leahy did a half an hour," Harwood says today, waving a hand, "in the car, kind of a *recitative* about what he thought about Vermont and what it ought to be and all that."[42]

Marcelle, invariably described by print reporters as "pretty" or "attractive," needed little fashioning; there is an almost palpable presence when the camera focuses in on her, describing her early attraction to Leahy. It was something Tod saw from the first: "Marcelle was very easy to work with. She just had a star power, and a charm, and a smoothness that you could just see was totally necessary for him." In the film, she talks about her whirlwind courtship by Pat, blushing as she does so.

And the family, from Leahy's grandparents to his youngest children, take center stage as well. Black-and-white still photos of Leahy's stonecutter grandfather, of the Leahy Press and of Leahy himself as a boy dressed with a jack-o'-lantern head for Halloween—viewers could be excused for forgetting that the election was supposed to be a referendum on inflation and Vietnam and corruption in Washington.

"The Leahy Walton film," Tod says now, laughing softly at herself, "that's how I always remember us all referring to it." *The Waltons*, of course, had begun a nine-season run on CBS just two years earlier, and the show's credits—which always involved the many Walton sons and daughters saying goodnight to the closing strains of a harmonica—had already become an equally long-running and affectionate joke in the popular culture.

This is not to say that Tod's film is a Hollywood production—far from it. The production values, in line with the budget, are low. As the *Free Press* would diplomatically put it, "Generally the documentary film has an unrehearsed appearance and one of its few technical difficulties is occasional jumpiness that may have been caused by splicing."[43]

And in point of fact, much of *Senate '74* functions in a very workaday manner, with Leahy duly answering questions duly asked, by friends and acquaintances designed to represent various voting constituencies. (Sideburn-wearing student standing on the University of Vermont green: "Are you willing to support a reduction in the defense budget?" Leahy: "Certainly. Especially when they seem to have money to spend on such things as a nerve-gas factory. This is abhorrent!")

Still, the film does have real charm, much of which lies in its few strands of what can only be called Hollywood tinsel, its occasionally open embrace of television's ubiquitous dramatic framing and celebrity culture. In this way, the made-for-TV campaign film was precisely the sort of early postmodern innovation that Richard Mallary was incapable of embracing, Patrick Leahy was incapable of refusing, and hence offered one last clarified distinction for voters choosing between them in the final days of the campaign.

"No one's going to watch a thirty-minute commercial," Harwood reassured his own troops, none of whom relished Leahy's sudden after-dinner dominance of their family television screens. And if they did watch, Harwood hastily added, they would likely be miffed that their favorite game shows had been pulled in favor of some politician's horn blowing.

This, the Mallary folks agreed privately, would be the final downfall of Clarabell, the moment when Leahy's hunger for the media spotlight would, at long last, consume him.

ELECTION DAY

November 5, 1974, was overcast and cold, and rain pattered off and on during the day. Like the day of the final debate, the weather was enough to dampen the enthusiasm of all but the truest-believing volunteers. Experts had already been predicting low turnout, with voters generally disillusioned in the wake of Watergate and its myriad related scandals. If 280,000 Vermont voters were eligible to come out to the polls that day, the consensus was that 100,000 or more might stay home out of mild disgust—but as the rain continued, even those estimates were revised downward.

Only college reporters initially showed up at Leahy's election party, including a young Chris Graff, who would later become a much-respected AP bureau chief. The cream of the state's political press were all in Montpelier, of course, to watch history be made: the election of the youngest senator in Vermont history, forty-five-year-old Richard Mallary.

But very quickly after the polls closed, a warning flare went up just shy of the Canadian border: the first town to report, tiny Holland, Vermont, with just over two hundred households and a solidly Republican voting history, went unexpectedly for Leahy. Clearly, Marcelle's dogged French-speaking campaign swings in the Northeast Kingdom had found fertile ground.

More red flares quickly went up from small towns to the south in conservative Rutland County, towns like Tinmouth, where dairy farmers had long provided a bulwark against growing Democratic strength in Chittenden County. All across the state, it rapidly became clear, Leahy had apparently made many small traditional GOP towns a wash: Jay (28–27), Bloomfield (21–17), Westfield (94–96). *We're in deep*, thought Harwood, tracking results in Montpelier. Already he and Knox knew they were in for a long night, and it was only a little past 8 p.m.[44]

For the Leahy folks, whose outlook had been grim, the news started off very well, and rapidly got better and better. In addition to strong vote totals where they had worried about getting any support at all, they were reaping unexpectedly huge margins in safe spots. Chittenden County was of course the treasure trove: Burlington was Leahy's by 2 to 1, outdone only by Winooski, where Leahy's Catholicism and working-class pitch upped the margin to 3 to 1 (1,312–379).

And significantly, Bernie Sanders and the Liberty Union Party had been held to less than 5 percent, no small feat given Sanders's own impressive statewide barnstorming. "I got maybe 4% of the vote," Sanders —now Vermont's other US senator—says today, "as Leahy occasionally reminds me."[45]

By 11 p.m., the momentum had clearly shifted—the bulk of the state's reporters had by then made the decision to quietly abandon the Mallary rally, where most of the "Republicans . . . seemed worn out," although they "stayed on their feet or rested in the few chairs and hoped for the best." But forty-five minutes north on Route 89, they found the Leahy affair at the Burlington Ramada Inn crackling with electricity, now packed with over three hundred supporters. Much to the reporters' delight, "balloons, streamers and free drinks flowed," and at around 11:25 Leahy finally left the hotel room where he had been closeted with friends and family since the polls closed.

It took a few long moments to reach the microphone—and to range his parents and Marcelle's parents next to him on the stage—but when he did, Leahy gave the crowd the sort of gruff, deadly-dry, tongue-in-cheek humor that would become his trademark. "A funny thing happened on the way to the Naramore polls," he began in a hoarse shout, a comment that was interrupted "immediately by applause, wolf-whistles and cheers."

Only those who knew Leahy best would note that his dark tie was the same he had worn for his announcement eight months previously, and in most of the key segments in the campaign film—not because it was lucky, but because it was the only decent tie he owned. But that now seemed likely to change.

"Give 'em hell, Pat!" one man yelled. "What do you think I'm doing?" Leahy shot back to more laughter, and then broke down into giggles himself. And then he continued, with mock solemnity, "I was told that I should write two speeches for this event tonight—one if you lose, and one if you lose badly." Then, patting the air to quiet the guffaws of the crowd, he said more soberly, "Look, it isn't over yet, folks. But I think we're going to pull this off."[46]

And indeed, it wasn't over. Back in Montpelier, Mallary was still hearing from his campaign consultants in Boston that he was behind by only some five hundred votes, although the Vermont reporters tracking the results had that margin at roughly fifteen hundred. But by 1 p.m., the congressman was moving slowly toward acceptance. The result clearly rankled, however, and Mallary—like any politician pinched and caught in a similar position—was struggling with his options and his emotions.

"Apparently the results are fairly clear," Mallary announced to the remaining reporters; "1,500 votes evidently separate us, with 95% of the votes in." Still, he added ominously, "I have no idea if I will seek a recount. I rule out nothing."

But only a few minutes later, out of the glare of the spotlight, Mallary's fundamental generosity reasserted itself. At 1:10 he telephoned Leahy in his room at the Ramada, a call taken by David Schaefer and then passed off to the candidate. "Pat, look, I'm sorry to have dragged this out, but the figures were fairly close. I'll be around this week, and if there is anything I can do to ease your way in, please let me know."[47]

True to form, the Leahy campaign had Sandy Milens present to capture the moment, a soon-to-be famous shot that Leahy would later autograph to media guru David Schaefer: "Dave—It wouldn't have been possible without the help from you and Jane. Patrick."

It was a gracious concession, and it finally allowed Leahy—sapped in every muscle, with the entire family now in tow—to return to the Ramada ballroom at about 1:30 a.m., where the swollen, partially drunken crowd had been chanting "We want Patrick!" since word of the concession call had seeped out. At the official news that Mallary had conceded, though, there was complete bedlam. The crowd couldn't be quieted for a full five minutes (and in fact it would be after 3 a.m. when the party finally ended).

When Leahy had them again, had them as quiet as they could be made to be, and had thanked everyone he could think of, he made a point of bringing the campaign full circle, as was only right and fitting and true: "I think my support has come from all over Vermont. I want to represent the whole state, and that's what we're seeing." He swept his hand over the crowd, and looked out over the faces of all his supporters, not one of whom—regardless of age—had ever seen a US senator from Vermont of their own political party before. There was a fascination shining in their eyes, a wonderment, something he found hard to put into words himself.

But he tried: "We started this thing with a small circle of friends. The *Free Press* called us the children's crusade. Well, my friends, we have grown to the big circle you see here tonight. Thank you all."[48]

POST-CRUSADE VERMONT

If the Naramore poll had seemed to cant the Vermont political world briefly back onto its traditional axis, Leahy's stunning upset of Mallary forcibly wrenched it off again, and the shock waves continued long after Election Day. The *Burlington Free Press*, having closed its preelection coverage with the observation that "two factors do not seem to have had a significant effect upon the US Senate race . . . the fate of the economy and the Watergate affair," humbly opened its post-election analysis with the line, "Nationally, the Leahy victory fitted a general pattern of Democratic wins, in the wake of the Watergate scandals and the economy."[49]

And Leahy would be coming into a freshman Senate class with a stellar cast of Democrats who had run aggressively and successfully on reform, Gary Hart and John Glenn among them. A new era was visibly dawning.

In his own defense, Vincent Naramore pointed to the polling results he had achieved in the two *other* 1974 marquee races—the race for governor between Tom Salmon and Walter Kennedy, and the US House race featuring Jim Jeffords and Francis Cain. In both cases, Naramore's numbers actually proved respectably accurate. He had predicted a 56–38 result in the former case, which actually finished 57–38; and 57–27 in the Jeffords–Cain race, which actually tallied 53–40. Naramore was simply at a loss to explain why he had so badly blown the race between Leahy and Mallary. But Leahy himself was never in any doubt: "The blockbuster had to be the movie," he said.[50]

With Naramore's other accurate readings as a sort of ersatz control, it's hard to avoid the conclusion that Tod's "Leahy Walton film"—and the campaign's aggressive decision to air it in a handful of thirty-minute blocks around the state—eclipsed the impact of any other single final factor. In their endless fascination and experimentation with media, the Leahyites had managed to debut a political weapon whose potency shocked even themselves. No one more so, in fact, than director Dorothy Tod. Yes, Tod was elated that Leahy had won, and that a Democrat would now sit in the Senate. Yes, she enjoyed the attention suddenly being paid to her work. And she had found Leahy and Marcelle to be unfailingly gracious, kind people, and finds them so to this day. But at the same instant, she found herself distinctly uncomfortable with the raw influence her own artistic medium could have in a relatively tiny media market like Vermont.

A new phase in the political arms race had commenced, and Tod didn't like the feel of it. "There was too much power in it," she says now, closing her eyes and shaking her short silver hair, as though to clear the thought of it—"just that you could do a half-hour film, and suddenly somebody's a *senator.*"

Tod struggles to put her discomfort—her particular brand of fear, really—into words: "That was the time of Marshall McLuhan and the medium is the message, and all of a sudden you were already into the —the *machinery* of it. I felt like suddenly I was just this instrument in this larger shift."[51]

Yet a key part of the reason that Patrick Leahy was now headed to the Senate, rather than Dick Mallary, was that Leahy's own instinctive, gut reaction to this transformation was just the opposite.[52]

Leahy knew that he was being sent to Washington to battle not just the oil monopolies but the system rigged to empower them, a system embodied by a corrupt Republican administration, and that he would need both to be and to play the Top Cop at a level he had thus far only imperfectly imagined. He knew, in short, that his personal film would now need to do what it is in the nature of blockbusters to do: produce sequels. And at just thirty-four years of age, with six long years to run before his next election, US Senator-elect Patrick Joseph Leahy could not have been more ready.

Ninety-Ninth of One Hundred

Arguably, no one was more stunned by Patrick Leahy's against-all-odds Senate victory than the senator-elect himself. Yes, he and Marcelle had never lost hope, but even Leahy's own optimistic internal polls had predicted a tough seven-point loss just days before the election. Dorothy Tod's "Leahy Walton film," as it turned out, had very suddenly changed everything.

And now the candidate who had done the least to plan for the transition to Washington, DC, would have to get serious about those complex logistics, and quickly.

But the unvarnished truth was that Leahy had been burning the candle at both ends and in the middle for months—managing multiple prosecutions and an internal police sting operation as state's attorney, in addition to campaigning frenetically from one end of the state to the other—and he was drained, utterly exhausted. Which is how Leahy and Marcelle and Paul Bruhn and his girlfriend all wound up in the Virgin Islands together that November, on the island of Saint Croix.

It was the sort of fantasy vacation neither of the couples had ever managed before, but Leahy felt that they all richly deserved it. Bruhn had given a year of his life to a groundbreaking twenty-four-hour campaign effort. Marcelle had worked as hard as any of the full-time paid staffers, and cared for the couple's children into the bargain. Leahy owed them all a huge debt, and a week or two of sun wouldn't be a bad down payment.

Still, he was no fool—the campaign/transition team kept the senator-elect's whereabouts on a need-to-know basis. No single word in a wintertime political story raises Vermont eyebrows like the adjective "Caribbean."

It was at their Saint Croix hotel that Leahy formalized an offer that had been more or less implicit during the weeks following the election: he wanted Bruhn as his chief of staff in Washington. Bruhn had proven his ability to design, staff, and lead a crack team, but more crucially, as Bruhn now boils it down, "Patrick knew I was completely loyal, completely supportive. We had a very tight relationship. There was just no one else there as a possibility."[1]

It would be a very youthful operation—Bruhn was actually seven years younger than his wunderkind boss—but that hadn't hurt them any in the election. Just the opposite, in fact. The campaign's innovative approach to media was part of a broad generational and technological shift, and Leahy had every reason to believe that he and Bruhn were the best team to play at the forefront of those cultural changes post-Watergate.

Finally, Bruhn flew back to the mainland to begin the heavy lifting. Leahy had another few days in the sun, and then he and Marcelle packed their own bags. But coming home was no chore, even with winter closing in. He was returning to the state that had just made him both the youngest, and the only Democratic, us senator in its history. Its people had placed an astounding amount of trust in him, shown him a great deal of love, and Leahy couldn't help but break into a smile every time he went over it all again in his mind.

Of course, quite nearly half the state had voted for Mallary.

The Republican establishment, and many of the media outlets that had long undergirded it, were still collectively aghast at Leahy's come-from-behind victory. Was the state's new junior senator an outlier? Or the harbinger of an actual coming Democratic majority? How much of the election could be attributed to a historically unpopular and unethical president, rather than any true shift from what would later be termed red to blue?

Predictably enough, at least in hindsight, it wasn't long after touchdown that Leahy discovered just how fleeting his postelection honeymoon was destined to be.

The trouble started with the current occupant of Leahy's Senate seat, the "Dean of the Senate," George Aiken. Vermonters had sent Aiken to Washington, DC, for thirty-four years running, and his Senate seniority had been a huge boon to his small state. By 1974, Aiken was a beloved institution in his own right at home, and perhaps most famous nationally for arguing that the United States should unilaterally declare victory in Vietnam and then simply bring its troops home—not Aiken's actual words and, as historian Mark Stoler has persuasively argued, not Aiken's actual meaning.[2]

It went without saying that one didn't challenge Aiken in the Green Mountain State, but that of course was the problem: Leahy hadn't waited for Aiken to signal his retirement before launching his campaign for Aiken's Senate seat in March of 1974. There had been a good deal of pearl-clutching at the time. The *Rutland Herald* set the bar with an editorial slamming the Democratic candidate for having "the temerity to announce his candidacy for the U.S. Senate before Sen. George Aiken made known his plans to retire."[3] Of course, it was in part Leahy's early and aggressive start that had kept the Democratic field clear and allowed Bruhn the time to construct and deploy the machinery of a statewide campaign — the early start had been effective politics, in short. But Aiken was not about to let bygones be bygones. The *Burlington Free Press* captured the Dean's revenge:

> As the 93rd Congress came to a close, eight of 11 senators, knowing they wouldn't be back for the 94th because of retirement or defeat, quit before their terms were up. That made it possible for some of their successors to be sworn in early.
>
> But Aiken of Vermont would have none of that.
>
> "My contract runs to midnight Jan. 2," he let it be known. "When I have a contract, I like to keep that contract."[4]

Whether Aiken's reading of his contractual obligations might have differed had Dick Mallary been the senator-elect in question, the world will never know. But given that seniority in the US Senate is as painstakingly determined as in the case of identical twin crown princes — precedence of a single minute is enough to separate members of the incoming class — Aiken's pronouncement had the effect of shuffling Leahy as near to the back of the line as it was possible to shuffle.

In fact, Vermont's now extremely junior Democratic senator eventually wound up ninety-ninth out of one hundred in seniority (and would quite possibly have been seated dead last had not a ticklish series of recounts barred New Hampshire's John Durkin from the Senate until September 1975[5]). And the chill from Aiken's Senate offices remained palpable during the transition. But as far as Leahy was concerned — although he kept respectfully mum at the time — it was only to be expected. In 2009, after decades of public silence where Aiken was concerned, he finally confided to *Vermont Business Magazine* that his relationship with Aiken had actually soured years before.

"I'd applied in law school for an internship with Senator Aiken's office, and he was very nice about it," Leahy said. "But he pointed out that my family were Democrats, so there were no internships available. I remember saying at the time that when I have an intern program, I'm not going to ask anyone about their politics. I'll pick them on merits. It's easy to say when you're a law student living in a basement apartment. But 10 years later, when I was a senator, we started an intern program and it's totally on merit."[6]

But even George Aiken's displeasure couldn't dull the magic of the Senate. On his first trip to the capital after the November election, Leahy arranged to meet with one of the senators on the Senate Democratic Steering Committee, the group charged with making all Senate committee assignments. While they chatted, a chime sounded, indicating a roll-call vote on the Senate floor. "Come on with me while I vote, and we can keep talking," Senator Frank Church of Idaho told Leahy. Leahy hung back; he wasn't sworn in yet.

"Don't *worry*," the senator said, shouldering into his suit jacket and hustling Leahy out the door. "Senate rules allow senators-elect on the floor." And when the doorman rose to block him at the door to the chamber, Church smoothly made the necessary introduction: "This is our new senator from Vermont."

The doorman cautiously scanned his list, and then his face broke into a smile. "Right! Senator Leahy. Welcome, sir, and come on in."

Leahy still shakes his head at the memory. "I almost had to look behind me to see who he was talking to. It was the first time anyone had called me 'senator.' As I walked in, my knees were shaking. And it struck me that only weeks before I was trying murder cases and those stressful settings hadn't bothered me a bit. But this . . . I was kind of overwhelmed, but it was nice that among those on the floor Senator Robert Stafford came over and greeted me warmly."[7]

As a student at Georgetown, Leahy had watched debates from the gallery; now, less than a decade later, he was himself looking up at the spectators from the Senate floor. The moment left him with a powerful glow and a heady sense of optimism. The trouble with Aiken was fleeting, after all—Aiken was leaving the Senate, and so theoretically the Aiken grudge was leaving as well.

But not so in practice, it turned out. Aiken had been very close with Senate Majority Leader Mike Mansfield, so close that Mansfield, Aiken, and Aiken's administrative assistant, Lola Pierotti (whom Aiken would marry after the death of his first wife), would eat breakfast together most mornings in Washington.

Political scientist Garrison Nelson, at that time a legislative aide to Leahy, remembers the dynamic well: "Every morning, Mansfield and Aiken and Lola would have breakfast together in the Senate Dining Room. And they'd read the paper and harrumph over it together. So here's the Republican and the Senate Democratic leader as close as can be, and Mansfield was just not going to give Patrick the time of day. And that was clear."

That early frost between Leahy and the majority leader showed itself in a hundred small ways. Mansfield would tap his watch just as Leahy had begun to feel his feet under him when making a speech on the Senate floor; Nelson came to the Senate floor one day to staff Leahy and found himself unexpectedly expelled from his seat by the majority leader, citing the technical rule rather than the common practice.[8]

Fortunately for the Leahyites, Vermont's other senator was more warmly inclined. Former Vermont governor Bob Stafford—himself appointed to the Senate just four years previously—made it clear that anything in his power to give was Leahy's for the asking. Stafford's wife Helen sent Marcelle a handwritten note, offering help and friendship. Most crucially, Stafford offered Bruhn's transition team a spare office in his own Dirksen suite, a bit of generosity that genuinely touched Leahy when he first heard the news from his chief of staff.

And as it turned out, Leahy and Bruhn would look back fondly on that single spare Stafford office, after moving in to their own new accommodations. The only office space left, when the ninety-eight senators ahead in line had finally been accommodated, was a series of dingy basement rooms located somewhere in the shadowy netherworld between the Dirksen and Russell Office Buildings, below ground level but with small transom windows near the ceiling that looked out into dirt-filled window wells.

"We did have windows, by a very strict definition," Bruhn says dryly. "And there was occasionally a little tiny bit of light."

The *Burlington Free Press* took the opportunity to close an otherwise upbeat piece on Leahy's committee chances with a just a pinch of salt in the wound: "Meanwhile, [Leahy's] administrative assistant, Paul Bruhn, has been organizing the staff and setting up Leahy's office, which is in the basement of one of the Senate office buildings."[9]

Vermont's largest daily (mostly its solidly pro-Nixon editorial board) had clearly been biding its time since the events of election night, and when the editors saw their first opportunity, they took it with a vengeance. As chiefs of staff go, Bruhn was indeed relatively young and inexperienced, although senators have absolute latitude in staffing their Washington offices. But it was the fact that Leahy had authorized the maximum pay scale for his incoming chief that the *Free Press* would hit hardest. The damning facts were laid before the public in an editorial helpfully titled, "Leahy's Overpaid Staff."

> Leahy's chief aide is a man 27 years of age who possesses no academic or professional qualification whatever for the job he will attempt to perform, yet he is being paid the maximum salary for Congressional aides — $37,050. This is only about $5,500 below the salary of a U.S. Senator which Leahy himself will receive.
>
> Other Leahy staff members, most of whom have had little or no experience in government or public service, will receive princely salaries which must appear both unconscionable and provocative to Vermonters — particularly in this time of economic recession.

Bruhn and his team might well have disputed the idea that their salaries were "princely," considering DC's infamously high cost of living, but the actual numbers seemed beside the point. It was a clear shot across the bow of Vermont's first Democratic senator, a warning that he could expect both a deeper scrutiny and a tone markedly sharper than that typically used during the Aiken years. The closing lines were a small masterpiece of vituperation: "The question is not whether Leahy has the right to hire inexperienced hangers-on and reward them with outrageous salaries at the taxpayers' expense. The question, rather, is why a U.S. Senator from the small state of Vermont would wish to exercise that right in a manner so insulting and at a time so inappropriate."[10]

In their DC basement office, the inexperienced hangers-on with the princely salaries took due notice and continued trying to make their subterranean space habitable.

Pat Leahy had always been one to move rapidly in any institutional setting; his legal training and his sober manner had always soothed superiors, opened doors, secured competitive scholarships and promotions and appointments. And very naturally and immediately, he began to develop what would become lasting, genuine relationships with some of the older members of the body, the southern senators in particular, men like John Stennis and James Eastland of Mississippi, and Richard Russell of Georgia.

It was a charm offensive, no bones about it, but Leahy's sincerity and his clear willingness to get to work won him points immediately.

Leahy's own incoming freshman class—dubbed the "Watergate class" for the number of Democrats who had won on the issue—*Time* magazine called "particularly impressive," and for good reason. John Glenn, the former astronaut, had finally taken one of Ohio's Senate seats by a 2-to-1 margin; Gary Hart, George McGovern's 1972 campaign manager and "a sort of 'Marlboro Man' turned politician," had "swamped" his incumbent opponent in Colorado by a 3-to-2 margin.[11]

Leahy had met Hart for the first time in December when they were both asked to appear on a DC television program themed around new young reformers in the Senate. Hart was struck not just by Leahy's youth (at thirty-eight Hart had thought he would likely be the youngest of the class), but by his gravitas and his clear focus as a defender of the Constitution.

"From the very beginning," Hart says now, "he staked out a pretty strong platform as a constitutionalist. Having been a lawyer and a prosecutor, he obviously felt strongly about the Constitution in general, but the First Amendment very particularly. I admired how astute he was then."[12]

Hart considered himself a serious reformer, especially with regard to superfluous military weapons systems, and he felt from the first that he and Leahy could work together. "I think [Leahy] was psychologically and politically a reformer—that is to say, he wanted to shake things up not just to be shaking them up, but to try new things and be innovative and creative. I was very much in that mode as well."

But beyond the feeling that here was someone with whom he could partner legislatively, Hart simply liked Pat Leahy, from the first. "He was young, bright, and very congenial. Very down-to-earth, homespun. We were very good friends." Their senses of humor gibed. Occasionally, when Leahy thought that a DC discussion was getting fanciful or too inside-the-Beltway, Hart said, Leahy would puncture the preciousness of it all by "lapsing into Yankee talk," in the broad accent of "a northern Vermont dairy farmer." And Hart would "respond by doing Durango cowboy talk alongside him."

And there was the commiseration factor: Hart wound up ninety-eighth in seniority.

Both Hart and Leahy spent weeks getting to know the eighteen members of the Senate Democratic Steering Committee, primarily responsible for staffing committees, and in the end the committee did as well by the freshmen as it was able. Vermont's junior senator actually got his first choice when it came to committee assignments: Senate Agriculture (Leahy had promised again and again on the campaign trail that Vermont farmers' concerns would be his first priority in DC).

But he had narrowly missed his second choice, Judiciary, and in that he found himself honestly disappointed. Apart from the politics of sitting on Agriculture, secretly he had wanted Judiciary above all. He felt he was amply qualified, and it was where he believed he could eventually make his mark. But freshmen can't be choosers.

That left Leahy's third choice: Senate Armed Services. That left Vietnam.

By 1975, the prolonged war in Southeast Asia was a stunning military debacle, by any standard. It was a year of one crippling, humiliating retreat after another for the government of South Vietnamese president Nguyen Van Thieu. The North Vietnamese Army began a months-long series of offensives just after the New Year and drove much of the opposition before it, rapidly capturing several major cities within weeks and touching off floods of refugees. Phuoc Binh, the provincial capital of Phuoc Long, fell to the Viet Cong in a week. In Cambodia, the Khmer Rouge closed the Mekong River as a South Vietnamese supply corridor, starving Phnom Penh. Russia had renewed its support for North Vietnam with a vengeance.[13]

South Vietnam's second-largest city, Danang, fell in March, after three days of rocket attacks. Thousands of refugees "waded into the sea, among them mothers clutching babies; many drowned or were trampled to death as they fought to reach barges and fishing boats."[14] The North Vietnamese offensives continued to escalate throughout the winter of 1975, and the North's battlefield successes continued to mount.

Still, US intelligence agencies maintained their prediction that Saigon itself would not fall before the rains came in May, slowing hostilities. Beyond that, and in the absence of substantially increased military assistance from the United States, they refused to speculate.

Time had summed up Leahy's 1974 Senate campaign thusly: "Leahy, a State's Attorney for Chittenden County, kept plugging at a theme with peculiar appeal to Vermonters: there was no place for partisanship in replacing 'the strong independent vote we've had for 34 years,' the vote of retiring G.O.P. Senate Dean George Aiken."[15] And the nonpartisan characterization was true enough. Leahy *had* very carefully filed down the sharp edges of his anti-Vietnam stance, and he had presented himself in many ways as a capable, middle-of-the-road, law-and-order Democrat.

But Leahy had also made it amply clear, to those listening carefully, that he meant to oppose the war in Southeast Asia—both Vietnam and Cambodia, open and secret campaigns, the entire far-flung military commitment to Indochina. And to that end, he had asked not for the diplomacy-centric Senate Foreign Relations Committee—typically the choice of Democrats with an internationalist bent—but Armed Services, where the GOP and hawkish Democrats had long held sway.

And the fact that Leahy had actually won a place on Armed Services, as a freshman inclined to scrutinize or even deny funding to the Pentagon for Vietnam, was no accident. Senate Democratic leadership was clearly preparing to make good on its election-year promises to wind down the war. And so in spite of selecting the hawkish John Stennis of Mississippi as chair, the Steering Committee had also fashioned a potential antiwar majority with a contingent of intelligent, skeptical freshmen at its core: Leahy, Hart, and John Culver of Iowa, a former marine captain who had once played fullback on Harvard's football team with Ted Kennedy.

Still, although the makeup of Armed Services was now nine Democrats to six Republicans, Chairman Stennis was himself considered a highly reliable vote for military reauthorization. And Thomas McIntyre of New Hampshire—once a staunchly pro-war Democrat and now of the opinion that in service of Vietnam "our nation is tearing itself apart"— seemed fully capable of swinging either way in early 1975.

Which is to say that the Steering Committee had given the White House and the Pentagon an Armed Services Committee that was balanced on a knife's edge, theirs to win or lose.

But although the situation in Vietnam was chaotic, voting to cut off support to troops in the field remained a wrenching decision—and one for which Leahy would certainly be pilloried as well as applauded. He had followed every last move of Vermont's delegation on the subject before he came to the Senate, and he well knew just how sharp a break he was contemplating with Vermont's traditional Republican support both for the White House and for the US military commitment.

Leahy's predecessor George Aiken, ironically enough, had become famous as an early Republican advocate for withdrawal from Vietnam—when in fact Aiken had said and meant nothing of the kind. In October of 1966, Aiken had actually said, "The United States could well declare unilaterally . . . that we have 'won' in the sense that our armed forces are in control of most of the field and no potential enemy is in a position to establish its authority over South Vietnam." Such a rhetorical move, Aiken argued, would allow not for precipitous or even phased withdrawal but for a face-saving "gradual redeployment" around "strategic centers."[16]

In other words, US troops would be free to leave the more dangerous interior of the country and move to create lasting strongholds along the coast.

This move Aiken saw as a way to build a standoff that might arguably lead to a lasting peace. But it was amply clear throughout the 1966 speech that Vermont's senior senator saw US forces in Southeast Asia for long years to come. And Aiken "objected vehemently" when Democrats began to use the so-called "Aiken formula" to justify an actual American pullout.

Although Aiken became skeptical of White House and Pentagon overreach as he neared his final days in the Senate, his vote for military authorizations had never been in any real doubt. As Mark Stoler frames it, "With half a million men in the field, nuclear war a possibility, and his beliefs regarding the American commitment and presidential power, Aiken would not vote to cut off military appropriations. . . . In the short run, he was forced to conclude pessimistically there was simply nothing he could do to stop the Administration."[17]

But Leahy was not content with criticism and pessimism. And neither, he increasingly suspected, was a working majority of the Armed Services Committee. As he had told *Time*, "There is going to be a coalition of people down there in the Senate now doing things in a different way. Some of us will have gotten in there tenuously, and we will have to prove ourselves by making some changes. I know I will."[18]

The idea that the Watergate class would catalyze a cohesive voting "coalition" was an optimistic notion, certainly. And Leahy had ventured it before he had really experienced firsthand the titanic forces driving the war in Southeast Asia. It was gut-level hope, nothing more.

Of course the White House also understood that Leahy and other freshmen senators had "gotten in there tenuously," and given the stakes surrounding the 1975 military appropriations process, the president's men were not in any way inclined to wait for a freshman to find his feet.

★ ★ ★

It was at his first Armed Services posture hearing in February that Leahy would see just how persuasive — and threatening — a show America's military brass could stage. As its name indicates, the posture hearing provides a moment early in the legislative session for the Pentagon and the Joint Chiefs and other players to sketch the nation's military posture vis-à-vis its traditional enemies and potential threats. Those general considerations are then funneled down, over the course of the following months, into discussions of the various proposed military appropriations.

The Good Fight, Hart's 1993 memoir, captures the elaborate Kabuki that characterizes the military appropriations process:

> Nothing attracted extremes more than defense matters. The Pentagon annually offered a budget it knew to be loaded with items it would not get and, truth be known, probably did not even want. These were bones to liberals and those who wished to build a record of "cutting military spending." This artificial waste (as opposed to real waste) would be hacked off in committees and on the Senate floor to the crocodile tears of the services, all of whom had let their congressional friends know ahead of time the list of expendable items. There was the other side of the coin also. Superhawks would add items the military did not request and sometimes did not want. Much of it was an elaborate, scripted ballet, a *pas de deux* designed to make a record of "being for a strong defense."[19]

In effect, posture hearings double as funding pitches, though often apocalyptic in tone and backed by the most persuasive data the intelligence community has to offer, both classified and unclassified. Hart found the presentations by the secretary of defense, the secretary of state, and others almost comically slanted, Henry Kissinger's estimate of Soviet prowess in particular. The secretary of state's famously thick accent and doomsday outlook dominated the hearing. Although the CIA's best secret intelligence tended to indicate a Soviet Union more clearly at or slightly below parity with the United States, the most prominent administration and military personalities were of one mind about the need for robust increases in military spending.

Like Hart, Leahy found himself increasingly jaded by the time the chairman called a late recess. The rhetoric had escalated to the point where he had to seriously wonder if they would all survive the afternoon coffee break.

But of the three freshmen, it was Culver of Iowa, the former Harvard fullback, who finally put a sarcastic pin to the dark balloon. Culver was a big man with a big voice, a major presence in a room. Just after Chairman Stennis had called the break—and with every senator's microphone still live—Culver leaned over to Hart and Leahy and said, loudly, "Did you ever wonder why the people who seem to care the most about Russia and national security speak with a *really* heavy accent?"

The microphone carried the words to the four corners of the room, and there was a stunned silence, and then the remaining crowd dissolved in nervous laughter. Kissinger and the other Eastern European hawks—the advisers "always wanting us to poke the Russians in the nose"—left as quickly as dignity would allow.[20]

★ ★ ★

By March of 1975, as Leahy remembers it now, "the phone was just ringing off the hook. Everybody was beating up on me." And "everybody" was an all-inclusive term: the personal calls came from President Ford and Secretary of State Kissinger and former secretary of defense Robert McNamara, as well as a carefully orchestrated Who's Who of "influential Vermonters." The vast majority of newspapers back home were happy to take up the drumbeat in support of the president.

Increasing the tension still more was Secretary of Defense Schlesinger's sudden admission in late March that "Saigon could be attacked in the current rainy season"—a worst-case scenario that the intelligence agencies had been denying for months. "All depended," Schlesinger suggested, turning the news to immediate advantage, "on whether the Saigon government could stabilize the military situation."

In other words, the secretary made clear, action in Congress was now the only thing standing between Thieu's government and a final, across-the-board, countrywide defeat in Vietnam.[21]

As the White House prepared its final push, Schlesinger asked for a personal meeting in Leahy's offices. Fortunately, space had become available aboveground in the Dirksen Building just weeks before, and Leahy's operation had been able to move into a more presentable location. Still, Leahy and his chief of staff agreed to the meeting with a certain bemusement. Secretaries of defense rarely came in person to freshmen senators' offices, but the vote in Armed Services was a true nail-biter.

And of course Leahy—now publicly leaning toward a no vote[22]—hailed from what had long been a conservative state, one with a very durable tradition of support for military action. Bruhn and his boss expected to be pressured, but what form that pressure would take they had no idea.

Leahy's chief of staff remembers the Schlesinger group filing into Leahy's new Dirksen office with a very particular air: "It wasn't that they were disrespectful, but they weren't totally respectful."[23] There was the suggestion that Leahy was well-meaning but perhaps didn't completely understand the situation on the ground in Southeast Asia; the tendency was to slightly overemphasize the honorific "senator" when referring to Leahy, as though Schlesinger and his advisers were reminding themselves anew of the fact each time they used it.

The erudite, pipe-smoking Schlesinger was infamous for his aloof manner, even with presidents (Nixon and Ford were both put off by it, in succession). With the thirty-five-year-old junior senator from Vermont, Schlesinger was highly precise and knowing, just a hair shy of patronizing. The heart of the secretary's case in late March was a document produced jointly by the CIA, the Defense Intelligence Agency, and the Bureau of Intelligence and Research of the Department of State.[24]

The joint intelligence assessment showed that Soviet and Chinese aid to the Viet Cong had doubled in 1974, an alarming datum certainly but one that perhaps deliberately left other readings of the information unspoken. Even with reductions to US military aid, for instance, "Saigon appeared to have received twice as much military aid as Hanoi in the past year." And if the North Vietnamese were making dramatic battlefield gains with far less in the way of resources, a skeptic might say that Schlesinger's private intelligence assessment was actually an indirect argument *against* continued funding: "In short, far from a brief for more aid, the document came close to an indictment of the government of South Vietnam for inefficiency."[25]

Leahy's pointed questions during and after the presentation did not sit well, clearly, and the air in the room grew increasingly chilly. "That may have been colored by where Patrick was on the war [publicly]," said Bruhn, "but they were a little bit disdainful of this very junior senator who was pushing them and asking very tough questions."

Finally, Schlesinger put away his pipe and gathered his paper and his aides to leave. He shook Leahy's hand and asked outright if the Pentagon could count on his vote.

Leahy pointedly did not answer the question. But he smiled broadly. "Thanks very much, Mr. Secretary," Leahy said, "I'm always glad to hear your point of view."[26]

In one way, the meeting wasn't all that different from the visit Leahy's father had received in Montpelier decades earlier from a self-appointed group of Republican businessmen, offering friendly advice about how business might pick up for a printer willing to give up either Catholicism or voting Democratic. Howard Leahy had given the little delegation a "sweet smile" and said, "Well, I'll do neither. Thank you."

And Secretary Schlesinger and his staffers had clearly done no better.

★ ★ ★

The White House's final ploy was as insufferable as it was inevitable: arguing that if Congress failed to provide the $722 million for South Vietnamese military aid requested by the Pentagon, then Congress alone bore the blame for a North Vietnamese victory.[27] The strategy was designed both to increase pressure on Congress and to act as a preemptive shifting of the blame if that pressure failed.[28] It was a deliberately slashing accusation, designed to sting, and Leahy and the rest of the Armed Services Committee felt it from every level of the administration.

Lest Americans think that their president didn't share the belief that Congress was to blame for stunning North Vietnamese battlefield gains, Ford took the opportunity of a golf vacation in Palm Springs to make his own feelings clear: "The ruinous decision to abandon the Central Highlands, Mr. Ford said, had been caused by North Vietnamese violations of the Paris agreements, and, in the words of a White House spokesman, 'by the effect on South Vietnamese morale of the prospect that the United States Congress would not approve any more aid in the way of ammunition and equipment that would enable them to fight for their own survival.'"[29]

And this general line of argument Ford laid out in a slightly more diplomatic form in an address to both chambers of Congress on April 10. The White House's final tactic was to point an argument sharp enough to gut a freshman senator, maybe one from a Republican state that had elected only one Democrat in its history.

Maybe only by a margin of, say, 4,406 votes.[30]

★ ★ ★

Thursday, April 17, 1975, a week after Ford's joint address to Congress, found the Armed Services Committee very much in session. The committee room was charged with expectation. Chairman John Stennis was characteristically controlled, in spite of the strong indications that his committee might well have enough votes to reject the White House request for $722 million in military aid. And, in truth, history sided with the senator from Mississippi; it had been years since he had been rolled in his own committee on an issue of any importance. The chairman's ability to deliver for the Pentagon would eventually result in both an aircraft carrier and an entire carrier strike group being named in his honor.

The seventy-three-year-old Stennis might have been hard of hearing, but his eye missed nothing, and if sweeping knowledge of committee procedure or Senate rule could sway the vote, his odds were excellent.

Leahy knew his own mind on the Vietnam question, and he knew Hart's; in fact, Hart had hardly been lobbied by the White House on the appropriation, so remote did the administration consider its chances. Culver had made it amply clear that he wouldn't vote a dime more for the war. But there were several senators who had been cagey right up until that morning. Harry Byrd Jr., Independent Democrat of Virginia, was one such enigma. Byrd had attended the Virginia Military Institute and had always been a resolute supporter of the military. But Leahy and Hart knew he had lost faith in the Vietnam effort.

"Harry Byrd was a kind of libertarian. He was an old Taft Republican, really," says Hart, "and he didn't believe we should be spreading troops all over the world. His argument was less a moral one about killing people than a fiscal one about spending money—Harry *hated* spending money."[31]

It was afternoon by the time the markup of the military appropriation bill reached the $722 million item for the South Vietnamese government, and when Stennis called for the first vote on that measure, the room was uncharacteristically silent.

The first surprise was Harry Byrd's no vote, which raised eyebrows around the room. Leahy felt his hopes rise, but he cast his own firm negative still without any clear sense of where the final tally was headed. Only with Republican William Lloyd Scott's party-crossing vote did the outcome finally become clear. As is tradition, Chairman Stennis voted last, with a poorly concealed scowl.

The vote was 8–7 against further military funding for the conflict in Southeast Asia.[32]

But Stennis was not finished, by any means. The chairman was not above using his poor hearing to his advantage, when the mood struck. "Senator Byrd," he called across the table in his soft Mississippi accent, fixing his eye directly on the Virginia senator. "Did I possibly mishear you? Did you *mean* to vote no?"

Byrd thought for a second. "I did, Senator," he said, then added, "They have lied to me long enough."[33]

Stennis digested that, then called a brief recess. Leahy was exultant; as a freshman he had quickly gotten used to the way that senior members of the Senate fashioned the bulk of legislation out of his viewing, but on the signal issue of the day, his own vote had arguably made a difference. Of course, the committee hadn't yet spoken definitively. The chairman had been rolled, and he was clearly unhappy about it.

And Leahy looked up just in time to see William Scott, the only Republican to vote no, following a desperate White House lobbyist named William Kendall out into the hallway.

Leahy's heart lurched, but it turned out that there was nothing to worry about: "In midafternoon, William Kendall, a White House lobbyist, called Senator Scott out of the committee meeting and made one last effort to persuade him to vote for additional aid. After a conversation of several minutes, Mr. Kendall informed the White House that Scott could not be swayed."[34]

Kendall's was not the last last-ditch ploy, though. Stennis came back with nearly identical appropriation language, but more than $200 million less on the bottom line: the White House was now supporting a $515 million item. It was clearly a move to appeal to the "old Taft Republican" in Harry Byrd. But again the vote was 8–7 against.

So Stennis cleared his throat, and sharpened his pencil: $449 million. The no vote held.

And sharpened it again: $401 million.

And again: $370 million.

Each time the skeptical coalition held; each time Leahy let out his breath only when Scott had repeated his negative. Leahy felt for the Virginian — Stennis was deliberately making it as hard as humanly possible on the Republican, forcing him to cross party lines again and again and again, against sums that looked at least comparatively affordable.

And the look behind his thick-framed glasses said that Stennis was prepared to go on like this all afternoon, or until the committee reached zero, but when he called an identical vote for an even $350 million, it was the yes coalition that crumbled: two of Stennis's own supporters thought $350 million too small a sum to make a difference in any event and sided with the no voters.

Stennis sat back in his chair with a sour look and said, "Well, I guess it makes no sense to take another vote." And then with a nod of his head, he called to the committee's assistant, "Please get the president on the line for me."

Later, when asked by reporters whether some way might be found around the committee's vote, Stennis was uncharacteristically peevish: "No, that's it."[35]

For Leahy—who had marched as state's attorney with antiwar demonstrators in the wake of Kent State, and who had lectured them on the ability of the system to address its own excesses—it was a sweet moment, a rush of vindication. A few years after Kent, he had made the case to antiwar Vermonters that sending Pat Leahy to Washington was their best hope to end the bloodshed, the institutional treachery, the epic waste of funds.

And now, almost miraculously, his single vote *had* mattered. The coalition for change he had casually mentioned to *Time* magazine had come together, and stayed together repeatedly when it mattered.

Leahy walked out of the Capitol Building that evening, and the soft DC springtime hit him like a kiss on the cheek. The Capitol and the Mall had never seemed more beautiful. He had been in public service his entire postgraduate life, and while that totaled less than ten years, it had been a decade packed with achievement, particularly on the criminal justice side—and yet, for the very first time in his public career, Leahy felt as though in some small part his actions had genuinely helped to alter the course of history.

And his hometown newspaper agreed wholeheartedly. The editors at the *Free Press* were delighted to emphasize Leahy's contribution:

> Leahy, as a member of the Senate Armed Services Committee, played an influential role in denying the additional aid to Indochina —an action which many observers believe precipitated the collapse of anti-Communist resistance in both Vietnam and Cambodia. And Leahy has been playing his "anti-war" stance for all it's worth.
>
> We are not certain that Congress should have appropriated hundreds of millions of dollars in additional aid when so much previous aid had been wasted or mysteriously "lost." We are reasonably certain, however, that the Senatorial exploitation of the aid issue dealt a severe psychological blow to the anti-Communist resistance in Indochina.
>
> Senator Leahy grandly declares: "When we make a mistake, there

seems to be a reluctance for some people to admit it." Yes indeed, Senator—yourself included.[36]

Following President Ford's brutal last-ditch talking points down to the last tittle, the *Free Press* editorial page made no bones about declaring that freshman senator Patrick Leahy had, in effect, all but single-handedly and with malice aforethought lost the wars in both Vietnam and Cambodia.

But even the savaging by his state's largest daily couldn't dampen Leahy's spirits after the Vietnam vote. He couldn't help but feel that he was on the rising end of a profound cultural change—within his state and his country. Vietnam was the most potent current metaphor for the two sides battling over that change, but the clash was there in almost every area of public policy, from health care and retirement security to the environment.

Like Hart and other Democratic reformers in Congress, Leahy felt that time was inarguably on his side. He had everything he needed but seniority, accumulated power in the institution. And if Aiken's historically long term was any guide, Vermonters might just be willing to return him to Washington long enough to make him truly a senator to be reckoned with. It might take decades, but he would work and wait.

Unless his own election to the Senate had been a fluke, an outlier to the broader trend, and the seeming rise of Democratic influence in Vermont an illusion produced by momentary Watergate disillusionment. Unless the voters thought better of things and threw him out on his ear.

There was always that, of course.

The Top Cop

The Second Children's Crusade

In July 1992, Leahy walked off the Senate floor and into an impromptu meeting that a trusted aide named Tim Rieser had scheduled for him in a nearby Capitol alcove. Seated there in his wheelchair was a man named Bobby Muller, a striking figure in his late forties, with longish white hair and black brows over dark eyes. In 1969, as a marine combat lieutenant, Muller had led a charge up a Vietnamese hill, only to be paralyzed when a bullet severed his spinal cord. And yet he had managed not merely to heal, but to create much of the nonprofit infrastructure available to Vietnam veterans in the decades following the war's end, organizations like the Vietnam Veterans of America.

Muller had pulled a series of long strings to get the meeting, but he felt that the senior senator from Vermont was uniquely positioned to help with the issue he had in mind. As Leon V. Sigal neatly frames it, "Leahy chaired the Foreign Operations Subcommittee of the Senate Appropriations Committee. In that capacity, he held the purse strings for foreign aid, assuring attention for his concerns in the State Department and the Agency for International Development."[1]

But Muller also had an intuition that Leahy was perhaps the only figure in Washington prepared to hear what he had to say, because he had come to talk about landmines, and from an admittedly crazy angle. Muller had decided that focusing on prosthetic limbs for landmine victims around the world—crucial as it was—simply wasn't enough. The key was to stop *creating* victims, to rid the world of antipersonnel landmines altogether.

A global ban. Not only in the seventy-eight countries in which they were already sown, but in all countries, everywhere. Forever.[2]

Muller's intuition, as it happened, was dead on. Well before he had finished his impassioned description of the problem—the fifteen thousand to twenty thousand victims every year, mostly children—Leahy was already remembering a small Central American boy, the son of a farmer, no different from any Vermont farm kid, really. A kid who left his farm one day to get some water from the nearby river.

★ ★ ★

For all his imposing physicality, Pat Leahy has always been a deeply sentimental man, and he has never made much of an effort to hide that fact. Today, it's not unusual to see Leahy choke up during an after-dinner speech, not a rarity to see him wipe away tears. Most often he is speaking about children when the mood turns misty in this way, children suffering at the hands of criminals or predators or outlaw guerrilla soldiers, and his raspy baritone will thin until it is all but inaudible. Very occasionally he will lower his head and put up a hand, to indicate his momentary helplessness.

It's a genuine wealth of feeling, and political audiences sense and react to that authenticity. The memory of two-year-old Beau Bishop's gruesome death at the hands of Eddie Trivento in 1966 will trigger just this sort of response.

But over the decades Leahy has also come to understand that his own sentimentality acts as a kind of witching wand for the emotional well-springs of his Vermont audiences, and for Americans in general—and that once tapped, those springs can easily power a campaign, or a crusade. And if it's register of emotion that distinguishes one from the other, then Leahy's decades-long drive to ban the use of antipersonnel land-mines can only be called a crusade.[3] In precisely the same way that Beau Bishop's 1974 death anchors Leahy's memories as a county prosecutor, another nameless Central American boy would bind him to the international landmine crisis two decades later.

He was eleven or twelve, as Leahy tells it, a dark-haired little boy in a field hospital on the Honduras–Nicaragua border.[4] Leahy had come as part of a congressional fact-finding tour; the year was 1985, and Congress was already squaring off against the White House over funding for the Contra rebels in Nicaragua. (The Reagan administration's arms-for-hostages deal, eventually disclosed in the Iran-Contra scandal, would not become public knowledge until November of the following year.) The boy had lost a leg to a landmine, while walking from his father's farm to the nearby river. Leahy couldn't look away. "He was hobbling around on a makeshift crutch. He'd been there several years, with no place to go."

Leahy found himself struck by the child's pluck, especially in such squalid conditions, his determined movement around the camp. Through a translator, Leahy asked whether the mine the boy triggered had been laid by the Sandinista government or the Contra rebels. "Well, he had no idea," Leahy says now. "He just knew his life was forever ruined."

The fact-finding trip hadn't been organized to find this particular fact — the orientation was on US policy toward the war in Nicaragua, and the Reagan administration's unwillingness to back away from the conflict. But Leahy found himself riveted by the young amputee. "I realized, now I get on a helicopter, I leave. I fly back to Washington, a day later I'd be in Vermont with my wife and kids, living in comfort and safety. I couldn't get this little kid out of my mind." He began asking his hosts more and more about the use of landmines in Central America. And by the time the helicopter lifted out of the camp, Leahy already had the glimmering of an idea.

It would take several years — and the return of Senate control to his own party — but in 1989 Leahy would succeed in creating a $5 million fund within the State Department's budget to provide prosthetic limbs for victims of landmines worldwide. The program would eventually be renamed the Patrick J. Leahy War Victims Fund, and over time it would extend help to victims in over a dozen countries.

But in 1989, it represented the first tentative movement the US Senate had made on the issue, and it did not go unnoticed. Bobby Muller at the Vietnam Veterans of America saw Leahy's passion on the issue, and thought he recognized a kindred spirit.

★ ★ ★

Now, in the alcove off the Senate floor, Muller thanked Leahy personally for his efforts in creating the fund for landmine victims. But then he began his real pitch. "The War Victims Fund is a wonderful thing. But I'd like you to consider going upstream on the issue a little bit, start dealing with the problem at the source, and get rid of the weapon itself."[5] The argument was heartfelt, and laced with barely contained frustration and excitement.

Muller invoked the international response to nerve agents following World War I. "There is a precedent for taking out a category of particularly vile weapons. But we need somebody to lead that effort, Senator," Muller said. "Would you be willing to be our champion?"[6]

Leahy hesitated for a moment, a relatively long one. He was genuinely moved, yes, but at fifty-two years of age he had also been in the Senate for nearly two decades, and he knew that advocates used the chivalric term "champion" only when the legislator in question was far more likely to emerge politically wounded than victorious. He also understood the vast reach of the US military in Congress. Leahy knew, for instance, that the army and the marines were currently relying on antipersonnel landmines in countries like South Korea, where more than forty-four thousand American troops and their South Korean allies faced an aggressive and unpredictable million-man North Korean force across the Demilitarized Zone.[7] The military's thinking had long been that without vast landmine buffers, the North might rethink the cost and benefits of a lightning attack across its southern border.[8]

Leahy's earliest days in the Senate had been served on the Senate Armed Services Committee; he had seen there how the military could stoutly maintain an overblown estimate of its enemies' capabilities, occasionally for decades, and he suspected that this was the case with the prospect of a North Korean invasion. (In 1997, he would go so far as to tell Canada's *Globe and Mail*, "If the primary defence of South Korea relies on land mines, they better start drawing up their terms of surrender."[9])

Still, he had also seen up close how weapons systems were guarded in the Armed Services Committee—passionately, jealously, not alone because they were supported by the military but because creating weapons created jobs. Parochialism leveraged patriotism, to the point where even the US military itself found it all but impossible to retire a weapon. Eliminating an entire *class* of weapons was pushing the very largest sort of rock up what might well be the steepest hill in the United States Senate.

And yet Muller was absolutely right. A country simultaneously exporting landmines and prosthetic limbs for their victims was not just a practical contradiction—it was a moral outrage.

The sifting of complex political and moral factors occupied a palpable few seconds, by Muller's estimation. "That's a good idea," Leahy said finally, with a glance at Rieser. He knew that Rieser supported the ban in concept, but also wanted to take a very careful legislative approach if his boss decided to pull the switch.

And then Leahy asked Muller a probing question of his own. "This will take years, Bobby. Are you ready to stay the course?"

Muller straightened in his wheelchair and cracked a small, sly smile. As it happened, staying the course was something he had learned to do particularly well. He says today, "In my thirty-five years as an activist, this is the most exemplary moment of democracy in action that I can remember. I pitched this guy, and I had nothing—I wasn't a donor, he didn't even know me—but I pitched him on the merit of an idea, something that would be the right thing to do.

"It's not like there are any landmines in Vermont, or anyone manufacturing landmines in Vermont. This guy just thought it was the right thing to do."[10]

★ ★ ★

Ultimately the Capitol alcove meeting between Leahy and Muller would send out four strong shoots, each quickly gathering strength and reach. First, Bobby Muller worked Washington from the advocate's side, eventually putting together and funding a very serious lobbying effort, employing top-flight Democratic and Republican lobbyists. Second, Jody Williams, the new day-to-day coordinator of the ICBL—the International Campaign to Ban Landmines—put in long hours outside the United States, shuttling from country to country, meeting one on one with like-minded nongovernmental organizations (NGOs) and nonprofits around the globe. Muller makes it clear, though, that both of these efforts were directed, in effect, out of Leahy's office.

Third, Leahy tasked Tim Rieser—perhaps his most trusted legislative aide and the man to whom Muller had first turned with his idea of a global ban—with forging a legislative path. Vermont-born, scary smart, and with a solid background as a public defender, Rieser fit the general profile of the Leahy staffer to a T. It's fair to say that he had become Leahy's go-to aide for particularly ticklish international situations, situations in which his even temper and easy diplomacy produced powerful results over time.

In the case of the landmine issue, Rieser felt that a complete ban was too outsize a move to make immediately; he had in mind a series of relatively small, coherent steps to build the issue's profile, steps that could be undertaken in the Senate itself. The initial step was a one-year moratorium on US export of antipersonnel landmines. Leahy wanted to go bigger sooner, but eventually he agreed to the strategy.[11]

Muller had hoped for something more immediately ambitious as well, but he made sure that the NGOs involved were all on the same page—Leahy's page. "And because it was such a modest proposal, it didn't get anybody's attention really—nobody was alarmed about it. They kind of let this one slide, because it didn't go high enough on their radar screens.

So an [export] moratorium for a year, fine. But that was just to kind of initially engage the issue in the political process."[12]

The last of the four shoots was Leahy's own personal campaign for the ban, and in many ways it was the most fascinating and least predictable. It would come, perhaps inevitably, to be called a "crusade," as was Leahy's first campaign for the Senate, because that remains the term reporters reserve for any openly emotional effort that seems to lift off from the well-worn grooves of traditional politics.

And raw, unfiltered emotion was certainly one of the keys.

Wherever Leahy went to speak about the problem of landmines, especially during the first year or two following his 1992 meeting with Muller, he would find his mind drifting back to the boy in Central America, and after a moment or two his eyes would begin to shine, and he would cry — simply, openly, without shame — as he told the story that defined the issue for him. Inevitably, the tears would stun and silence the audience, and then drive them to loud applause.

Muller found himself as startled as the rest: "I've got to tell you — politicians don't normally cry when they're dealing with an international issue like this. I think he impressed his colleagues for sure with the passion, and the seriousness."

Later, after Leahy had visited other war refugee camps, there would be other stories he would tell, and those stories would bring on the huskiness in his voice, stories from Bosnia, Latin America, Vietnam. On the Senate floor in October 2001, for instance, Leahy told of lifting a legless Vietnamese man into his first wheelchair, a man who had spent years dragging himself along on a makeshift wooden pallet. The wheelchair had been provided by the War Victims Fund: "He looked like a really small man. He had no legs. He was probably about my age. He was just looking at me, stoically. I didn't know what to expect, but I went over, picked him up, carried him and put him in his wheelchair. The expression never changed, but as I started to go back, he grabbed my shirt, pulled me down and kissed me. . . . It was his way of saying thank you."[13]

Muller, who shared the dais with Leahy at many events in support of the landmine moratoriums and the global ban, still marvels at the passion Leahy was capable of bringing to events that might otherwise have seemed perfunctory.

"You know, he went to the camps where the war victims were, and he actually saw the casualties over the years, and when he would be giving a talk, and wander back in his mind to those visits, tears would well up in his eyes," as Muller described it in 2007. In a 2015 interview, Muller continued to detail the empathic link between Leahy's memory and the ongoing campaign: "He would imagine the story and have tears running down his face. One of the things that gave us such an incredible advantage in our work on landmines was how Leahy would talk about it."[14]

It was a seeming paradox, of course. What made Leahy's display of emotion so moving was that it was clearly genuine—and yet what ultimately made it effective over time was that it was repeated periodically, documented on many occasions, as the campaign to ban landmines built momentum. Was it a genuine emotional release, then, or a manufactured version of it?

"His enthusiasm is so strong, you forget what the facts are," teased Senator John Warner, a Virginia Republican who had shared the chamber floor with his northern counterpart since 1979.[15]

It's finally impossible to separate Leahy the knowing, vote-counting, veteran legislator from Leahy the emotional ban advocate; they make up one highly engaged senator, often operating all but instinctively within a rapidly changing political environment. But it's also fair to say that Leahy was quite nearly as surprised as anyone else by the sudden emotional richness of his own presentation.

Leahy would eventually adopt the term "crusade" as a badge of honor, in fact, just as he did during his 1974 Senate campaign, but he would always insist upon deploying it with the requisite dash of modesty. In 2014, he explained his passion for the landmine ban to Bryan Bender of the *Boston Globe* in just this way, with a familiar story and a familiar result: "'I don't want to sound like I am on a crusade but nothing has gripped me as much since I have been here,' Leahy said, tearing up when recalling how he lifted a Vietnamese landmine victim into his wheelchair. ('He grabbed my shirt, he pulled me down, and he kissed me.')"[16]

Still, for all their surprising effectiveness, Leahy's efforts were not limited to hitting emotional grace notes. Far from it. The operation went forward on all traditional fronts simultaneously, as well. Where necessary, he was hands-on in the Senate, backed by the persistent support of Muller and Jody Williams's growing list of foreign and domestic allies. "It was almost like the work of a stealth team," Williams would write in 2013.[17]

"Leahy used his personal touch, handwritten postscripts to 'Dear Colleague' letters and face-to-face appeals, to line up 35 co-sponsors in the Senate, among them several Republicans, most prominently Minority

Leader Robert Dole (R–KS), a wounded World War II veteran," noted Leon Sigal.[18] Dole was also occasionally known to fall prey to tears on the Senate floor, particularly when the discussion centered on fallen soldiers and attempts to rehabilitate them. Leahy could scarcely have found an ally more perfectly in tune with the subject of his bill, and the tragic emotional key in which Leahy had instinctively moved to present it.

As Pat Leahy's third term in the Senate drew to a close, the campaign to ban landmines provided him an opportunity to hone a signature brand of emotionally charged, media-centered populism; and backed by the steady institutional work of Rieser, Muller, and Williams, it proved quickly and undeniably effective. Leahy's one-year moratorium easily passed the Senate, survived a conference committee, and President George H. W. Bush signed it into law on October 23, 1992.

It was a watershed moment. In spite of the export ban's relatively small effect on the US posture toward the *use* of landmines, Leahy had proved that the issue had power and resonance. He had found a way to impact the Senate through a palpable, righteous populism that drew in forces outside the walls of the institution.

And in 1993, with Bill Clinton newly elected, Leahy tripled down, passing an amendment to extend the export moratorium to three years, and by a vote of 100–0. (Muller still whistles at the count: "A hundred votes. *Unanimous.* I don't think you could actually get a hundred votes in the Senate to back the idea that the earth revolves around the sun.")

Of course, the export ban was simply setting the table. Now the idea was to take the entire effort up a notch, to constrain the US Army's own use of what Muller always coldly called "the weapon." Leahy's approach was to apply Rieser's step-by-step legislative strategy—a one-year bill followed by several multiyear reauthorizations—to an actual ban on use.

And so on June 16, 1995, working with Illinois representative Lane Evans on the House side, Leahy filed S. 940, The Landmine Use Moratorium Act. It called for a one-year moratorium on the use of antipersonnel landmines by US forces, with an important set of caveats. First, the one-year date was delayed for three years, to allow the military a chance to add the moratorium to its long-range planning. The language would take effect in 1999, if passed.

But more crucially, the bill specified that the United States "shall not use antipersonnel landmines except along internationally recognized national borders or in demilitarized zones within a perimeter marked area that is monitored by military personnel and protected by adequate means to ensure the exclusion of civilians."[19] The series of carve-outs was a tough pill for the international side of the ban campaign to swallow. Jody Williams had adopted a mantra to describe the ideal ban—"no exceptions, no reservations, no loopholes"—and Leahy's language ran afoul of that ideal in more ways than one.[20]

Leahy and Rieser had judged the scale of the opposition extremely carefully, however. This was no mere ban on export of a US munitions product, a product sold only by one relatively small firm at that. This was laying hands on US military strategy itself; the pushback would be fierce and directed at avoiding a precedent as much as anything else. The Korean DMZ would be the military's case in point, that was certain.

As Leahy saw it, the nuanced exception language stripped the military chiefs of their best arguments and put another handful of pro-military senators in play.

Still, even with its caveats, the one-year ban on landmine use touched off a firestorm. If, as Muller had remarked, the export ban hadn't made it onto the Pentagon's radar screen, the use moratorium seemed to be dead center. A string of military brass trudged up Capitol Hill, arguing that "APLS were an integral part of its war-fighting methodology."[21] And they weren't afraid to play their ultimate hole card, that the legislation would degrade military effectiveness as a whole.

Unexpectedly—and worrisome for Leahy—the State Department also jumped in with both feet, now maintaining that landmines were crucial not only to US military effectiveness, but the effectiveness of American allies. In effect, the one-year use moratorium would hamper American diplomatic as well as military efforts. And then came the State Department's own trump card: the limited ban could conceivably "contravene U.S. NATO obligations."[22]

Other than the facts that Leahy's one-year ban would gut military effectiveness, sabotage our diplomatic efforts worldwide, and destroy the most successful military alliance in the nation's history, the military and the Clinton administration seemed fine with it.

Leahy continued to make his own heartfelt pleas for the Landmine Use Moratorium Act, on the Senate floor and elsewhere. And these exhortations were undeniably effective. A little more than a month after introducing the legislation, he urged his colleagues: "Again, my bill calls for a 1-year moratorium on the use of antipersonnel mines. Not because the United States uses landmines against civilian populations the way they are routinely used elsewhere, but because without U.S. leadership nothing significant will be done to stop it. Like the landmine export moratorium that passed the Senate 100 to 0—2 years ago—and like the nuclear testing moratorium, my bill aims to spark international cooperation to stop this carnage. Time and time again we have seen how U.S. leadership spurred other countries to act."[23]

Still, under standard rules of play, the language would have been dead on arrival. The scale and stature of the opposition—and the gauge of the arguments they were willing to deploy—were all but overwhelming.

But Leahy had been in the Senate long enough to know that he would need his own trump card, when the moment came. And finally he played it: Senator Robert J. Dole.

More to the point, Senate Majority Leader Robert J. Dole.

At the same time that the "Contract with America" and the so-called Republican Revolution of 1994 had swept Newt Gingrich into power in the House, Dole had realized a lifelong dream of becoming the leader in the other body. Unlike his House counterpart, however, Dole was an old-school institutionalist par excellence; he and Leahy were old friends, had worked together for twenty years. He was also a man of certain stark contradictions. A red-meat Kansas conservative in many ways, Dole also believed fervently in the idea of bipartisanship, especially around core economic and emotional issues, particularly those touching on the military or disability. The landmine issue hit both, and squarely.

Since the export ban in 1992, Dole and Leahy had had what can only be called a meeting of the hearts on the issue. With Dole's cosponsorship helping to shield the bill through the committee process and providing cover for Republican senators on the floor, the Leahy-Evans Landmine Use Moratorium Act finally passed the Senate in August, 67–24.

Equally significantly, Dole was slowly but surely ramping up a campaign for the Republican presidential nomination in 1996, and given the GOP's tendency to nominate the elder statesman, he was the odds-on favorite to face Bill Clinton. And as Clinton would demonstrate by signing a Republican restructuring of welfare, the Democratic incumbent was adamant about leaving Dole no rocks to throw come the general election cycle.

Which is to say that on January 26, 1996, Bill Clinton somewhat reluctantly signed the Fiscal 1996 Foreign Operations Bill, which carried Leahy's landmine language.[24] Leahy was ecstatic; it would be the highwater mark of his legislative success on the issue. And it gave Muller and Williams and their far-flung network of allies precisely what they had been seeking all along: here was the concrete example to take to the world court of opinion.

It was time to fight openly and across the board for a global prohibition on "the weapon," to use Muller's term. That meant taking the crusade to the next level as well, taking the argument directly to the people, on a global scale. In October 1996, Leahy flew to Canada to join Jody Williams for the Ottawa Conference on Anti-Personnel Landmines. Williams had been working international meetings on the ban for five years now, and she had developed a feel for the particular dynamics of the room. From the first, it was clear that the energy in Ottawa was different, keyed to a higher level. For Leahy, it was a delightful change of pace to be in a room — at long last — where almost everyone had seen the light on landmines long ago and was prepared to act.

To top it off, Canada's foreign minister, Lloyd Axworthy, eschewed the boring closing remarks the assembled delegates had expected and ended the three-day meeting with a blockbuster announcement, as Williams recounted: "Anyone who hadn't been paying close attention when he started speaking was now riveted by his words. Essentially, he told the governments it was time to put up or shut up. Since they'd all pledged to ban landmines, there was no better time than now to get started. He concluded by saying that Canada was prepared to sign a mine ban treaty in Ottawa in December 1997 even if only one other country signed it with them."[25]

Axworthy had thrown down the gauntlet, starting a one-year clock to a second Ottawa conference, at which the governments of the world would either put up or shut up. It was a moment of authentic political courage, and it spurred the audience of activists to redouble their efforts.

That meant returning to the crusade, and Leahy did so with a vengeance. In November he joined Ambassador Madeleine Albright in addressing the United Nations, introducing a US resolution calling for a "vigorous" negotiation of an "international agreement to ban the use, stockpiling, production and transfer of anti-personnel landmines, with a view to completing the negotiations as soon as possible." The UN General Assembly passed the resolution 156–0, albeit with a handful of countries abstaining.

But Leahy had always had the deep, intuitive sense that actually passing the global ban, and moving a reluctant American president on the issue, would require a different sort of pressure altogether, an honest-to-God populist wave. And that meant taking it beyond the barriers of the political world and pushing an awareness of the landmine issue deep into the reaches of popular culture itself.

For Leahy, of course, that always meant Batman. More specifically, in this case it meant the famed DC Comics writer and editor Dennis O'Neil, the man who, in the 1970s and 1980s, had done more than any other single artist alive to make the Dark Knight and his arch-nemesis dark again.

★ ★ ★

It's fair to say that the Batman television series of the late 1960s nearly killed the franchise with camp. Sales of Batman comics plummeted, and the Joker himself was unceremoniously retired — until writers like O'Neil began to move the Dark Knight and Joker-oriented story lines away from broad comedy and back toward the troubled psychopathologies that had marked the first appearances of both the heroes and the villains of Gotham City.

By the late '80s, O'Neil was editing a far darker — and far more popular — clutch of titles, breakout stories like *Batman: Legends of the Dark Knight*, Frank Miller's *The Dark Knight Returns*, and the 1988 graphic novel *The Killing Joke*, all of which would ultimately inspire director Christopher Nolan's fantastically successful *Dark Knight Trilogy* some twenty years later.

And so in the late '80s and early '90s it wasn't unusual for Denny O'Neil to receive accolades and attention for his work at DC and Marvel. But it was highly unusual for that attention to come from the United States Senate, and in the form of a lunch invitation to the Senate Dining Room:

> I like Pat Leahy's politics and especially his humanitarianism and I liked Pat Leahy before I knew much about either because he invited me to lunch a few years ago, along with my wife and a number of other comic book guys. Senator Leahy, it turns out, is a Batman fan and not shy about saying so in pubic. Lunch was in the Senate dining room that day, and although my mistrust of what we're forced to call The Establishment is reasonably sincere, I have to admit that this butcher's kid from North St. Louis was pretty impressed with himself, sitting at a big table with a living, breathing senator, surrounded by the nation's movers and shakers.[26]

Leahy's interest in O'Neil and his fellow geniuses from DC Comics seems, from the first, far more focused and mutually productive than his Grateful Dead interactions. By 1992 Leahy had contributed the foreword to *Batman: The Dark Knight Archives*, a hardcover anthology of the first four Batman titles, in which he talked about his childhood love of the caped crusader. And before O'Neil really knew what had hit him, he found himself learning more about antipersonnel landmines than he could ever have expected.

> I mentioned the senator's humanitarianism, which brings me to our second encounter with him. In 1996, at the instigation of Jenette Kahn, then DC Comics' publisher, we did some comic books about the landmine problem. Before Jenette dragooned me into a meeting full of impressive people, I hadn't known there was such a problem. But there was, and is, and it consists of the existence of millions of small explosive devices scattered throughout the planet. . . . So the Super-man guys did a book, to be translated into the appropriate languages, which showed what landmines are and what to do if you see one, and we Batman guys did a book, in English, designed to raise awareness. And that's where we re-encountered the Senator.[27]

Clearly Leahy had been working several levels of the DC corporate and creative hierarchy to bring about the desired result. So when O'Neil jokes about being "dragooned" into a high-powered meeting by his publisher, and from there into producing the humanitarian story itself, the observation is far more correct than he had any way of knowing at the time. The truth was that Leahy was here, there, and everywhere, unabashedly exerting any and all forms of influence in pursuit of the ban.

The result was "Death of Innocents: The Horror of Landmines," issued in December 1996, a gorgeously drawn and surprisingly compelling Batman narrative, given its openly didactic aims. The plot is direct enough: when a Waynecorp employee is killed by a hidden mine in a faraway land called Kravia, a guilt-ridden Batman intervenes to find the victim's daughter Sarah, also missing in the accident. There he finds it nearly impossible to assign clear moral values in an environment rendered chaotic by years of civil war.

Leahy himself wrote the preface, a very spare version of the story he had told hundreds of times by 1996: "My own interest in landmines dates to a trip I took to Central America several years ago, when I met a young boy who had only one leg. His parents were farmers, his country was at war, and he had stepped on a landmine near his home. He had no idea who had put it there but it made no difference. His life was shattered."[28]

The issue was filled with very literal calls to action (Leahy offered both his phone number and his e-mail address), culminating in a final page directing calls and letters to the US Senate, the House of Representatives, and the White House. It was a strikingly direct attempt, on the part of DC Comics, to influence specific pending legislation.

"Because in real life, there's no Batman," the final editorial page concluded. "Children are dying. And you can help."

Ostensibly directed at children and teens in the United States, the high policy quotient makes clear that DC Comics, along with the Department of Defense and the State Department, actually had a larger audience in mind: the parents of those same children, and the not insignificant audience of adult collectors who continue to read Batman voraciously. An iconic franchise like Batman has traction at nearly every demographic level, and the design of the book sought to leverage that broad appeal.

For his part, Leahy had still another audience in mind. With the ink still fresh on the one-year moratorium on US military use of landmines, Leahy wanted every US senator to know that he was now taking the crusade to the final level: a lasting worldwide ban on "the weapon," to be memorialized in an international treaty currently being drafted by representatives from over forty countries.

Toward that end, he personally sent every one of his ninety-nine Senate colleagues a copy of "Death of Innocents."

Certainly there was the hope that a few might actually read it on a slow day, but more than that, it was a not-so-subtle demonstration of the popular reach of the issue. And if senators didn't take the point from the comic itself, they could hardly miss it in the *Washington Post*'s coverage of the venture.

The headline read, "Caped Crusader and Anti-Mine Crusader Join Forces."[29]

Leahy was no longer just a superhero fanboy. In the eyes of the press, and among the NGO community at work internationally on the issue, he was increasingly taking on the colorful outlines of a superhero himself. Paul Bruhn, Leahy's diehard 1974 campaign manager — the man who had labored to conceive and construct Leahy's ubiquitous Top Cop image — would have swooned. Nothing to date had so clearly validated Leahy's intuitive grasp of popular culture's leverage within and against traditional political culture.

Of course, the Princess had yet to join the crusade.

★ ★ ★

By 1997, Diana, Princess of Wales, was perhaps the most watched person on the planet. Her lavish royal wedding sixteen years earlier had drawn a television audience of nearly 750 million; her divorce in August of 1996 freshly whetted that audience's appetite for royal scandal. Tabloids were besotted with the idea of a modern-day princess — the demure woman whose virginity had been publicly declared prior to her nuptials — assuming the independent life of a single woman.

Or, more properly, a single woman celebrity. Crowds of paparazzi faithfully attached themselves to her each morning and trailed her into the wee hours like remoras.

But throughout her personal troubles, and in spite of long-standing friction with her husband and the queen, Diana's charity work had remained an inspiring constant.

Since the early 1980s she had been a patron of children's hospitals and countless other organizations built around the most daunting challenges of the day — AIDS, drug addiction, poverty, even leprosy. Among other ceremonial posts, she had served as the vice president of the British Red Cross, and it was through those connections that she had eventually come to act as patron to the Halo Trust, an organization founded in 1988 to tackle "civilian mine-clearance as an act of humanity."

And that was how, in the bleak middle days of January 1997, the world woke up to a series of startling images from Angola: the Princess of Wales herself, wearing a crisp white shirt, tan capri pants, and standard-issue mine-clearance gear — a blast shield and a gray bulletproof vest. There was footage of Diana walking carefully through a partially cleared field, crimson skull-and-crossbones signs staked into the ground all around her.

She calmly told one trailing reporter, "I'm very happy to do photo calls if it raises the issue, but only on that basis. And it's certainly nothing in it for me."[30]

It was a tectonic news event. Within twenty-four hours, the international campaign against landmines was experiencing a profound outpouring of support and awareness, a flood of donations and promises of help in instituting the global ban. Every activist in every nonprofit in every country involved in the campaign could feel that the ground had shifted immediately in favor of concerted international action.

It was as though the princess had touched the issue with a magic wand, and instantly the world had begun to understand.

Leahy marveled from afar. Here was his own basic notion — to inter-twine the politics of landmines with popular culture — taken to an almost miraculous level. Watching it, he immediately had another idea about where that wand could work its potent magic. Leahy still had Bob Dole's ear on the issue, and of course Dole's wife Elizabeth was in fact the pres-ident of the American Red Cross. And while Diana had stepped down as vice president of the British Red Cross in the wake of her divorce, she was still its best known patron.

And so it was that six months later, in mid-June, the princess swept into Washington, DC, and set about bewitching each branch of govern-ment and every arm of the media in turn.

On Monday, June 16, she brought the landmine message to an eightieth birthday party for former longtime *Washington Post* publisher and board chair Katharine Graham, attended by three Supreme Court justices, a handful of network television anchors, and the editors of the nation's top magazines. The next night, the Red Cross staged a Hollywood-style gala, complete with red carpet and tickets ranging up to $3,500. There, the four hundred high-powered guests listened to traditional folk music from coun-tries most plagued by mines, Cambodia among others, and Diana auctioned off a silver box engraved with the words, "With love from Diana, 1997."

Dressed in a sleeveless red beaded dress and seated between Dole and the British ambassador, Diana had never seemed more gracious and glamorous. Her speech following the dinner was clear and powerful and heartfelt.

Leahy absolutely gloried in it all. From his seat of honor at the Red Cross dinner, he could almost *feel* the landmine ban becoming a fait ac-compli in the minds of his colleagues — at least the select few who had been invited to attend. (Senator Strom Thurmond, then ninety-four, was particularly smitten. "I came to see a princess," he told a reporter point-edly. "After all, a man likes to look at a good-looking woman.") Of course, to make absolutely certain that the Senate didn't miss the significance of Diana's visit, that afternoon Leahy and Nebraska senator Chuck Hagel had spent a solid forty minutes on the Senate floor touting the visit and the international ban.

In all, the Red Cross event would raise $600,000 for prosthetic devices for the victims of landmines around the world. The spotlight on the land-mine issue was now blindingly bright, and thermite hot. The following day the princess would take the issue into a one-on-one meeting with First Lady Hillary Rodham Clinton.[31]

And, unbelievably enough, the fairy tale momentum continued.

Within a week of Diana's visit, a *second* princess had joined the crusade: Princess Astrid of Belgium suddenly came forward to address an international assembly of delegates meeting in Brussels to lay out the framework of an international ban.[32] Brussels was designed to function as a precursor to the second Ottawa Convention in December 1997, at which the rapidly evolving text of the ban was to be signed. Jody Williams was engaged in frenetic shuttle diplomacy, country to country to country, trying to keep the ban language strong and the spines of the major Western powers stiff.

The next major stop was Oslo, the penultimate meeting before all the world's delegates were to return to Ottawa for a signing. Only a few months remained on Axworthy's ticking clock.

And then, abruptly, Diana's light went out.

★ ★ ★

At about 10 p.m. on the night of August 31, 1997, news broke in Washington of an accident involving the Princess of Wales, then in France. Rapidly the outlines of the tragedy grew darker. (Online news sites were still a novelty, but that was where the story emerged and grew, making the death of Lady Diana one of the first blockbuster stories to ignite outside the confines of traditional media.) Within a few hours, the worst was confirmed: Diana and her "then beau" Dodi al-Fayed had died in a horrific crash in Paris's Pont de l'Alma Tunnel.

Their Mercedes was destroyed. The pile-up had produced enough raw force to drive the radiator into the laps of the passengers in the front seat. Diana and Fayed had been riding in the rear, apparently without seat belts. Later investigation would reveal that the car's driver, Henri Paul, was driving drunk and had slammed into a pylon; blame would also fall on a large knot of paparazzi chasing the car at high speed.[33]

Leahy was back in Vermont when word of the tragedy began to seep out. He and Marcelle were called out of a gathering by aides and given the broad strokes of the story, though at first there seemed some possibility that Diana might live. She had been taken to the intensive care unit at the Pitié-Salpêtrière Hospital in southeast Paris, Leahy was told, and he and Marcelle made it back to their farm in Middlesex still hoping that Diana might pull through.

But within a few hours, a call came confirming her death. The finality of it hit both Leahy and Marcelle very hard—they had both loved her warmth, her commitment to the issues, and found her delightfully human and likable. He had had one long lunch with her to discuss the landmine issue, and over the last year the two had struck up a delightful correspondence, including handwritten notes with best wishes for Marcelle and the family, which Leahy had found especially touching.

Leahy was always struck by her powerful bond with her own two boys, and he would later tell the Senate, in a speech memorializing her humanitarian work, "I saw first-hand how she became involved [in the landmine cause] not as a Princess but as a mother, a mother who knew how other mothers suffered when their children suffered. She spoke for all of us."[34]

But along with and to one side of his sadness at the senselessness of Diana's death, Leahy couldn't help feeling another loss: the loss of the princess's almost magical power to drive the landmine crusade to its long-anticipated conclusion. Without her gentle prodding, he began to worry, the issue might well continue to languish.

But again, fortune seemed to be determined to see the crusade through to the end.

The outpouring of sympathy, across the globe, was finding a multitude of ways to make itself felt, and to make itself effective. To take just one example, Elton John rewrote the lyrics of his 1973 song "Candle in the Wind," originally a tribute to Marilyn Monroe, to reflect England's grief over the loss of Diana, with proceeds to benefit Diana's various charities, including the landmine cause. The song exploded globally, very rapidly becoming the best-selling single of all time.[35]

If Leahy's tears had helped begin the landmine crusade, it seemed that now the whole world was weeping. Grief suffused the issue, driving events forward.

And as fate would also have it, the Oslo conference—the last stop on the itinerary of the global ban campaigners before Ottawa—was to take place on September 1, the day following Diana's death. Jody Williams writes in her autobiography, "Oslo, August 31, 1997. The day before the Oslo treaty negotiations would begin. It was 6:30 in the morning when [ICBL cofounder Stephen] Goose and I were jolted awake by the phone. . . . The global reaction to her death is well documented but in many ways still defies the imagination."[36]

When he had his own chance to address the conference, Leahy invoked Diana as a symbol of that globalized sympathy and desire to honor her memory: "Because of what she did and because of her death, the whole world is watching what we do here." The Norwegian foreign minister acquiesced. "We shall spare no effort . . . to achieve the goals she set herself."[37]

But if America had properly begun the fight against landmines, America was also determined—at the highest levels of the administration and the Pentagon—to squelch it. Leahy had leaned heavily on the Clinton administration to send a delegation to Oslo, and he had finally succeeded. But it was in many ways a pyrrhic victory. Diplomat Eric Newsom headed the us delegation; ironically enough, he had once worked as a lead staffer for the Foreign Operations Subcommittee of the Senate Appropriations Committee, with Pat Leahy as his chair, and in that position he had been something of a skeptic of the ban. In fact, Leahy and Muller had helped Newsom land the job at State partially in the hope of moving him out of the landmine conversation.

Now Newsom had brought a take-it-or-leave it proposal from the State Department: the United States would sign the ban as long as it excluded Korea, excluded "smart landmines," and did not become effective for nine years. The conditions were interlocking; dropping any of them would mean that the United States would not only refuse to sign, it was strongly implied, but actively oppose a ban.[38]

Leahy now faced the extreme level of opposition from his own government that he had always anticipated. He had been a senator long enough to sense when large political wheels were turning just out of sight, and he could feel the pushback on the ban in a hundred different ways. It had never been stronger. The thought of it disturbed him, but he was careful to maintain his game face for the press.

"I don't know if the Pentagon has mobilized like this since World War II to battle me on this issue," he quipped to the *Globe and Mail*. And when the reporter gave him the smile he was after, Leahy let fly again. "They went on high alert. I expected to hear klaxon horns sounding and the missile silos opening. I had a vision of three-star generals rappelling off the Dome of the Capitol and coming through my window to stop this assault on their weapons."[39]

Despite intense pressure from the us delegation, however, the rest of the world held firm. Over two weeks the ban language was strengthened and clarified. "And each 'no' empowered others to say the same, to hold firm in their intention to give the world a mine ban treaty with no loopholes, no exceptions, and no reservations."[40]

Finally—after one last attempt to weaken the treaty, albeit less than had originally been demanded—Newsom abruptly withdrew the US proposals. Washington had privately decided to take the fight to the capitals of the various countries that might be susceptible to direct pressure from the White House.

President Clinton, as he had told Bobby Muller privately in 1996, still wouldn't risk a breach with his generals.[41] It could hardly have looked worse for the United States, in terms of public relations: "The motion to adopt the treaty by voice vote evoked 'a roar,' Newsom recalls, with 'everyone standing on tables, people throwing papers in the air,' and amid the uproar 'the US delegation sitting like the Politburo, stonefaced.'"[42]

Some eighty-nine countries had now agreed to the specific language of a global landmine ban, to be signed in Ottawa in just a few months. It was a historic moment, what many were hailing as a new people-centered politics, with America seated stubbornly on the outside. No one was more frustrated with the American recalcitrance than the most prominent American at the conference, Pat Leahy. Crestfallen is the only word for his reaction to what he saw as the stonewalling of his own country.

And with the Oslo conference breaking up, Leahy was no longer inclined to be diplomatic about his bitter disappointment. He could barely contain his frustration at the administration, telling reporters that the ban was "an issue that could not be solved by the kind of frenzied all-night, eleventh-hour scramble that sometimes has been raised to an art form in this administration. There are simply too many countries involved, and the issues are too serious for that."[43]

It was a strange, bittersweet few months before the final December signing of the ban. In October 1997, the Nobel Peace Prize Committee honored the International Campaign to Ban Landmines and Jody Williams, its coordinator, in equal parts. The award again focused an intense, glaring spotlight on the campaign, and that attention would help raise the number of eventual treaty signatories in Ottawa from 89 to 122, including Japan, one of the Clinton administration's few remaining allies against the ban.

And certainly Williams had slaved for five long years to make the treaty ban a reality. But the act of singling her out for such an honor was almost immediately divisive within the small universe of international activists who had pushed the campaign to fruition, especially among those whose work on the issue predated Williams's tenure.[44]

A few months after the Nobel ceremony in Stockholm, the *New York Times* would run a long exposé of the tensions, filled with a bitter back-and-forth over the issue. Bobby Muller, to take the most vitriolic exchange, claimed that Williams "abused his trust by putting herself forward as a Nobel nominee in a letter she drafted for a US Congressman." Williams's response was equally cutting — that Muller's anger was sexist in origin: when "girls do all the work, boys want the recognition."[45]

The article raised a series of high-profile questions about how the award came to be directed to Williams personally, rather than "on behalf of" the ICBL, which would of course have direct implications on the prize money involved. Some activists thought it was recognition well-deserved; others saw unsavory maneuvering in the nomination process. The only true takeaway from the *Times* coverage was that the Nobel Committee's choice had served to fracture, rather than strengthen, the movement: "The Nobel announcement fell like a cleaver on the campaign."

Laudably, and significantly enough, Pat Leahy refused to be interviewed for the March *New York Times* piece. It was perhaps the only time he had ever turned down a media request on the landmine issue, certainly the only time he had ever resisted a chance to discuss it in the pages of the *Times*. Jody Williams was a Vermonter, of course, and as her senator — as well as someone who had seen her operate at a very high level internationally — he was lavish in his praise after the Nobel announcement.

But for his own part, Leahy had actually sent a separate nomination, suggesting that the Nobel committee honor Canadian foreign minister Axworthy and the ICBL jointly. Leahy's argument was that by almost single-handedly creating what would come to be known as the "Ottawa process," Axworthy had taken a leap of great personal and political courage. He would later remark of his nomination of Axworthy, "It is one of the easiest things I ever did."[46]

Muller agrees, but only to a point. For him, the push for a global ban on landmines properly began in an out-of-the-way alcove just off the floor of the US Senate, in 1992, when Pat Leahy thought for a long moment and then agreed to champion Muller's cause. Muller continues to be blunt about his own thoughts on the prize. His Long Island accent is no-nonsense.

When there was discussion about a Peace Prize, I thought it was a joke. But I said, "Look, if there should ever be a Nobel Prize for this effort, it's gotta be split. It's gotta be between Leahy and Axworthy, because these two guys brought the political strength, and they both in their respective ways made it happen." You know, they really *deserved* that recognition for the campaign. Leahy and Axworthy both. Leahy for bringing the issue to the fore, before anybody, and putting the United States in the position of leadership. And then Axworthy for capitalizing on that momentum.

But Leahy deserved the Peace Prize, without a doubt. And I was as public about it as often as I could be.[47]

Leonidas and the Three Hundred

**LEAHY VERSUS THE BUSH WHITE HOUSE,
MAY–OCTOBER 2001**

In Book 7 of *The Histories*, Herodotus recounts the bloody story of King Leonidas, circa 480 BC. The tale is set in Thermopylae, a narrow pass between towering mountains and the sea, directly in the path of the invading Persian army of King Xerxes. Defending that pass—and the heart of Hellenic culture beyond—were Leonidas, his three hundred handpicked Spartan warriors, and just a few thousand Greek volunteers picked up along the march to battle.

For his part, Xerxes commanded an army of fantastic size; for every man Leonidas could position in the pass, Xerxes could afford to send a hundred against him. Given this ludicrous imbalance, Xerxes postponed his attack, certain that Leonidas would flee once his scouts had counted the enemy forces.

Finally Xerxes grew indignant and ordered the Spartans captured or slaughtered. Still, by crowding shoulder to shoulder into the narrow pass, the Greeks managed to repel the Persians again and again and again.

Only after being betrayed—by Ephialtes, who led the Persians to a secret path around the pass itself—did Leonidas perish. But the battle raged on even then, as his surviving men fought the Persians for his corpse, using broken swords and hands and teeth.

This, says Luke Albee, Pat Leahy's onetime chief of staff, this is what it felt like to face off against the Bush team on so many of its dearest priorities in so narrow a window of time, especially in the frantic months after 9/11 and during the 2001 anthrax attacks, when the new administration had a stiff patriotic wind at its back and Leahy's own Senate offices were ordered evacuated not once, not twice, but three separate times. It felt like holding the pass, facing down the onslaught.

"I just remember being in the capital with [Leahy], where you're trying to do all this stuff and you have 90 percent of your staff not even there, you're out of your offices, and you know the whole administration — Justice and the White House and the Department of Defense and the intelligence agencies — they're all staffed and ready to go.

"And we're always outgunned to begin with [against the administration], but I just remember feeling then like Leonidas and the three hundred Spartans. It was really something."[1]

★ ★ ★

The East Room of the White House is palatial by almost any standard: eighty by thirty-seven feet, with a ceiling rising more than twenty feet and punctuated by Bohemian crystal chandeliers. The flooring is a gleaming and elaborate oak parquet. Its designation on the original floor plans was "Public Audience Hall," before less monarchical, more democratic messaging prevailed.

Still, American presidents tend to use the East Room for receptions and announcements and bill-signings meant to overawe, formal state dinners, or the introduction of a long-anticipated Supreme Court nominee. Today, though — May 9, 2001, at 2:40 p.m. — the room is being used to introduce a group of circuit court nominees, eleven judicial hopefuls who might ordinarily have received only a quick introduction in the Rose Garden, in unobtrusive knots of two and three.

No DC insider can miss the point: President Bush intends to place an *extraordinary* amount of importance on the tier of benches just beneath the Supreme Court. This afternoon is clearly the launch of a very serious long-term push to fill any and all empty circuit court seats. The Bush candidates will roll out in very rapid succession, and they will be very carefully chosen indeed. But in particular Bush wants these initial choices to be seen and discussed as widely as possible. They've been chosen as much for symbolism as substance.

The subtleties are not lost on Pat Leahy, of course, standing and chatting in the front row. In fact, if any one person in the assembled audience is meant to be overawed by the setting — if any one senator is meant to appreciate the several messages layered smoothly into today's event — it is Leahy himself. As the ranking Democrat on the Republican-controlled Judiciary Committee, he will lead the opposition to some, if not many, of Bush's conservative nominees.

It is a role he played to near-deadly effect during the January confirmation hearings of John Ashcroft. The *American Prospect* predicted that after "Pat Leahy and Ted Kennedy [tore] out John Ashcroft's entrails" over the nominee's history of racially charged statements, Ashcroft would survive, but as damaged goods.[2] Damaged or not, Attorney General Ashcroft is himself now seated in the front row with Leahy, just a casual handshake and a joke away, another small sign there to be discerned in today's staging. It is Ashcroft's birthday as well, and it's hard to wonder if even that detail hasn't been a part of the planning. Certainly these particular nominees — Ken Starr's former protégé John Roberts among them — represent the sort of birthday present that might well keep on giving to the nation's conservative top law enforcement officer.

A *Washington Times* reporter sidles up and cheekily asks Leahy's opinion of this crop of nominees. "Encouraging," Leahy offers after a moment, and then winks. "Had I not been encouraged, I wouldn't have been here today." In fact, Leahy is the only Democratic lawmaker present, for reasons of his own.[3]

As is his habit, Leahy has brought along a black Nikon DSLR, and as he small-talks and jokes with those seated around him, he snaps a quick photo or two. For every photo he takes, of course, there are three he doesn't — often at a potentially historic event, Leahy uses the camera simply to observe carefully, to note key elements in isolation. With the camera, he can stare unobtrusively, yet somehow become a part of the background. The Nikon is camouflage and poor man's spy gear all in one.

Now, as the nominees file in to applause, stepping up onto the three-tiered riser at the front of the room, searching a bit awkwardly for their names on tape at their feet, Leahy uses the camera to frame the group as a whole. For the early Bush administration, it is a strikingly diverse selection: each of the riser's three tiers has one woman and one minority candidate, almost exactly balancing the number of white men.

But Leahy is more intrigued by the fact that two of the eleven are actually nominees originally selected by Bill Clinton, nominees who have been until now methodically denied confirmation by Republicans in the Senate. White House press secretary Ari Fleischer is already whispering to reporters that it is "an unprecedented act for a president to renominate a judicial choice . . . made by a president of the other party."[4]

And indeed, a casual viewer might well read this group of nominees as an olive branch, from a president looking — as the 2000 campaign phrasing went — to be a uniter, not a divider.

Leahy snaps the group shot and has to smile to himself. Just two months ago, the Bush administration announced that it would break with half a century of precedent and bypass the American Bar Association altogether when ranking its nominees, opting instead for the advice of the conservative Federalist Society—an "early warning missile" in the coming fight.[5] And just two weeks ago, Senate Republicans announced that they would scrap the so-called "blue slip" practice of allowing home-state senators to single-handedly defeat nominations they opposed—a practice they vehemently insisted upon during Clinton's presidency and used to defeat a wide range of Clinton nominees.[6]

So it seems clear enough that President Bush and his allies, for all the show of moderation and civility and peace offering here in the East Room, are preparing for something more like full-scale war in the long term.

But there is not a hint of truculence in the president's remarks this afternoon. After noting Ashcroft's birthday, Bush goes on pleasantly, introducing next his personal counsel, Alberto Gonzales. "Judge Gonzales is a great friend of mine who, fortunately, is my lawyer and is a part of the process, judicial selection process." The White House counsel's quick smile is shy, but otherwise his face is unreadable. In the words of Gonzales's eventual biographer, "He ooze[s] a mortician's calm."

Although unspoken, there is a strong sense among many in the room that Gonzales himself may well be a high-profile nominee in the not-too-distant future; speculation has swirled that Bush's lawyer, one of the few Hispanics in the administration and one of the few men alive with the president's complete trust, will quickly be short-listed for the Supreme Court.[7]

But for now, Gonzales is not simply a "part of the judicial selection process," as his boss blandly puts it—he is the point man charged with remaking the judiciary, aligning it more consistently with the strict constitutional aims of the Federalist Society. Gonzales has spent late nights interviewing candidates personally—he had done fifty such interviews by March—and in many ways today is his day, too.[8]

"I urge senators of both parties to rise above the bitterness of the past," Bush goes on mildly, "to provide a fair hearing and a prompt vote to every nominee. That should be the case for no matter who lives in this house," he adds, not looking at Leahy, but clearly directing his words in that direction, "and no matter who controls the Senate."

The reference is to the evenly divided Senate—so evenly divided, in fact, that Democrats (with their fifty seats) actually held the majority from January 3 to January 20, when the switch from Vice President Al Gore to Vice President Dick Cheney shifted the tiebreaking vote. For seventeen short days, Leahy had realized a decades-long ambition of running the Judiciary Committee. And as its chair, he had allowed himself a single sentimental ritual at the opening of his first hearing: having Utah's Orrin Hatch present him with a gavel made for him by his son Kevin during a high-school shop class.

It had been a sweet, long-awaited moment, especially for a former prosecutor, and Leahy had clearly relished it—only to see the majority seesaw back just barely out of reach less than three weeks later, and Hatch duly take up his own gavel and the chair.

It is this excruciating taste-and-loss of power that Bush is referencing, and whether intended or not, it has the feel of picking at a still-fresh wound. But Leahy simply gives another ghost of a smile.

Because the senior senator from Vermont knows something that few people in this very knowledgeable room know: his fellow Vermont senator, Republican Jim Jeffords, will vote *against* Bush's first budget tomorrow, rejecting the Texan's signature call for $1.35 billion in tax cuts at the expense of a vast array of domestic priorities like education—special education in particular. Jeffords's vote will not stop the massive tax cut, but it will help clarify just how far from the political center Bush has already moved, only months after the most closely divided election in American history.

And beyond that, Leahy is privy to a deeper secret still. Jeffords is far closer to switching parties, and throwing control of the evenly divided Senate to Democrats, than anyone in the Republican Party suspects. It isn't a sure thing by any means, but Jeffords is seriously disaffected, and his discussions with Minority Leader Tom Daschle are bearing a certain undeniable amount of fruit.

In short, Bush's team aren't the only ones with a plan for the broader war.

As it turned out, it took all of fifteen days for Vermont Republican Jeffords to make that short but momentous walk across the Senate aisle. An entire parallel universe—one in which dazed Republicans were suddenly forced to surrender their working Senate majority and turn their committee gavels over to jubilant Democrats—unspooled as a consequence during the last weeks of May 2001, helped immeasurably by what seemed for all the world like studied indifference from the White House.

For weeks, in fact, reporters remained convinced that the switch could not be real *because* the White House seemed to care so little: "Top Republicans told the *Times* that the best evidence that Mr. Jeffords is not, at the moment, about to leave the party is that the Bush White House is not on the phone to Mr. Jeffords or his friends trying to dissuade him from doing so."[9]

The truth, though, was that the White House was acutely aware and intimately involved, and at the highest levels. Jeffords was called to meet so often with the vice president in the weeks leading up to the budget vote and his incipient party switch that Cheney's Capitol Hill hideaway was dubbed "the torture chamber."[10] But once *inside* the torture chamber, Jeffords would invariably find that Cheney was merely there to press him on proposals he had already rejected, rather than breaking new ground.

It was an odd dynamic, a sort of pronounced bureaucratic stutter. "I started to get the sense that the administration was simply trying to find a way to survive the next few days," as Jeffords would later puzzle it out, "promising me something, almost anything, and then throwing it overboard once it reached the conference committee."[11]

So it was not that the White House didn't know how perilously close Jeffords was to the exits, despite its retroactive spin to the contrary.[12] As would become apparent during the Iraq War, self-assurance and inflexibility had quickly ceased to be the administration's opening strategic posture and had become instead its self-defining existential characteristic.

Predictably, then, it was a tense three weeks for Jeffords. But for the Judiciary Committee's ranking member, one Patrick Joseph Leahy, there was a radiant, dreamlike quality to the way the world suddenly reimagined itself. Just three weeks after being publicly admonished by the president to make nice no matter who was in power, Leahy found himself suddenly yet inexorably hoisted back into power — and with GOP calls for comity and bipartisanship still too fresh for the media to forget them.

June 6, Jeffords's last official day as a member of the Republican caucus, was particularly surreal.[13] Flower arrangements poured into the offices of the newly minted Independent, so many that every flat surface was wildly in bloom; desks and filing cabinets blocked the halls as offices were horse-traded. Jeffords's own mahogany desk was physically carted from one side of the Senate to the other, delaying the Senate's opening gavel. The Democrats' standard Tuesday lunch became an impromptu, high-spirited steak-and-salmon celebration. Jeffords himself finally entered the room, to cheers and a standing ovation, and as the senior Vermont senator, Leahy was naturally there to squire him about, the unofficial master of ceremonies.

The Leahy home on State Street in Montpelier (*center*), shown here in the wake of the devastating flood of 1927. The Leahy Press, the family's livelihood, was attached to the rear of the house. Courtesy of the Vermont Historical Society.

Barred from the basketball court by a lack of sight in one eye, Leahy made a point of showcasing his superior abilities with the other—on the rifle team. From Leahy's 1960 Saint Michael's college yearbook, *The Shield*. Leahy is at bottom row, second from right, with glasses.

The newly appointed twenty-six-year-old Chittenden County state's attorney speaking at the retirement of the outgoing state's attorney, John Fitzpatrick, in Burlington in 1966. Judge Edward J. Costello is seated between the two men. Costello's son Paul today describes this image as "a reflection of the time when the Irish had come into their own in Burlington." Photo courtesy of Paul Costello.

Leahy brought an entirely different approach to the state's attorney's office, at once reformist, innovative, and media savvy. Case in point: this late-'60s photo of Leahy taking target practice with members of the Burlington Police Department. Photo: Burlington Police Department.

Leahy's early announcement for the Senate race of 1974. To several very substantial obstacles—he was just thirty-four, a Catholic, and a Democrat—Leahy added the ire of a political establishment that thought he should have waited for Republican legend George Aiken to announce his retirement from the Senate. Photo: Sandy Milens.

The Senate campaign of 1974 was a study in aggressive tactics and superior technology. As state's attorney, Leahy had his sedan equipped with two Dictaphones and a telephone handset, a rarity and a distinct advantage. Photo: Sandy Milens.

Vermont filmmaker Dorothy Tod and her cameraman Adam Gifford, on the campaign trail with Leahy during the long summer months of 1974. It is no exaggeration to say that Leahy owed his stunning victory in significant part to the campaign film he invariably referred to as "the blockbuster"—a project also wryly dubbed the "Leahy Walton film" by Tod and her crew. Photo: Sandy Milens.

The early 1974 election results were immediately electrifying for the Leahy campaign. Watching from his room at the Burlington Ramada Inn, Leahy was jubilant, quite nearly to the point of levitation. His wife Marcelle was more cautious, and with good reason: the contest would last into the wee hours, and the candidates would finally be divided by just over four thousand votes. Photo: Sandy Milens.

Leahy takes Congressman Dick Mallary's concession call at 1:10 a.m. Mallary had briefly threatened to call for a recount, but within the hour his fundamental generosity reasserted itself. The Leahy campaign could finally address the giddy crowd still waiting in the Ramada ballroom. Photo: Sandy Milens.

The crowd at Leahy's 1974 victory party seems riveted to a sight they have never seen before: a Democratic United States senator-elect. But whether Leahy's upset victory was a Watergate-era fluke, or the harbinger of an emerging Democratic majority, would remain an open question well into the 1990s. Photo: Sandy Milens.

September 11, 1975, Senator John Stennis of Mississippi, chairman of the Senate Armed Services Committee, greets Secretary of State Henry Kissinger. Beneath the smiles authentic tension lingers: Leahy (*rear*) and Senator Harry F. Byrd of Virginia (*right*) had voted just months before to deny an urgent White House–backed appropriation for the conflicts in Vietnam and Cambodia. "They have lied to me long enough," Byrd remarked in casting the pivotal vote. Courtesy of the Associated Press.

Leahy huddles with Bobby Muller, founder of Vietnam Veterans of America, at a 1997 news conference calling on President Clinton to support a global ban on landmines. Although Leahy would eventually prod the Senate into historic support for the ban, resistance from the Clinton administration would prevent the United States from joining 122 other countries at the signing ceremony later that year in Ottawa. Courtesy of the Associated Press.

On September 19, 2001, eight days after the 9/11 attacks, Attorney General John Ashcroft (*center*), Judiciary Committee Chairman Pat Leahy (*left*), and Senator Orrin Hatch of Utah (*between them at rear*) hold a joint press conference to demonstrate a united front in the face of the terrorist threat. Within days, that unanimity would be replaced by the emerging GOP "9/11 hardball strategy"—a concerted attempt to advance unrelated Republican goals and judicial nominations under the banner of counterterrorism. Photo: Tom Williams, courtesy of Getty Images.

October 26, 2001, the East Room of the White House. After six weeks of bruising legislative infighting, President George W. Bush signs the final version of the USA Patriot Act. While Leahy had succeeded in making the act's provisions less worrisome for advocates of civil liberties, his hardest-won victory was a sunset to force a reconsideration of the legislation once the passions of 9/11 had cooled. Courtesy of the Associated Press.

With the Patriot Act signed, Leahy was free to do what he had wanted to do for weeks—visit Ground Zero and see the devastation and cleanup efforts there for himself. Here, Leahy and aide Bruce Cohen prepare to board an FBI helicopter near the East River. Photo: Julie Katzman.

Left to right, Barry Meyer, chairman of Warner Bros. Entertainment, actor Clint Eastwood, and Leahy at the grand opening of the Warner Bros. Theater at the Smithsonian National Museum of American History, in February 2012. Leahy had long been a proud champion of Hollywood on Capitol Hill, but his sustained push for Internet piracy legislation would provoke national scrutiny of that relationship. Photo: Kris Connor, courtesy of Getty Images.

While Leahy's war with the administration of George W. Bush was fought on many fronts, it's fair to say that Attorney General Alberto Gonzales—who entered the Bush family circle as Governor Bush's personal lawyer—was the most consistent focus of his wrath. Gonzales would resign under pressure late in the summer of 2007, owing in large part to Leahy's sustained congressional scrutiny. Photo: Andy Nelson, courtesy of Getty Images.

Leahy and his wife Marcelle at the 2012 Williston, Vermont, premiere of *The Dark Knight Rises*, the final installment of Christopher Nolan's *Dark Knight* trilogy. The senator's relationship to the Batman franchise is remarkably complex, involving not simply acting in and writing for Batman productions, but grafting various elements of the caped crusader myth onto his own evolving political story. Photo: Bruce Jenkins, from the *Burlington Free Press*, July 15, 2012, © 2012, Gannett-Community Publishing. All rights reserved. Used by permission and protected by the copyright laws of the United States. The printing, copying, redistribution, or retransmission of this content without express written permission is prohibited. Courtesy of *Burlington Free Press*, www.burlingtonfreepress.com.

Leahy escorts Alan Gross and his wife, Judy Gross, to a waiting air force jet immediately following Gross's release from a Cuban prison on December 17, 2014. Leahy and his staff were pivotal in securing Gross's release, one of several breakthroughs that allowed for the Obama administration's historic rapprochement with Havana. Courtesy of the Associated Press.

(Precisely how much of a hand Leahy had had in Jeffords's decision remained between the two men, though Majority Leader Daschle would credit Leahy with significant influence, and Jeffords himself would thank Leahy in *My Declaration of Independence* for "quiet support behind the scenes."[14] To the assembled Democrats and the swarming media, though, the *consigliere* connection seemed perfectly clear. If possible, Leahy's stock within the caucus climbed even higher.)

But of the day's myriad pleasures for Leahy, most deeply satisfying of all was calling the Judiciary Committee into session even *before* the thorny issues of the organizing resolution had been settled. With outgoing chair Orrin Hatch's permission, Leahy had opened the morning with a lightning hearing on Bush's controversial faith-based initiative.

The session was almost giddy, marked from the start by an easy banter between the three old hands who had all coveted the chair during the last month. And also marked, of course, by the delicious return of the gavel:

> Chairman LEAHY: The Committee will be in order. I wanted to follow a tradition that I have followed now for 20-some-odd years. I have chaired probably half a dozen different Committees at different times. I have been twice in the minority, three times in the majority, which gives you some indication of how the Senate changes all the time.
>
> What I have always done is started a new Committee with a gavel that my son made for me in high school. I know I embarrass him every time I mention that, but this is the gavel I have always used and so that is where we will start.[15]

Leahy had spent twenty-six years in the Senate tirelessly boosting all things Vermont, from maple syrup to Green Mountain Gringo Salsa, but in the last few weeks that boosting had taken on an increasingly bright political charge. The "Don't Mess with Texas" bumper stickers that had come in a brash wave to DC with much of the Bush administration had now been answered by a boomlet of fresh green "Don't Mess with Vermont" stickers, and the larger David-and-Goliath narrative came into focus: small states, and blue states, matter. Even a pebble can stop a tank, if it gets wedged in there just right.

And the fact that the bumper stickers had been the brainchild of Leahy's office strongly suggested that there were more Green Mountain pebbles where that one came from.

Inescapably, the word "Vermont" itself began to suggest a certain large-scale, if still largely inchoate, response to the early ideological overreach of the administration. And Leahy, for one, was not going to stop invoking both the place and the rapidly evolving concept on this day of all days.

> Chairman LEAHY: Vermont is a very special place. You may have read a lot about it. I am sorry. Go ahead, Orrin. I will stop if you stop.
> Senator HATCH: I have to admit it is a very special place. . . .
> Chairman LEAHY: Joseph Smith [the founder of Mormonism] was born there, don't forget, don't forget. I was in the town of his birth on the day of his birthday about a week or so ago, Senator Hatch. I want you to know I was there.
> Senator HATCH: You would do well to pay more attention to what he had to *say*.[16]
> [*Laughter*]

Hatch's portion of offhand repartee contained more than a germ of seriousness, because banter and cross-party friendships could only stretch so far, finally. As before Jeffords's switch, the Judiciary Committee was still painfully even in its divide, and eventually the partisan pressures would mount dramatically. And nowhere more so, or more quickly, than over the president's push to remake the judiciary in a markedly more conservative image. From the start, Leahy had in mind a very carefully nuanced counteroffensive on judicial nominations, but it boiled down to this: meet any hint of accommodation or moderation on the part of the administration with a double helping of Senate goodwill and actual bipartisan cooperation, but meet the first sign of a "lurch to the far right" with skepticism, delay, or outright opposition.

It was left to Senator Charles Schumer of New York to deliver the message in the bluntest terms, a taste of a long-running Leahy-Schumer good-cop, bad-cop dynamic to come. "The idea of having just one slate of right-wing judges is gone," Schumer insisted. "There will be some conservative judges but we will exert moderation. We won't get our way but [Bush] won't get his way either."[17]

And Leahy made it clear immediately that he would reassert two of the very qualifications that Bush and his counsel Alberto Gonzales had spent long months de-legitimizing: blue slips and the rankings of the American Bar Association. Along with the olive branch to match the president's — a very quick start to the nominee hearing process — Leahy didn't hesitate to show his own stick: nominees would need to be vetted by the ABA and cleared by their home-state senators, as in years past. And even Bush's carefully chosen initial group of eleven had one "blue slip problem" —

Terrence Boyle, a former aide to North Carolina Republican Jesse Helms, was being opposed by North Carolina Democrat John Edwards.

In short, Leahy's was at root the old-school, institutionalist understanding, and the days and weeks following the switch in Senate power saw him move authoritatively to reassert it. But Bush, and his political strategist Karl Rove, had already given a much different set of marching orders within the administration. And although it would take some months for Leahy and his staff to catch on, the change was aggressive, long-term, and undeniable.

Just as Jim Jeffords had understood, only after weeks of back and forth, that Bush and Cheney had little use for compromise, especially under pressure, Leahy and his staff would very quickly learn that Bush's initial olive branch had apparently come from a tree otherwise denuded.

★ ★ ★

The second list of Bush nominees, like the first, was designed to make a point—but in this case a point jagged enough to draw first blood. Released on June 22, this second, smaller slate of names read like a conservative dream team, and as such it presented an immediate, pressing challenge to Leahy. Among other names, the nominees included "Judge Carolyn Kuhl, a former Reagan administration lawyer who was at the forefront of some of its efforts against abortion; University of Utah professor Paul Cassell, known for his legal work against the 'Miranda' rights that police read to suspects; and federal magistrate Terry Wooten, once a top aide to Sen. Strom Thurmond, R-S.C."[18]

For most observers it was a surprisingly conservative list, particularly following the change in power in the Senate, but in context it shouldn't have surprised anyone; Bush's already clear default pattern in such moments was to double down, to project unstinting muscularity and to act always on behalf of a putative mandate, mostly heedless of new circumstances. This posture was a clear hit with committed conservative action groups. "It doesn't seem that the president has altered his standard as the political landscape has changed," the Conservative Free Congress Foundation marveled.[19]

As with Jim Jeffords, the tough line on judges was turning out to be the only line, and the Bush White House was making it crystal clear to friend and foe that it had no intention of softening its position. Judges were Bush's long-term legacy, and his team was determined to power over or through any Senate obstacles.

"It was a kind of Bush / Karl Rove in-your-face thing . . . they were just moving ahead full-bore on their conservative agenda," says Ed Pagano, Leahy's chief of staff after Luke Albee. Unlike Albee, Pagano is decidedly low-key, and he makes his final point clear by way of deliberately bland understatement and a smile. "So it was—a different atmosphere," he says, choosing his words.[20]

For Leahy—who was not only staunchly pro-choice, but also, as a young state's attorney, an early crusader for proper application of *Miranda*—this newest slate had to seem almost deliberately provocative. For all his disgust at Eddie Trivento's crime, back in 1966, state's attorney Pat Leahy had read the child-murderer his *Miranda* rights a full five times in one day, so scrupulous was he in those early months after the watershed high court ruling, and so concerned about having his case later overturned. It was a strongly formative set of experiences.

Still, Leahy was determined not to be goaded now into an overreaction. He felt he had defined a workable way forward, and he remained determined to showcase the accommodating qualities of the new Judiciary Committee—important as a way of inviting further accommodation from the White House, but also for building credibility with Senate moderates and the media should that accommodation not be forthcoming. With the Republicans' loss of Jeffords, though, the Senate—and the world of possibility—had changed, and by tradition Bush would need to recognize that.

If anything, however, the weeks following produced less and less cooperation from the administration. Leahy and his staff began to have the sense of a long conveyor belt, moving leading lights of the conservative movement methodically from the wings to center stage. And the administration seemed to be focused almost exclusively on pushback, rather than negotiation.

It was a palpable, qualitative difference from recent practice. "During the Clinton years, [Republicans] were open for business," as Luke Albee phrases it. "You give us one of our judges, we'll give you two of yours. That sort of thing. That was their working assumption. Now it was different. Now they just said, 'Forget it. No way. We want 'em *all.*'"[21]

But of course there were other pressing demands on the new chairman's attention during the summer of 2001. Chief among them, the FBI —an organization Leahy himself liked to refer to as "the crown jewel of investigate agencies"—seemed unable to stem a tide of scandals and cover-ups, which had in turn spawned multiple overlapping investigations, each of which seemed to produce more evidence of serious mismanagement and wrongdoing.[22] The list of blots on the FBI's reputation grew yearly: botched raids at Ruby Ridge and Waco; famously botched investigations of the 1996 Olympic bombing and alleged nuclear spy Wen Ho Lee; revelations of highly placed spies and moles within its own organization, including Robert Hanssen and James J. Hill.

Leahy worried a great deal that the White House would make the situation worse with an ideologically rigid candidate, possibly even one without the requisite minimum of experience. As it turned out, Robert Mueller was Bush's pick for director, and to Leahy's satisfaction, the White House at least publicly presented the seasoned California US attorney as a candidate specifically chosen to pass bipartisan muster.

Finally, after months of wrangling, it seemed that Leahy's olive-branch strategy was having some visible effect.

"All institutions, even great ones like the FBI, make mistakes," Mueller observed at the opening of his confirmation hearings. "The measure of an institution is in how it *responds* to its mistakes. I believe the FBI can, and must, do a better job of dealing with its mistakes. If I have the honor of being confirmed by the Senate, I will make it my highest priority to restore the public's confidence in the FBI, to re-earn the faith and trust of the American people. The dedicated men and women of the FBI deserve nothing less, and as director, I would tolerate nothing less."[23]

The words had hit precisely the right note with the committee and its chairman. The Bush administration's latest move gave Leahy hope that they were all somehow finding their strides, whatever their governmental branches and political parties, swinging downhill after a long few months of laboring up a dicey, unfamiliar slope. Hope grew that September would bring at least a small measure of sanity, along with the autumn chill and the flaming leaves of the Japanese maples.

SEPTEMBER AND OCTOBER 2001

The car arrives for Leahy at a bit after nine in the morning. As is his habit, Leahy says good morning to the driver and carefully folds his tall frame into the front rather than the back seat, then pulls some notes from his briefcase to study on the way to the Supreme Court Building. He is a featured speaker at an annual meeting of circuit court judges there, later in the morning, and he wants to put his thoughts for the talk straight in his mind.[24]

September morning light pours in through the windows as the driver heads them back down Ridge Drive to Georgetown Pike.

Leahy's congressional residence is a modest two-story home, at least by the upscale standards of leafy McLean, Virginia. Just one long touchdown pass from the green-and-gold end zone of the Langley High football field, it seems at once unremarkable and remarkably American. But the house does have several notable features of more than passing usefulness to the chair of Senate Judiciary: it backs up onto an expansive stretch of woods, greatly enhancing its sense of privacy, and it is less than a mile from the CIA's Langley headquarters, greatly enhancing its sense of security.

Basic bodily security is far from Leahy's thoughts at the moment, but over the next three months it will become an extraordinarily pressing problem, to be considered at nearly every moment of every day. By Thanksgiving, a Secret Service detail will be guarding him twenty-four hours a day, seven days a week. At that point, Leahy will be thinking twice not only about every plane that passes overhead, but also about every letter that he opens, every trace of dust his finger finds clinging to the desk in his Capitol Hill hideaway office.

But for the moment he is absorbed in the talk for the conference — and of course in mental preparation for a Judiciary hearing later that afternoon, on President Bush's new drug czar nominee, John Walters. As is becoming par for the course, Leahy doesn't think much of Bush's choice. Walters has been known to dismiss evidence of sentencing disparities by race as "urban myth," to take just one potential flashpoint, and he has long favored jail time over treatment.[25]

The driver has the radio playing softly, and something from the stream of chatter breaks into Leahy's consciousness — something to do with an explosion at the World Trade Center. Initially he thinks little of it; recently his morning station has been running historical audio of key moments in history, and he assumes that this is a clip from the 1993 Trade Center bombing. Still, he asks the driver to turn it up, and then very quickly realizes that the report is reflecting real-time chaos in New York City.

Within another moment, Leahy has a friend in New York on the phone. The friend is watching television and passes on the earliest speculation: an apparent accident, a one-in-a-million mistake.

But pilot error seems crazy to Leahy. "What kind of weather do you have there today?" he asks. "Clear as a bell," the friend replies, "but I guess the pilot got lost."

"That's impossible," Leahy mutters. "You can't hit that tower by mistake on a clear day. This is a terrorist attack. Has to be."[26]

Already he is wondering whether to hold to the day's itinerary, but the car is now just moments from the Supreme Court Building, and Leahy makes the snap decision to continue on his way. Once there, the very façade of the building—fashioned of Vermont marble, something the grandson of Vermont stonecutters ordinarily never fails to bring to mind —seems reassuring, all but impregnable.

But on the way into the building, one of Leahy's staffers gets word of a second plane hitting the second tower at 9:03 a.m. There is no denying it now: the dawning national awareness that the United States is experiencing a coordinated wave of attacks. Uncertainty and anxiety begin leaking quickly into everything around him. People are already beginning to stream out of buildings around the Capitol, aimlessly, wandering, cell phones clutched tightly to their faces. A few are already in tears.

Quickly, Leahy calls Marcelle, who has been out for a walk around their McLean home, and tells her to turn on the television. With a promise to call back when he reaches his office, Leahy rings off and then goes directly to the ornate East Conference Room on the second floor, to wait for Chief Justice William Rehnquist. Again, in the characteristic silence of the building, and amid the elaborately carved oak paneling and the period oil paintings of the early chief justices, it's hard to believe the urgency of events under way in New York City.

Leahy is already processing the likely fallout, though, if in fact the unknown attackers have managed to evade both airport security and the various US intelligence agencies. It's a dead certainty that his committee will be one of the central tools the nation will use to investigate and respond to this attack. He knows his own life has just been upended, in more ways than one.

When Chief Justice Rehnquist enters, Leahy immediately draws him aside, whispering, "Bill, before we start, I believe we have a terrorist attack."

Before Rehnquist can react, a loud "muffled boom" echoes through the room. From the window, a dark plume of smoke can already be seen rising thinly across the Potomac River. It is 9:37 a.m., and a third plane —American Airlines Flight 77—has just struck the west face of the Pentagon itself.[27]

The American war zone has just expanded to include the capital.

Although the Defense Department is already moving to ground all air traffic in US airspace—an unprecedented emergency move—at this precise moment no one knows how many more planes-turned-bombs are still aloft. And given that the Supreme Court Building houses a coequal branch of the US government, Leahy knows that he has no choice but to evacuate.

Yet there is a frightening lack of official acknowledgment and information, as though no hands are at the switch: Washington's emergency broadcast system has yet to sound (in fact it never will), and fire alarms —the sign for evacuation of the House and Senate—are silent on Capitol Hill. Congress's long-standing evacuation plan is not in evidence.[28] Cell phones are already crashing as the system becomes hopelessly overloaded. Those who find themselves on or near the Hill have only wildly conflicting media reports and their own instincts to consult.

Leahy's instincts take him back to his people, his Senate staff, still across Constitution Avenue at the Russell Senate Office Building. Their safety is uppermost in his mind.

Once outside and on the move, he can see hundreds of workers and tourists exiting the Capitol—clearly an evacuation is under way, although the fire alarms haven't been triggered.

Still, it is orderly until—just at 10:15—there is what sounds like a loud explosion, and suddenly the streets between the Capitol and Union Station are full of people running and screaming. "We have to get out of here!" a man screams repeatedly.[29]

Sirens are now wailing from different directions around the city. At one point, a Capitol Police officer recognizes Leahy moving past him on the street and suddenly comes forward to hug him quickly before moving on.

It's like the Kennedy assassination, Leahy finds himself thinking, the same shock and unguided anger, the same sudden outpourings of fellow feeling. He had been in DC as a law student in 1963, and there is an eerie, fatalistic sense of déjà vu now.[30]

By the time Leahy reaches his office, he finds that most of his younger staffers have refused to leave—they're worried about the confidential information out on their desks and computer screens. "Out!" Leahy yells, startling them up out of their seats. He claps his hands loudly. "Everybody out! Out, out, out! Hurry it up!" True to a policy he established years before, Leahy is himself the last to evacuate, following the staffers out into the daylight.

Along with a small army of others like them, Leahy and his people wind up in a small tense knot under the leafy trees in Senate Park. Here and there members of Congress are huddled around radios, trying to pick out useful information from the stream of chatter; the Emergency

Broadcast System has yet to be used, and there is no official information going out over the airwaves.

Senator Joe Biden—who offered to take the Senate floor for a speech in defiance of the terrorists, but was turned away by officers enforcing the evacuation order—sits now on a park bench, alone, cell phone pressed tightly to his ear.[31] Leahy takes the moment to call Marcelle again, to tell her the few details he knows and to reassure her that his staff is safe. Even from her vantage point in McLean, Marcelle feels that the world has gone terrifyingly off the rails. She will later recall, "Pat had his cell phone, and he kept in touch. He told me not to go near any government buildings. And don't go near the CIA building near our house. So I immediately got on the Internet and e-mailed all our kids to tell them Dad's okay, and I would be the conduit for information. . . . And when I went outside it was dead silence, absolutely silent—even the birds had stopped singing. *No sound.* And when I walked back across the street, a jet went over and I could look up and see that it was loaded with bombs."[32]

Marcelle, who had once been a surgical nurse at the area hospital, tries to call to see if they can use her help again. But they aren't answering. So she takes her expired ID and drives there to offer her services: "I told them I'd empty trash cans if that's what would help." But the hospital isn't overwhelmed, and for the worst reasons. As Leahy himself delicately frames it, "Most every victim was dead or being taken care of with local first-aid at the Pentagon. There was nothing in between."[33]

The longer Leahy and his staffers stand in Senate Park, the stranger the sights they see. Every now and again police officers move past the park carrying shotguns, or trundle past in armored vehicles; evacuated workers stream by, many in tears. From the park, one can see snipers in black occasionally seeking purchase on a rooftop, and the word is that the White House is now guarded by agents brandishing automatic weapons in the streets.

Like Biden, Leahy feels a combination of frustration and anger that is rapidly hardening into defiance. If nothing else, he is going back into his own damned Senate offices, evacuation order or no. "I want the Congress right here," he tells a reporter who questions his defiance of the order. "I'm not going to run."

And there he and his inner circle stay until 4 p.m., fielding what phone calls make it through the overloaded system and beginning a process of thinking about how the US government should respond.

Later that afternoon, Leahy and several aides walk over to the 4th and D Street home of communications director David Carle. It is an unlikely war room: a diminutive green two-story on a block of three-story town houses. There they gradually set up a de facto communications hub, each of them working a cell phone or monitoring a television screen or both, and then pooling what information they manage to gather.

For Carle, trying both to play host and Leahy communications director simultaneously, there is a clear sense of solidarity, of moving through the crisis together, but it is impossible not to sense the helplessness in the group as well. For a staff and a senator accustomed to ample Senate resources, and the power to compel serious action in official Washington with a single phone call, the sudden exile and the lingering confusion are baffling, dispiriting. Everyone in the room seems utterly drained. It has been the most emotionally grueling day that any of them can remember, and no one knows for sure whether it is over yet or not. No one knows if there are more planes, more explosions, more secret folds to what seems like a meticulously coordinated terrorist plot.[34]

It is there, at Carle's neat, quiet little home, that the Associated Press finally reaches Leahy, after hours of chaos and failed attempts. What sort of response, the AP reporter wants to know, should the United States mount to the attacks? It is precisely the question Leahy has been asking himself over and over since hearing the first reports from New York City that morning in the car. But it is perhaps as fraught a question as he has ever fielded in his long years as a senator.

Leahy pauses for several long seconds, and when he answers it is loudly enough that the staffers all briefly stop their own cell phone conversations wherever they are.

"I would strike back with terrible fury," he says very deliberately into his cell phone, anger suddenly edging his voice in a way that snaps his aides' heads around.

When Leahy walks back to the Hill later that evening, accompanied by a pair of police officers, he enters what amounts to a fully militarized zone: massive surface-to-air missile launchers are positioned among the trees, and jets come streaking up the mall, their undersides bristling with ordnance, before screaming away into the distance.

★ ★ ★

By the next day, September 12, the initial flush of anger had cooled for Leahy, but powerful emotional currents were everywhere, and building rather than dissipating. The Senate was pointedly back in session, for the specific purpose of condemning the September 11 attacks, and speaker after speaker rose to excoriate the terrorists and declare full support for the president.

Leahy's own speech began in careful, measured, almost ministerial tones, but when he recalled an old friend killed at the twin towers — a retired FBI official named John O'Neil — his pacing slowed, his tone suddenly suffused with grief. "When I listened to the news at a little after 5 this morning, I heard the name of a friend of mine, who went into the building to help with the rescue."[35]

Leahy's voice thickened, and he was forced to stop for a moment. "And the building came *down*," he managed to finish. The Senate chamber was uncharacteristically silent.

But after another moment, Leahy looked up and took his speech in a distinctly different direction. He went on to lay out what would quickly become his own signature case to the American people — that no act of terror must ever be allowed to stampede America into surrendering the legal underpinnings of a free, democratic society. He would not be the only public figure making this case, of course, but for most the accent would be on retribution, punishment, and swiftness of response.

Leahy, however, found himself in a unique position: there was no real question but that he would personally spearhead the Senate's response to the attacks.

Beryl Howell, a senior counsel for the Judiciary Committee who would work very closely with Leahy on the Patriot Act over the next two months, remembers it as a foregone conclusion: "Leahy was looked to because he's a master legislator, but still lots of senators — the chairs of some of the other committees who were working on [legal responses to 9/11] — could also have tried to assume the role of being in charge. But, you know, there wasn't even a competition. It was clearly going to be Patrick Leahy."[36]

Even now, just one day after the attacks, Leahy could feel the pressure building to legislate overnight, a sort of political pressure he had seen and felt before but now palpable at an unprecedented intensity; even now, with the ashes still smoldering, he could feel a gathering surge of support for almost any action of seeming substance in response to the attacks, no matter how quickly sketched or how questionable in effect.

Just that morning, in fact, Attorney General Ashcroft had transmitted, from an undisclosed location, a series of stern directives to his assistants and legal advisers in the Justice Department: they were to map out changes in current law to do "all that is necessary for law enforcement, within the bounds of the Constitution, to discharge the obligation to fight this war against terror."

And Ashcroft made it clear that the reading of the Constitution that had guided Congress's hand for the last several decades was far too restrictive. He wanted a substantially broader interpretation, a mind-set based not necessarily on constructing cases that would hold up in court, but on allowing officers to disrupt putative plots quickly—whether or not a later court might disallow evidence.[37] It amounted to a "better to ask forgiveness than permission" strategy, and it would quickly come to guide the Justice Department to an extent alarming to both parties.

In practice, much of the Justice Department's immediate reevaluation amounted to "catalog[ing] gripes about the legal restraints on detectives and intelligence work," some of which "had been bouncing around the FBI and Justice Department for years."[38] And the same was true that morning in the Senate: suddenly bills and amendments that had gone down in flames months or years earlier were being dusted off and quickly put back into circulation. The trend was already clear.

And so when Leahy made his case, for the first time after 9/11, he did so as much out of gut instinct as intellect, out of instincts and reflexes built up over a lifetime as a prosecutor and a legislator openly dedicated to balancing citizen rights against the power of the state. And on the Senate floor the day after the attacks, he slowly articulated a blend of action and caution, and called for crafting law enforcement tools that wouldn't later devolve into weapons to be turned on law-abiding citizens.

> As our leaders have said here this morning, we stand here not as Democrats or Republicans—we stand here together. We will be supportive of our President, and of our institutions, and of each other. Because this challenge to our freedom is going to be answered by the strength of our democracy.
>
> Trial by fire can refine us, or it can coarsen us. If we hold to our ideals, then it strengthens us. Our people, our values, our institutions are strong. President Roosevelt spoke of the "arsenal of Democracy." That arsenal is our ideals, our values, our freedoms, our community—that sustains us, that propels us forward. . . .
>
> I am confident that as a nation we will seek and serve justice. Our nation—my neighbors and friends in Vermont—we demand no less. But we must not let the terrorists win. If we abandon our democracy to

battle them, they win. If we forget our role as the world leader to defeat them, they win.

But *we* will win. And we will maintain our democracy, and with *justice* we'll use our strength. We will not lose our commitment to the rule of law no matter how much the provocation, because that rule of law has protected us throughout the centuries. It has created our democracy; it has made us what we are in history. We are a just and good nation; we will remain a just and good nation. But we are a nation capable of a terrible fury, and our enemies must know that.[39]

It was already a balanced, well-structured argument—partially because Leahy had spent most of the night rolling it through his mind—but it is one that he would continue to nuance and expand upon through the coming weeks.

But beyond the argument's coherence and the appropriate elevation of the rhetoric, there was from the beginning a certain inherent moral courage to it that would not come clearly into focus for years to come.

For even now, little more than twenty-four hours after the attacks, Leahy was already one of the only powerful voices arguing restraint, arguing deliberation—arguing for some small but significant pause, delay enough to carefully calibrate the legislative response to the actual needs of a terror-aware, twenty-first-century law enforcement community. Even "normally privacy-minded lawmakers, including Sens. Dianne Feinstein (D–Calif.) and Charles Schumer (D–N.Y.), had no intention of questioning efforts to push a bill through quickly. Even Rep. Bob Barr (R–Ga.), a conservative and dedicated privacy advocate, couldn't offer much hope."[40]

Again, Leahy could feel already, even as he surrendered the floor, that any delay—no matter how brief by Senate time—risked everything.

Luke Albee puts it in simple terms: "It was a lonely place to be saying slow down."[41]

One other part of Leahy's speech went more or less unnoticed at the time as well, a short but heartfelt tribute to the tenacity and the durability of the Senate as an icon of democracy. They were the words of a man deeply in love with the institution itself, laced with an understandable dash of survivor's bluster: "And we know that quite possibly this building was the target of the plane that crashed. But we know that this building must be open because the people's business is done here. And no country and no terrorist, no matter how evil, no matter how twisted, no matter how diabolic, can close the symbols of the United States democracy."

It was all but impossible to imagine, even on September 12, but an attack of a much different sort was already being planned, one every bit as evil and twisted and diabolic, but one that would in fact succeed in shuttering nearly all the symbols of United States democracy for a stretch of long, turbulent weeks.

And all of this on the strength of less than a dollar in postage.

★ ★ ★

The first real indications of how profoundly the political climate had changed came the following day, during consideration of a routine spending bill for Commerce, Justice, and State—also known as the CJS Appropriations Bill. The CJS bill had been proceeding in torpid but orderly fashion prior to the attacks, but now it became the obvious vehicle for a rush of provisions and amendments to deal with the terrorist threat.

The most far-reaching of these was the "Combating Terrorism Act," put forward by Orrin Hatch and Dianne Feinstein. The legislation had been written originally during the Clinton years but had gone nowhere, and for understandable reasons. In the name of addressing changes in technology—expanding the government's authority to trace telephone calls to include e-mail, for example—the bill also vastly expanded the reach of that power to trace, allowing it without a warrant on a loosely defined "emergency" basis, and extending its reach to anyone very loosely defined as a "terrorist."[42]

No longer would a court order be necessary, under the Hatch-Feinstein amendment, and no longer would the *content* of telephone or e-mail conversations necessarily rest outside the scope of these emergency powers. And as Senator Carl Levin pointed out, the changes weren't even limited to terrorism but reached into a host of other more pedestrian criminal classifications as well.

In the past, Leahy had had little trouble derailing this very amendment, and he offered the same sort of reductio ad absurdum that had always made it clear the bill was not ready for prime time: "I guess some kid who's scaring you with his computer could be a terrorist [under this vague definition] and you could go through the kid's house and his parents' business and everything else under this, it's that broad.

"But again," he finished, waving a hand, his rough baritone generously laced with sarcasm, "the Senate can *vote* for whatever they *want*."[43]

But the legislative physics of the situation were utterly different now. In the last two days, the Senate had abruptly relinquished the feel of a deliberative body; instead, it had morphed into something more akin to a supermassive black hole, its strange new gravitational force drawing anything related to terrorism relentlessly through the process at unprecedented speed. To stand in the way of such high-velocity bills risked very real political injury, risked open public condemnation in the name of the 9/11 victims and their grieving families.

The session, then, became a case study in acquiescence; even the strongest objections were phrased with a certain wistfulness, an understanding that they had little place in the chamber currently.

The Combating Terrorism Act, unthinkable just days before, passed by unanimous consent, with less than an hour of debate. Only Leahy and Senator Carl Levin offered any real critique of it.

Stopping far-reaching counterterrorism legislation was an absolute impossibility, then. And in fact Leahy himself badly wanted to modernize the statutes surrounding surveillance and the terrorist threat. The 9/11 attacks had painfully demonstrated the need for a significant update of the laws. The key would be negotiating beforehand precisely what went in, and what stayed out.

And, perhaps, how long what went in *stayed* in.

★ ★ ★

But there were more severe political aftershocks to follow.

On Sunday, September 16, five days after the attacks on New York and Washington, Leahy and Senator Hatch, the ranking member of the Judiciary Committee, joined the attorney general for a classified briefing and a frank discussion of the need for antiterror legislation. By all accounts it was a productive and collegial meeting. In a crucial concession, and in the interest of speed, Leahy had agreed to negotiate directly with the White House on behalf of the Senate, forgoing the committee process entirely.

Afterward, Leahy and Hatch held an impromptu stand-up press conference outside the Justice Department to stress their unified front—Democrats united with Republicans, legislative branch united with the executive.

In his prepared remarks and in his responses to reporters' questions, Leahy continued to articulate the issue in terms of painstaking balance: "We will take whatever steps are necessary to protect our nation and to seek out those who caused this horrible, horrible murderous deed. But we'll do it within our framework, our framework of laws and our Constitution. If we don't . . . then in some ways the terrorists win."

Hatch, for his part, stressed the same balance, but with something of the opposite emphases. "We both want to make sure that that's done within the realm of the Constitution, we meet Constitutional prerequisites and considerations. But we also know that we need to modernize some of our lives to make sure that we don't leave a stone unturned in response to terrorists."[44]

This agreement on everything but where to place the accent continued amiably through the question and answer, with Leahy promising, "You do it right the first time. By doing it right, though, means you obey the Constitution," and Hatch nodding along, only to add, "We're not going to put up with terrorism in this country, and we'll do whatever it takes Constitutionally *and otherwise* to get rid of it" (emphasis mine).[45]

Still, it was in the main a solid show of solidarity; no one expected perfect harmony as details of the legislation began to float to the surface. The purpose of the Sunday press conference was simply to communicate to the American people that their government was speaking with one voice.

All of which made Ashcroft's own press conference, held the very next day at FBI headquarters with Director Mueller, that much more stunning.

Without any advance notice to either Leahy or Hatch, Ashcroft walked up to the bank of microphones and announced that the administration's pending legislation—*although the sweeping measures would not be finalized for two more days*—would need to be passed more or less immediately.

"Now, we will be working diligently over the next day or maybe two to finalize this comprehensive proposal," Ashcroft said, slowly and carefully, "and we will call upon the Congress of the United States to enact these important anti-terrorism measures this week."[46]

Friday, it seemed, was Ashcroft's deadline, for a bill he would deliver on Wednesday. The attorney general was giving the Congress of the United States just a little more than forty-eight hours to pass the voluminous bill that would later come to be known as the USA Patriot Act.

There was no need to draw the obvious conclusion, that anyone who took longer than several days to turn around the administration's hastily drafted legislation was either actively or passively inhibiting law enforcement, especially given that Ashcroft had opened the press conference by referring darkly to "associates of the hijackers that have ties to terrorist organizations" and who "may be a continuing presence in the United States." Delay was danger, plain and simple.[47]

The direct implication was that "we were going to have another attack if we did not agree to this immediately," Leahy says now, drawling out the words with evident disgust. He and his staff were shocked. "It was really unseemly," Beryl Howell politely puts it.[48]

It was their first real taste of 9/11 "hardball."[49] But not their last, of course. Within a month's time, the administration and their GOP allies in Congress would be routinely framing much of their preexisting policy wish list as a crucial response to the attacks—including, in a neat yet painful irony, Bush's long slate of Heritage Foundation–approved judicial nominations.

The White House made it clear through the GOP leadership that this line was now a unified talking point: "The holdup of these nominees threatens the war on terrorism because these judicial vacancies need to be filled as soon as possible to act on law enforcement requests." Reporters immediately confirmed that there was no evidence such requests were languishing, but that fact seemed all but beside the point.[50]

★ ★ ★

While Ashcroft's public demand for immediate passage of his sweeping legislation hadn't poisoned the well altogether, it had made the water more than a little bitter to the taste. Just moments before a September 19 Capitol Hill meeting to exchange their respective first drafts, a very hoarse Senator Patrick Leahy appeared on NPR's *Talk of the Nation* and quickly made it clear that he and the attorney general had "met several times during the weekend, and we've been on the phone, obviously a great deal during the day and the evenings and so on trying to put together packages that work."

But Leahy dismissed outright the idea of a two-day congressional discussion of the intricate bill. Trying to reassure the American people that they were safe from terrorism by passing a hastily drafted bill would be like trying to legislate against "paralyzing snowstorms or hurricanes," Leahy maintained, and then added, in a sly dig at Ashcroft, "it's like King Canute. It's not going to happen."[51]

The passing reference to Canute—reputed to be so arrogant that he commanded the waves (unsuccessfully) to cease crashing upon his shore[52]—notwithstanding, Leahy was still committed to working diligently with the administration to pass a careful, useful bill quickly. But an inevitable frostiness had already replaced the sense of camaraderie that marked the days immediately following the attacks.

When the two sides met later that morning "in an ornate room in the

Capitol to exchange proposals," Ashcroft's point man, Assistant Attorney General Viet Dinh, "made a beeline for a seat near the head of the conference table. Leahy and his colleagues raised their eyebrows and shook their heads. Only members of Congress were supposed to sit at the table, one of the Senators told Dinh, asking him to sit with the rest of the staff."[53]

The check on the Justice Department's aggressive posture was no accident: both parties in Congress realized that the moment had come to assert their own prerogatives, to use those prerogatives or lose them. Leahy was joined by Senators Hatch and Richard Shelby, among others from the Senate, while House Majority Leader Dick Armey brought with him John Conyers and a small handful of others from the House.

Alberto Gonzales was there representing the White House, but remained mostly silent and alert, as was his habit.

Ashcroft began by having his own department's forty-page proposal passed out. It was a sobering document. In some ways it tracked with the 165-page proposal that Leahy would pass out next: the attorney general wanted wiretaps to cover suspects rather than phone numbers, to permit surveillance as the target moved from phone to phone; "pen and register" and "trap and trace" laws updated to include e-mail and other electronic modes of communication; and he wanted to significantly bolster money-laundering scrutiny.[54] And both approaches rejected the idea of a national ID card.

But in other ways the Justice Department's proposal broke radical new ground. It did away with court scrutiny of wiretaps altogether in two instances: "first, when obtaining the contents of communications of 'computer trespassers,' and second, in emergency situations where the provider of Internet or other telecommunications services believed there was an immediate danger of death or serious physical injury to any person."

In practice this would allow any Internet service provider to voluntarily (or under FBI pressure) and secretly allow the FBI to tap e-mail correspondence, for instance. Similarly, under the draft bill, the administration would have the authority to obtain "any educational record or other information in the possession of an educational agency or institution 'in investigating or preventing a Federal terrorism offense.'"[55]

The most dramatic provision, though, concerned the attorney general's powers of detention. "It called for the indefinite detention of any noncitizen the attorney general 'has reason to believe may further or facilitate acts of terrorism,' as well as the unrestricted sharing of grand jury and eavesdropping data throughout the government."[56]

The Bush White House wanted the power to wiretap and detain suspects of its choice, without charges or court oversight in certain cases, for as long as it saw fit. Period.

As Leahy and others leafed through the Ashcroft draft, the room filled with a low murmur of disagreement, and disbelief. The only restraint that the administration had shown, as far as Leahy's team was concerned, was in leaving any new death-penalty provisions *out* of the draft. (Even for committed death-penalty supporters like Bush and Ashcroft, it was hard to argue a deterrent effect on suicide bombers.[57])

Leahy's own proposal was passed out next, and it benefited from following Ashcroft's more jarring draft, at least with the congressional group assembled at the table. The 165-page USA Act draft was much longer, but designed to facilitate current approaches and live as much as possible within current oversight regimes. Predictably, coming from a former prosecutor, it was heavy on practical, nuts-and-bolts measures to strengthen actual enforcement, without creating liabilities for the prosecutors who would eventually try terrorist suspects.

Among other provisions, Leahy's draft sought to triple the number of border security agents on the northern border of the United States; to increase the number of language specialists and translators at the FBI, as well as the number of judges expediting FISA (Foreign Intelligence Surveillance Act) orders; to increase funding for counterterrorism at the Department of Justice and for the FBI's technical support center; and to criminalize terrorist attacks against mass transportation systems.[58] Combined with the areas where it agreed with Ashcroft's draft — updating surveillance to match current technology, for instance — Leahy's draft was forward-leaning but clearly mindful of judicial oversight.

And as such, it was precisely what Ashcroft had told his deputy to avoid.

It was an inherently twisted dynamic from the start: the Bush administration had vowed to change the face of law enforcement, to burst the box of typical policing — therefore, only something that genuinely outraged congressional privacy advocates could hope to reach that bar. Ironically, rejection of the administration's ideas at this first meeting would have told Ashcroft's team that they were more or less on the right track to please their several bosses.

But from a purely pragmatic standpoint, there was a solid foundational overlap between the drafts. It seemed at least possible that the administration would accept nearly all of Leahy's provisions. The fight would be over Ashcroft's controversial expansions of executive branch authority.

"There were a lot of people in the room, both Republican and Democrat, who were not about to give the unfettered power the attorney general wanted," Leahy now insists. In fact, Dick Armey—one of the most ardent conservatives in Congress—was already privately talking up the idea of a "sunset"—a provision requiring that the law be reauthorized at some point in the near future, after the furor around the attacks had dissipated.[59]

The sunset provision was even then beginning to seem like the only answer to the powerful new legislative physics that Leahy had confronted during the discussion of the Hatch-Feinstein amendment: it might be the only way to defer any truly lasting decisions until cooler heads had time to prevail.

Still, Leahy sought to strike an upbeat note with reporters outside the conference room. "We're trying to find a middle ground, and I think we can. We probably agree on more than we disagree on."[60]

Once back in his offices, Leahy let the pose of "surprising agreement" drop. He sat down with his point person on the bill, Beryl Howell, and they exchanged impressions of the meeting. Both had been deeply disturbed and a little depressed by the reach of Ashcroft's proposal, and the casual way the attorney general had put forward an idea like indefinite detention. It was painfully clear that Ashcroft would fight for those extraordinary powers, that he was ready and even anxious to argue their centrality to a post-9/11 mind-set, and that denying them was going to be a battle royal.

Finally, after they had both vented, Leahy boiled down his directives into two points and ticked them off on his big fingers. "One, let's not do a knee-jerk reaction on this bill," he told Howell. Even if Ashcroft returned to his short timeline and began to beat them up in the press, they had to stay focused. They had to demand the time necessary for careful legislating. "We're going to proceed calmly. And we're going to get it right."

He held up the second finger. "And we're not going to be rushed into a sunset either."[61]

Although a sunset was looking more and more like the only effective way to deal with the Bush administration's aggressive push in a tense national moment, Leahy was an old hand with sunset provisions, and he knew that they could have distinct downsides as well.

"Because with the lure of a sunset," Leahy went on, "you can write a bad bill. You can say, Oh let's just try this out, or let's just try that out, it'll go away in a few years anyway. And then people stop pushing for the best bill they can get in the original drafting. Now we've got to get the best bill we can get, so I'm not putting the sunset on the table yet—no matter what the House says. So we just keep the sunset in our back pocket."

Leahy laced his fingers together over his shirtfront, leaned back in his chair and gave Howell a slow nod, and closed his eyes to just a canny slit. For the first time since the attacks, he seemed comfortable again with the basic process of things, the tumblings of the legislative universe.

"We stay mum on the sunset for now, Beryl," Leahy repeated.[62]

And so began a month of substantive, intense—and often fantastically strained—negotiations. Howell did far more than merely serve as Leahy's point person on the overall legislation; she also coordinated and integrated the work product of the several other committees charged with polishing smaller pieces within their own bailiwicks, such as the Senate Intelligence Committee and the Senate Banking Committee, tasked with addressing terrorist money laundering.

Each day, teams of negotiators worked around a huge conference table in the Senate Judiciary Hearing Room, Room 226 of the Dirksen Senate Office Building—so many teams from so many agencies and departments that Howell occasionally lost track of who was in the room, arguing for or against which provision.

Leahy would stop by the hearing room as often as his schedule allowed, but Howell would brief him at length each evening, without fail, either in his official offices or sometimes in his hideaway office in the Capitol.[63]

It was a grueling process, reformulating some of the most complex and arcane procedures in American jurisprudence. Outside Room 226, though, another set of negotiations was being conducted in the klieg-light court of public opinion, and there, for the first time in a very long time, Leahy found himself substantially handicapped.

His gruff voice and grave demeanor still carried great weight; it wasn't that. Leahy remained the chair of Judiciary and had the weight of a Senate majority firmly behind him. But his message was clearly not what a frightened nation wanted to hear. His argument was that the situation was epic in its complexity and required time enough for proper, thoughtful action—otherwise we risked a permanent diminishment of our constitutional freedoms. And some risks would have to be accepted in a free society.

The administration, however, was more than happy to simplify. President Bush, in remarks to employees at the Federal Bureau of Investigation on September 25, two weeks after the attacks, said, "I see things this way. The people who did this act on America, and who may be planning further acts, are evil people. They don't represent an ideology, they don't represent a legitimate political group of people. They're flat evil. That's all they can think about, is evil. And as a nation of good folks, we're going to hunt them down, and we're going to find them, and we will bring them to justice."[64]

★ ★ ★

By the end of September, Howell was a wreck. As the negotiations reached their most difficult phase, she had attempted to bring civil libertarians and Justice Department officials together—only to have Ashcroft's team leave the room en masse when it came time for the ACLU and Center for Democracy and Technology watchdogs to speak.[65]

But there was an even deeper problem: no one on Ashcroft's team had any actual power to deal. As a result, Howell—who had Leahy's full proxy to negotiate—would reach a crucial understanding with her counterparts, only to have them return later with different instructions and points of view, upsetting days of work.

So Howell and Bruce Cohen met with Leahy and told him that someone had to put his foot down, and only Leahy's foot would do the trick. Someone in the negotiating room had to be able to speak authoritatively and bindingly for Ashcroft.[66]

Leahy said he understood completely, and left the room immediately. "I don't know what he did, or whom he talked to," Howell says now, but results were not long in coming. Within the space of a few hours, White House Deputy Counsel Tim Flanigan strode into Dirksen 226, making it clear to Howell and Cohen that he could now deal directly for both the White House and Ashcroft.

It seemed to be just the breakthrough that both sides needed.

With Howell and Flanigan paring the talks down as much as possible to just themselves, they hacked and compromised their way through the thorniest issues: most crucially at that point, Flanigan "agreed that the government would not use evidence about US citizens obtained in an illegal matter under US law, and that a court would review information before it could be shared among intelligence and law enforcement agencies with the United States."[67] They shook hands on it, and went back to give their principals the news.

Leahy was overjoyed. He drove back to his house in McLean that night feeling like a great weight had been rolled from his chest. He could live with what Howell had gotten, and best of all they could *act* — the strain of being the only voice for thoughtful delay was wearing on him. With this new agreement, "he'd done what he could to protect civil liberties . . . but he had also moved to quickly bolster law enforcement and counterintelligence operations. No one could accuse the Democrats of coddling terrorists."[68]

Leahy swept into his office the next morning in high spirits. The deal, as codified overnight, rested in piles on his polished wood conference table. And promptly he was joined by Ashcroft, Senator Hatch, Michael Chertoff, from the Justice Department's criminal division, and the ever-unreadable Alberto Gonzales.

But Ashcroft and Hatch were not so inscrutable. They brought a much different mood into the meeting, and before the discussion could even formally begin, Ashcroft broke the silence by saying he had rethought his agreement with some of Flanigan's concessions. It was clear from the reactions of Hatch and Gonzales that they had known this was coming.

Ashcroft was backing away from the agreement, he told Leahy very directly, and returning to where it had stood before Howell and Flanigan's breakthrough.

Leahy's jaw dropped, but the attorney general went on, impassively. The administration would return to its insistence that the FBI and other law enforcement agencies be allowed to share wiretap and grand jury information with the CIA, the National Security Agency, and other intelligence agencies — and that *without* the limited court scrutiny Leahy and Howell had fought to keep.

And they would also return to a broader definition of terrorism, and an insistence that statutes of limitations be abolished for any such offenses.[69]

Leahy was absolutely flabbergasted. He struggled with the stark new direction of things, and managed to say, "John, when I make an agreement, I make an agreement. I can't *believe* you're going back on your commitment."

Ashcroft was unrepentant, reiterating that some of the concessions

Flanigan had agreed to would weaken the bill unacceptably. It was clear that the attorney general planned, now that he knew the outer limits of what Leahy could agree to in order to close a deal, to deliberately push Leahy beyond those limits.

And within a few more minutes the meeting had ended, with a tension so profound you could almost pat it with your hands.

But that tension would only grow, in fact: within the hour, Ashcroft and Hatch had called a hastily scheduled press conference to accuse *Leahy* of dragging his feet on a measure designed to keep the American people safe. "I think it is time for us to be productive on behalf of the American people. Talk won't prevent terrorism," Ashcroft said in the blunt, take-no-prisoners tone he and the administration had adopted since the attacks, adding that he was "deeply concerned about the rather slow pace" Leahy had unilaterally forced upon the White House.

At which point, Hatch stepped up to sharpen the sting for anyone who had missed it. "It's time to get off our duffs and do what's right," Hatch chided.[70]

Alerted to the attack later in the day, Leahy was at first unbelieving, and then livid. Not only had Ashcroft scuttled a solid agreement by going back on his word, but he had done so knowing that just minutes later he would be berating *Leahy* publicly for the ensuing delay. It was a lack of integrity Leahy had a hard time believing, but there was no denying the accusations coming his way even now, as relayed by CNN and the rest of the networks.

In Leahy's mind, the administration's brazen politicization of the crisis, its seeming indifference to the erasure of basic civil liberties, and now its clear double-dealing made an increasingly airtight case that Congress should never trust any administration — but this one in particular — with the sweeping powers being demanded.

It was a particularly post-9/11 Catch-22: no White House that demanded unchecked police powers could be trusted with such powers.

But Leahy struggled to convey this brazenness to the media, as a whole still very much in the thrall of Bush's tough-on-terror rhetoric. And so, by way of analogy, he reached finally for the story of the most corrupt law enforcement official he had ever known: Paul Lawrence, the undercover narcotics agent he and the Burlington Police Drug Task Force had caught fabricating drug buys in a sting operation in 1974.

Confronted by the *New Yorker* for delaying the progress of Ashcroft's draft of the Patriot Act, Leahy told the Lawrence story from start to finish, from Lawrence's days as supercop to the sting with a Brooklyn cop code-named "the Rabbi," and he leaned hard on the consequences of that bust. The governor had finally had to release seventy-five people from prison because of Lawrence's corrupted evidence, and that wasn't the worst of it. "'The tragedy was that many of them really *were* drug dealers, but we had to let them out because of Lawrence's role,' Leahy recalled. . . . 'But the most awful thing was that there was one person who couldn't be pardoned. He had committed suicide.'"[71]

Leahy went on to draw the moral for the *New Yorker* columnist: "'I have great respect for law enforcement,' he said. 'But we also need checks and balances. As they say, absolute power corrupts absolutely.'" It went without saying that in this analogy, the Bush administration was looking increasingly like a cop gone bad.

It was a tough new tack, but Ashcroft's latest moves had seriously shaken Leahy. There was something more disturbing here than just the collapse of the deal, or even Ashcroft's double-dealing, he felt. It was painfully clear that Ashcroft felt that there would be no repercussions —that there *could* be no repercussions—for this duplicity in a post-9/11 political environment. He seemed that unconcerned.[72]

This was beyond 9/11 hardball, really, because hardball—even as a mere metaphor—still implicitly honored the basic rules of the game. This was different. This had the feel of someone who had left the field altogether, but had very pointedly taken the bat along, to attack whenever and whomever he saw fit along the way.

★ ★ ★

The USA Act that came to the floor on October 11, 2001, was a far cry from Leahy's original bill. On the positive side, it would give law enforcement a host of new tools with which to pursue suspected terrorists; it would break down some of the walls that had prevented domestic law enforcement from sharing information with the nation's intelligence agencies, and vice versa; and it would aid in stemming the flow of money to suspected terrorists. But it also allowed for far more in the way of governmental surveillance than Leahy was comfortable with, and it spread that surveillance very broadly; it allowed the government these powers, in various exigencies, without court approval.

But at this point, that simply couldn't be helped. Leahy's experience with the Combating Terrorism legislation had taught him that the Senate, at this strange political moment, would ultimately side with the administration in any pitched battle even vaguely connected to the emerging War on Terror.

The legislative road didn't end with passage of the Senate bill, however — he could still hope for improvements down the road when the House and the Senate hammered out their differences. He could win back in conference some or all of what he had lost. That would be the time for celebrations or recriminations.

But there was one last painful moment to be endured in the Senate.

Wisconsin senator Russ Feingold, like Leahy a respected advocate for civil liberties, insisted on putting forward three amendments designed to offset the new executive branch powers — all of them things Leahy would have included gladly, but for the fact that they threatened to upset the agreed-upon package, mixed bag though it was.

Majority Leader Daschle tried to head Feingold off both publicly and privately — arguing that opening up the amendment process could very well lead to a far worse bill — but Feingold would not be deterred.

And so Leahy — the Senate's foremost warrior for civil liberties — was forced to stand on the floor of the Senate and acknowledge that his handful of hard-fought victories in the negotiation process would not hold, in all likelihood, if put to a series of majority votes. It was even more galling to be arguing, in effect, *for* the provisions that Leahy himself had rigorously opposed and which Ashcroft had forced through the process after backing away from their more nuanced agreement: "The Administration agreed to my proposal on Sunday, September 30, but reneged within two days. . . . Frankly, the agreement of September 30, 2001, would have led to a better balanced bill. I could not stop the Administration from reneging on the agreement. . . . In these times we need to work together to face the challenges of international terrorism. I have sought to do so in good faith."[73]

When all was said and done, Feingold's three amendments were tabled, or killed, by overwhelming majorities. And Feingold was finally the lone vote against the USA Act, 96-1. (The next day the House passed a very similar version of the bill, 337-79.)

Feingold's was a vote of conscience, but Leahy's chief of staff at the time, Ed Pagano, makes very clear that Leahy had a different path of conscience to walk: "I certainly respect [Feingold's] stance on it. But the person who was in the trenches was Pat Leahy — he was trying to fight and make it better because he knew absolutely that it was going to pass. Sometimes the easy vote is the no vote, when you *don't* have the responsibility. It was

Leahy's responsibility as chair of Judiciary to improve what we thought was a very flawed, overbroad draft from the Bush administration."[74]

Leahy had known in his heart, the moment that Flight 77 hit the Pentagon, that his own life was changed forever. And here it was in the black and white of the USA Act, S. 1510. He had used every last erg of his expansive legislative power to head off what he considered abuses of the Constitution, but even now the Senate bill had far too many trapdoors, if a given administration were inclined to exploit them. He knew he would be attacked by self-styled patriots for not giving the administration 100 percent of what it wanted, and by civil libertarians for putting his name to the bill at all.

The attacks of 9/11 continued to influence and confuse and distort the workings of the institution he loved.

There was only one chance left to reassert some sort of real oversight — the moment when the House and the Senate would reconcile their two versions of the bill. With much struggle, the House had managed to insert a December 31, 2006, sunset provision into its version, which meant that the provision was fair game for the final conference.

Now that he had gotten the best basic bill that he could, Leahy could stop being cagey, stop keeping mum. He wanted the sunset, and wanted it badly. That way, Congress would could take another run at these issues, if not more than one, when time had lent a bit of perspective to the changes wrought by the legislation.

There was one small problem, of course: the only thing that Ashcroft and the White House professed to hate more than even a momentary delay in counterterrorism legislation was the idea that such legislation might vanish altogether, almost magically, in just five years' time.

But before either side could position itself properly for the endgame, it turned out there was another game entirely.

Just three days after the House passed H.R. 3108, an obscure young intern in Tom Daschle's office picked up a letter from a stack in her lap and slid her letter opener about an inch into the flap.

The return address was 4th Grade, Greendale School, Franklin Park, NJ, 08852. And the powder that all but leapt out of the small cut in the envelope, whitening the front of her dark skirt, looked at first like baby powder to her. But a sinking part of her knew it couldn't be baby powder, not with the rank scent of mildew that began to fill the room.

And not with the way the powder behaved.

Because even as Grant Leslie remembered her training and forced herself to freeze, the powder began inexorably to do the impossible. Rather than falling to the carpet, a portion of the particulates began to climb slowly—like a thin smoke all but worried apart by a breeze—into the breathing range of the interns all around her.

Leonidas and the Three Hundred
OCTOBER AND NOVEMBER 2001

Almost immediately, the powder in the Daschle letter was identified as anthrax. Leslie and the other interns — as well as a handful of others potentially exposed — were given prophylactic doses of Cipro and told to go home and watch for any symptoms of either cutaneous or inhalational anthrax.

By the end of that evening, researchers at the US Army Medical Research Institute of Infectious Diseases at Fort Detrick, Maryland, had provided final confirmation: the powder was indeed anthrax.[1] Clearly the anonymous mailer had decided to follow the primary wave of media attacks with a secondary strike at the very heart of the US government. And the strain of anthrax was exceptionally virulent, what senior scientist John Ezzell called "the face of Satan . . . the closest thing I've seen to weaponized anthrax."[2]

As David Willman points out in *The Mirage Man*, his painstakingly researched account of the 2001 anthrax attacks, Ezzell never actually said that the powder *had* been weaponized, only that its properties approximated something that a state-sponsored entity might create in pursuit of an enhanced biological weapon. Its "highly aerogenic" properties, its ability to climb into human breathing range when disturbed, were pronounced; it was "energetic," according to another highly placed USAMRIID scientist, Peter Jahrling, and "professionally made."[3]

Given that such energy and mobility are the ideal result of any bioweapons program utilizing anthrax, and given that various state programs around the world had experimented with additives designed to lend anthrax spores just this power of flight, it was all but a foregone conclusion that Ezzell's comment would be seized upon by the Bush administration as proof that the attack was international, and perhaps Iraqi, in origin.

For years the misperception would persist—in spite of overwhelming evidence to the contrary—that the Daschle letter had contained anthrax coated with silica or polymerized glass, or bentonite, a claylike material once favored by Iraqi bioweapon designers.[4]

Yet the debate over weaponization quickly served—and serves to this day—to displace and obscure the far more apposite truth: these particular spores betrayed a profound and potentially unprecedented level of design and acumen.

It's fair to say that the powder in the Daschle letter astounded and frightened every hardened bioweapons researcher who examined it. For one thing, it more or less refused to be examined. Its tendency was to drift up and out of sight; when it did finally succumb to its own fragmentary gravity and settle, it could "reaerosolize" again and again, under the slightest impetus. Even a researcher moving a fingertip softly against the *outside* wall of a sealed tube would be enough to reagitate the powder within. The spores contained in the Daschle letter could almost effortlessly reaerosolize and float five or more feet up into breathing range, more than a month after being spilled.[5]

This bioweapon could fly, then, under what amounted to its own power, and that power didn't appear to diminish with time.

The Daschle strain contained spores or groups of spores measuring reliably between one and three microns—just large enough to be retained by the body rather than exhaled, and just small enough to avoid being snared in the respiratory tract's mucus or filtration systems. The anonymous mailer had taken a germ designed by nature to be potentially lethal and made it reliably so.

Given that the average postal envelope is fashioned from paper with pores of between ten and twenty microns, it quickly became clear as well that the sealed envelopes carrying the powder would not have acted as containment vessels, but rather as continual delivery systems as they moved through the postal system.

Along with the air-conditioning systems, mail delivery was immediately halted in the Capitol and the Senate Office Buildings. Given the tide of letters and parcels that rolls in and out of the seat of American government each day, the sudden cessation of delivery and the quarantine of already received correspondence produced absolute organizational chaos.

Chaos, that is, in every Senate office but one: Suite 437 of the Russell

Building, the offices of Senator Patrick Leahy of Vermont. Leahy's operation was not caught off guard because it had already, in point of fact, made a key internal decision to stop opening all mail three days *prior* to the discovery of the Daschle letter.[6]

The Leahy camp's comparatively cool presence of mind, and aggressive early action, look all but precognitive in hindsight. On October 12, when NBC News had first reported the discovery of a live anthrax letter in its corporate mailroom, Leahy's chief of staff Luke Albee had digested the news and drawn an immediate bottom line: "I just went and talked to our office manager Clara Kircher, and I said, 'If these zealots are targeting the press, then they're coming after us next.'"[7]

This frank bottom line Albee then worked up as a more formal memo to Leahy, with the deliberately proactive title, "Taking Security in Our Hands." The memo pulled no punches, and finished with the lines, "In light of the latest anthrax news at NBC, WSJ [the *Wall Street Journal*] and the State Department, Clara and I have decided to stop opening all mail until we can get some guidance from the 'experts' charged with protecting us. . . . It seems quite plausible to me that a member of Congress could be on their mailing list."[8]

From that moment on, any mail addressed to Leahy was diverted to a remote location. By the time the Daschle letter was received three days later, Albee's operation had already more or less adjusted to the change in routine.

Beryl Howell still shakes her head in wonder at the accuracy of Albee's call: "It was unbelievable that he had taken those precautionary steps. He thinks on a chessboard ten steps ahead. And in this case, Luke saved lives."[9]

Albee's decision to shut down mail handling was a bold one, and it's fair to say that it was distinctly unpopular with the Senate sergeant at arms. Kircher defended the stoppage at a meeting of fellow Senate office managers later in the day on the twelfth, to the surprise of the group, but no other Senate office saw the wisdom of following suit. Leahy, however, solidly backed his staff. Albee had been chief of staff for some seven years, and the senator had an extremely high level of respect for Albee's occasional gut-level decisions.

"He totally trusted us," Albee says.

But having anticipated the Daschle letter didn't entirely relieve the feeling in Albee's gut, nor did seeing a new level of security suddenly erected in the buildings where he spent his workdays. He had still a persistent, nagging sense of threat: "And right-wing commentators had *really* noticed Leahy for the first time. Leahy had really become a target then for the opposition."[10]

The truth is that authorities severely underestimated the power of the Daschle anthrax at every turn. Officials first thought that sealing off Daschle's office would be sufficient; when testing showed that the spores had spread far beyond that limit, they would expand the protective bubble first to the sixth floor, then to the southeastern quadrant of the Hart Building, before eventually shutting down all of Hart—and then, in rapid succession, the Rayburn, Longworth, and Cannon Buildings.

Finally, the House of Representatives itself was closed at the order of Speaker Dennis Hastert for three days of environmental scanning.

Equally mystifying was the official stance on prophylactic Cipro prescriptions. The Cipro wave began with the twenty-three Daschle staffers and three Feingold staffers that nasal swabbing determined had been exposed to the bacterium; they, in addition to five of the Capitol Police, were prescribed the drug immediately.[11]

But within days Cipro was being much more freely dispensed from one of the medical offices in the Capitol, to those who had been exposed, or even to those who were simply worried about exposure. The medical authorities refused to be pinned down on who should or shouldn't ingest it, always ultimately placing the onus on the patient.

Leahy's legal team—Beryl Howell, Julie Katzman, and Bruce Cohen—all made the pilgrimage to the office. "It was like going to the nurse's office in high school," Howell says, with a laugh in her voice. "And they handed us out the Cipro. It was pretty strong Cipro they gave us, and it was hard on the stomach."[12]

Katzman, who was pregnant at the time, recalls the unsettlingly iffy quality of the medical advice as much as the wait in line. "I stood on line for a long time, but when I talked with the doctors, they said they thought I *shouldn't* take it. They said in theory it would be okay—and the manufacturers of the drug were saying it was okay—but they also advised me not to take it."[13]

The mixed messages didn't end there. "Ultimately they gave it to me, and said if you *feel* like taking it, take it. But they advised me at the same time *not* to take it. They said, it's up to you."

Finally, Katzman opted not to take the drug, because "the chances of my having been exposed were so slim." But it's a measure of the deep uncertainty and the paralyzing tensions of the moment that the Hill's best clinicians would actually send a pregnant woman off with a filled prescription for a drug they had advised both for and against ingesting.

★ ★ ★

The Daschle anthrax letter was the nightmare come true that bioterrorism experts had feared and predicted for years. But for Leahy and his staff, in at least one way it was that much worse: the nightmare had that exhausting looped-narrative quality of the very worst dreams, the sense that you've found yourself in this story before, and every exit door turns out to be an entrance back into the horror.

On 9/11, just weeks before, they had found themselves suddenly forced from their offices, working from their own DC homes and apartments, from restaurants and nearby Starbucks outlets. For the better part of two days, they had been exiles wandering the capital, trying to respond to the worst terrorist threat in history with what amounted to one hand tied behind their backs.

Now it was happening all over again, and in the most exacting stage of the endgame on the USA Patriot Act.

Informed that they would have to evacuate their Dirksen Building negotiating quarters almost immediately, Howell and her assistant David James made a series of mad dashes through the crowded Judiciary Committee hearing room, transferring drafts and notes onto thumb drives, grabbing key stacks of paper — but always with the eerie sense that these stacks might themselves be infected.

Finally, when they had whittled down what they needed into what they could carry away, Howell and James confronted the $64,000 question: where to go? "We vacated our offices and then we were meeting in places in the Capitol I didn't know existed. In hallways and under eaves and behind corners."[14] They sat cross-legged for hours under the Rotunda, notes and drafts in their laps, lowering their voices as bystanders passed.

Ultimately, no space was large enough or private enough to house their entire negotiating operation, and the lack began to wear on them all. Finally, though, they found a space just barely large enough to house at least the nerve center of Howell, Katzman, and James and one or two others: Leahy's secret hideaway office in the Capitol Building.

As Capitol hideaways go, Leahy's was posh. Adjacent to the Speaker's hideaway, very narrow but with high ceilings, views of the National Mall, and a working fireplace, it was one or two notches from the most desirable of the Senate holes-in-the-wall. But it was designed for private one-on-ones; as a practical work space, it was a well-appointed broom closet, with barely enough outlets and chairs for four people to occupy without knocking knees.[15] By the time they had everyone hooked up to a power source, the room was festooned with wires and plugs and extension cords. Still, it gave them a tiny pied-à-terre, a space to call their own, and the team began to take a certain pride in their ability to function regardless of their surroundings.

The Justice Department and the White House still had endless space and personnel and man hours to throw at their final machinations for swaying the bill. And they had the club of 9/11 to swing at Democrats whenever an argument over warrants or judicial oversight got heated. With the anthrax attack, and the ensuing panic over it, that club had gotten even heavier.

But the Leahyites had heart. Howell worked long hours in spite of a debilitating nausea from the Cipro—a nausea that came and went for weeks—forcing herself through draft after mind-numbing draft of the evolving bill. When she went home, she would find her kids still frightened of planes, and ducking reflexively whenever one passed overhead.[16]

This was the moment when Luke Albee felt the situation was like that of Leonidas and the three hundred Spartans, hemmed in by countless antagonists—but surviving battle after battle, and giving better than they got. Leahy and his team had found a way to do the people's business in spite of hijackers and anthrax mailers and gut-wrenching fluoroquinolone-class antibiotics, and they were now working against the clock to execute one final but key defensive maneuver against the executive branch itself.

It was indeed, to use Albee's deliberately understated phrase, "really something."[17]

★ ★ ★

On October 17, all the principals gathered in Speaker Hastert's office for the final negotiation. Hastert was already under fire for his decision to close not just the House office buildings for anthrax testing, but the House of Representatives itself. By the next morning the front page of the *New York Post* (a paper that had also been a target of the anthrax mailer) would be screaming, "WIMPS: The Leaders Who Ran Away from Anthrax," but for now Hastert seemed unperturbed and called the meeting to order.

Leahy and Daschle spoke for the Senate majority; Hastert, Congressmen Jim Sensenbrenner, Barney Frank, and Dick Armey represented the House. Tim Flanigan, joined by Assistant Attorney General Viet Dinh, had the power to speak for both the White House and the Justice Department, although Leahy harbored dark doubts, given his experience earlier in the month with Flanigan's supposed authority to deal.

In some ways, Leahy liked what the House had been able to secure better than his own product from the Senate: it included stronger court oversight, though nothing like what he would have ideally preferred, and a five-year sunset. But after talking with Armey and Frank, Leahy was convinced they could do better—a four-year sunset, so that the administration would have to seek reapproval of the package again in 2005.

In any event, framing the discussion as a choice between sunsets—rather than between a sunset and no sunset—seemed a solid approach, and Leahy and Armey began by arguing for the four-year span. But Tim Flanigan took the maneuver *en passant*, and made an impassioned presentation against *any* sunset provision.

It had to do with the very nature of the threat the nation now faced, Flanigan argued. "We're feeling *very* strongly about the sunsetting. This is not a war of a fixed duration. And it will not change the culture of law enforcement and national security if we basically make this a short-term fix."[18]

Like Ashcroft, Flanigan was pushing the idea that this law, along with others the administration would seek, was deeper than the nuts and bolts of surveillance—at a deeper level, it was about radically changing the culture and the mind-set of law enforcement. Anything else was dangerously passive, pre-9/11 thinking.

But the composition of the group of lawmakers Flanigan faced was formidable. Leahy aired again all his concerns about the expansion of executive branch authority, from the wiretapping to the detention provisions—and he made it clear that even with a sunset, the administration would be getting far more from a Democratic Congress than Bill Clinton had gotten from the GOP after the Oklahoma City bombing. Armey was no less direct or forceful, and his objections came from the opposing side of the political spectrum, the more libertarian wing of the GOP.

And Congressman Barney Frank, of course, was Barney Frank, as pugnacious and formidable a debater as had ever been sworn in to Congress.

In concert, the three produced a full-fledged counterassault on Flanigan's basic argument, becoming in the process what Ed Pagano now laughingly calls "something like the Three Amigos of civil liberties."[19] All of them wanted a four-year sunset and made it clear collectively that they couldn't sign off without it.

It was a lot of rhetorical firepower to discharge in such a relatively small space. So much so that Flanigan was silent when they finished, and Daschle took advantage of the lull to see if the administration was bluffing.

"Mr. Flanigan," Daschle ventured, "does this mean the president will veto the bill?"

There was some risk in asking the question openly—Daschle knew that Hastert was looking for an excuse to kill the sunset, and a veto threat would amply fill the bill. Flanigan paused for a long few seconds.

But then—whether because the administration was also feeling the heat to move the process to a conclusion, or whether it was partly a small personal olive branch to make up for the abrupt Ashcroft reversal earlier in the month—Flanigan "gave a wry smile and acknowledged that, no, it was not the administration's position to veto over the sunset."[20]

And that was that.[21]

Leahy left the room feeling as though the skies were finally starting to clear, after five weeks of dark insanity. He had the four-year sunset in his pocket, and stronger court oversight than he had had reason to expect just days previously. The bill still wasn't perfect by any stretch of the imagination, but in a capital city where children still flinched as planes tore overhead, and the House of Representatives was shuttered for fear of the air within it, it was the absolute level best he or anyone else could do.

And now, if the administration abused the powers it was being given, he would have another solid crack at the law in four years.

At the elaborate East Room signing of the USA Patriot Act on October 26, Leahy told a group of reporters beforehand that the act was an attempt to move the United States "out of the Dillinger days of law enforcement" and into a posture sustainable over the long term against nimble and deadly terrorist cells. Make no mistake, though, he told them pointedly, it was Congress's duty—and especially the duty of his own Judiciary Committee—to provide "constant oversight" as the law went into effect.[22]

Just moments later, standing just over the seated president's left shoulder as Bush signed the USA Patriot Act into law, Leahy leaned down with his Nikon and focused in for an extreme close-up. It was, as always, Leahy's habit to record history in the making.

The room burst into applause. But when a smiling President Bush looked up from the newly signed legislation, his eyes widened just a bit, clearly startled to see Leahy still peering down at him through the camera's powerful lens.

Message delivered.

★ ★ ★

With the USA Patriot Act finally complete, Leahy suddenly had liberty to do what he had wanted to do for weeks now—make the trip to the site of the fallen towers in New York, as he had visited the Pentagon's crushed west face in the days following the attacks. And so they met at Union Station near the Capitol, on Friday, November 2, just a bit after dawn—Leahy and two of his most trusted aides, Bruce Cohen and Julie Katzman.

Amtrak's new Acela express would have them in New York City by lunchtime, and it offered business-class seating and breakfast on the train, but Katzman couldn't help being struck by the lack of security. After 9/11, almost overnight, plane travel had become a gut-churning, time-consuming gauntlet, but the train station felt "like a soft target," which made Katzman nervous for the opposite reasons—especially so, given that she was three months pregnant.[23]

Leahy was determined to see Ground Zero, although it was still smoldering, the last spiky ruins of the towers not yet fully demolished. Of course, he would not be the first VIP to visit the site; the last month and a half had been marked by a slow, steady pilgrimage of the country's most prominent political leaders. By this point, in fact, the New York authorities had developed a relatively smooth routine, and from Penn Station the Leahy trio was quickly transported downtown to a staging area several blocks from Ground Zero.

There the smell was already pervasive—not so much the smell of fire or ashes, but a sharp chemical smell, drifting, inescapable. They were given bulky yellow breathing masks and hard hats, and briefed about security precautions and the progress in cleaning up the site. And then —accompanied by FBI representatives—a guide led them directly onto the site of the attack.

Even after weeks of television footage, it was difficult to process the sight: dark, tortured masses of steel, huge trellises of it still rising into the air but canted at crazy angles; massive hills of debris, unrecognizable but giving up disturbingly intimate details as one approached, a scrap of a calendar, a piece of a shoe. All of it cloaked in dark smoke, slowly breathing from the piles.

And everywhere over the site, up on the small hills and grouped at the edges, were first responders in bright neon vests, firefighters in full gear, all working doggedly at a task that would take years to complete.

As Leahy moved over the site, shoes already covered with ash and dust, breaking with his tour here and there to speak with grieving firemen and exhausted policemen, it was as though he could feel the layers of anguish continuing to silently accumulate at the site. It couldn't be clearer that this place was a wound that had yet to close, nearly two months on. Fresh hurt continued.

Amid the smoke, the strange and disquieting stench of the debris, Leahy found himself transfixed, watching the sorting of the rubble, the still desperate search for parts of human bodies. Today he can only describe it by way of incomplete comparison: "It was so very much worse than any crime scene I had ever been to as State's Attorney."[24]

Even among those professionally dedicated to helping the city recover there was and would be further trauma, inevitable emotional aftershocks. Even now, weeks after the fact, every dogged advance ran afoul of some new heartbreak. Every time a bulldozer blade cut the earth, it risked dishonor.

And in all of this there was a faint echo of Leahy's own deeply conflicted feelings about the massive response to the attacks he had helped fashion on Capitol Hill. The truth was that the USA Patriot Act was in many ways still an industrial-size bulldozer where a scalpel was needed.

Leahy believed firmly that the act would help break down the walls that had prevented the FBI and other intelligence agencies from sharing clues to the 9/11 attacks. But the act relied on the discretion of a president and his administration, and already the Bush Justice Department had made it clear that it would pursue the broadest, most far-flung possible readings of the legislation. Leahy's own remarks about the bill on passage had been riddled with his lingering doubts:

> I have done my best under the circumstances. . . . My efforts have not been completely successful and there are a number of provisions on which the Administration has insisted with which I disagree. . . . In these times we need to work together to face the challenges of international terrorism. I have sought to do so in good faith. We have worked around the clock for the past month to put forward the best legislative package we could. While I share the administration's goal of promptly providing the tools necessary to deal with the current terrorist threat,

I feel strongly that our responsibilities include equipping such tools with safety features to ensure that these tools do not cause harm and are not misused.[25]

Later, flying in a sleek blue law enforcement helicopter over the mountains of accumulated debris at Fresh Kills Landfill on Staten Island, Leahy could look out his window and see in graphic terms what had so upset the protesting firemen: of horrible necessity and in spite of the exhausting work of the teams of spotters at Ground Zero, inevitably this vast dumping ground would become the final resting place of many of their colleagues.

Leahy returned to Washington emotionally exhausted—from the epic tensions playing out at Ground Zero, from the spate of horrors and sharp public conflicts with the administration that had filled the preceding months. He wanted nothing more than to rest, catch up with his family, and guide the Senate Judiciary Committee to a more stable and productive footing. A return to normal, albeit a new normal.

More than anything, he wanted to get out of the reactive mode into which they had all been forced, to reach a place from which the committee could accomplish the work of overseeing the War on Terror—work that seemed capable of occupying a lifetime—but also pursue a wide range of goals unrelated to it. Leahy had taken to insisting that if America shredded the Constitution in pursuit of security, the terrorists would win; but a part of him felt that they had *already* won, by narrowing the agenda of the United States government to all terrorism, all the time.

But none of these wishes would come true. Quite the opposite, in fact.

Within a matter of days, it would be Luke Albee's nagging sense of personal threat to Leahy himself that would be dramatically borne out, Albee's belief that his boss was still somehow "on the screen" of an ideological zealot.

A pattern of threat that began on 9/11 would continue to unfold with the sort of dark narrative persistence that ordinarily marks only the Marvel and DC Comics universes: the broader terrorist attacks of September, narrowing in October to bioterrorist attacks on the iconic buildings Leahy shared with his colleagues, before finally shrinking in mid-November to the size of an average postal envelope, this one addressed very particularly.

To Senator Leahy, Russell Senate Office Building, Washington, D.C., 20510–4502.

From a familiar return address: 4th Grade, Greendale School, Franklin Park, NJ, 08852.

The CDC had long suspected at least one more anthrax letter, judging from its mapping of the cross-contamination found in the congressional mail system. Still, it had taken a full month to locate what would now be called the Leahy letter; all mail impounded after the October 15 discovery of the Daschle letter had been stored in fifty-five-gallon barrels, and each barrel had to be painstakingly processed by workers in hazmat suits at a secure location. And yet the FBI couldn't be sure that the letter hadn't somehow passed through the Russell Building before landing in the secure location—the building would need to be shuttered and examined, again.

The familiar sense of dread and contamination returned immediately. Following a full staff briefing by the Centers for Disease Control in the LBJ Room of the Capitol, Albee received his own call from the FBI. It turned out they wanted to interview him about potential exposure and who might want to target Leahy. "I was sitting in my office in the Russell Building and they said, 'We want to interview you,' and I said, 'Great—come on up.' And they said, 'We're not coming in that building.'"

Albee can laugh now, with a can-you-believe-it look, but there's still a palpable disillusionment—even a trace of anger—in his tone a dozen years later.

"Honest to God, they said, No *way* we're coming up there."[26]

★ ★ ★

Leahy was very careful about giving his own answer to the question: why Leahy? His years as a state's attorney had taught him not to speculate about a criminal's animosity toward himself or his office. The downsides were too steep, either exacerbating the fixation of a disturbed criminal still at large, or deepening his own sense of understandable paranoia. Or perhaps both at once.

And Leahy was no stranger to the idea that someone might simply loom up at him out of nowhere, for no reason. In 1983, in fact, he had been attacked walking to the Capitol from his Russell Building offices, right there on the West Terrace. A disturbed man had simply run up and struck him in the face, before pulling away to mutter "things that were indecipherable."

Leahy had been unhurt, really, and back on the Senate floor within the hour, but he knew that the world had a lot of damaged people in it, and that a prosecutor or a senator sometimes offered a sudden focus for their rage.[27]

And so when asked, as he was many, many times during the last weeks of November, Leahy demurred. Not only did he "not attach much significance to the fact that both he and Daschle, the Senate majority leader, [were] Democrats," but Leahy tried his best to shut down such speculation altogether, maintaining that "it could just as well be a person who picked two names at random, or picked them because we're [he and Daschle] in different buildings. Who knows what it is?"[28]

But whether there was a "lone wolf" at large with a personal vendetta or not, the fact was that Leahy's life had been transformed yet again, this time into something that felt each day more and more like a remarkably fast-moving techno-thriller. He and his staff were evacuated as teams of hazmat-suited specialists swabbed his offices in the Russell Building for telltale spores. *USA Today* breathlessly reported that scientists at Fort Detrick had purchased a small ultra-sophisticated robot to open the Leahy letter while preserving any potential forensic evidence. The story was picked up in countless outlets, although the truth was finally a good deal less outré.[29]

Leahy held a joint press conference with the FBI, at which the bureau unveiled a cool $1.25 million reward for information leading to the arrest of the "cold-blooded murderer" (1–800-CRIME-TV was the number to call, accentuating the surreal, quasi-fictional feel to unspooling events).[30]

But most lastingly, Leahy was now detailed a security team twenty-four hours a day, seven days a week. The team was omnipresent. Where he went, they both followed and preceded him. In official Washington, the impact on others was lessened; post-9/11, more than a few public figures were being so guarded. But in the quiet of Vermont—where individual members of the state's congressional delegation may well wander in alone to the local diner or farmers' market on weekend mornings—the security detail turned heads.

Leahy tended to joke about the guards to put his friends back home at ease. And the part of him that used to love the sound of the police siren on a deserted road back in his state's attorney days occasionally took a childlike delight in the power now arrayed around him.

Marselis Parsons, who had known him since Leahy's days as a state's attorney, remembers the day that Leahy entered the WCAX studio for an interview, trailed by a tall, silent, lantern-jawed security guard. "And the guy was wearing a dark raincoat. Patrick whispers to me, 'Ask him what he has under his coat,' and the guy lifts it up to show us—an Uzi or some semi-automatic rifle. And they came and went in this big dark SUV."

Viewed from the quiet of Vermont, the around-the-clock detail could only come to seem like overkill as the days passed. "I think there was a legitimate fear for his safety for a while," Parsons explains, "but most of us thought the security detail lasted way too long. I mean, posting Capitol Police at the bottom of the hill in Middlesex, Vermont?"[31]

But in Washington, the real-world techno-thriller continued, and the threat remained both authentic and pressing. Scientists reported that the Leahy letter contained billions of spores, enough to kill one hundred thousand innocent people.[32] When they did open it, it was after three solid weeks of meetings and dry runs, in a specially prepared room within Fort Detrick's BSL3 Containment Lab. The letter inside was very similar to the Daschle letter, either the rantings of a crazed killer, or a very clever simulation of same.

And to point up the threat even more, a bedridden ninety-four-year-old widow in Oxford, Connecticut, died suddenly of anthrax exposure on November 21; suspicion fell on cross-contamination in the mail her caretakers brought in daily and placed by her bedside. Even those with only the most fleeting exposure to the envelope's microscopic trail of spores could die.[33]

The man to whom the letter was actually addressed couldn't avoid being hyper-aware of all this. But that worry didn't relieve him of the responsibility to steer the Judiciary Committee through the continuing turbulence. And as the tumultuous year came to a close, it looked to close with a bang: the Bush administration had just announced its already-controversial policy on military tribunals for enemy combatants, and Attorney General Ashcroft was due before the Judiciary Committee to defend it, as well as his use of the new Patriot Act.

For three hours, under the eye of the frenzied media, it would be Leonidas squaring off against King Canute, with Leonidas holding the gavel.

But if anything the chair of Judiciary went into the much-ballyhooed confrontation the underdog. Not only was Ashcroft exceedingly familiar with the workings of the Judiciary Committee, and a highly nimble executive branch player to begin with, but he also understood very well the rhetorical high ground he occupied immediately post-9/11. No one in America, with the possible exceptions of the president and vice president, understood it better.

By preference or of necessity, Ashcroft was already well on his way to making invocation of September 11 the first part of any answer to any question about any policy his department undertook. And the questions had mounted sharply in recent weeks, questions about the continuing detention of some eleven hundred suspects following the attacks, in many cases without formal charges, and about the administration's assertion that it could legally eavesdrop on the conversations between these suspects and their lawyers.[34]

Characteristically, when senators filed into the Judiciary Room from the Senate chamber, they found Ashcroft already calmly seated, fully prepared, waiting on them (he would point out in his first brief memoir that his father recommended showing up early, rather than merely on time).[35] He could not have forgotten his rough treatment during his January confirmation hearings. Now he would have a chance to take the fight to those who had opposed him.

The attorney general's opening lines eschewed the traditional flattery of the committee and the chair to lock the focus squarely where he desired it. His very first clause reached the 9/11 touchstone: "On the morning of September 11th, as the United States came under attack, I was in an airplane with several members of the Justice Department en route to Milwaukee, in the skies over the Great Lakes. By the time we could return to Washington, thousands of people had been murdered at the World Trade Center; more were dead at the Pentagon; 44 had died in the crash to the ground in Pennsylvania. From that moment, at the command of the President of the United States, I began to mobilize the resources of the Department of Justice toward one single, overarching, and overriding objective: to save innocent lives from further acts of terrorism."[36]

Ashcroft did not pull the next punch in the slightest: "To those who scare peace-loving people with phantoms of lost liberty, my message is this: your tactics only aid terrorists, for they erode our national unity and diminish our resolve."[37] It was, as the New Yorker's Jeffrey Toobin noted at the time, a signature instance of Ashcroft's deliberately binary approach to the threat—"action or inaction, speed or delay, engagement or surrender," and in this case good versus evil.[38]

Given that Leahy had been loudly questioning the constitutionality of the new rules earlier in the week, not to mention asserting that the administration's "preference for unilateralism" threatened the bipartisan spirit ushered in by the attacks, it was hard to see Ashcroft's last rhetorical strike aimed anywhere else.[39]

But Leahy did not rise to the bait. He had succeeded earlier in the month in eliciting testimony from other Bush officials—most notably Michael Chertoff, then head of the Criminal Division at the Department of Justice—that the military tribunal policy would not be used as broadly in practice; now he wanted Ashcroft on the record confirming that narrower reach. And so after a few pleasantries, he drilled in:

> Chairman LEAHY: But with all the changes and switchbacks and everything else and the statements that have come from different parts of the administration, my question is still basically: Does the administration—whether these are legal or not, is my understanding correct that the administration, one, does not intend to use military commissions to try people arrested in the United States; two, the military commissions would follow the rules of procedural fairness used for trying U.S. military personnel; and, three, the judgments of the military commissions will be subject to judicial review? Are those three points—is that understanding correct? Is that your understanding?
>
> Attorney General ASHCROFT: I cannot say that I have that understanding in the way that you have it. I do not know that the United States would forfeit the right to try in a military commission an alien terrorist who was apprehended on his way into the United States from a submarine or from a ship, carrying explosives or otherwise seeking to commandeer an American asset to explode or otherwise commit acts of terror in the United States.
>
> Chairman LEAHY: But not my question, General.

It was a theme the committee's Democrats sang in harmony—that the Departments of Justice and Defense now claimed authority to detain Americans on American soil without charging them, and to invade their attorney-client relationship at the discretion of the commander in chief, although war had never been formally declared. A claim of such authority was outrageous and should be disavowed.

But here Ashcroft had recourse to the administration's most durable and elemental argument: terrorists are evil, and the evil have no civil liberties to invade. In a remarkable and chilling moment, the attorney general pointed out how each constitutional right in turn, if conferred upon terrorists, could lead to violence and tragedy—pointedly ignoring the fact that the subject under discussion was *suspected* terrorists in custody, the vast majority of whom would turn out to be altogether innocent of terrorist plotting: "Al Qaeda terrorists are now told how to use America's freedom as a weapon against us. They are instructed to use the benefits of a free press—newspapers, magazines, broadcasts—to stalk and to kill victims. They are instructed to exploit our judicial process for the success of their operations. . . . Mr. Chairman and members of this Committee, we are at war with an enemy that abuses individual rights as it abuses jetliners. It abuses those rights to make weapons of them with which to kill Americans."[40]

The metaphorical contortion was breathtaking: civil liberties had become hijacked airliners, to be stopped at all costs. If the eleven hundred detainees still in custody contained even a single evildoer, in the emerging nomenclature of the Bush White House, the only safe option was to deny the full gamut of civil liberties to them all.

From his seat at center stage, Leahy peered down at the unflappable attorney general and saw a man who had finally, at long last, found the magic armor and broadsword he'd been seeking his entire political life. He was combating Evil, and what he did was therefore categorically Good. And the attorney general's discretion about using that armor in other, unrelated arenas was clearly dwindling. Within a few months, Leahy would openly confide to the *New Yorker* that in his opinion Ashcroft was using his "popularity from the anti-terrorism campaign to push his agenda on social issues, particularly abortion and gun control."

"In many ways, Ashcroft has created a far more political department than any Justice Department since I've been here," Leahy would fume. "I think it's beneath the dignity of the Justice Department."[41]

★ ★ ★

By January 2002, the White House was prepared to telegraph its ongoing strategy in what was now known internationally as the War on Terror (although White House insiders would consistently refer to it as GWOT, the Global War on Terror). The president and his administration were clearly already deep in preparations to forcibly overthrow Saddam Hussein's regime in Iraq, and the outlines of an administration-wide sales campaign came methodically into focus.[42]

In his January 2002 State of the Union address, George W. Bush accomplished the huge rhetorical and strategic shift from Afghan training camps and Osama bin Laden to the Iraqi regime and Saddam Hussein in just a few deft paragraphs.

"Our war on terror is well begun, but it is only begun," Bush warned. "If we stop now, leaving terror camps intact and terror states unchecked, our sense of security would be false and temporary." White House speechwriter David Frum had developed a powerful phrase to draw together Iraq, Iran, and North Korea into one short list for aggressive US action. Bush delivered it dramatically: "States like these and their terrorist allies constitute an axis of evil, arming to threaten the peace of the world."

The phrase carried as well a faint echo of Reagan's "evil empire," but it went Reagan one better. Given that Iraq was presented as the worst of the three evils to which Bush served notice that January night, it allowed the administration to argue that Saddam Hussein and his ilk were the most evil of the evildoers—evil squared, in effect.[43]

Leahy watched from his second-row seat at the front of the House chamber and felt increasingly unsettled. The whole rhetorical fan dance was unnecessarily inflammatory, and the focus on Iraq as the next stop in the War on Terror was at once deeply misleading and arrogant. Leahy began to strongly suspect that the White House was laying plans to attack Iraq with or without congressional approval—no one in the House chamber that night could have missed the president's intensity on the issue.[44]

But Leahy left the speech with an answering sort of intensity, a resolve to slow down the White House's sprint to war certainly, but beyond that to finally manage and rein in the overwhelming forces unleashed by the terrorist attacks of 9/11. There was a panicky feel—a heedlessness, and at worst a mindlessness—to American actions over the last year and a half that threatened disaster if it weren't checked.

It was passing strange, in a way, how completely the administration's aggressive early posture—both ideologically and militarily—had alienated Leahy, who had worked very smoothly with George W. Bush's father. George Herbert Walker Bush had offered respect and friendship, mostly regardless of party, and as a result he had been able to count on Leahy's vote when he needed it. ("I protected him on a couple of things, where he needed appropriations," Leahy remembers, and in a gesture of return respect, the senior Bush would tell his staff to leave Leahy's name off their whip list for votes that might hurt him back in Vermont. "He helps out when we need him—I'm not going to call him for this.")

Leahy had spent real quality time at the White House then, and their wives had been surprisingly close, with Barbara Bush always asking after "the beautiful Marcelle." The two men were given to playing little good-natured pranks on one another, and laughed about them for years.

And so when George W. Bush moved into the Oval Office, Leahy had expected more—if not the same relationship he had enjoyed with the father, then maybe an echo of it. And there had been a dutiful series of meetings in the early months. Several times the younger Bush had offered him breakfast in the little study off the Oval Office, poached eggs and bacon for Leahy and oatmeal "porridge" for the fitness-conscious Texan. They had talked about W's parents, and a few mutual friends, but when it came down to business, George W. Bush consistently offered his administration's conservative talking points, and that was the practical extent of the discussion.[45]

The president seemed always blithely secure in his own ability to get most if not all of what he wanted; the unspoken message was that he didn't actually need Leahy's back-channel help, especially in a post-9/11 environment.

Of course, that had left Leahy no position at the table except square opposition. "My strategy was to be independent," as Leahy sums it up. "George W. Bush learned that I wasn't playing. What I told him was where I'd be."

And on Iraq, Leahy found himself moving inevitably into opposition of an invasion. Again, he prepared to dig in his heels in the Senate, and in the press—what heels he had left after the struggle over the Patriot Act, that is.

But this time, at least, he wouldn't be fighting alone.

★ ★ ★

Leahy's suspicions were borne out dramatically over the next several months. Following the State of the Union, it was Vice President Cheney and the newly created White House Iraq Group ("a collection of senior staff members who met regularly to discuss how best to promote the White House's message on Iraq") who pitched the argument to the public's ears. Cheney, like the president, dispensed with doubt altogether. "Cheney didn't offer any evidence to back up his claims about Iraq's WMDs. But his assertions were bold and clear: 'There is no doubt he is amassing [weapons of mass destruction] to use against our friends, our allies, and against us.'"[46]

Colin Powell's much-ballyhooed February speech to the United Nations raised a host of terrifying possibilities—nerve agents, mobile laboratories, anthrax stores hidden on constantly moving train cars—but failed to deliver much in the way of solid, tangible evidence. "But despite Mr. Powell's tone of urgency, it was far from clear that he had convinced his audience of the need for military action."[47]

And that was the ongoing signature of the White House's Iraq push, in Leahy's view: it was a fine mesh of meticulously coordinated talking points, but behind the mesh there seemed consistently to be very little evidence. And given the rapid approach of the midterm election season, the timing of the Iraq War Resolution was itself suspect. Karl Rove had been signaling that terrorism and war would be the twin touchstones of the GOP election strategy.

As Leahy saw it, the key to managing the Iraq war debate—to the extent that it *could* be managed—was to drag it forcibly back into the Congress, where it belonged. Rove and others had been hinting broadly that the president needed no new authorization for an invasion, because legislation passed in the immediate aftermath of 9/11 already allowed the pursuit of al-Qaida members "wherever they may be found." (Cheney's continued assertion that al-Qaida had a working relationship with Saddam Hussein, long after the connection had been soundly debunked, can be traced in part to this legal rationale—to admit that al-Qaida was not in Iraq was to admit that in fact the president needed to return to Congress for additional authorization to invade.)

And so in the humid final days of July 2002, Leahy and Senator Dianne Feinstein of California submitted Senate Concurrent Resolution 133, "Expressing the sense of Congress that the United States should not use force against Iraq, outside of the existing Rules of Engagement, without specific statutory authorization or a declaration of war under Article I, Section 8, Clause 11 of the Constitution of the United States."[48]

In one way, it was pure symbolism. After a brief media stir, the resolution would languish in the Foreign Relations Committee; the president and the War on Terror still had powerful momentum in public opinion, and no senator wanted to guess wrong should Saddam be found, in fact, to possess near-nuclear capabilities.

But it's fair to say that the concurrent resolution was an irritant around which a pearl of opposition began to form. It was a reassertion of congressional authority in tension with what the White House commonly referred to as the "unitary executive branch," and at least one respected Republican, Richard Lugar of Indiana, joined Leahy and Feinstein in a public break with the White House.[49] It touched off a series of fiery speeches in opposition, from staunch liberals like Ted Kennedy and dyed-in-the-wool institutionalists like Robert Byrd (Kennedy called the drive to war "an extraordinary policy coup" by neoconservatives like Cheney and Donald Rumsfeld[50]).

But as in the days following 9/11, a certain strain of patriotic hysteria marked any attempt to sift the actual evidence of Iraqi weapons programs. Back home in Vermont, Leahy was more likely to be approached on the street by war backers than by skeptics. "The majority of people were in favor of that war," he is quick to remind an interviewer. "That's what was going on at home. I had a man come up to me, madder than heck in Vermont, who pointed to a 9/11 tattoo on his arm.

"He said, 'I put that there on 9/11 because of what Saddam Hussein did to us.' And I said, 'Saddam had nothing to do with 9/11.' And the man said, 'Oh, yes he did. I heard Dick Cheney say so, and he wouldn't lie about something like that.'

"And I thought to myself, *Oh, bless you.*"[51]

The unity of 9/11 had given way to an air of almost unparalleled mistrust, on both sides of the issue. And so for us senators, the discussion finally reduced itself to one extremely quiet, extremely secure room on the third floor of the us Capitol, a locked room containing the CIA's classified National Intelligence Estimate (NIE).

The ninety-page document represented the last, best case for war. And its assertions were stark: Iraq "has chemical weapons" and "is reconstituting its nuclear weapons program." Yet the report also indicated that there was substantial disagreement within the government over the accuracy of those assertions. Dissents were relegated to footnotes, however, and the report's final pages; the bold assertions were front-loaded, phrased and framed for dramatic effect.

According to a number of experts in the field, like Peter Zimmerman, the scientific adviser to the Senate Foreign Relations Committee, the report was really something of an elaborate confection. The dissents in and of themselves were "pretty shocking."[52] And so in a strange turnabout, it was the opponents of the war resolution who began increasingly to urge their colleagues to go and read all the way through the report.

"I actually went and read the intelligence. They kept it in a secure room above the Senate, with big thick doors," Leahy now makes a point of noting. And it's no small point of pride. As investigative journalist

Michael Isikoff notes, "Senate aides would later calculate that no more than a half-dozen or so members actually went to the secure room where the highly classified NIE was kept under lock and key."[53]

When he discusses that NIE, Leahy's face slowly takes on the particular look of dismissive disgust he reserves for George W. Bush–era politicization and fabrication. "So I read it. There was *no* involvement [of Iraq with al-Qaida], *no* WMDs, they knew that. You had people like [Ahmed] Chalabi and others [who] kept trying to meet with me, and I refused to meet with them. . . . My God, the biggest *fraud*, Chalabi. Curveball, they called him."

A curveball, indeed. The National Intelligence Estimate would eventually come "to symbolize the entire WMD foul-up," and it's tempting to think what the vote count on the Iraq War Resolution might have been, had more than six US senators taken the time to actually read it.[54]

★ ★ ★

By the time the Senate took up the war resolution, on the evening of October 10, 2002, pressure had mounted palpably. The White House had long since secured the votes for passage, but administration and Pentagon surrogates were hard at work trying to limit the size and credibility of the opposition. "The administration brought a *lot* of pressure," Leahy remembers, especially on those in purple states or who were up for reelection.

The talk on the floor was both anxious and aggressive. "You're out of your mind," one pro-war Democrat whispered to Leahy. "Maybe some of this stuff is ambiguous, but do you have any idea how the American people feel? They want this thing."

Leahy did his best to whip support against the resolution, but the last-minute momentum was in favor. He and Senator Patty Murray of Washington settled on a similar response to the hand-wringing: "If you're going to lose a Senate seat, this is worth losing a Senate seat, because this is a huge move internationally—it's real, it's for keeps, and it's wrong."[55]

Famously enough, Hillary Clinton had come to the opposite conclusion. In a much-anticipated speech (she was already widely expected to seek the presidency in either 2004 or 2008), New York's freshman senator expressed strong support for the resolution, while calling on President Bush to "work hard" for a UN resolution authorizing combat, and to approach war only as a last resort. Notably, she ranged the White House's assertions that Saddam had direct contacts with al-Qaida and was rebuilding his WMD programs as "facts" which were "not in doubt."[56]

(In some ways, it was a watershed moment not simply for Clinton, but for the Democratic Party writ large. For his own part, Leahy would ultimately endorse 2008 presidential candidate Barack Obama over the woman and senator he had known far longer, and in so doing he would make it clear that the Iraq invasion and its disastrous consequences were paramount in his mind. "Many around the world have lost respect for America and the hope that America once gave them," Leahy would tell the *New York Times* in January 2008. "We need a president who can reintroduce America to the world and reintroduce America to ourselves."[57])

By contrast, Leahy's own floor speech emphasized the administration's missteps and groundless assertions, and made the case implicitly that it couldn't—and constitutionally shouldn't—be trusted with the decision on war with Iraq. He mocked the "new product" roll-out of the potential invasion, and excoriated the NIE: "We have heard a lot of bellicose rhetoric, but what are the facts? I am not asking for 100 percent proof, but the administration is asking Congress to make a decision to go to war based on conflicting statements, angry assertions, and assumptions based on speculation. This is not the way a great nation goes to war."[58]

He saved what he believed to be the most affecting argument for last, and for Leahy of course it couldn't help but be: the unsettling parallels opponents saw between the Iraq War Resolution and the Gulf of Tonkin Resolution (1964) that escalated the war in Vietnam. "That resolution was used by both the Johnson and Nixon Administrations as carte blanche to wage war in Vietnam, ultimately involving more than half a million American troops, and resulting in the deaths of more than 58,000 Americans."

It was well after midnight when the United States Senate finally voted on Senate Joint Resolution 46, and the tally was a lopsided 77–23. In the end, all Republicans but one (Senator Lincoln Chafee) stuck with the president, as did a majority of Democrats.

Predictably perhaps, all Democratic senators with presidential aspirations (Biden, Clinton, Edwards) were in favor. (Bernie Sanders, the lone independent in the House of Representatives and a later presidential candidate himself, was decidedly not.)

It was a depressing loss. But as completely as he had ever felt anything in his twenty-eight years in the Senate, Leahy felt that he had made precisely the right call. And unlike the days following September 11, 2001, during which he and his staff had made up most of the opposition to the White House's push for unilateral executive power, there was now a solid, tested core of liberal and progressive senators he could count on the next time the administration chose to play 9/11 hardball.

The Bush White House seemed on a course to squander the nation's post-9/11 goodwill. And assuming Democrats could hold their razor-thin majority, that would be the time to look into the politicization of the Department of Justice.

Of course, the White House had no intention of leaving the Senate in Democratic hands. And in terms of politicization, Leahy hadn't really seen anything yet.

★ ★ ★

In the run-up to the 2002 midterm elections, the White House was divided about how best to approach the election. Karen Hughes, the president's longtime Texas counselor, argued that staying above the electoral fray "would send a powerful, unifying signal" to the nation. It would also quiet the criticism that had begun to solidify against the White House's ubiquitous use of 9/11 as an ongoing theme, as a constant spur to Congress, as a sort of political Swiss Army knife.

Karl Rove, on the other hand, pushed for full-scale engagement. "I argued that any short-term goodwill from this above-the-fray behavior would be overwhelmed by the disadvantage of his party's losing ground in Congress. . . . My argument, and mounting evidence that Democrats in Washington were obstructing Bush, carried the day."[59]

Two issues defined that obstruction, as far as Rove was concerned: Democratic insistence that some Homeland Security employees be unionized, and Leahy's refusal to advance the entire slate of conservative judicial nominees put forward the previous year. It's fair to say that removing the gavel from Leahy's hand was a very powerful impetus for the White House, and one that eclipsed many other more pedestrian concerns.

It was personal, in a word. The two parties had always disagreed about judges, and unionization. The difference now, however, was that the president of the United States could accuse Democrats on the ballot of weakening the country's response to the terrorist threat.

And he could move poll numbers dramatically when he did so.

In the last weeks of the midterm campaigns, the GOP's soft-on-terror charge against the Democrats reached its nauseating apex: Vietnam veteran Max Cleland, a freshman senator from Georgia and triple amputee, was targeted as soft on the War on Terror by his Republican opponent, Saxby Chambliss. The vehicle was a now infamous commercial campaign that juxtaposed Cleland with photos of Osama bin Laden and Saddam

Hussein, and falsely charged that Cleland had opposed the creation of the Department of Homeland Security.[60]

In his autobiography *Heart of a Patriot*, Cleland writes of the ad, "It showed Osama Bin Laden's photo, Saddam Hussein's photo, and my photo alongside, as if I were a terrorist as well. A voice-over stated that I had voted against President Bush's Homeland Security proposal a number of times. The ad was an absolute distortion of reality."[61]

John McCain and Chuck Hagel—two other highly decorated veterans —publicly denounced the spots. But the damage was done.

And the midterm campaign as a whole, leveraging Rove's handpicked candidates with the president's soaring approval ratings on questions of security, was brutally effective. When the dust had cleared on election night, the results were stark: in a year when the party in the White House typically lost seats, the GOP picked up eight seats in the House. And with a two-seat pickup in the Senate, they flipped Senate control quite exactly, from 51–49 Democratic, to 51–49 Republican.

It was a galling result, and Leahy spent the day after the election effectively incommunicado at the family's Middlesex farm. His Senate office did release a statement summarizing the achievements of his short fifteen-month tenure as Judiciary Committee chair.

The *Washington Post* couldn't resist a bit of snark: "'I hope the new majority will carry forward many of our priorities,' Leahy's statement said, a prospect that's about as likely as Montpelier hosting the next Republican National Convention." And the *Post*'s background paragraph about Leahy's home state helpfully noted that "in recent years, Vermont may have surpassed New York and Massachusetts as the most despised state among Republicans."[62]

The incoming GOP majority was not shy about making their feelings known publicly, but in private the sense that Leahy and Jeffords had gotten exactly what they deserved was all-consuming. "Then there's the off-the-record vitriol," wrote the *Post*, "which can be summarized—and sanitized—to 'Let Them Eat Ben and Jerry's.' (Or 'commie-flavored ice cream,' as [GOP strategist Ed] Rogers calls it.)"

And Rogers for one was willing to go a good deal further. When asked if there were any plans afoot for political payback to Vermont's senators, he all but licked his chops.

"There hasn't been time yet for thoughtful retribution planning," he said.[63]

The Top Cop Rises

Nemeses and Archenemies

It hurt to lose the Judiciary gavel again in January 2003, and to return to the minority as ranking member—again. There was no denying the sharpness of Leahy's disappointment. Of course the American people were still frightened, less than two years out from the events of 9/11, but there seemed more to it than that. It was as though the voters simply couldn't make up their minds for any significant period of time, even with the two major political parties separated by an increasingly vast gulf on most issues of consequence. Senate majorities seemed perpetually balanced on a knife's edge, ready to topple one way or the other at a moment's notice.

And Leahy's prominence as a White House critic had earned him a particular animus from the party now warming the seats of power in the Senate. Perhaps most painful of all, he would have to watch from what amounted to the sidelines as Republicans put together the 2005 revisions to the Patriot Act required by Leahy's own hard-fought sunset provision.

But oddly enough—with every branch of government now ideologically disposed to lean its way—the Bush administration seemed continually to be lurching from one debacle to another. The defining twin tendencies of the White House—aggregating "unitary" executive power and ushering in spectacularly unqualified loyalists to wield it—were combining to tear the president's second term down the middle.

The preemptive war in Iraq, turned over in significant measure to private contractors, produced a rash of scandals, involving everything from gargantuan contracting overruns to the torture photos of Abu Ghraib.[1] No weapons of mass destruction, the raison d'être for the invasion, were ever found. Bush secured reelection in 2004 with just a 2 percentage-point win in Ohio, a backhanded rebuke to Karl Rove's plans for a growing GOP majority. In August 2005, Hurricane Katrina made clear how far FEMA had fallen as an agency, headed as it was by a soon-to-be infamous Bush loyalist with almost no experience in disaster preparedness.

When Sandra Day O'Connor announced her intention to resign from the Supreme Court later that year, George W. Bush shocked Republicans and Democrats alike by nominating his own White House counsel, Harriet Miers, to fill the slot. Like Alberto Gonzales, Miers had begun her years with the Bush family as George W. Bush's personal lawyer and seemed to have few credentials beyond her status as the president's confidante. Even fire-breathing conservatives drew the line at Miers, with Ann Coulter observing that "Miers is a good bowler . . . which, in all honesty, is the most impressive thing I've heard about Miers so far."[2]

Bush finally withdrew the nomination before the month of October was up, perhaps the most disastrous roll-out of a potential Court justice in modern memory. Even for the ranking member of Judiciary, then, it was a target-rich environment.

And out in the countryside, Leahy could feel a powerful wave continuing to build as 2006 approached. More than anything else, voters were demanding basic competency from their government, an end to the parade of loyalists.

If anything, Leahy underestimated that frustration. When the wave finally drew back, Democrats were firmly in control of both the House and the Senate again, with the presidency in 2008 seemingly the Democrats' to lose.

It was at this particular moment, in the heady weeks following the 2006 midterm wave election, that incoming chair of Judiciary Pat Leahy decided to take a closer and long-overdue look at the Gonzales Justice Department.

★ ★ ★

It would be inaccurate to say that Pat Leahy never liked Alberto Gonzales. Like Joe Biden, who famously pronounced Gonzales "the real deal" at his confirmation as attorney general, Leahy felt a certain genuine appreciation for Gonzales's extraordinary life story.[3] The man's roots in Humble, Texas, an impoverished community outside Houston, growing up in a house without telephone service or hot water, made Bill Clinton's politically marketable upbringing in Hope, Arkansas, seem downright privileged by comparison.

It would, however, be accurate to say that Leahy never truly *respected* Alberto Gonzales.

Gonzales—who worked in the mid-1990s for Vinson & Elkins, a pricey Houston law firm—originally made his bones with the Bush dynasty working as in-house legal counsel to then-Governor George W. Bush. His record from that period was a checklist of dirty jobs performed for his client, including keeping the younger Bush's brushes with the law out of the public eye, in at least one case by avoiding jury duty.[4]

And for Leahy, that early water-carrying defined Gonzales, in all the worst ways. When Leahy is asked to describe the man Bush nicknamed "Fredo," his expansive forehead creases with displeasure. "Well, Gonzales really—I think the president owed Gonzales because he helped hide his drunk driving, which would not have helped him in the election." He pauses, shakes his head, and then lowers the boom: "*Remarkably* unqualified to be attorney general."[5]

Along with Vice President Cheney and White House lawyer John Yoo, Gonzales had aggressively forwarded the notion of the "unitary executive" post-9/11. He had quickly made himself master of a certain signature brand of obscurantism, as well, and if questioned about the underlying philosophy or legal opinions, Gonzales seemed to be able to stall inquiry nearly indefinitely—always mild-mannered and courteous, but rarely willing to admit responsibility or full recollection of the events in question.[6]

There was something outright offensive in all of this for Leahy. His heart had always been with the justice system, from his earliest days as a prosecutor. The passion is still remarkable today, at the start of Leahy's eighth term in the Senate. "I feel very strongly about law enforcement," Leahy makes clear, before turning to the subject of Alberto Gonzales. "The only thing in my office that has my name on it is the plaque that says Chittenden County State's Attorney and, mounted above it, my badge. The thing is, if law enforcement breaks down, *everything* breaks down. That's why I've been so tough when things have been done wrong in law enforcement."

One of Leahy's favorite stories, in fact, involves a private meeting during his law school years with US Attorney General Bobby Kennedy, who maintained that he would take on the executive branch and prosecute his own brother's friends if push ever came to shove.

From that vantage point, Gonzales seemed absolutely the worst sort of candidate for attorney general: excessively deferential to the president, and eager to advance and defend even the most controversial applications of the "unitary executive" theory—enhanced interrogation, indefinite detention, secret and warrantless bulk data collection.

To Leahy's doubtful eye, there was something about Gonzales not merely subservient, but verging on the craven. "I remember blowing my stack at him at one of the hearings," Leahy admits, anger again edging his voice. "He said, 'Well, as a member of the President's staff . . .' And I said, 'You're *not* a member of the President's staff! You are the Attorney General of the United States of America! You're not *Secretary* of Justice —you're the Attorney General! And you work for *all* of us!'"

And so it was no surprise that within weeks of the 2006 Democratic sweep, the incoming chair of Judiciary was sharpening his knives for a suddenly vulnerable administration, and for Gonzales in particular. Leahy was suddenly everywhere in the news, finger pointed sternly at the White House and the Department of Justice. He issued calls for information about "detention of terrorism suspects, abuse of detainees and government secrecy . . . reviving dozens of demands for classified documents" that had been "rebuffed or ignored by the Justice Department." Calling the Bush administration "obsessively secretive," Leahy made clear that he was willing to fight now with all the power of the Senate behind him.

"I expect real answers," he warned reporters, "or we'll have testimony under oath until we get them." How to compel testimony under oath from a famously dismissive White House? "I expect to get the answers. If I don't, I believe we should subpoena them."[7]

And just that quickly, a standoff loomed.

But as with the long battle over judicial nominations he had waged during his last stint as chair of Judiciary, Leahy would play the long game. He made it clear that he would exhaust all other options before turning to the nuclear. "I'm not trying to set up the idea of a confrontation for the sake of a confrontation. I hope people in the administration will listen. We'll try it that way first."

It was an interesting and revealing bit of phrasing. Leahy resolutely insisted that he wasn't setting up the idea of a confrontation *for the sake of a confrontation*, and that was true. But he never denied that he was, in fact, setting up the idea of a confrontation.

Because that was also true.

On the afternoon of December 7, 2006, David Iglesias—the up-and-coming US attorney from the district of New Mexico—was making his way through the Baltimore-Washington International Airport when a text lit up his cell phone: "Call Mike Battle."

Battle was the director of the Executive Office for United States Attorneys, and when Iglesias reached him a few moments later, Battle was brief, almost curt: "David, the administration wants to go a different way."

Iglesias was stunned. It was immediately clear that he was being fired, over the phone, without warning. Yet his reviews by the Justice Department's EARS team (Evaluation and Review Staff) had been extremely positive in both 2003 and 2006. Among other honors, he had been hand-picked in 2001 to chair a committee directly advising attorney general John Ashcroft on immigration and border issues.

Iglesias had every right to believe the surprise call might well be a promotion, a reward from an administration he had served with high distinction. The thought of actually being terminated made it hard to catch his breath. "What's going on, Mike?"

"I don't know," Battle responded, his own voice tight. "I don't want to know. All I can tell you, David, is that this came from on high."

And with that, Iglesias had been fired, without notice, and for reasons that seemed purposefully obscured.[8] He had been given just seven weeks to find another job. And the irony of the date didn't escape him: it was Pearl Harbor Day, and the other US attorneys who were summarily terminated that day couldn't help wondering if the timing was a whimsical calling card left by someone high in the reaches of Main Justice, or even the White House.

But one thing Iglesias knew for sure. He wasn't going without a fight, and his first tentative move was to reach out to his closest friends among the ninety-three US attorneys for information.

It gradually became apparent that nine US attorneys in all had been terminated without cause, seven on December 7, 2006, and two earlier in the year.[9] It was unprecedented to remove a group of US attorneys midterm, a move made all the more confusing because among the group were more than a few rising superstars, prosecutors like Iglesias who had seemed to be on a fast track to higher office and greater responsibility.[10] Some were told that the firing was no commentary on their performance, that the attorney general merely wanted to allow others the résumé boost of serving as US attorney; others, like Iglesias, were given no reason at all.

But if performance was not explicitly at issue, that left politics.

The US attorneys were supposed, in an ideal world, to be working outside the political sphere. Not that any of the nine were Pollyannas about the realities of the Bush White House — they knew that a premium was placed on loyalty. Bud Cummins, let go from his position as US attorney for the Eastern District of Arkansas, made it clear in a private phone call to Iglesias that he had always understood that politics would inevitably play a part in his career. But as far as Cummins knew, his politics and values had been entirely in sync with the White House, especially post-9/11: "Look . . . no one's pretending here that they aren't judging you as much on your political standing as on your case-to-case merits. That just comes with the territory. As much as the Justice Department is charged with impartially upholding the law, it is also expected to implement the priorities of the administration. I didn't have a problem with that. In fact, I wholeheartedly approved of the mandate handed down to us. Who wouldn't? We were fighting terrorism, protecting the homeland in a clash of civilizations. It wasn't hard to get behind that agenda."[11]

And yet, Cummins had been peremptorily moved aside and replaced by a young protégé of Karl Rove, Tim Griffin. The thirty-eight-year-old Griffin had a very particular sort of résumé, including stints at the Republican National Committee, the Bush-Cheney Florida recount team, and the special prosecution of Henry Cisneros, Bill Clinton's HUD secretary. It was the sort of hyper-partisan background that would have made Griffin essentially unconfirmable under normal circumstances.

But the years immediately following 9/11 were anything but normal, and the White House had used the War on Terror to push for an obscure, little-discussed provision in the 2005 revisions to the Patriot Act. As recounted by Iglesias,

> In the early spring of 2006, some nine months before Mike Battle called me, Bush had signed into law a package of "Improvements and Reauthorizations" to the 2005 USA Patriot Act, the centerpiece of his antiterrorist legislative drive. Buried in the surfeit of legal tweaking and tuning was a brief amendment to the same section 546, of the US Code 28, that, since 1789, had served as the basis for the hiring and the firing of US Attorneys. Under the statute, any interim appointment to the post would expire after 120 days, if the Senate had not confirmed a candidate by that time. The administration's tactic was simple and inspired: suspend the 120-day provision. It was a move that effectively lifted oversight of the US Attorney selection process from Congress and transferred it to the White House. Bush, in short, could select anyone

he wanted, for whatever reasons, and hold it as an interim appointment for as long as his pleasure was served.[12]

And that was when the penny dropped for Iglesias. The wholesale firings, with the approaching holiday season as cover, provided an extremely convenient opportunity for the White House to replace seasoned and successful prosecutors with the sort of loyalists who might ordinarily never pass muster in the United States Senate.

Slowly but surely, the disparate legislative and personnel gambits resolved into what looked increasingly like a unified political strategy, directed from "on high," as Mike Battle had tersely put it. "As a way of ensuring the continuing party loyalty of US attorneys, it was nothing short of a masterstroke, giving the president wide room for an end run around the Senate confirmation of US attorneys."[13]

Iglesias himself was convinced as well that his own firing, along with several others, was precipitated by his unwillingness to pursue trumped-up voter fraud charges in his state, a national push with its own distinctly political dimensions. New Mexico, like Florida in 2000 and Washington in 2004, had experienced a historically tight election in recent years. US attorneys in those states might conceivably have changed the course of those elections by bringing fraud charges in the weeks and months before Election Day, and if not, the record of prosecutions for voter fraud alone might have provided justification for other later "voter caging" measures (requiring state-issued ID, for example).

But Iglesias, and US attorneys like John McKay of Seattle, had declined to prosecute. The voter fraud cases were essentially baseless, and although he had experienced some grumbling from New Mexican Republicans, Iglesias had held off. Now he had the sharp feeling that the fraud prosecutions had been part of a larger invisible loyalty test. "As the scandal developed, it seemed that we were paying the price for refusing to prosecute spurious and potentially disruptive voter fraud cases."[14]

Taken as a whole, it was breathtaking. The seeming politicization, and possible perversion, of an elite arm of the US justice system; legislative skulduggery involving the Patriot Act, facilitated by a GOP 9/11 hardball strategy and enacted under the original hard-won sunset provision; and, too, the wily presence of White House strategist Karl Rove just barely discernible at the top of the organizational machinery.

The White House couldn't have hatched a scheme more precisely calibrated to arouse the wrath of Patrick Joseph Leahy if they had tried.

★ ★ ★

California Senator Dianne Feinstein, Leahy's longtime ally on the Judiciary Committee, had lost two US attorneys in the wave of firings, and before the first rumors had finished skittering across Capitol Hill she and Leahy had formed a grim, united front. Almost immediately, they introduced the "Preserving United States Attorney Independence Act," which would return Section 546 of US Code 28 to its original form and restore the Senate's crucial role in the confirmation process.

And there was nothing mild mannered about the rollout. Feinstein charged that "the Bush Administration is pushing out U.S. Attorneys from across the country under the cloak of secrecy and then appointing indefinite replacements without Senate confirmation."

Leahy took the rhetoric a half-step further, telegraphing the direction of the Senate hearings he was already planning to hold. "Political gerrymandering of these important posts is wrong and an affront to our criminal justice system. It is vital that those holding these critical positions be free from any inappropriate influence and subject to the check and balance of the confirmation process."[15]

Predictably enough, Attorney General Gonzales offered a bland, blanket denial to any implication of wrongdoing—"We in no way politicize these decisions"—even as he admitted that US attorneys had been removed. "That on occasion in an organization as large as the Justice Department some United States Attorneys are removed or are asked or encouraged to resign, should come as no surprise."[16]

And Gonzales agreed to testify before the Senate Judiciary Committee on Thursday, January 18, 2007, to answer the mounting questions about the US attorney firings.

But something strange and amazing happened the day before that testimony, on Wednesday the seventeenth: the White House suddenly dropped its years-long resistance to court monitoring of its warrantless wiretapping program. The *International Herald Tribune* captures some of the surprise that Leahy felt: "The Bush Administration, in what appears to be a concession to its critics, said Wednesday that it would allow an independent court to monitor its warrantless electronic-eavesdropping program. . . . The Attorney General sought to portray the administration's change of posture as anything but grudging."[17]

Leahy was indeed surprised. He had been at loggerheads with Bush officials for nearly five years over just this provision. And in his experience, especially in the years following 9/11, this White House conceded precisely nothing.

The timing of the concession was intriguing as well. The White House clearly wanted to offer Senate Democrats an olive branch, but Leahy suspected there was much more to it than building relations with the party now in power. It seemed as though, suddenly, the administration was more concerned with deflecting attention from the nine fired US attorneys than with guarding the workings of one of its most cherished antiterrorism initiatives.

Leahy's instincts told him it was time to attack.

At the Thursday hearing, rather than thank the attorney general for finally coming around to his way of thinking, Leahy and the rest excoriated Gonzales for taking five years to make such a basic concession to civil liberties. It was the worst grilling the attorney general had endured to date, leading the *Montreal Gazette* to report that "Leahy tore a strip off Attorney-General Alberto Gonzales." And the raw Canadian metaphor wasn't far off the mark.[18]

"President Bush has not been helped by having a rubber stamp Congress for six years," Leahy growled to the reporter after the hearing. "There's been nobody to say No." It was in effect a declaration of war, and Leahy paused before adding a final colorful touch. "We're not intimidated by the administration."

The choice of words was fascinating, an almost word-for-word prefiguring of the most famous five words Leahy would ever speak, for director Christopher Nolan's cameras, just six months later.

In more ways than one, the Top Cop was on the rise.[19]

By February 2007, the mounting pressure from Leahy and Feinstein and Mark Pryor of Arkansas was producing dramatic results. Interim US attorney Tim Griffin, Karl Rove's handpicked candidate to replace Bud Cummins in the Eastern District of Arkansas, abruptly announced that he was withdrawing himself from consideration for a permanent appointment. Griffin made no attempt to hide his disdain for the senators who had taken issue with his manner of coming into the job.

"I'm not going to get fair consideration from Senator Pryor, or the Judiciary Committee, particularly under Leahy," Griffin told the *Washington*

Post. And given that he wouldn't be needing the goodwill of the chair of Senate Judiciary anytime soon, he added, "I decided that there was nothing to gain by submitting myself to that circus."

Senate Republicans managed to block consideration of the Feinstein-Leahy bill to return to the previous system of limiting interim appointments to 120 days, but the measure was gaining ground. Already the *New York Times* was calling the firings and the related Patriot Act maneuverings "a political purge" conducted by an administration that had "made partisanship its lodestar."[20]

It was at that critical moment that the Justice Department made perhaps its worst decision since originally green-lighting the firings: Gonzales and his lieutenants suddenly reversed course and began to argue that the nine US attorneys had, in fact, been fired for performance reasons. "From time to time," Gonzales ventured, "we make an evaluation as to whether we believe we can put in people who can produce better results, who can do a better job."[21] Similar hints and aspersions followed in short order.

And that was the final straw for Iglesias and the other fired US attorneys. Now, with their jobs commandeered, they were facing what amounted to an active campaign of professional slander. In New Mexico, Iglesias held a press conference on his last full day as US attorney for the District of New Mexico. He stood in front of enlarged charts and graphs, showing the robust productivity of his office.

"I would have no objection to someone calling me and saying I'd lost my political support," Iglesias said carefully. "But they said it's performance, and I've got lots of data showing that's not the case."

And then Iglesias, a veteran and a former military lawyer, used an incendiary bit of Vietnam-era slang to characterize the call out of nowhere that had upended his life. He called it a "political fragging."[22]

Suddenly the scandal had a face, and a voice.

And Leahy now had a group of extremely compelling (and willing) witnesses. When four of the fired US attorneys came before the Senate Judiciary Committee on the afternoon of March 6 — David Iglesias, Bud Cummins, Carol Lam, and John McKay — the group gave subtle but unmistakable indications that they saw no reason to protect the administration that had once forwarded their careers. To the contrary, their joint statement, read by Carol Lam, played its own version of 9/11 hardball: "As the first United States Attorneys appointed after the terrible events of September 11th, 2001, we took seriously the commitment of the President and the Attorney General to lead our districts in the fight against terrorism. We not only prosecuted terrorism-related cases but also led our law enforcement partners at the federal, state, and local level in preventing and disrupting potential terrorist attacks."[23]

The implication was clear. Not only were the firings unprecedented and a creeping corruption of the independence of the US attorneys as a whole—they had made the nation less safe from terrorist attacks as well.

Iglesias found himself marveling at the theatrical nature of the hearing room, the way that it allowed Leahy to shape the message that emanated from its courtroom-like setting: "It was fascinating to see these veteran lawmakers put together the first inchoate narrative of the story, keenly analyzing the political and legal implications of what was even then unfolding before them. Like press conferences, hearings can be a form of high theater, and the assembled senators were playing it for maximum dramatic effect."[24]

Instinctively, Leahy reached for his own personal touchstone of governmental corruption and malfeasance, the Nixon administration and Watergate: "These actions we've heard of from the administration—I really believe they undermine the effectiveness and professionalism of US Attorney's offices around the country. Not since the Saturday Night Massacre—when I was a young lawyer and President Nixon forced the resignation of the Watergate prosecutor Archibald Cox—have we witnessed anything of this magnitude. The calls to a number of US Attorneys last December by which they were forced to resign were extraordinary—I don't know of any precedent for it. What is more disconcerting—unlike during Watergate—there was no Elliot Richardson . . . seeking to defend the independence of the prosecutors."[25]

The March 6 hearings in the House and the Senate Judiciary Committees were a public relations tour de force. Suddenly the inside-baseball aspects of the scandal made visual sense; here were the fired US attorneys themselves, a diverse and relatable group of professionals, clearly exceptional minds and compelling witnesses all. Following the hearing, several prominent senators called for the resignation of the attorney general. Republican Arlen Specter hinted darkly that "one day there will be a new attorney general, maybe sooner rather than later."

The White House, too, seemed painfully aware that the dynamics had changed. On March 9, Gonzales finally came to Leahy's office for the sit-down the administration had avoided for the last two months. That fact alone, that the attorney general had come to Leahy, rather than vice versa, told the political establishment a great deal.

In a triumph of understatement, the *Washington Post* would describe the encounter as a "tense, hour-long meeting."

But the White House clearly realized that the administration was at a distinct disadvantage; Gonzales had come ready to deal. And the results were undeniable. The White House agreed "not to oppose legislation that would eliminate the attorney general's power to appoint US Attorneys without Senate confirmation," assuring passage of the Feinstein-Leahy Preserving United States Attorney Independence Act. Gonzales himself "also agreed to allow the [Judiciary] committee to interview five top-level Justice Department officials as part of an ongoing Democratic-led probe."

Most dramatically, the attorney general announced that he "was accepting the resignation" of his chief of staff, Kyle Sampson, who Gonzalez said had been in charge of the process that had produced the firing list.[26]

Leahy maintained his sternest countenance, but inside he was ecstatic. At a stroke he had in hand his Patriot Act revision, his initial knot of Justice Department witnesses, and his first resignation.

And the following Tuesday, on the heels of those negotiated losses, Gonzales gave what could only be called a disastrous press conference at the Justice Department on the firing scandal. Standing without a podium before a portrait of Bobby Kennedy (which Leahy must have found supremely ironic), Gonzales radiated discomfort. And his trademark obscurantism — divorced from a legal or quasi-legal setting — seemed like simple contradiction at best, and stonewalling at worst. Dana Milbank perfectly captured the hemming and hawing:

> Attorney General Alberto Gonzales faced the cameras for all of nine minutes yesterday, but he managed to contradict himself at least four times as he fought off calls to resign over the firings of US Attorneys.
>
> "Mistakes were made," he said in fluent scandalese, but "I think it was the right decision."
>
> "I am responsible for what happens at the Department of Justice," he posited, "but "I . . . was not involved in any discussions about what was going on."[27]

Not only were the optics of the March 13 press conference deadly to the administration's case, but Gonzales chose to double down on one of the most controversial aspects of the scandal — that Iglesias and the others had been let go not because they had lost the president's goodwill (which would speak only to the president's "pleasure"), but because they were subpar US attorneys.

Ominously for Gonzales, the president was finally compelled to weigh in on the firings. Trapped by reporters all asking the same questions, Bush looked supremely uncomfortable. He was "frankly not happy" about the way his attorney general had handled both the firings and the ensuing uproar. But he added carefully, "I've heard those allegations about political decision making. It's just not true."[28]

The e-mail trail from the White House to the Justice Department, however, was finally beginning to emerge. And those messages, taken in total, told a very different tale indeed.

As early as September 2006, it turned out, Kyle Sampson had written others that by avoiding the Senate confirmation process, "we can give far less deference to home-state senators," particularly Democratic senators like Feinstein and Pryor. He had also written about the need to hire only "loyal Bushies," a pithy phrase that would be scrutinized ad infinitum over the next six months.

Rather than confirming that one deputy at Justice had enforced a political standard in hiring and promotion, the correspondence suggested that there wasn't a top Gonzales deputy who *hadn't*.

And the e-mail revealed something more important: that Gonzales himself had not been truthful when he had stated that he was out of the loop on the firing scheme. In fact, according to e-mail between Justice and the White House, "Gonzales had participated in a meeting about the purge, contradicting his earlier statements."[29]

Leahy was understandably beside himself. His earliest and worst suspicions about Gonzales had been confirmed, and as far as Leahy was concerned, all pretense of civility was at an end. In fact, only a few days later the attorney general and Leahy found themselves by chance at the Supreme Court for the same conference. Gonzales, spying Leahy standing alone in one of the ornate hallways, hurried over and tried to engage in a bit of off-the-record contrition. He quickly asked for a private meeting later that day to "figure out what was going on."

Leahy stopped him midsentence with a pointed finger. "No," he said flatly. "The next time you're going to talk to me about this it's going to be [in] an open hearing under oath."

If the meeting in Leahy's office five days previously had been tense, this was openly angry. So uncomfortable was the tableau, in fact, that Chief Justice Roberts—looking to say a quick, friendly hello to both men—did an abrupt about-face and just continued walking.[30]

But perhaps most tantalizingly, e-mail from January 2005 showed

White House political strategist Karl Rove himself asking "how we planned to proceed" in the firing of some US attorneys. Rove, "keenly interested" in replacing Bud Cummins, had later been intimately involved in an elaborate plan to move his own protégé Tim Griffin to a mid-six-figure political berth at Justice, and from there to Cummins's post as US attorney for Eastern Arkansas.[31]

And that was all Leahy needed.

With the e-mail disclosures, he now had the grid coordinates of the White House, and, with obvious relish, the chair of Judiciary commenced what would be a months-long campaign of rhetorical mortar fire. "Every day it's almost like a drip, drip of a faucet. Something else comes out, and we get these hurry-up calls from the White House: 'Oh, by the way, there's something else we wanted to tell you.' My response is, Feel free to tell us anything you want, but you'll be telling us under oath."[32]

Again, the embattled White House tried to negotiate from what was an increasingly weak position. Within days an offer to have Rove and other White House advisers testify privately, off the record, surfaced in the media.

Leahy was curt, and in just five words made it clear he was dispensing with middlemen and media interlocutors. He was now addressing Bush himself.

"I don't accept his offer," Leahy said.[33]

★ ★ ★

In the months and years immediately following the attacks of September 11, Attorney General Ashcroft had always come before Congress wielding what seemed a magic sword. Ashcroft attacked with 9/11, parried with 9/11, and given the prevailing mood in the country, he had bested Leahy again and again. President Bush, for his part, had seen no need to compromise or woo the Senate. The White House had its agenda, and senators and representatives were admonished to get on board or face an indignant pummeling in the media, and then defeat at the ballot box.

Leahy had been one of the very few to stand up to the administration's pressure tactics — often deployed in the service of nakedly unconstitutional initiatives — but he had done so in very measured language. He'd had to walk a very fine line as chair of Judiciary, in order to satisfy the nation's urge for aggressive action and yet protect the fabric of American civil liberty. He had spoken earnestly, carefully, passionately, and yet, for the most part, quietly.

But 2007 was another atmosphere altogether. In many ways and on many separate issues, the administration had badly miscalculated, and the White House was now openly in retreat. And Leahy could be heard very clearly, throughout the sweep of American media, baying in pursuit.[34] Anger and outrage became his tools of choice, deployed mostly consciously and increasingly edited and distributed for the YouTube generation.

Case in point: Leahy's grilling of Bradley Schlozman.

Schlozman had been one of the earliest Bush appointees to the Justice Department's Civil Rights Division, and according to an e-mail later released, he had made a point during his tenure of ferreting out and replacing "liberals" and "democrats" (not to mention "commies" and "mold spore") with "real Americans" and "right-thinking Americans."[35] Having established his loyalty to the satisfaction of the administration, Schlozman had been the recipient of the first US attorney slot vacated under the plan worked out by the White House and Gonzales's chief of staff. He replaced Todd Graves, US Attorney for the Western District of Missouri, in March 2006.

And once in place as interim US attorney, Schlozman quickly brought indictments against four liberal activists for voter fraud — in the weeks immediately preceding the 2006 midterm elections. Graves had deliberately slow-walked the very same charges, which he considered flimsy at best.

As it happened, Democrat Claire McCaskill still prevailed over Republican Jim Talent in a very close race, but not, Leahy suspected, for lack of trying on Schlozman's part.[36]

In short, Bradley Schlozman was the entire US attorney firing scandal in miniature.

Leahy couldn't have asked for a more perfect foil in Schlozman. With his crouched posture, high, nasal voice, and tendency to wince uncomfortably as Leahy bored in, the former interim US attorney presented an instant icon of administration mendacity.

LEAHY: You didn't think that when the US Justice Department
stepped in it would have any effect that close to an election?
SCHLOZMAN: Well, there was no individual who was possibly going
to be disenfranchised or who was —
LEAHY: That's not my question at *all*, Mr. Schlozman, and you know
it. Did you really think that bringing — having the Department of

Justice bring a charge like that that close to the election would have no effect on the election? I'm not talking about an individual being stopped from voting. But it would have had no effect on the election?

SCHLOZMAN: I did not think it was going to have any effect on the election in this case, no, Senator.

LEAHY: You're *amazing*. I—do you read the papers at all?

SCHLOZMAN: I do.

LEAHY: You watch the news at all?

SCHLOZMAN: Occasionally, yes.

LEAHY: Do you ever watch it *before* an election?

SCHLOZMAN: Senator, I mean I've . . . I've watched the news on occasion. . . .

LEAHY: Would it have affected the prosecution? Would it have affected your ability to bring the prosecution if you'd just waited a few weeks until the election was over?

SCHLOZMAN: The Department of Justice does not time prosecutions to elections.

LEAHY: [Exploding] Well, *yes they do*! [Holding the red manual aloft] That's what the manual *says*! And you, rather reluctantly I felt, admitted that you actually did read it when you became the interim US Attorney. The fact is—would it have changed the outcome of your prosecution had you *waited* a few weeks to bring it?

SCHLOZMAN: I don't know . . . I doubt there would be, have been any impact on the actual prosecution. But again I did what I did—

LEAHY: [Riding over Schlozman's voice] That's my conclusion too.[37]

Leahy's anger and frustration are certainly audible, and highly watchable. But the chair of Judiciary also seems, on close examination, in nearly full control of the outburst; within seconds his characteristic poker face is back, with the occasional icy smile, and he continues the intense cross-examination without a flutter or a missed cue.

At this point, the scandal had drawn together most of Leahy's personal strengths into one neat, consumable package: his ability to question closely and thunder appropriately; his ability both to be and to act the overseer of the overseers, the Top Cop addressing the egregious lapses of the nation's highest law enforcement organization; and finally, the capability of delivering all of that to a larger audience via the ubiquity of emerging technology.

It was pure Pat Leahy, in other words, facing off against what much of the country now saw as pure George W. Bush.

As was becoming clearer with each passing day, the Justice Department under Alberto Gonzales had countenanced not only the overt politicization of its prosecutorial function, but the politicization of its very prosecutors themselves. Schlozman may have been the starkest example, but with other RNC operatives like Tim Griffin now operating as interim US attorneys across the country, it was difficult to avoid the conclusion that Karl Rove's plans for a permanent majority had superseded most every other consideration.

But how to force Rove's testimony? There Leahy was stymied, utterly. It was clear that the White House had drawn a very bright red line around its own inner circle of advisers.

On the brighter side, though, that left Gonzales outside the line.

Further outside every day, in fact. The attorney general's former chief of staff Kyle Sampson had now disputed Gonzales's own testimony: "I don't think it's accurate," as Sampson carefully put it. Another top deputy, Monica Goodling, had resigned after invoking the Fifth Amendment in a bid to avoid testifying before Leahy's committee. And White House political director Sara M. Taylor had abruptly announced her resignation as well.

Gonzales himself was said to have "retreated from public view" in order to spend "hours practicing testimony and phoning lawmakers for support" in advance of appearing before Leahy's committee. But Leahy had worked the other former prosecutors on the committee hard, including the GOP senators like his old friend Specter.

For the most part, Fredo's pleas were falling on deaf ears.[38]

It was worth remembering that Bush's nickname for Gonzales was not a shortened form of Alberto, but rather drawn straight out of Francis Ford Coppola's *Godfather* trilogy, in which Don Corleone is nearly brought down by an unprincipled traitor but finally saves the family by having his own weaker older brother Fredo put down.

And so, after waiting three months for another chance to question Gonzales directly and under oath, finally, on July 24, dressed in an uncharacteristically sober black jacket offset only by a mint-striped tie, Leahy opened the oversight hearing without much in the way of pleasantries. Never had he looked so stern, seated in the center of the long, draped Judiciary table, glaring down at the attorney general. On the heels of his welcome to those packed into the hearing room, Leahy went immediately to the heart of the matter:

> The attorney general's lost the confidence of the Congress and the American people. But through oversight we hope to restore balance and accountability to the executive branch.
>
> The Department of Justice must be restored to being worthy of its name. It should not be reduced to another political arm of the White House. . . .
>
> With the department shrouded in scandal, the deputy attorney general's announced his resignation. The nominee to become associate attorney general requested that his nomination be withdrawn, rather than testify under oath at a confirmation hearing. The attorney general's chief of staff, the deputy attorney general's chief of staff, the department's White House liaison and the White House political director have all resigned, as have others.
>
> I would joke that the last one out the door should turn out the lights, but the Department of Justice is too important for that. We need to shine more light there, not less.[39]

Leahy's cutting reference to the wave of resignations afflicting Justice left Gonzales stone-faced at the witness table, but it accomplished its purpose: to highlight the way in which the US attorney scandal continued to act as the straw that broke the camel's back, finally prompting the resignations of a host of Bush officials who had narrowly survived the other serious scandals of Bush's second term.

When he stood to administer the oath to the attorney general, Leahy —ramrod straight and face solemn—paused dramatically to emphasize the words, "and nothing *but* the truth." No one in the packed hearing room missed the point.

But as was his wont, Gonzales responded with the mild, courteous mien that had made him such a difficult figure to pin down all along. His tone always seemingly helpful and deferential, he managed to respond again and again without answering the highly specific and well-honed questions put to him. Quickly the hearing developed a pronounced rhythm—Leahy or Republican Arlen Specter whittling an issue down to a sharp point; Gonzales returning to a large, long narrative response; Leahy or Specter refocusing the issue and insisting upon an answer; Gonzales refusing, for a host of various reasons.

GONZALES: Senator, you're asking me a question that is related to an ongoing controversy which I am recused—I will say the president's tried very hard. . . .

SPECTER: Oh, no, no. I'm not asking you a question about something you're recused. I'm asking you a question about constitutional law.

GONZALES: You're asking me a question that's related to an ongoing controversy.

SPECTER: I'm asking you whether you can have a constitutional government with the Congress exercising its constitutional authority for oversight if when the president claims executive privilege, the president then forecloses the Congress from getting a judicial determination of it. That's a constitutional law question.

GONZALES: Senator, both the Congress and the president have constitutional authorities. Sometimes they clash. In most cases, accommodations are reached. In very rare instances, they sometimes litigate it in the courts.

SPECTER: Would you focus on my question for just a minute, please?

GONZALES: Senator, I'm not going to answer this question, because it does relate to an ongoing controversy in which I am recused.

(Booing)

LEAHY: I would note, please, we'll have decorum in here.

Leahy, as always, insisted upon order, but here too it seemed as though the firings scandal was the final straw, even for the protesters. One woman went so far as to wear "a pink negligee and a sign proposing 'Give Gonzo a Pink Slip.'"[40]

Before the first hour had passed, it was clear that Gonzales's testimony would be something more akin to anti-testimony, a very long series of recusals and protestations of faulty memory and ongoing legal proceedings. And if he had hoped to retain the backing of the committee's Republicans, Gonzales had chosen precisely the wrong strategy. Specter, to take the most glaring example, was soon openly mocking the witness: "Well, let's see if somehow, somewhere, we can find a question you'll answer."

It was a brutal afternoon for the attorney general, as one senator after another homed in on the administration's most egregious assertions of executive power and privilege. From the Abu Ghraib torture scandal, to warrantless wiretapping, to the Justice Department's use of a political litmus test in hiring, Gonzales answered without being more than nominally responsive.

He had not been aware, he couldn't quite remember, in deference to ongoing legal proceedings he couldn't really say.

But it was in response to Leahy's own blunt questioning that Gonzales was repeatedly forced into evasions that had the reporters in the room shaking their heads at one another. If one or two evasions were enough to shield him from Specter or Kennedy, Gonzales seemed to feel safe only behind seven or eight when answering the chair. Possibly the most ludicrous of these exchanges concerned Monica Goodling's adoption of a political test in hiring, and her own admission that doing so had crossed an ethical, perhaps even a legal line.

> LEAHY: She testified under oath that she crossed the line. Were you aware that Ms. Goodling was doing so?
>
> GONZALES: That she was crossing the line? No.
>
> LEAHY: Were you aware that she was asking about political allegiances in vetting career Justice Department?
>
> GONZALES: I don't recall being aware of that. If I'd been aware of that, that would have been troubling to me.
>
> LEAHY: Do you know whether other officials at the White House were aware she was doing that?
>
> GONZALES: Not that I'm aware.
>
> Let me just mention I'm aware — and I think I became aware after the U.S. attorneys were asked to resign — there was an issue that I became aware of where Ms. Goodling apparently asked a potential career hire into the D.C. U.S. attorney's office improper questions.
>
> So at some point I did become aware of that. But otherwise I can't recall being aware of other instances where she may have asked improper questions.

If this was the deliberate strategy that Gonzales had disappeared from public life to develop and rehearse, Leahy could only shake his head. It was a profound misreading of the public mood and, correspondingly, the mood of the Senate.

Leahy's impression of Gonzales from the beginning had been of a man swimming wildly out of his depth, yet continually promoted because his loyalty to George W. Bush was implicit and unquestioning. And as he watched the attorney general shift dubiously back and forth, claiming to have been unaware or out of the loop or unable to answer a series of questions that spoke directly to the basic workings of the Constitution itself, Leahy couldn't help thinking that Gonzales had been the perfectly wrong candidate to lead the Justice Department in the continuing wake of 9/11. Closing the hearing, he spoke to Gonzales directly, his voice low:

> You've come here seeking our trust. Frankly, Mr. Attorney General, you've lost mine. You've lost mine. And this is something I've never — this is something I've never said to any cabinet member before, even some of whom I've disagreed with greatly. . . .
>
> I know this committee will do its best to try to restore independence and accountability and commitment to the rule of law to the operations of the Justice Department. I know I'll be joined by a lot of senators, Republican and Democratic, in that. I take no pleasure in saying this, but I'm seriously, gravely disappointed.

Asked today to characterize the July 24, 2007, hearing that finally broke the back of the Bush Justice Department, Leahy has to search for appropriate words. He finally offers two: "Just pathetic."[41] And certainly that viewpoint was very broadly shared in the moment. Over the several days following, both Republican and Democratic senators called for the attorney general's resignation, as did a large number of prominent editorial pages.

The US attorney firings scandal had reached political escape velocity, and, predictably enough, Batman wasn't far behind.

It's one of several reliable laws that govern Leahy's media personae: *As a media discussion of Leahy and his political issue of the moment lengthens, the probability that the whole narrative will be translated to the Batman universe approaches 1 (certainty).*

In this case it was Dana Milbank, who had been mining comedy gold from the Gonzales Justice Department for years. The bit was slugged "The Caped Crusader from Vermont," and perhaps no other single piece has ever shown more clearly the way in which Leahy's cultivation of the Batman fandom returns actual political dividends.

> *Somewhere in Gotham, the Batphone rings. Loyal butler Alfred (played by Robert Byrd) summons Bruce Wayne (Leahy). It's Commissioner Gordon on the line, and the news is grim: A villainous alliance has been formed by the Riddler (Karl Rove), the Penguin (Dick Cheney), the Joker (Alberto Gonzales) and Catwoman (Harriet Miers). . . .*
>
> *Enter the caped crusader, who has flown in from Vermont wearing a Batman-gray business suit and Batman-black loafers. He strikes back at Gotham's criminal masterminds with his signature weapon: the news conference. Meeting reporters in the Judiciary Committee hearing*

room, the Dark Knight encounters so many Batmicrophones on his Bat-lectern that he has to hold his Batspeech in his hands.

"The Administration has produced no documents!" Leahy growled.

POW!

"No adequate basis for noncompliance!"

BANG!⁴²

That the opposing stories insisted upon by the Judiciary Committee and the White House could now be reduced to the good/evil duality of a comic made clear how completely Leahy had dominated the conversation. All signs were pointing in the right direction. Leahy felt in his bones that Gonzales was within days of resigning.

But to his real surprise, another long-hanging shoe dropped first.

It was, in fact, White House strategist Karl Rove who first announced his resignation that August. Standing before a waiting helicopter with the president on the thirteenth, Rove surprised reporters not only with the announcement itself but with his seeming inability to get through it without weeping. Rove "struggled to read" his short statement, reporters noted in their puzzled accounts, "overcome by emotion" and at times "close to tears." If nothing else, the outburst suggested that even for the administration's most hardened political operative, the pressure had become all but overwhelming.

Leahy, for one, wasn't moved by the tears, telling reporters, "There is a cloud over this White House, and a gathering storm. A similar cloud envelops Mr. Rove, even as he leaves the White House." Leahy's satisfaction with Rove's abrupt exit was real, but also bittersweet. For a few months more, he and Senator Specter would make noises about continuing to pursue Rove's testimony under oath, but Leahy more or less knew that when Rove boarded that White House helicopter, no congressional summons would ever bring him back.

(And of course, Rove would continue to taunt him from afar—that was something the political strategist made clear immediately. "I realize that some of the Democrats are Captain Ahab and I'm the great white whale," he told a gaggle of waiting reporters with a smile. To make sure no one missed the sound bite, he repeated it. "I'm Moby Dick and they're after me." It more or less went without saying which particular Democrat was Ahab.⁴³)

A more unalloyed satisfaction would come two weeks later, when

Gonzales announced his own resignation as attorney general on August 27, 2007. His statement was brief, and he left the room without taking questions.[44]

David Iglesias, for one, found himself exhilarated but also undeniably touched by a certain tragic sense, the feeling that "simply put, Alberto Gonzales lost his way. He chose loyalty to Bush over fealty to the Constitution and his sworn duty to uphold it."[45]

It had taken seven turbulent years—and the gavel of Senate Judiciary had changed hands no fewer than five times in the meanwhile—but Leahy had finally managed to clean house at the Department of Justice. Along the way, he had become inarguably the single most effective counterbalance to Bush-era presidential overreach, the Democratic Party's most potent congressional weapon. And Pat Leahy had become an increasingly intriguing and well-known avatar in various arms of the popular culture, as well.

And so when PBS set out to produce an October *Frontline* documentary on Dick Cheney's pervasive influence in strengthening the powers of the executive branch, the opening montage more or less wrote itself:

ANNOUNCER: For three decades, Vice President Dick Cheney led a secretive and bitter behind-closed-doors battle to restore presidential power.

MARTIN LEDERMAN (Office of Legal Counsel, 1994–2002): He believes that the president should have the final word, indeed the only word, on all matters within the executive branch.

ANNOUNCER: After 9/11, there were enhanced presidential powers to detain, render, interrogate, wiretap.

Sen. PATRICK LEAHY (D–Vermont): Mr. President, it is time to have some checks and balances in this country!

JANE MAYER (the *New Yorker*): It's a direct showdown constitutionally between the president and Congress.

ANNOUNCER: The latest clash is over secret Justice Department findings authorizing the CIA to engage in the harshest interrogation techniques ever.

Sen. PATRICK LEAHY: Mr. President, we are a democracy![46]

★ ★ ★

The resignation of Alberto Gonzales was a powerful conclusion to a complicated story, but Leahy's life in 2007 was a thick braid of long-running narratives, more than one of which was undergoing startling development.

Nowhere was this truer than in the FBI's continuing investigation into the anthrax attacks of 2001. Working very quietly, agents with the Amerithrax task force had finally begun to lay the foundations of a solid case against a senior biodefense researcher at Fort Detrick named Bruce Ivins.[47] An initial search of Ivins's home turned up little of use, but later that week agents spied Ivins coming out with a bag of trash at 1 a.m., just in time for the weekly garbage pickup. Ivins's behavior seemed both suspicious and out of character; the agents stopped the truck a few blocks away and retrieved the bag that Ivins had discarded.

Wrapped in standard suburban garbage, they found two scholarly treatises on the use of DNA nomenclature to send coded messages.

It was a captivating find. The first anthrax letter, the NBC News letter, had made use of boldfaced Ts and As, and investigators had from the first suspected that they contained a coded message of some sort, although clearly a very simple message. Over the next several weeks, one of the FBI researchers, Darin Steele, applied the basic principles of DNA structure to create a working translation key for the Brokaw letter. He found two messages, both very short.

In fact, the first message that Steele decoded was just three letters long: PAT.[48]

To say that Leahy had been frustrated by the progress of the Amerithrax investigation is to vastly understate the case. In the months and years following the late-2001 attacks, he, along with Tom Daschle and the attorney general, had received detailed confidential briefings from leadership at the FBI, but Leahy had never been convinced that actual progress was being made. In fact, he had been increasingly convinced of the reverse.

Leahy's anger on the subject simmered for years, but by 2007 it was threatening to boil over on a semi-regular basis.

In early September of that year, I sat down with the senator for the first of the handful of long one-on-one interviews that inform this narrative. We met at one of his favorite restaurants in downtown Burlington, the Rusty Scuffer, and we spoke first at some length about the US attorney firings and the resignation of Alberto Gonzales, which had taken place just days previously. Leahy was clearly still on a high from the ritualized combat in the Judiciary Committee; he was relaxed and in his element, chatting easily and joking with the owner of the restaurant, an old friend.[49]

"Hey Patrick," the owner said, shaking his hand. "You're getting a lot of print."

"Don't you believe a word of it," Leahy advised, eyes smiling over his coffee, and they wished one another's wives well. But when I shifted gears to ask whether he was satisfied with the pace and the progress of the anthrax investigation, his mood darkened immediately. His white brows knitted together, and he radiated displeasure.

"No!" he answered, at a volume that drew a few looks from the front of the restaurant. "No!" he said again, in what would have to be described as a slightly muffled shout.

And then immediately he was contrite. "I'm a little sensitive on this one," Leahy began, "because two people died touching an envelope I was supposed to open." He sat back in his chair, and then started again. "I feel badly for them, and for their families. And we spent three years, Marcelle and I couldn't go *anywhere* without heavily armed people around us. Finally, I said, This guy's not going to try anything, and our family wants our privacy back."

Another moment of thought before he continued. "I wish they had turned this investigation over to some good sheriff or police chief somewhere. I think it's been very badly handled." Finally, Leahy pursed his lips and lowered his voice a little. "I have a theory. But what I want to know is why me, why Tom Daschle, why Tom Brokaw?"

I said that the targets, taken as a whole, suggested a genuinely unbalanced suspect, someone driven by the sort of purified right-wing ideology that perceives both the media and Democratic power brokers as equivalent threats to the Republic. He and Daschle, I pointed out, were both the targets of daily vitriol on conservative talk radio.

Leahy laced his long fingers together, and it was clear that he had spent a good long time working this particular mental puzzle. "I don't think it's somebody insane. I'd accept everything else you said. But I don't think it's somebody insane. And I think there are people within our government—certainly from the source of it—who know where it came from."

He tapped the table with his knuckles, to let that settle in. "And these people may not have had anything to do with it, but they certainly know where it came from."

The implications were clear, and heavy. To a certain extent they tracked the theories laid out in the years following the anthrax attacks by a college professor and microbiologist named Barbara Hatch Rosenberg. Rosenberg had maintained for years, both on the Internet and in forums domestic and international, that the US government had either culpability in or suppressed knowledge of the anthrax attacks—or both.

In fact, during the summer of 2002, Leahy had called a meeting in his Capitol Hill office with four FBI officials, and then invited Rosenberg as well. Although the surprised FBI agents were decidedly cool to Rosenberg and her take on the attacks, Leahy and his staff insisted that her concerns and theories be vetted.

Beryl Howell, Leahy's "point person for all things anthrax," would later make clear to the *Atlantic* magazine that Leahy was not siding with Rosenberg or her theories—but that the senator was determined to make sure the bureau pursued *all* leads, regardless of which direction they pointed. "'Whether or not Rosenberg's suspicions about [the bureau's first suspect Steven] Hatfill were correct was really not my business,' Howell says. 'It was really law enforcement's prerogative to figure that one out.'"[50]

Unquestionably, the anonymous anthrax mailer had created a weapon that exceeded the average government official's capacity for reasoned thought, for belief.[51] The spores seemed to inhabit some purely, darkly imaginative space, comprehensible only in the vocabulary and the conceptual architecture of science fiction. It was a superweapon, in a phrase, and over time the FBI had had no choice but to develop the inevitably matching behavioral profile of a supervillain.

"His thought processes," they warned at a November 2002 press conference, "are organized and rational during his criminal behavior. . . . He is a non-confrontational person, at least in his public life. He lacks the interpersonal skills necessary to confront others. . . . He may have become mission-oriented in his desire to undertake the mailings. He may have become more secretive and exhibited an unusual pattern of activity."[52] As Daschle puts it, "the FBI was leaning toward the theory that these mailings were the work of an individual, a 'lone wolf,' as agency behaviorists put it . . . [an] 'angry male loner.'"[53] The bureau had provided some clarifying detail in an earlier letter mailed to over thirty thousand microbiologists, seeking tips or information: "Based on his selection of the Ames strain of Bacillus anthracis one would expect that this individual has or had legitimate access to select biological agents at some time. This person has the technical knowledge and/or expertise to produce a highly refined and deadly product. This person has exhibited a clear, rational thought process and appears to be very organized in the production and mailing of these letters. The person might be described as 'stand-offish' and likely prefers to work in isolation as opposed to a group/team setting."[54]

Implicit in the description was that very precise, perverse admixture of genius and sociopathology that roils every comic book universe: a trusted and respected scientist—perhaps a government scientist—lending his superior public gifts to unprecedented private violence, in an attempt to foster an anarchy that will consume society itself.

And there was much about Fort Detrick senior bioweapons researcher Bruce Ivins that fleshed out the FBI's profile, once they had dug below the surface of his seemingly staid suburban life. Here, without doubt, was a dark, tortured—and torturing—soul.

A wealth of evidence suggested that Ivins had been living through a strange series of aliases for years, in fact, and that he used those alternate identities—as well as the US mail—to harass and threaten those he thought had slighted him.

He wrote graphic and violent anonymous material on the Internet, often in pursuit of female celebrity fixations; he described detailed homicidal plans to various therapists, plans targeted at acquaintances who thought him sweet and harmless; he confessed that sometimes he would lapse into fugue states, and disappear for long hours in his car at night, hours of which he later had no memory whatsoever; and he had been fixated for decades on a sorority, Kappa Kappa Gamma, having been rejected by one of the sorority's sisters as a young man, and in revenge had burglarized and stalked a wide range of KKG houses over the years, on multiple college campuses across hundreds of miles. There was reason to believe that the particular Princeton mailbox used to send the deadly letters was also known to him: "Nearly straight above the mailbox, on the fourth floor of an office building at 20 Nassau, is the Princeton chapter of Kappa Kappa Gamma. Ivins had painstakingly researched the locations of scores of KKG chapters throughout the East."[55]

The psychology was strange and turbulent, yes, but also almost straightforwardly pulp-fictional. He had been known to speak of himself as two Bruces living in one body, one the Bruce that earned honor and recognition from the US government for his research, and the other a darker side capable of seemingly any violent thought or action. Among the evidence ultimately presented by the FBI was a short autobiographical poem Ivins wrote to a former female colleague capturing this evil-twin dynamic. It read, in part:

> I'm a little dream-self, short and stout.
> I'm the other half of Bruce—when he lets me out.
> When I get all steamed up, I don't pout.
> I push Bruce aside, then I'm Free to run about![56]

But beyond the undeniable psychopathology they discovered, the Amerithrax task force had also assembled a very powerful circumstantial case against Ivins. Using technology unavailable when the anthrax letters had been sent originally, scientists were able to profile the DNA of the Daschle and Leahy spores—distinctive genetic "morphs" helped trace the powder back to a flask of material in Ivins's custody since the 1990s. Of all the scientists who might have had access to the material from the flask in question, only Ivins had spent large amounts of time alone at night in an anthrax "hot room" in the weeks before the first and second waves of anthrax letters.

There was, as well, an extremely powerful motive to threaten the nation with anthrax. Ivins had held a joint patent on a "next-generation anthrax vaccine" with four other USAMRIID scientists since 1994—a potential monetary windfall—but the Bush administration had made it increasingly clear that in lieu of a direct threat, funding for the vaccine's development and production was to be terminated.[57]

Ivins knew from personal experience how fear and war could spur development in his particular subfield; he had been part of the team that had rushed to prepare anthrax vaccine for soldiers during the Persian Gulf War. He had seen firsthand how quickly America's defense establishment advanced even questionable military projects in the rush to war. Amerithrax task force members theorized that after the attacks of 9/11, Ivins saw his opportunity to raise the threat level around a domestic anthrax attack, and seized it.

If that was in fact Ivins's plan, it proved spectacularly successful: the US Defense Department did in fact quickly ante up hundreds of millions of dollars to forward Ivins's next-generation vaccine. His prized project was stalled no longer.

And had Ivins lived, he would have stood to collect substantial royalties from his co-invention. But as the FBI drew its net tighter, Ivins blew up at a group therapy session on the evening of Wednesday, July 9, 2008, and threatened to kill his colleagues at USAMRIID. He told the stunned group that he "had a list of those he intended to kill. He had a bulletproof vest and was going to obtain a Glock handgun with the help of his son."[58] From there it was only a matter of days before Ivins was forcibly hospitalized, and once released, only a matter of days before he carried out the suicide he had threatened to his therapist.

Bruce Ivins killed himself with a deliberate overdose of Tylenol and codeine before charges could be formally preferred. And with his death, the answers to a myriad of pressing Amerithrax questions were lost forever.

Why had Ivins selected the various political and media targets for his deadly letters? Why, among the others, Pat Leahy? The investigators offered several theories, all of them built of circumstantial rather than direct evidence. Both Leahy and Daschle were high-profile pro-choice Catholic senators, relevant given that Ivins and his wife (herself president of the Frederick County Right to Life chapter) were socially conservative Catholics with connections to a host of antiabortion organizations. Leahy and Daschle were both profiled negatively in a Right-to-Life newsletter found in the Ivins home during an FBI search.[59]

But more crucially, Leahy had made himself the single most high-profile impediment to the Bush administration's conservative agenda, and later—in the panicky days following the 9/11 attacks—to its War on Terror. Ivins, "a longtime student of the news media and national politics," would have followed the back-and-forth over judicial nominees —which officially made Leahy the bête noir of the Right.

And again, in the immediate aftermath of the attacks on the Pentagon and the twin towers, Leahy would be the highest-profile Democrat arguing for restraint and moderating the pace of America's response. Ivins had every reason to cheerlead as the United States jumped to a wartime footing. In a September 26 e-mail to a former colleague, he boasted that unlike others in his therapy group, he was ready for war, and made it clear that war implied confronting anthrax, and hence the need for an effective vaccine: "I just heard that the Bin Laden terrorists for sure have anthrax and sarin gas. . . . The news media has been saying that some members of Congress and members of the ACLU oppose many of the Justice Department proposals for combating terrorism, saying that they are unconstitutional and infringe too much on civil liberties. . . . Osama Bin Laden has just decreed death to all Jews and all Americans. But I guess that doesn't mean a lot to the ACLU."[60]

In his final sentences, Ivins directly echoes the language of the block-printed notes inside the two waves of anthrax letters ("Death to America.

Death to Israel"). Of course, at the time of the message's writing, the first wave of letters had yet to be found and opened — which makes this particular e-mail one of the more incriminating pieces of evidence in the Amerithrax file. And by "some members of Congress," Ivins must certainly have been referring primarily to Leahy, who dominated the coverage and was for a span of weeks in September 2001 the only prominent senator openly pushing back on Ashcroft's original draft of the USA Patriot Act — and doing so in the name of civil liberties.

Still, was Ivins's animus toward Leahy strong enough to account, or partially account, for his coding the name "Pat" into the first wave of anthrax letters, as a clue to his second wave of targets?

David Willman, author of *The Mirage Man* and one of the most careful students of Ivins and his methods, doesn't believe so. In Willman's reconstruction, "Pat" is an exclusive reference to a former colleague with whom Ivins had been obsessed for years, Patricia Fellows. Ivins was shocked and dismayed, as Willman sees it, when his original anthrax letters produced no reaction in the media — and only *then* decided to launch a second wave. As Willman framed it in an e-mail:

> Ivins grew greatly agitated and frustrated in that yawning interregnum between when he mailed the first batch of letters, on Sept. 18, 2001, and the first report of the index victim's symptoms, on Oct. 4, 2001. Sixteen days! Put yourself in the perpetrator's shoes: He's executed this diabolical, attention-seeking scheme — and no one has noticed. My point is that Ivins in all likelihood expected the first letters to hit with shock-and-awe force. Therefore, I don't think it can be assumed that Ivins had originally planned to send a second batch, ultimately postmarked Oct. 9, 2001, and addressed to Sens. Leahy and Daschle. So, I would not agree that Ivins probably knew — as he was preparing the original letter, mailed on Sept. 18 — that he would be sending a second round.[61]

It's a compelling psychological reading, and Willman's caution is well taken. But if we cannot assume that Ivins *had* planned a second wave of letters, with "Pat" as a clue tucked into the first, we cannot necessarily assume that he *hadn't* either. Certainly there could have been other logical causes for the mailer's mounting agitation in the wake of his first biocrime. These were felonies of meticulous planning, and the possibility of a second wave of letters might have been a part of that elaborate overall design.

With his love of codes and clues and personal vendettas — and with only a few DNA-derived letters to play with — it doesn't seem out of the realm of possibility that Ivins might have settled on a double reference, a way of targeting and taunting two Pats at once. This was, after all, an obsessive given to making target lists and "anger lists," lists he would consider at great length. Certainly he must have shortened that mental list of targets and considered it again and again, rendering it down finally into his own cold sort of haiku.

Would it never have occurred to him that Leahy and Fellows shared the same three-letter, one-syllable nickname? We will never know, not really. Ivins made certain of that.

★ ★ ★

Even as the Amerithrax task force laid its thick dossier of evidence before the public, even as a skeptical Tom Daschle came to accept the bureau's conclusions as solid,[62] Leahy remained convinced — and very publicly so — that the FBI had failed to ferret out the entire network behind the attacks. That alone was an explosive thought, and an even more explosive statement to enter into the public record.

But after having been briefed in Vermont by FBI director Mueller on August 7, 2008, concerning the small mountain of evidence now pointing to Ivins, Leahy chose a packed Judiciary Committee oversight hearing nine days later to amplify the allegations he had first laid out for me the previous September.

Voice low but steady, and pausing throughout for emphasis, Leahy alleged the existence of a full-blown criminal conspiracy, in language borrowed very deliberately from his days as a courtroom prosecutor. He had always had the instincts of a performer; he had spent long years honing his capacity for the sound bite. But behind this particular bite lay long years of resentment and anger and fear for his family. All of which gave five of Leahy's sentences in particular a palpable force:

"If [Ivins] is the one who sent the letter, I do not believe in any way, shape or manner that he is the only person involved in this attack on Congress and the American people. I do not believe that at all. *I believe there are others involved, either as accessories before or accessories after the fact. I believe there are others out there. I believe there are others who can be charged with murder."*[63]

It was a powerful statement, delivered with calculated gravity, and it was immediately effective — Leahy's colleagues Arlen Specter and Charles

Grassley would quickly echo Leahy's suspicions and his language, as would the editorial board of the *Washington Post*.[64] Left unspoken in the charged Washington committee room, though, was the most far-reaching element of the allegations Leahy had laid out in the Rusty Scuffer a year earlier: that one or more of those theoretical accessories might actually be part of the government of the United States.

But there is no reason to think that Leahy had changed his mind.

Ivins's death by Tylenol was an ending to the Amerithrax saga that only a conspiracy theorist could love. A lone wolf researcher who killed himself just before the discoveries of a trial—the very neatness of the conclusion was certain to gin up decades of Internet speculation. New Jersey congressman Rush Holt summed up the danger: "I don't want it to reside in the court of public opinion. Then we'll end up with something like the Lee Harvey Oswald case. There [will be] too many people in whose minds the case is never closed."[65] But that die was cast. The Internet was alive with skepticism.

Yet it was precisely the neatness of the supervillain story line that animated the tabloid coverage of the FBI's announcement regarding Ivins. Whatever differences remained in the year 2008 between the doppelganger cities of New York and Gotham vanished altogether in a frenzy of mythmaking. The *New York Post*, which had itself received one of the deadly anthrax mailings in 2001, assigned Ivins one supervillain handle after another. "'Thrax Man," they called him initially, a "dangerous and deranged lunatic"; within a few days they had switched to "Dr. Anthrax," and then oddly, "Omega Man." (For good measure, they also labeled Ivins a "Kreepy Kappa Lover.")

For its part, the *New York Daily News* opted for "Anthrax Doc" and "mad scientist," before veering briefly to "Dr. Death" and then finally settling on "Dr. Doom" in an otherwise sober August 11 editorial.[66] And this cross-pollination between reality and graphic novel didn't stop with the tabloids.

Far from it. During the very week that bioweapons designer Bruce Ivins was being involuntarily committed to Sheppard Pratt psychiatric hospital, even as he was threatening to kill his Fort Detrick colleagues and himself, Warner Bros. was staging a series of splashy mid-July premiers for the second installment in Christopher Nolan's acclaimed *Dark Knight* trilogy. *The Dark Knight* featured Christian Bale in the role of the

Batman, and the late Heath Ledger in a much-anticipated tour de force as the Joker. And confronting the homicidal supervillain in one key dramatic scene—in a speaking role, no less—was Senator Patrick Leahy.

Suddenly everywhere one looked, during the summer of 2008—from the somber committee rooms of Capitol Hill, to twenty-four-hour cable news and the silver screens of thousands of American and European multiplexes—there was the Judiciary Committee chairman confronting not just the run-of-the-mill criminals he had always faced down as a prosecutor, but supercriminals at play on a global scale.

For all practical purposes, the lurid DC and Marvel comic book universes were now finally indistinguishable from Leahy's own.

For Love of the Batman

THE DARK KNIGHT AND COICA/PIPA/ SOPA TRILOGIES

In mid-1994, Leahy received an unexpected but extremely intriguing phone call. On the other end of the line was Robert Daly, then cochairman at Warner Bros., inviting him out to Los Angeles for a one-day walk-on in the upcoming *Batman Forever*, starring Jim Carrey and Nicole Kidman. Daly knew of Leahy's highly public fanboy interest in the caped crusader, and he thought the senator would get a kick out of spending a day prowling around the set.

It would be an understatement to say that Leahy was delighted, but he was also scrupulous—he insisted on paying his own way to the filming, and noted that fact to *Variety* the following year.[1]

Jim Carrey's career had yet to hit its zenith, and his early box-office appeal made the film a major financial success. Opening weekend set a new all-time record, and only Pixar's *Toy Story* earned more in 1995.[2] Leahy's cameo role, a silent partygoer at the Riddler's ball, went more or less unremarked upon.

But Leahy *had* gotten a real kick out of it all—the sun, the shoot, the stars, the premiere—and the following year, 1996, he found himself out in California again, at the Warner Bros. Burbank studios, filming a similar walk-on for *Batman & Robin*. It was the fourth (and doomed to be the last) in the original series of Warner Bros. Batman films. George Clooney, star of the television drama *ER*, was slated to replace Val Kilmer as Batman.

Again, Leahy was one of a hundred faces at a wild ball invaded by the film's arch-villains, Arnold Schwarzenegger and Uma Thurman, but this time out the camera found Leahy more often. He was grouped standing with some of the principals in the crowd, and while he delivered no lines, he was called upon to react dramatically to the lines of the speakers around him. With his height, his large smooth head, and prominent glasses—and resplendent in a Hollywood tuxedo—Leahy was difficult to miss. If his acting was a bit broad, so was the acting and tone in general. Director Joel Schumacher, according to actor John Glover, would sit on a crane and yell through a megaphone, "Remember, everyone, this is a cartoon!"

Almost from the beginning the film was beset by withering criticism. Schwarzenegger's one-liners fell horribly flat; on the other hand, critics complained that the codpieces and nipples on the batsuit weren't quite flat enough.

In the end, *Batman & Robin* (1997) was almost universally acknowledged to be the worst Batman film ever made, not an easy distinction to secure. Clooney apologized profusely for it and later mused, "I think we might have killed the franchise." (Over the years, Clooney has made a small cottage industry of these apologies, so much so that by 2014, *Vulture* could run a fairly long compendium titled, "A Brief History of George Clooney Apologizing for Being a Bad Batman.")[3]

Yet Leahy was smitten by the whole process. He was a fan of Batman films, yes, but now he had had a real taste of the process by which Hollywood synthesized those dreams—a process at once exacting, artistic, frenetic, surreal. Even the horrible reviews had been an absolute hoot to read.

Still, for all his enthusiasm, it would be a full decade before Leahy landed another Batman cameo. But when it came, that call would be more than worth the wait.

WHY SO SERIOUS?

In one way, it was a short, routine midsummer flight from Washington to Chicago. But from another angle, Leahy had come an extremely long way: from a gangly kid with one good eye, soaking up 1940s Flash Gordon and Batman serials in a tiny theater in Montpelier, to a thirty-year-plus veteran of the US Senate on his way to film a small but visible role in the second installment of Christopher Nolan's already acclaimed *Dark Knight Trilogy*. A small *speaking* role, opposite Australian sensation Heath Ledger.

It staggered the mind.

And the truth was that Leahy was all but beside himself with excitement and had a very hard time containing it. (Although his high-profile cameo was supposed to be on the down low, Leahy would himself let the cat out of the bag in just a few weeks' time—a *Roll Call* "spy" would hear the senator casually regaling his barber in the Russell Senate Office Building with an account of the filming, sparking a flood of Batman-themed squibs in the media.[4])

But more than simply another Batman credit, this film shoot in July 2007 was also the clear culmination of a long mutual love affair with Hollywood itself.

From his earliest days in the Senate, Leahy had gravitated to the social swirl that the motion picture industry could and often did produce in the capital. Jack Valenti, the dashing longtime president of the Motion Picture Association of America, had made a point of taking young Pat Leahy under his wing in the mid-1970s; Valenti and his wife Mary Margaret invited the Leahys to their home and to their favorite DC-area restaurants. He acted, as Leahy would later movingly characterize it, as a "mentor."[5]

Leahy was more than flattered by the gracious attention. Valenti was a physically small man with an eye-poppingly impressive résumé: he had been a decorated bomber pilot in World War II, as well as a trusted special assistant to President Lyndon Johnson, and—as president of the MPAA—he was on a nickname basis with both Hollywood and DC's A-lists. He had actually been in the motorcade when President Kennedy was shot and killed in Dallas.

With his brilliant smile and brilliantined hair, Valenti worked the halls of the House and the Senate like visiting royalty—except for the "visiting" part. Jack Valenti was a permanent fixture, and everyone in Washington well knew it.

Valenti's nearly forty years as MPAA president overlapped almost entirely with Leahy's own long career, and their relationship grew stronger and more complex as the decades passed. Along with their shared reverence for filmmaking as an American institution, the two men shared a very vocal pride in their Italian heritage. It was a friendship that eventually took on distinctly sentimental overtones. Valenti would single out and charm Leahy's mother at national Italian American events here and there, and Leahy would regularly attend advance screenings of first-run films at the MPAA headquarters, where Valenti made sure that the dinners "always included at least one Italian dish."[6]

(Never one to miss a social or political nuance, Valenti occasionally catered to Leahy's Irish side as well, joining him for a premier of *Angela's Ashes*, the film adaptation of Frank McCourt's best seller, at the Irish ambassador's residence in late 1999.[7] Fortunately McCourt had once been a schoolteacher, as it fell to him to hush the DC dignitaries, who were in particularly high spirits: "Would you be *quiet* back there? The ambassador is speaking!")

In April 2007, when Valenti eventually passed on to what he was known to jokingly call "the great screening room in the sky," his onetime mentee and lifelong friend not only attended the funeral but served as an honorary pallbearer.[8]

Touching down in Chicago just three months later, Leahy was determined to acquit himself on-set in a manner that would have made the old Hollywood master proud. But he was nervous down deep, in spite of his wife Marcelle's presence and reassurances. Being cast and showing up for work was one thing; performing in an environment where sixty seconds of finished film might cost a million dollars or more—that was another matter entirely.

This Time, This Place, the Valenti memoir that Leahy still had stashed in his official desk on the Senate floor, spends a good amount of time discussing the risks to a near-celebrity of moving for any length of time in the rarefied realm of actual celebrity. Valenti was no stranger to this feeling of playing far above his own comfort level.

"It's tremendously difficult to maintain your handhold on the side of the mountain at a level where so few ever climb, where the vista is so splendid, where the air is so thin," the old bomber pilot mused, before making it clear that in Hollywood, as in war, failure is not an option. "But you can't look back or down; it's too terrifying."[9]

A quirk of Christopher Nolan's directorial modus operandi: he typically refuses a second unit and director, to ensure consistency in his vision and work product. This insistence makes for a significantly longer shooting schedule, but it's hard to quarrel with success—each of his Batman films creates a brooding, almost bullying sense of place.

Batman Begins, with its focus on mysticism and deep origin myth, Nolan filmed in large part overseas, from the Vatnajökull Glacier in Iceland (standing in for Bhutan) to the Mentmore Towers in Buckinghamshire, England. But when the *Batman Begins* script called for Gotham itself, Nolan selected not New York but the major American metropolis where he had lived out his own origin story: Chicago.

Nolan's goal was to reenvision Gotham as a vast but profoundly realistic metropolitan landscape, "New York cubed" in the shorthand adopted by the film's design team.[10] Chicago's stark skyscrapers served their needs precisely, and in truth city officials had been delighted to replace New York in Nolan's imaginary universe.

For his second film, Nolan had again selected Chicago, and so after Leahy and Marcelle were picked up at O'Hare International, they found themselves being driven into an area of the city more or less commandeered by Nolan's crew. The old Chicago Post Office, the Richard J. Daley Center, the IBM building on Wabash Avenue, the Chicago Theater, Millennium Park—Leahy was more than a little impressed by the long list of iconic Chicago structures now serving, or being prepped to serve, as Gotham film sets.[11]

But at the moment of Leahy's arrival, the lion's share of the project's energy was focused on the vast conglomeration of buildings situated on East Wacker Drive, the Illinois Center Buildings. Production teams swarmed the plazas. The lobby of Hotel 71, at 71 East Wacker, had been made over into Bruce Wayne's upscale penthouse, green screens swathing the windows so that views over the city could be added later.

And at 111 East Wacker, Building 2, a lobby on one of the lower floors had been lavishly converted into the setting for Gotham prosecutor Harvey Dent's fund-raiser—the backdrop for one of Ledger's more gripping moments of insanity.

Leahy and Marcelle were steered to a series of trailers laid out beside Building 2, one of which was reserved for the couple if they felt like relaxing or napping during the long delays in filming. But Leahy had no intention of sleeping. The energy of the set was infectious, and he was determined to soak it in while he had the chance.

And there was another reason for Leahy to be a bit on edge: in this scene, he would actually have to *act*, among the film's principals. And Nolan—a man Leahy knew only "slightly through some mutual friends" —was a notorious perfectionist, always looking to push the envelope to achieve his signature brand of realism.[12] Nolan's stated theme for *The Dark Knight*, after all, was "escalation" —the sense that both the film and the trilogy, spurred by the Joker's anarchic violence, were intensifying, complicating, all but imploding.[13]

In short, Nolan wanted both stunning violence and unstinting realism, including the stunts and effects. It was not the most comfortable combination for an amateur actor from Vermont who had never spoken a line on film, and whose last Batman credit had involved watching a heavily accented Arnold Schwarzenegger attack Poison Ivy's "jungle party" in his Freezemobile ("All right, everybody—chill!").

Leahy, wearing his best senatorial suit and tie, walked into the large makeup trailer still feeling the mix of exhilaration and trepidation. Slumped in the makeup chair next to his own was a tall good-looking young man in cutoff jeans and an old T-shirt, longish hair hanging in a tangle to one side of his face.[14]

After a moment, the young man leaned over and stuck out his hand, gave a suddenly brilliant smile. "I'm Heath," he said.

Ledger was then nearing the pinnacle of a brilliant early career—just twenty-eight, he had already won an Oscar nod for his work as Ennis Del Mar in *Brokeback Mountain*, as well as a New York Film Critics Circle Award. He had multiple feature films under way, from blockbuster to stylishly independent. And of course he was only six months or so from the "accidental overdose" of painkillers, anti-anxiety drugs, and sleeping pills that would end his life.

Ledger would be found unconscious in his Lower Manhattan apartment on January 22, 2008, his heart stopped by a horrific cocktail of pharmaceuticals: oxycodone, hydrocodone, diazepam, temazepam, alprazolam, and doxylamine.[15] Today's Chicago shoot would be one of his last, and that untimely death would lend his turn as the Joker a certain undeniable iconic stature. Buzz would build accordingly, and somewhat ghoulishly, in the interval between the death and the release of *The Dark Knight* in July 2008.

The Joker's chilling three-word taunt—"Why so serious?"—would eventually be on everyone's lips.

Leahy took in the series of photographs framing the mirror in front of Ledger's chair, all various depictions of the Joker's disturbing makeup, from every angle, to help the makeup artists recapture the signature look from day to day. It was hard to reconcile the twisted images and the good-natured, shaggy-haired Australian in the chair beside him.

"I'm Patrick," Leahy said, shaking Ledger's hand and then adding hastily, by way of some sort of explanation, "from Vermont."

As the afternoon wore into evening, and evening into night, Leahy's trepidation began to get the better of his exhilaration. As his time on camera grew closer, Leahy learned more about the mechanics of his confrontation with the Joker. A knife, for instance, would be held to his throat

—although "held" would be putting it mildly. Nolan's push for realism demanded that Ledger grab Leahy's head and force it violently up to the edge of the knife.

At least the knife itself—when Leahy looked it over briefly prior to the shooting—seemed harmless. It was plastic, light in his hand. "That doesn't even look real," he marveled to the prop handler.

The man just chuckled before pocketing the knife. "Wait until you see it in the movie," he said, moving away. "You'll think you could shave with this baby."

The hour got later, and the tension in the vast room grew palpable. Eventually Leahy learned the reason for some of that mounting anticipation—the Joker and Batman had yet to meet face to face on set, and tonight would be their first actual filmed confrontation. "There was quite a bit of time before we actually got to the scenes where they appeared together," says Nolan's wife, Emma Thomas. "Everyone waited for those moments—they were really something to see. It was amazing to watch Heath and Chris [Christian Bale] work together."[16]

With all the actors finally collected in the ballroom, but for the Joker and his henchmen, Nolan briefed everyone on what to expect. The Joker would come into the ballroom, fire his pump-action shotgun in the air, and then proceed to move through the partygoers, ad libbing as he went, until he reached his mark for the confrontation with Leahy.

Leahy was preparing himself to act surprised when the door did fly open and the blast from the shotgun—blanks but much louder than anyone expected—scared the ballroom into actual stunned silence. Leahy puts his hand on his heart remembering it: "Everybody was like, 'Ayyy!' I mean, you really *jumped*. And Ledger was really frightening. You didn't have to act scared."

And suddenly the Joker was standing in front of him, very much in character, the ghoulish makeup far more disturbing than the photographs he had seen in the trailer earlier. And as Leahy now freely admits, he blew it initially. "We're not intimidated by thugs," was Leahy's line, to which the Joker would reply mildly, "You remind me of my father," before brandishing the knife and spitting, "I *hated* my father!"

But when they ran through it the first time, Ledger wasn't playing; he threw Leahy "halfway across the room."[17] It was very much like being manhandled by a psychopath, actually, and it was a mortifying moment for Leahy. "The first time he did it, I crashed into the back of the set, and stuff's just falling all over me." Leahy actually puts his head in his hands, thinking about it. "And I was so *darned* embarrassed."

They ran the exchange dozens of times, from this angle and that, with Ledger punching Leahy, throwing him aside, every variation of momentary violence. But in almost every take, Leahy came out of the throw unpredictably, stumbling, not surprising for a man in his late sixties more used to the ultra-controlled processes of the US Senate. Finally, a stuntman playing one of the Joker's henchmen—an actor Leahy had actually worked with in *Batman & Robin*—suggested a work-around.

"Look," the big henchman proposed, "when Heath throws you back, I'll catch you and threaten you with this shotgun. We'll be in the back of the scene at that point, and you just give me a look when you've got your feet under you, and then I'll just walk away threateningly. Good?"

It worked, and the physical problem was solved. But Nolan continued to take different versions of Leahy's line itself. He was unsure whether he wanted real fear in Leahy's voice, or sharp defiance.

Finally, Nolan opted definitively for the latter, and Leahy was "directed to act like the prosecutor he once was, with a take-charge attitude."[18]

It was a truly amazing moment, when set against the long arc of Leahy's political career: the very same Top Cop image that Leahy had developed as a young Chittenden County state's attorney—the image Paul Bruhn had then fashioned into a winning senatorial persona—now being explicitly deployed by a major Hollywood director to a worldwide audience.

It wasn't that Leahy had come full circle; that metaphor captures the reprise of the familiar theme, but fails by suggesting a tailing off, a foreshortening. It was more as though Leahy's signature prosecutorial image were still in the process of expanding, of amplification, executing a widening spiral that had already carried it over four decades to larger and more appreciative audiences with every turn of the gyre. Audiences now fully global in scale.

Top Cop, indeed.[19]

With his own turn complete, Leahy could now give himself over to his own profound love of the movies. He could delight in the surreal sights that filmmaking inevitably generates, like the elaborate faux staircase and fireplaces added to the ballroom that had been only months before a mostly empty lobby. He felt more one of the cast now, and with the anxiety gone, he saw more of the easygoing humor.

When Maggie Gyllenhaal steps in to stop the Joker's rampage, Ledger turns and stalks over to her, drawling the words, "Well, hello, beautiful!" and primping his lank hair as he goes. The final angle didn't show Gyllenhaal, who had actually left the set; instead, a big bearded extra about her height was positioned to help Ledger keep his glance at the right level.

And so when Ledger approached the stand-in with the beard, and delivered the line, "Well, hello, beautiful!" a voice rang out from the back of the room—"You already made that film, Heath!" No one missed the reference to *Brokeback Mountain*, and everyone dissolved into laughter.

Michael Caine, reprising his role as Alfred, drifted over to Leahy, and they chatted about *The Cider House Rules*, shot primarily in Vermont and for which Caine won an Oscar in 2000. They had a good friend in common, Putney writer John Irving, who had also won an Oscar for *Cider House*. Leahy was struck by Caine's friendliness, his genuine affability. He knew that some actors stayed in character on set, but Ledger and Caine worked in the opposite way. They seemed fully able to switch their characters on and off, like a light switch, saving everything for the camera.

At one point, Caine turned to Ledger, who was chatting with some other actors, and said loudly, "Heath, I don't think it's very nice of you to come over here to the US and throw a US senator around the set, not very nice at all."

Ledger looked puzzled. "What do you mean?"

"The Distinguished Gentleman," Caine continued, hooking a thumb at Leahy. "He's a US senator, you know."

"Now, wait just a *second*," Ledger protested, walking over with his ghastly face turned sharply to one side in mock-suspicion. "He said his name was *Patrick*. From *Vermont*." Then he made a show of pausing in thought before turning to one of the directorial assistants and cocking an eyebrow. "Uh, am I going to be in some sort of trouble now?"

As the Leahys prepared to leave, at nearly four in the morning, Ledger drifted over to Marcelle and gave the joke one more twist. "Listen, Marcelle, I'm sorry I had to be so rough on your husband back there." It was the Joker at fault, Ledger maintained, dragging his tangled greenish hair away from his face and turning up the slash of red at his lips in a smile.

Marcelle smiled back and said, "Oh, Heath, that's all right." She paused, then turned back and patted his arm maternally. "But you really want to work out those issues with your father."

And it was a wrap.

★ ★ ★

The July 2008 world premier of *The Dark Knight* was held not in Chicago or New York or Los Angeles or Tokyo or even Beijing, but rather in Montpelier, Vermont (population 7,750), and that a full two days before anyone else in the world got a look at Nolan's artistic exercise in escalation. But Leahy hadn't simply managed to cajole Warner Bros. into debuting the film in his tiny but picturesque hometown (in a theater just a moment's stroll from the door of Leahy's childhood home at 136 State Street). He had also prevailed upon the company's CEO Barry Meyer to attend himself and to help raise more than $100,000 for the Kellogg-Hubbard Library—the quiet Main Street sanctuary where Leahy had retreated as a kid to read his Dickens and Stevenson and Batman.[20]

If anyone harbored any lingering doubts that Montpelier's favorite son had achieved true Bigfoot status in both DC and Hollywood, Meyer's presence alone seemed to dispel them once and for all. Even Meyer himself couldn't quite seem to believe where he was or what was actually happening.

"I think I can safely say, without having to check with anyone," he joked to Vermont Public Radio's Jane Lindholm, "that this is the first time Warner Bros. has ever had a world premiere of a movie in Montpelier, Vermont. Or anywhere in Vermont for that matter."[21]

In that same interview, Meyer gave a bit of insight into the origin of his relationship with Leahy, but only a bit. Apparently the two men had met several years prior to *The Dark Knight* for a "five-minute meet-and-greet" but soon fell into a pleasantly rambling hour-and-a-half discussion about the Batman universe and the motivations of its various villains. "And, you know, we became friends after that," Meyer adds. It remains unclear whether the original meet-and-greet was in a DC or a Hollywood context, whether it was a social or a business gathering, or a mingling of both.

What is amply clear is that the friendship progressed quickly and produced almost immediate collaboration. By February 2007 Meyer was introducing Leahy to a packed MPAA symposium on "The Business of Show Business" as "a real ally to the entertainment industry . . . as good a friend and champion as our industry has ever had (even going so far as to contribute an Oscar caliber—although not Oscar winning—performance in *Batman & Robin*)."[22]

In part, that 2007 symposium had been designed to foreground the movie industry's rapidly growing anxiety over illegal downloading and streaming of its intellectual property. And when Meyer called Leahy a "champion" for the industry, he was no doubt referring to a series of initiatives that would soon be surfacing at multiple levels of the US government, all aimed at protecting Hollywood's intellectual property rights worldwide. In hindsight at least, Meyer's introductory remarks almost seem to verge on the preemptive, in anticipation of increased attention to Leahy's role as a legislative warrior for his industry:

> Webster's defines "integrity" this way: "firm adherence to a code of moral or artistic value; soundness; incorruptibility."
>
> Webster's defines "character" this way: "moral excellence and firmness; strong reputation."
>
> I define character and integrity this way: Ladies and Gentlemen, the Senator from the State of Vermont and Chairman of the Senate Judiciary Committee—Pat Leahy.[23]

As it turns out, Meyer's preemption was premature. In general Leahy's 2008 pop-cultural tour de force—*Dark Knight* speaking role, movie premiere, and personal attendance by the CEO of the world's third-largest television and entertainment company—aroused far more admiration than complaint.

A few curious entertainment writers queried the company about Leahy's connections to director Christopher Nolan but received only bland nonstatements in response: "Publicity representatives had no knowledge of any special connections between Christopher Nolan and the current chairman of the Senate Judiciary Committee, though maybe they're just playing their cards close to the vest."[24]

But at least one outlet—*Vulture*, a popular online entertainment site—raised a very public eyebrow. "What Is Senator Patrick Leahy Doing in 'The Dark Knight'?" writer Brent Simon wanted to know. Simon called Leahy's turn "one of the more bizarre cameos of the summer," then went just a wee bit further, joking that "Leahy saw what that *Wedding Crashers* cameo did for fellow Senate maverick John McCain, and is now out to get his own Cheddar."

Out to get his own Cheddar. It was a joke, but a palpably charged joke nonetheless.

Simon's snark was double-edged—par for the course at *Vulture*. Part of the point was that the risqué *Wedding Crashers* did absolutely nothing for McCain, and *The Dark Knight* might well do even less for Leahy. The cheeky comparison of Leahy to a rapper who might actually use the slang term "cheddar" was clearly meant to be ludicrous. And every article written about Leahy and Batman over the previous fifteen years had stressed that all royalties from the senator's appearances benefit charity, in perpetuity.

Still, the idea that Leahy's *Dark Knight* cameos betrayed a hunger for something *other* than money was born—"cheddar" as screen time, power, social connections in Hollywood—as was the corresponding idea that such a hunger might be exploited by savvy Hollywood executives. It was not yet an actual meme; a meme implies sudden, viral transmission of the idea or behavior in question.

That would come later.

★ ★ ★

In the event, everyone bet big on *The Dark Knight*—Nolan, Warner Bros., Ledger, Meyer, and, in his own way, Leahy—and everyone won big. Very big. The *International Herald Tribune* captured Meyer's moment of success—when the opening-day receipts were tallied:

> Early on a Saturday morning about three weeks ago, Barry Meyer pulled a sheet of paper from the fax machine in his home office, inhaled deeply and held it up to the light of a nearby window. The number on the fax was eye-popping: $66 million, plus change.
>
> Ka-ching. The opening day U.S. box office receipts for the Batman film "The Dark Knight" had just set a record. And for myriad reasons—including the late Heath Ledger's delicious turn as the Joker—the blockbuster is still filling theaters at a pace that may land it just behind "Titanic" on the list of top-grossing films.[25]

Nolan's second installment of the *Dark Knight Trilogy* proved a stunning artistic and critical achievement for one reason above all others: it managed to complete the work of dispelling, for the foreseeable future, the camp sensibility that had long hampered the franchise, and to reduce as much as possible the gap between dark fantasy and painfully realistic human pathology. In that, it drew more heavily from the slasher genre than it did from the 1960s television series.

Heath Ledger, in the performance of his short career, invested the

Joker with precisely the sort of disturbed psychopathology intended by his creators, particularly the artists and writers who had reimagined the character in the mid-1970s.[26] The slash of lipstick across Ledger's chalk-white face is not Romero-perfect, but rather a testament to self-abuse. The iconic makeup looks as though it hurt Ledger's Joker to apply it. Michael Caine put it best: "Instead of a naughty clown, Heath played him as a maniacal psychopath, a murderer."[27]

And yet the audience is never treated to an origin story, by which the Joker's trauma might be explained or rendered comprehensible. Very much the reverse, in fact. Nolan wanted the viewer to confront the Joker as a force of (human) nature: "The purpose of The Joker for us was always that he has no arc, he has no development. He doesn't learn anything through the film, he's an absolute. He cuts through the film sort of like the shark in *Jaws*."[28] Ledger's death by overdose in the weeks before the film's release simply enhanced this effect. Audiences in effect saw Ledger both dead and alive, tragic in either instance, and never has a Batman film felt more relevant, more completely of its moment.[29]

It was this *artistic* triumph—even more than the $534 million *The Dark Knight* would eventually earn—that would render Pat Leahy's tiny speaking role so culturally powerful, and ultimately so politically charged.

It's fair to say that *Batman & Robin* (1997), in which Leahy had last appeared, had been generally regarded as a crime against both movie-goers and the comic-book franchise as a whole—to be associated with it in any way was seen as its own lifelong punishment. But Nolan's *Dark Knight* trilogy was different from the start, that rare project that disarms both highbrow and box-office skeptics. *The Dark Knight* in particular bewitched critics, pitched as it was "at the divide between art and industry, poetry and entertainment," and from its opening week forward it broke record after record.[30]

And the money was nothing compared to the cultural capital the film was clearly generating hand over fist. *The Dark Knight* would not only become the highest-grossing film of the year, its characters and catch-phrases ubiquitous, but the reviews would be for the most part sublime. It would garner eight Academy Award nominations. Ledger would go on to win a posthumous Oscar for his supporting role; the film and its villain would romp at the Critics Choice Awards, the People's Choice, the Golden Globes.

What was it worth, in *non*monetary terms, to play in an A-list production directly opposite Bale and Ledger in what was quickly becoming not just a summer blockbuster but a major cultural touchstone?

But for the most part, as 2008 came to a close, Leahy and his communications people fielded requests from interviewers seeking the human interest side of his participation in Nolan's triumph, the philanthropic aspect, the new wing of the Kellogg-Hubbard Library, the humorous, pun-heavy angles. It was an ongoing public relations bonanza for Leahy's office. (When reporters crowded into that office a year later, to witness Leahy's pre-confirmation conversation with the newly nominated Sonia Sotomayor, they found *Dark Knight* posters still stacked prominently on the senator's desk for signature. And predictably enough, even the white-hot Supreme Court nomination story expanded to include mention of the caped crusader.[31])

Leahy was riding very high, higher than ever before. And perhaps understandably, then, his office's general attitude toward the few pundits who grumbled here or there about his luck in snagging the cinematic comet of 2008 could be summed up in more or less three words: *Why so serious?*

★ ★ ★

Of course, the following years would see some very serious antipiracy legislation introduced into the US House and Senate. Very serious, indeed. Meyer's characterization of Leahy as a champion for his industry wasn't overstating the fact in the slightest. Global theft of its intellectual property was Hollywood's number one concern, far and away, and Leahy turned to that problem with a vengeance in 2010.

It's important to note, though, that this push against copyright theft wasn't a snap decision on Leahy's part, but rather a position he had evolved toward over more than a decade, and more or less reluctantly. As far back as the year 2000, Leahy had used a Judiciary Committee hearing to dramatize the ease with which music could be stolen over the Internet. Using Napster, a peer-to-peer file-sharing service eventually driven out of business by legal troubles, he had managed to impress his Senate colleagues by illegally downloading the Grateful Dead's hit "Touch of Grey" (although the process took so long that Leahy joked to the committee that his pirated version should be called "Touch of White").

But while genuinely concerned at that point, Leahy had still been on the fence about congressional intervention. On the one hand, he knew the members of the Grateful Dead personally, and when they—or Lars

Ulrich of Metallica, for instance — came to Capitol Hill, it was hard not to agree in principle with their vocal complaints. And yet his belief in the continuing freedom of the Internet was a strong guiding principle as well. It left him in an uncomfortable philosophical bind.

"Obviously artists deserve to be paid. But our responsibility in the Congress is not to stifle innovation," Leahy temporized.[32]

Still, as the pace of twenty-first-century technology continued to accelerate, Leahy saw the increasing ease with which online piracy could be accomplished. And of course during those same years he had been discussing the problem sympathetically with Jack Valenti, for whom global piracy was something of a Great White Whale. In his star-studded 2007 memoir, a slowly failing Valenti still managed to distill his organization's top priorities to their essence: "My ultimate goal was to make sure the American movie could move freely on all continents, compete fairly in all marketplaces, and be protected from thievery in every part of the world. The latter objective, though I did not know it at the beginning of my movie career, was to become the prime activity of the MPAA, summed up in the clearly stated maxim: 'If you cannot protect what you own, you don't own anything.'"[33]

Leahy has always been sympathetic to an institutional argument — in this case, that the institution of American cinema itself was uniquely threatened by the rapacious global piracy enabled by emerging technologies. And as he would argue again and again, from a profusion of slightly different angles, theft was theft, and as a onetime prosecutor he was now inclined to side with those being relieved of their intellectual property, in spite of the dangers inherent in attempting to regulate more firmly a notoriously self-protective Internet. As Barry Meyer framed the argument at his 2007 MPAA symposium, "It shouldn't be 'illegal' when it's a car theft statute that's broken, and only 'unauthorized' when it's a copyright law."[34]

With the first decade of the twenty-first century drawing to a close, Leahy finally felt he understood where the line needed to be drawn. And so in September 2010, he introduced S. 3804, the Combating Online Infringement and Counterfeits Act. Like its more famous progeny, SOPA and PIPA, the 2010 act would be known and discussed forever after exclusively by its alien-sounding acronym, COICA.

And Leahy had developed a bit of media-ready shorthand for his solution to the paradox that had troubled him originally.

"The internet needs to be free — not lawless," he declared.[35]

★ ★ ★

As introduced, COICA was not an especially long bill, but it was extremely potent by design. Under its provisions, the attorney general would be empowered to pursue crippling injunctions against websites the Department of Justice determined to be "dedicated to infringing activities," further defined as being "primarily designed" or used to market copyrighted material. The bill laid out a process and a system of criteria by which a federal court might adjudicate the matter and, if the court agreed with the attorney general, order the domain name in question to be suspended or locked by the Internet registry in charge of it. In technical parlance, the service provider in question would be compelled to "prevent a domain name from resolving to that domain name's Internet protocol address"; practically speaking, the web address of the "rogue website" would simply cease to function, bringing up only an error message instead.

The pirate site would, in a very real sense, cease to exist.

As legal remedies go, such a shutdown order would have the dual advantages of being both immediate and complete. Entertainment industry executives, who insisted that their losses to global piracy ran into the billions, saw this new approach as an elegant solution to their perennial problem.

But it would not be putting too fine a point on it to say that digital rights activists were collectively aghast. In their reading, COICA would allow the government, for the first time, an effectual means of censoring the Internet, the ability to black out sites based purely on their content.[36]

But the tools available to the Justice Department in the proposed legislation didn't end there. US credit card companies would be prohibited from processing payments to the site in question. And Leahy's original bill also envisioned the creation of two public databases, one a list of domain names against which the Department of Justice had secured injunctions, and another a list of domain names the DOJ found highly suspect but against which it had *not* acted: "The Attorney General shall maintain a public listing of domain names that, upon information and reasonable belief, the Department of Justice determines are dedicated to infringing activities but for which the Attorney General has not filed an action under this section."

In other words, the Justice Department could take a certain amount of action without court approval. Clearly the idea was to allow the attorney general a means of graduated response to allegations of online piracy. Suspected piracy websites, and their domain registries, could be pressured to halt their "infringement" activities simply by being listed and duly notified. And of course the list was also meant to warn customers and potential commercial partners away from the "rogue" site.

But for digital rights activists, this last provision was almost more troubling than the court-approved shutdown of a website. It would create — in the instantly heated rhetoric of the controversy — a blacklist. And it would do so almost entirely outside the scope of due process.

Critics of the bill rapidly threw up a host of other objections. They pointed out that in its early days, YouTube had carried a great deal of unlicensed material — but that shutting it down in 2006 would have stifled the ensuing explosion of creativity and commercial innovation. A group of eighty-seven prominent Internet engineers argued that COICA would undermine and fragment the Internet's central domain name system and drive users to domain systems located elsewhere in the world.[37] And the bill's wording was said to be too vague to survive legal challenge.

But the vast majority of the controversy surrounding COICA would be reduced to two very blunt charges, both of which were unfailingly expressed as rhetorical nitroglycerine: Leahy's was a "censorship bill" that would all but end free speech online, and it would "create a blacklist" that would make Hollywood's own experience with blacklists pale by comparison.

In short, COICA would "break the internet."[38] And Leahy quickly found himself savagely caricatured — by longtime allies in Silicon Valley and online rights communities — as the madman wielding the sledgehammer.

He was stung, to say the least. Of course, this wasn't his first rodeo, by a good long shot. He wasn't naïve about the controversy that COICA would stir; he had known all along that it would be a real battle, and draw real blood. But he'd thought that, at the least, his opponents would acknowledge his own long-standing — even originary — support for and loyalty to the Internet. After all, in 1995 Leahy had been just the second senator to launch a Senate website (Ted Kennedy had beat him to the punch). In the mid-1990s, he had cofounded the Congressional Internet Caucus, a bipartisan group of House and Senate members dedicated to nurturing the new digital technologies; and he was regularly singled out for "Golden Mouse" awards by the Congressional Management Foundation, in recognition of his consistently early adoption of new technology.

For over a decade, reporters had been calling the tech-savvy Judiciary chairman "the cybersenator," and it was an image of himself that Leahy clearly loved, and which his staff touted whenever possible.[39]

In very much the same way that he had wholeheartedly embraced new campaign technologies during his long-shot 1974 Senate run — and overwhelmed his decidedly traditional opponent — Leahy had seen the Internet coming, and he had run with it. He had immediately incorporated Internet protection into his existing Senate repertoire as a constitutionalist, a passionate guardian of free speech.

In 1996, to take just one potent example, he had opposed the Communications Decency Act — which was trumpeted as a way to block access by children to sexually explicit websites — on free-speech grounds. Given the law's framing as child protection, Leahy was courting political disaster, but he stood his ground — and was "vindicated" in 1997 when the Supreme Court struck it down as unconstitutional. He refused to see the new medium hobbled, even in the name of shielding youth.

"I sent child molesters to prison. But I yield to nobody in the Senate on the First Amendment," he told the *New York Times*. "I am just not going to vote for a law that is so broadening that you could finish up closing down just about every library."[40]

The Internet *was* free speech, to Leahy. In fact, it was everything with which he had rapturously associated himself over the course of his political life — youth, popular culture, entertainment, economic expansion. And of course it was a profoundly visual medium, and in that way played directly into Leahy's complex, lifelong obsession with photography and film.

To suddenly be cast, on the strength of a what he saw as a few mischaracterized provisions in a single thirty-two-page bill, as Big Brother come to strangle the Net in its infancy — that could only hurt. But again, Leahy wasn't new to controversy, or to lawmaking. And so rather than lash out, and rather than sit pat with what might well develop into a losing hand, he did what senators do: he amended. And, shrewdly, Leahy waited until four days after the November midterm elections to file that amendment.

The "Manager's Amendment" to S. 3804 was a measured response to the criticism that had been leveled at the bill. That is to say, it eliminated the so-called "blacklist" provision that would have allowed the Department of Justice to list publicly the sites it suspected of piracy but which it had chosen not to pursue. But it did not eliminate the listing of those sites against which injunctions had been secured — and more crucially, it left in place the central procedures by which the attorney general could effectively remove from the web those sites "primarily dedicated" to infringement. Leahy felt it was as far as he could go without pulling all the bill's teeth.

And at least initially it seemed that the Manager's Amendment might thread the needle—Leahy's committee voted it out 19–0 less than two weeks later. Predictably, however, critics in the digital rights community were not mollified. Yes, the amendment lessened the concerns around "blacklisting," but it was still a "censorship bill" for all that.[41]

Ultimately, it would be Senator Ron Wyden of Oregon who would win the battle of rhetorical escalation—and manage to kill COICA by placing a Senate hold on it through the 2010 lame-duck session. The day after the amended COICA bill passed out of Judiciary, Wyden announced at a separate Senate trade hearing that he would "take the necessary steps" to make sure that COICA didn't pass the Senate.

"It seems to me that online copyright infringement is a legitimate problem," Wyden began, "but it seems to me that COICA as written is the wrong medicine. Deploying this statute to combat online copyright infringement seems almost like using a bunker-busting cluster bomb when what you really need is a precision-guided missile."[42]

And with Wyden's publicly announced hold, and time running out on the lame-duck legislative session, the so-called blacklisting bunker-busting Dark Ages–stepping censorship cluster bomb was effectively dead.

THE SEQUELS: *THE DARK KNIGHT RISES* AND THE PROTECT IP ACT

Leahy had been deftly and momentarily outmaneuvered, but certainly not beaten. As a thirty-five-year veteran of the Senate, he knew better than most that significant changes in the status quo usually require a campaign spanning years rather than months. COICA had been a bruising battle, not the war—and a battle in which the timing of the 2010 midterm elections had substantially empowered his opponents. The new 112th Congress would allow him maximum flexibility.

And Leahy was determined to fight the issue out again, all the way this time, because he was still convinced that the US economy (particularly the motion picture and recording industries) was directly threatened by Internet piracy. It was the sine qua non of his thinking on the subject: stealing was wrong, period, whether online or in three dimensions, and as a former prosecutor he was determined to address the rampant theft that had become almost casually accepted in the early twenty-first century.

While it's fair to say that Leahy, out of fear that innovation might inadvertently be stifled, had for a decade or more resisted calls for congressional intervention to prevent online piracy, he was now a firm believer that Congress had an obligation to act. And he had begun to tie that belief emphatically and methodically to his own core identity as a prosecutor — always a sign that he was all-in on an issue.

It wouldn't be any easier the second time out, of course. The battle over COICA had made it clear that he would be targeted, and brutally, by longtime allies in the free-speech and digital-rights communities. And they would be waiting for him to come forward with a new bill. But there it was.

If the rule of law was going to have any real meaning in the online world, Leahy strongly suggested, it would be because even longtime champions of Internet freedom saw that digital theft was out of control, and moved to end it. Only Nixon could go to China, in other words, and only Leahy and other strongly pro-Internet senators like Al Franken — who had made an early name for himself as an advocate of Net neutrality[43] — could make the case that the time to act on digital piracy was now.

And the COICA collapse hadn't been a total loss. In fact, the general push against piracy was already bearing fruit off Capitol Hill. The pressure of the controversy had brought Internet providers like AT&T, Comcast, Verizon, and Time Warner Cable to the table to hear the complaints of the entertainment industry directly, with the result that a voluntary deal seemed to be taking shape:

> The new procedure, which is expected to go into effect next year, is known as a graduated response, and establishes a series of six warnings that an Internet service provider, or I.S.P., can send a customer whose account shows signs of infringing activity.
>
> These warnings escalate from simple email notifications to a set of "mitigation measures," like slowed connections or a block from Web surfing altogether. As the steps progress, a user must acknowledge to his I.S.P. that he understands the notice, and the user can also contest the complaint.[44]

The voluntary agreement would also set up a clearinghouse called the Center for Copyright Information, designed to oversee the new system. Leahy watched the voluntary deal coming together through the spring of 2011 and thought it was fine, so far as it went. But he wasn't inclined to hold back a new version of COICA.

Or at least not entirely. With the voluntary agreement falling into place to help regulate the competing American interests, Leahy made the decision to direct his new bill entirely at "non-domestic infringing domains" —or in his personal shorthand, "foreign rogue websites." This time out, no one would be able to argue that his bill would lead to the shutdown of YouTube or Facebook or any other American site, large or small.

It was one of a number of concessions that Leahy and his drafters would make to the criticisms of COICA. They would also leave out the so-called blacklisting procedures. Under the new draft bill's procedures, the attorney general would first have to bring an infringement action against the individual operating a website—and only if that action proved unsuccessful could the Department of Justice then move against the domain name itself. In that way, due process would be strengthened.

So with these careful emendations in place, on May 12, 2011, Leahy, with eleven cosponsors, introduced the Preventing Real Online Threats to Economic Creativity and Theft of Intellectual Property Act, known quickly thereafter as PIPA.

But it's fair to say that critics saw PIPA as COICA reborn, a zombie bill in many ways more threatening than its predecessor. Not only did the new bill retain the process whereby the Department of Justice could effectively "disappear" a domain from the Internet, but PIPA made that disappearance total and complete. In addition to requiring that domain registries block the "rogue" domain from resolving, and that financial services companies refuse to process all transactions associated with it, search engines like Google and Internet advertising companies would now be required to eliminate the offending domain from their search results or client lists.

And while "foreign rogue sites" were the only ones targeted for actual shutdown, all these third parties would be drawn into the legal action, and shielded from legal risk themselves only if they complied rapidly and satisfactorily. Google or PayPal would be immune to a lawsuit from the infringing site itself, that is, but not from action by a Justice Department displeased with their level of cooperation.

PIPA also created a *private* right of action for copyright holders, allowing them a whole series of legal options under the act. *TechDirt* didn't mince words: "This is yet another case of regulatory capture, in which a private industry is being granted additional, extraordinary and unnecessary powers to stifle new technologies and innovation, because in their estimation it infringes on their copyrights. Remember the long list of new innovations that the entertainment industry has so deemed, including (but not limited to): player pianos, radio, cable TV, the photocopier, the VCR, the DVR, the MP3 player, YouTube, etc."[45]

And even though PIPA was specifically limited to nondomestic domains, technology writers for outlets like Techdirt, Wired, and Huffington Post still found the bill's definition of an "Internet site dedicated to infringing activities" hopelessly broad.

As with COICA, the draft of PIPA was immediately converted into the most explosive rhetorical sound bites, with subtlety sacrificed to impact. Critics charged that the new antipiracy bill was another censorship bill, and in particular its new potential restrictions on search engines amounted to the same sort of authoritarian government suppression that Google had once bowed to in Communist China.[46]

★ ★ ★

Leahy was determined to move the new bill forward with as much overwhelming institutional force behind it as he could muster. Ron Wyden had been his principal obstacle the last time out, and although Leahy very pointedly reached out to his COICA antagonist for suggestions on PIPA, he suspected that another hold might well be in the offing. No stranger to the hold process himself, Leahy knew that the best way to get a hold lifted quickly was to pressure the holder from within—to show that a strong majority of senators wanted a debate, if not a vote.

So immediately after introducing PIPA with eleven cosponsors, Leahy and advocates for the bill began an all-out push for public Senate backers. And all the while, the chairman was working to keep his committee members on board with the new iteration. As with COICA, Leahy would draw PIPA very smoothly through the Judiciary Committee, with Democrats and Republicans united. The new piracy bill, like the old, enjoyed unusual unanimous support from the committee.

Not only would it pass out of committee only two weeks after being introduced, but the May 26 executive business meeting discussion of it lasted less than ten minutes.

And that, pointedly enough, was the morning Wyden chose to publicly announce his hold on PIPA. As would be the case in the online community at large, Wyden noted none of the changes meant to make the bill more palatable, focusing instead on the newer features that had provoked even stronger concerns.

"In December of last year I placed a hold on similar legislation, commonly called COICA," Wyden announced on his Senate website, "because I felt the costs of the legislation far outweighed the benefits. After careful analysis of the Protect IP Act, or PIPA, I am compelled to draw the same conclusion. I understand and agree with the goal of the legislation, to protect intellectual property and combat commerce in counterfeit goods, but I am not willing to muzzle speech and stifle innovation and economic growth to achieve this objective."[47]

It was a direct broadside, but of course Leahy had seen Wyden's hold coming, and he prepared his committee's July 22 report in part to parry these latest charges from the Oregon senator. Drawing search engine operators and online advertisers under the bill's injunction process—in addition to financial processors—was absolutely critical, Leahy argued, in order to counter the elaborate façade of legitimacy created by the foreign rogue sites. Such sites "are easily accessible by entering domain names that sound legitimate into the users' search engines; they often accept payment through well respected credit card companies; and they often run advertisements from trusted companies. All of this presents an appearance of legitimacy to the virtual store. . . . In many cases, American consumers may unwittingly be giving their credit card information to overseas organized crime syndicates when visiting rogue Internet sites."

PIPA's critics might choose to stress the dangers of Big Government; the July Judiciary report countered by painting the dangers of Big (foreign) Crime. National security, the report stated bluntly, was directly threatened by the same organized crime syndicates targeted by PIPA.[48]

Leahy had seen COICA fall in part because the opposition had been willing to escalate the rhetorical fight quickly and decisively, and such escalation went more or less unanswered. He wouldn't make that same mistake twice.

As summer came to a close, Leahy was pursuing his strategy of overwhelming institutional force. Along with the unanimous, bipartisan vote out of Judiciary, his push for cosponsorship was bearing real fruit: by December, the number of official cosponsors would reach forty-one, an overwhelming vote of confidence in the bill's future. Wyden's hold was in place, but Leahy was in communication and offering tweaks to the bill that might bring the Oregon senator on board—or at least mollify him enough to lift the hold and allow debate. And Leahy knew that a companion bill was coming forward in the House, which would significantly increase the momentum for some sort of final compromise.

But the overworked Judiciary chairman also had a secret, a secret he very much meant to keep this time out.

The Bat Signal was in the sky again.

★ ★ ★

The telephone call had come from England, months before. It was Christopher Nolan's wife and coproducer Emma Thomas, wondering what dates Leahy might be available to shoot a cameo for the third and final installment of her husband's *Dark Knight* trilogy.

Given that this was the first indication that there might be a part for him in *The Dark Knight Rises*, Leahy was briefly flustered. "What dates?" he repeated.

"Well, you did such a good job in the last one," Thomas went on smoothly, "of course we want you again."[49]

The date turned out to be the first weekend in September, and the location was Los Angeles, with temperatures in the eighties, a challenge given that some of the scenes on the docket required snow and heavy winter costuming. But the heat couldn't dampen Leahy's spirits. He lived for the movies, always had.

As had become his habit over the years, Leahy paid his own expenses to LA, but the smoothly functioning production machine took him in hand at touchdown. As it turned out, the City of Angels was only one of eleven cities on three continents to be used for principal photography; clearly *The Dark Knight Rises* would be a much different affair from Nolan's brooding, Chicago-centric *Dark Knight*. Gotham itself would be mostly pieced together using Pittsburgh, New York, and LA, the latter partially because it had become the director's home and offered plenty of open streets and canals for the exterior chases and shootouts.

Escalation, the scriptwriters' theme for the second film in the trilogy, had now morphed into the unabashedly "epic" for the final installment: "The third film's emerging themes and story lines suggested another genre shift: neither hero's journey nor crime drama, *The Dark Knight Rises* would encompass the tone and wide-scale destruction of an epic disaster movie or war film."

The phrase "epic disaster movie" was writer Jonathan Nolan's, but he was quick to add, "hopefully without losing any of the emotional heart."[50]

And although Leahy saw some of the larger, more far-flung sequences being filmed during his weekend in Los Angeles, his own short scene was of the more emotional and focused sort. This time out, Leahy was slated to play a scene in which Bruce Wayne is forced off the board of directors of Wayne Enterprises by rival John Daggett. Daggett is fronting for the film's central villain, an unstoppable mercenary named Bane with a unholy mission to incinerate Gotham City.

"Board Member #2," Leahy's unnamed character, is a loyal supporter of Wayne's who angrily opposes Wayne's ouster, and in that way Leahy's character in the third Nolan film more or less reprises his role in the second, giving his character a certain continuity through the trilogy. (In a similar way Nolan's uncle, British actor John Nolan, would be reprising his own role as Douglas Fredericks from *Batman Begins*. The Nolans favored such continuity, and it added to the familiar — even familial — atmosphere on set.)

The boardroom scene would be shot in downtown LA, at 550 South Hope, on the ninth floor of the California Bank & Trust Building. The existing conference room had already been adapted to resemble the severe-chic boardroom from Chicago's AMA Plaza, used four years earlier in *The Dark Knight*.

This was a vastly different shoot from Leahy's last, different in fact from any he had done previously. Those three previous shoots had all been part of a party scene in their respective films, the typical place to drop in a celebrity cameo. Party scenes allow for more ad lib and less unrelenting focus on an amateur — easier for director and visiting actor both. But while still an ensemble, this boardroom scene was far tighter in its focus, and more intimate in terms of cast.

The shot contained thirty actors, with fourteen seated down either side of a long glass conference table and Morgan Freeman and Christian Bale standing and facing one another at opposite ends. The blocking was interesting: Leahy found himself seated seven seats down, just at the center of the scene, with his back to the camera as the point of view follows Bale into the room. John Nolan was seated next to Leahy, with John Daggett (played by Australian actor Ben Mendelsohn) directly across the glass.

The placement allowed a tight two-shot when Nolan and Leahy were called upon to rise to Bruce Wayne's defense, and it also promoted a sense of direct confrontation between Leahy and Daggett — very much in the spirit of Leahy's challenge to the Joker in *The Dark Knight*.

There was no deliberation over how Leahy should deliver his single line this time out. Board Member #2 was angry. Period.

And certainly Leahy was far more at home seated and barking at an antagonist across what might easily have been a Judiciary Committee conference table. The exchange was designed to be charged, but repressed and ultimately controlled, particularly compared to the Ledger-inspired mayhem of Leahy's last film shoot.

> LUCIUS FOX: All right, ladies and gentlemen. This meeting will now come to order.
> JOHN DAGGETT: Now, I'd like to point out that we have a non-board member here [referring to Bruce Wayne]. Which is highly irregular, even if his family name is above the door.
> DOUGLAS FREDERICKS: Bruce Wayne's family built this company.
> BOARD MEMBER #2: [Stabbing finger at Daggett] And he himself has run it—
> JOHN DAGGETT: —into the *ground*, sir.

While the afternoon shoot was different in feel and tenor from the late-night party atmosphere of *The Dark Knight*, there was no less of Hollywood for Leahy to savor. He spent the time before, during, and after the actual filming chatting and drinking it in. He found Morgan Freeman charming and "very down to earth, but intense" once the lights were on. Like Heath Ledger and Christian Bale, Freeman seemed able to turn his character on and off like a switch.

But Leahy actually found himself spending as much or more time with the cameramen and the various still photographers working the shoots he visited that weekend, talking shop. To a person, they were all happy to answer his questions and to pass on some of the tricks of their trade.

As always, the quick dip into Hollywood was bracing, and Leahy savored every minute of it. But there was a sense of parting, as well. There might well be more Batman movies to come, involving other directors and other casts and crews—but Nolan had made it clear that *The Dark Knight Rises* was the last hurrah for this particular extended family. Other successful directors had found ingenious ways to extend a trilogy forward into more sequels, or backward into several prequels, but for Christopher Nolan, it seemed, a trilogy was three movies and no more.

On Sunday Leahy returned to Washington, with no one the wiser but his own inner circle. With *The Dark Knight*, he had let the secret of his cameo slip a year before the premiere, which hadn't mattered ultimately; in fact, it had contributed in a small way to the Ledger-centric buzz already building around the film. But with the legislative and media battles around the Protect IP Act now fully joined, Leahy had no intention of letting the cat out of the bag this time. He well knew that opponents of the bill were looking for anything to use as a cudgel against it.

What PIPA's sponsor didn't know, and wouldn't find out for several months yet, was that those same opponents were keeping certain epic secrets of their own.

★ ★ ★

On November 9, 2011, a relatively small group met for a brown-bag lunch discussion in the Mountain View, California, offices of Mozilla, producer of the popular open-source web browser Firefox. Mozilla's open meeting space was designed to be relaxing rather than imposing, featuring plush comfy couches and recliners, and the thirty-odd people who attended were notably on the younger and less formal end of the professional spectrum.

But as with most Silicon Valley gatherings, this one was deceptively casual.

Among the group were key congressional staffers, well-placed employees at Google and other top Internet firms, and "individuals from non-profits in the Internet space including Demand Progress, Center for Democracy and Technology, Public Knowledge, EFF [Electronic Frontier Foundation], Fight for the Future, and the Stanford Center for Internet and Society."[51]

To the more practiced eye, the assembled represented a critical mass of extremely well-connected high-tech and public-advocacy activists. To a person, they were true believers: the Internet must remain free, and SOPA/PIPA both courted censorship.

A Mozilla vice president, Harvey Anderson, cohosted the meeting with Elizabeth Stark, a Stanford Law School student allied with Fight for the Future. Fight for the Future had recently enjoyed big success in attacking another antipiracy bill, Senator Amy Klobuchar's Commercial Felony Streaming Act (CFSA); the group had used Justin Bieber, whose career began by covering other stars' copyrighted material on YouTube, to make the case that CFSA would stifle creativity and commerce. And their "Free Bieber" campaign (complete with web page depicting a sad Bieber behind bars) ultimately generated hundreds of thousands of signatures on petitions to scotch Klobuchar's bipartisan anti-streaming bill.[52]

Discussion at the Mozilla meeting focused largely on a new companion bill to Leahy's PIPA—the Stop Online Piracy Act, or SOPA, which had been introduced in the US House just two weeks earlier. SOPA was, in many ways, more alarming to Internet activists than PIPA. In their eyes, SOPA was PIPA on steroids, containing all the negatives of Leahy's bill and adding a few more for good measure.

SOPA went further in terms of defining creative activity as infringement, making it more likely that a YouTube mash-up of popular songs, say, would be legally actionable, and increasing liability risk for tech companies. "It lowers the barriers to who can be considered liable for IP theft, saying that sites that don't do enough to prevent piracy—such as search engines—can also be held liable for infringement."[53]

The dramatic high point of the meeting came when the DC staffers made it amply clear that barring serious and dramatic opposition, SOPA and PIPA would indeed pass out of Congress and into the hands of a White House that seemed inclined to support a version of the bill. As with PIPA, SOPA had broad bipartisan support and over thirty cosponsors. This was not a drill, a staffer for Representative Zoe Lofgren stressed. Unlike COICA, SOPA/PIPA seemed sufficiently powerful to become law, and that within a few months' time.

The air went briefly out of the room. "There was a real sense of gravity, people realized this was an all-hands-on-deck moment."[54]

And that was when the Fight for the Future contingent floated what amounted to the high-tech nuclear option: a blackout of the web's most popular and ubiquitous sites—sites like Google and Mozilla and YouTube. The idea was a day of collective online action, to be called American Censorship Day.

As Fight for the Future's Tiffiniy Cheng and Holmes Wilson envisioned it, normal users going to Google on this day of action wouldn't see the familiar primary colors of Google's logo—instead they would see a black page with a notice about the censorship dangers of SOPA and PIPA.[55] And the activists proposed a head-spinning timeline: going forward with American Censorship Day in just one week's time.

Needless to say, those attending from tech supergiants like Google were intrigued but very much noncommittal; they needed to take the idea back to their organizations and make their own pitches. Could all commerce be ceased for a day without massive complications? Would a rushed or failed protest set back the cause?

Eventually, the brown-bag group on the comfy couches at Mozilla considered an option less dramatic than a day of complete darkness—that of encouraging companies to participate in American Censorship Day to the extent they felt comfortable doing so, with some ceasing operations and others engaging in smaller but helpful actions, like blacking out their familiar logos or supplying a contact-Congress tool.

The meeting ended on an equivocal note. It simply wasn't clear how many of the larger organizations and companies were prepared to buy in so completely and so quickly. But the Fight for the Future activists were determined to press the issue, and they quickly lined up all the nonprofits they had targeted.

And by the weekend, Mozilla had come through. Harvey Anderson had managed to persuade Mozilla's top management, in record time. After all, this was Silicon Valley, where being nimble was a necessity.

With dizzying swiftness, American Censorship Day ballooned in scale. Joining Mozilla were Reddit, Boing Boing, Techdirt, and finally Tumblr — all sites capable of sending vast amounts of web traffic to Fight for the Future's carefully designed SOPA/PIPA protest site. All carried a dramatic censorship graphic.

And while Google, Facebook, and other Internet giants didn't black out their operations on November 16, they did send a joint letter to Congress, a letter they also published together in full-page ads in the country's largest daily newspapers.[56]

The result exceeded the activists' wildest dreams. Depending on the pundit, it was the New Economy facing off against the Old Economy, New Media like YouTube battling Old Media like Hollywood and the recording industry. The most cynical read was that the fight was really between the lawyers and DC lobbyists recently acquired by high-tech powerhouses, attacking K Street, the longtime home of comfortable, well-established DC lobbying firms. Or a California subway series, between Hollywood and Silicon Valley.

But no matter how one characterized the combatants, Armageddon had begun. Of that there was no doubt.

★ ★ ★

By early January 2012, the drive to kill what critics now almost universally referred to as SOPA/PIPA was still gaining palpable momentum. Wyden had been unmoved by Leahy's attempts to address his concerns in the legislation, and the coalition that had come together on American Censorship Day was growing daily. The most intense spotlight had moved to the White House, where two We the People petitions on whitehouse.gov had very quickly garnered more than fifty thousand signatures each, asking Obama to veto the bills should they pass.[57] It was clear that the administration was deeply uncomfortable with critics' strident comparison of SOPA/PIPA to the sort of authoritarian control over information practiced in Iran and China. A response to the We the People petitions was said to be in the offing.

And opposition to the bill back home in Vermont was reaching a boil as well. Leahy appeared on Vermont Public Radio's noontime call-in program, *Vermont Edition*, on January 12, and it was clear from host Jane Lindholm's summary of her mail on the topic that Fight for the Future's campaign had taken firm hold in the state.

By this point, Leahy's response was all but automatic. And it was deliberately stripped down to its barest, least objectionable elements:

> Partly [PIPA] comes from my own predilections as a former prosecutor — I've always felt that *stealing* something should be against the law. And if people *steal* things . . . where they get the money online, that should be *stopped*, or whether it's out of a bricks-and-mortar store on Main Street. But it's worse than that — we have counterfeit drugs. . . . Some of it can be traced back to organized crime, and you have somebody who buys drugs online for their heart condition, or their child's illness, and they bought a counterfeit drug, and their child *dies*, or they die — that should be stopped. I think most people agree with this. I think if you steal something, you should not be able to make money out of stealing. We all agree on that.[58]

Of course, Leahy's attempt to frame the subject in terms of universal agreement (stealing is wrong, kids dying is tragic) also purposefully avoided the contentious parts of the bill. But in the same way that opponents of the bill had jettisoned subtlety and focused on a worst-case reading of the bills, Leahy seemed clearly out to make stark, elemental points to the Vermonters listening.

PIPA had brought both sides of the aisle together as few other bills had, he insisted. "Now I've had numerous hearings on this bill. We've twice marked it up in the Senate Judiciary Committee, where every Republican and every Democrat voted for it, and now it's going to come up to a vote." Both the Chamber of Commerce and organized labor strongly supported the bill — something else that only happens once in a blue moon.

It was, again, the institutional argument: the Senate overwhelmingly liked the bill, Republicans and Democrats, as did a host of traditional constituencies, and two years of hearings had given the bills a very thorough airing. The process had been robust. Now a debate and a vote would decide the issue.

But Leahy well knew that stressing the dangers to children or the agreement between the Chamber and labor was not the way to appease the online revolutionaries. For that, he would have to concede something, and it would have to be something valuable. It was the same move he had made late on COICA, a manager's amendment designed to disarm the opposition. But in this case, rather than jettisoning a minor element, Leahy clearly felt the need to cast off some serious ballast. He told Lindholm: "There is one concern that's been expressed by Senator Wyden and others, one major concern, on the domain name provisions. That I've been meeting [on] with people throughout the time I've been home, and my staff has been meeting with them in Washington. . . . I've authorized my staff to tell those other senators that I am willing to hold that back in the final piece of legislation, in the Manager's package, which would hold that back, give us more time to study it, so we can focus on the others. That in itself will remove a lot of the opposition that we now have."[59]

As potential concessions go, this was major. The basic objections to the domain registry provision—that forcing registries in the United States to lock out a range of addresses would make foreign registries more attractive and thus change the current architecture of the Internet—had been one of critics' strongest tools since the COICA debate.

But the scope of Leahy's public concession speaks directly to the pressure PIPA faced by mid-January, and the chair of Judiciary may well have known more about the bill's increasingly gloomy prospects than was then being reported in the media. The vote on PIPA was scheduled for January 24, just twelve days hence, and Leahy's unexpectedly large olive branch suggests that a cancellation of the vote may already have begun to loom as a possibility.

Of course, the prospective sop to critics raised another series of questions: since requiring that registries freeze out rogue websites was the central enforcement provision of both COICA and PIPA, how would it then achieve its basic goals? And if domain registries would be able to continue working with "rogue" infringing websites, why would search engines and advertising companies still be forced to drop them, and remain liable if they didn't?

These questions, and others like them, Leahy implored the Senate to leave to the amendment process. And then, just before Lindholm redirected the interview, Leahy previewed his final line of argument. Venting his frustration with those who said they hadn't known about the bill until recently, Leahy insisted that "for two *years* we've had information out there. . . . Certainly some of the companies like Google knew about it, because they spent tens of millions of dollars on K Street lobbyists in Washington."

This sharp, preemptive attack on Google's credibility might have seemed to come out of nowhere to a Vermonter listening in on January 12. After all, Google hadn't blacked its website out on American Censorship Day the previous November; rather, the company had contented itself with a sternly worded letter.

But as Leahy seemed to be hinting, that was about to change, dramatically. And in less than one week.

★ ★ ★

The White House finally weighed in on the controversy on January 14, but given what was to happen on January 18, even the president's considered opinion on the matter seemed suddenly dwarfed in scale.[60] Fight for the Future and the other groups that had constructed American Censorship Day were back, and together they were pushing hard for a sequel to the original SOPA/PIPA blackout protest, this one fully global in scale. Many of the web's largest and most beloved companies were already firmly on board.

And when Google finally announced publicly on the seventeenth that it would be participating in the protest the next day, the last piece fell into place. Suddenly Leahy's willingness to trade away PIPA's central enforcement mechanism made perfect sense. His personal intelligence sources, always excellent, couldn't have missed the approach of a storm this massive.

The January 18 Internet blackout was the biggest online protest ever. Over 115,000 websites participated in the blackout, including Google, Wikipedia, Craigslist, Reddit, Tumblr, and WordPress. Facebook, the second-most visited site in the United States, did not use its social network in the protest, but its CEO Mark Zuckerberg issued a statement against SOPA and PIPA on his Facebook page, which had nearly sixteen million followers.[61]

While Google opted to block out its logo and to link to an anti-SOPA/ PIPA petition but otherwise allow searching to continue unimpeded, Wikipedia went entirely dark and let its users—162 million of them— know exactly why the site was unavailable.

The results were—quite literally—like nothing the world has ever seen.

Google alone secured over seven million signatures to its petition. Another four million e-mails were directed through the websites of the Electronic Frontier Foundation, Fight for the Future, and Demand Progress. Social media erupted, and the SOPA/PIPA controversy thrust most every other subject aside. Twitter in particular fomented the uprising. Tweets by celebrities like Ashton Kutcher and Kim Kardashian drew in tens of millions of younger Americans who might otherwise have remained blissfully unaware of Congress's workings. Senator Wyden later told the *New York Times* that "lawmakers had collected more than 14 million names—more than 10 million of them voters."

And the deluge of digital outrage fueled an impressive amount of impromptu old-school activism as well: protests broke out in major (mostly left-leaning) cities, and telephone calls flooded into the offices of senators and representatives.[62]

Predictably enough, support for the bill drained away within hours. Ten Senate cosponsors abruptly reversed alliances, and by day's end nineteen total had expressed opposition. Within twenty-four hours, 122 members of the House of Representatives had suddenly joined the opposition. Republicans in particular immediately saw the dangers of being associated with SOPA/PIPA, and the political advantage to be had in opposing it.[63]

And before the day was out, "the opposition turned illegal . . . when the online hacker group Anonymous brought down the Justice Department's Web site." Major portions of the Internet were executing a vast, collective, angry spasm, and as January 19 came to an end, no one knew precisely where it would end.[64]

Leahy, who was less than a week out from the Senate debate on PIPA, pushed back as hard as he was able. Again he took to the Vermont Public Radio airwaves to make his case, but it was clear that the massive protest—and his implicit framing as villain—had gotten under his skin. His tone was much sharper and less avuncular than was his wont when addressing a hometown media outlet.

Mitch Wertlieb's introduction made clear that Vermont's senior senator was not amused. "Yesterday the wildly popular online encyclopedia site Wikipedia went black, to protest the Protect IP Act, known as PIPA. . . . Senator Patrick Leahy introduced PIPA in the Senate, and we caught up with him yesterday morning to get his thoughts. The Senator was, to say the least, unimpressed with the self-imposed blackout by Wikipedia."[65]

"Unimpressed" would be one way to phrase it; another would be to say that Leahy was genuinely peeved. He had seen the erosion of support in the Senate, and as with the COICA debate, he believed the facts were being misrepresented to protect the financial interests of the Internet giants. When Wertlieb asked about Google's position, Leahy pounced: "I think they [Google] just paid, what was it, five hundred million dollars to settle the fact that they had these counterfeit drugs being sold online, which hurt a lot of people's health. They're making billions and billions of dollars from these people who are selling counterfeit goods, selling stolen goods, on their search engines."

Leahy had been too long in the business to let his irritation get the better of him during a broadcast. But like it or not, he found himself essentially back in campaign mode, and he had always been strong when it came to staying on message, bringing the heat again and again. And now, with Google and others so blatantly on the attack, it wasn't a question but that fire had to be returned.

When asked if he would be open to more direct negotiations with the alliance of companies that had powered the January 18 blackout protest, Leahy deftly maneuvered around to the Google attack again, driving it home: "You know, we asked Google and others to testify—we had a whole lot of hearings on this—and it was *beneath* them to come and testify, they didn't want to bother. Now they are actually starting to talk with us. . . . Maybe the five hundred million dollar fine they paid attracted their attention."

And he was adamant that the vote would go on. "Oh yeah, Tuesday. I'm flying back to Washington tomorrow, we're going to meet all weekend long on this. I'm open to any suggestion. . . . Let's have a real honest debate."

But the fact that the vote was being openly questioned, even by local media outlets, was in a sense its own answer.

It was a performance designed to hold the dam for a few days at most. But outside of the tight focus of Leahy's staff and the Judiciary Committee, the popular protest continued to spread. The ferocious 2012 GOP presidential primary was still under way, for instance, and one by one the Republican hopefuls publicly lambasted the bills (it was an added bonus that Leahy had long been a bête noir for the Right).

A GOP debate hosted by CNN in Charleston, South Carolina, on January 19 took up the SOPA/PIPA issue directly. Newt Gingrich didn't mince words, and as someone who had personally dueled with Leahy as Speaker of the House, he seemed to relish not mincing them. "The bill in its current form is written really badly and leads to a range of censorship that is totally unacceptable. Well, I favor freedom."[66]

Mitt Romney, who had spent the bulk of the debate trading savage thrusts with Gingrich, more or less mirrored the former Speaker's response, ending with, "And so I'd say, No, I'm standing for freedom."

And Ron Paul, who had spent the night being more or less ignored at the far end of the stage, suddenly had his moment: "I was the first Republican to sign on with a host of Democrats to oppose this law—" Paul was cut off by the crowd's enthusiastic response, intriguing given that it was really the only instance during the debate when a candidate highlighted, rather than downplayed, his work with Democrats. It was the one issue all night that seemed both to electrify and to unify the fractious GOP audience in Charleston.

And that, perhaps, was the political straw that broke the camel's back.

The next morning, word came early: Senate Majority Leader Harry Reid effectively pulled the plug on PIPA, and the House quickly followed suit with SOPA. Significantly, Reid announced the indeterminate delay of the vote in a tweet, the medium used to foment and focus so much of the resistance over the last seventy-two hours.[67]

It was clear that Democrats in general, and Leahy specifically, had digital fences to mend, regardless of whose reading of the bills one preferred. The political damage was real, and widespread.

Still, Leahy was not yet ready to let bygones be bygones. PIPA represented five years' worth of very hard work, and whatever its flaws, he genuinely believed that it would stop the drain of American profits into the bank accounts of foreign copyright pirates. There was a bitter edge to the statement his office released hours after Reid's stand-down order. "The day will come when the senators who forced this move will look back and realize they made a knee-jerk reaction to a monumental problem. . . . Somewhere in China today, in Russia today, and in many other countries that do not respect American intellectual property, criminals who do nothing but peddle in counterfeit products and stolen American content are smugly watching how the United States Senate decided it was not even worth debating how to stop the overseas criminals from draining our economy."[68]

But a few days later, on January 23, Leahy used a nearly empty Senate chamber and the nomination of a US district judge from Nebraska to deliver a final word on PIPA in an entirely different key. His tone seemed now authentically more in sorrow than in anger, and there was an almost elegiac quality to the lines. The ordinarily authoritative chairman seemed regretful, though he clearly continued to see the demise of the antipiracy effort as driven by a deliberate misreading of the bill rather than fully honest concern. It was a statement full of considered pauses, almost wistful at certain points.

> Now I've remained flexible on this. I've listened to people both for and against the legislation, made changes in it along the lines suggested by others, such as Senator Wyden. I took seriously the concerns about the domain names system provisions, said we would fix that in the manager's amendment. So I regret that we're not going to go forward with it this week. I regret that so much misinformation has stopped it. I thank Majority Leader Reid for trying to schedule debate on this serious economic threat. And I understand that, when the Republican leader recently objected, and a number of senators who'd cosponsored and long supported the effort jumped ship, he was faced with a difficult decision. And I understand as leader, he did what he had to do. But I hope after a delay, we can come back together and work on this.[69]

Of course, 2012 was a presidential election year, and realistically the chances for resurrecting an antipiracy bill in the months before the hotly contested vote were slim to none. No one wanted to risk waking the Internet dragons again, now that the world had seen the widespread havoc they were capable of wreaking.

And of course 2012 would be notable for another reason: the July release of *The Dark Knight Rises*, the much-anticipated final blockbuster in Christopher Nolan's Batman trilogy.

★ ★ ★

Unlike his appearance alongside the late Heath Ledger, Leahy's final cameo for Christopher Nolan had remained a well-kept secret. Only on the eve of the Fourth of July, 2012—just two weeks before the US opening of *The Dark Knight Rises*—was the Associated Press offered the news. And almost immediately, the AP snippet (which mentioned only that Senator Patrick Leahy would be playing a scene with Christian Bale and Morgan Freeman) began to crop up in newspapers around the country, framed with the predictable puns and joking references to Batmobiles, Robin, and evil villains in tights.

But not everyone was content to joke this time around. Just months before, the coalition against SOPA/PIPA had raised what amounted to a massive army, most of it in the scant space of a few days. And that army —composed of Internet activists, privacy and Net neutrality advocates, bloggers, and social media habitués—had never disbanded; it couldn't disband, really, any more than it could be said to have formally assembled. It continued to exist as a massive and far-flung network of links, contacts, and websites, powered by the sorts of powerful and often aggressive emotions and personalities that dominate the web.

And that network was watching to make sure that SOPA and PIPA died childless.

Within days of the AP story, Demand Progress (one of the larger sponsors of the January 18 blackout protest) had created HolyConflictOfInterest .com, a page devoted exclusively to protesting Leahy's long-standing and ongoing connections with Time Warner, owners of the Batman franchise and Nolan's reboot of it. What drew the eye immediately was a technicolor six-panel graphic, designed to look like an actual page from a 1970s-era Batman comic book.

A screamer headline reads, "The Adventures of LEAHY & TIME WARNER." A dialogue between Batman and his disillusioned ward makes up most of the text:

ROBIN: Holy Conflict of Interest, Batman!
BATMAN: I know, Robin. It's hard to stomach. . . . His name is Patrick Leahy, Chairman of the powerful Senate Judiciary Committee. He rakes in a ridiculous amount of cash from Hollywood and sponsors Internet censorship bills on their behalf. . . . But the icing on the cake is that the Hollywood moguls feed his ego by letting him appear in summer blockbusters—like *The Dark Knight*!

At that point a panel depicts the Joker threatening a terrified-looking Leahy with a knife—an actual still from Leahy's *Dark Knight* cameo. The Joker demands, "Censor the 'Net, Leahy—or you won't be gettin' a stupid cameo in the next Batman movie!"

And the narrator finishes the piece by advising readers that "Batman and Robin are too put off to help, so it's up to you to tell Leahy and Congress to stop shilling for Hollywood by censoring the Internet."

HolyConflictOfInterest.com offered visitors to its homepage the most poisonous caricature of Leahy available—that he was tyrannically powerful and openly corrupt yet also somehow a weak, hopeless egotist in thrall to the suits at Time Warner—and in that way it expanded upon some of the scorched-earth tactics that had finally killed SOPA and PIPA. Demand Progress had seen the way that the media were drawn to Leahy's Batman obsession; the caped crusader and Leahy's loyalty to him were absolute catnip for reporters, when the pairing surfaced every few years, and it had long been a staple of Leahy's own public relations operation.

Leahy's antagonists were now shrewdly looking to turn that raw pop-cultural power to their own political advantage.

And in the wake of the historic January 18 Internet blackout protest, Demand Progress's Batman-themed attack bore immediate fruit. Many of the newspapers and websites that had duly carried the human-interest news of Leahy's cameos in *The Dark Knight* and *The Dark Knight Rises* now seemed more than happy to offer their readers a delicious comic-book twist: Batman's biggest fan in the Senate—the venerable Vermonter who donated his silver-screen royalties to his childhood library—was now being openly accused of leading a double life of self-serving corruption.

Leahy was used to attacks from the right-wing media; he had been their poster child for liberal politics for decades. But this was criticism across the ideological spectrum.

Even deep-blue sites like the *Huffington Post* gave the story serious play. Local Vermont reporters ran with it as well. The coverage was still replete with puns, but all the jokes now cut the other way. "US Sen. Patrick Leahy's cameo in the forthcoming *The Dark Knight Rises* is shining a bat-signal-sized spotlight on the senator's coziness with Hollywood," wrote Andy Bromage for *Seven Days*, Vermont's largest arts weekly, in a column titled "Holy Slamming-Leahy's-Ties-to-Hollywood-and-Batman, Batman!"[70] The previous week's column had skeptically detailed the donations Time Warner had made to Leahy over the years.[71]

As in 2008 with *The Dark Knight*, the final installment of Nolan's acclaimed trilogy would premier in Vermont—Williston, Vermont, this time out, to allow a larger local audience to attend a sneak preview a full day ahead of the New York City premier, and five full days before the rest of the world.

Again, Warner Bros. CEO Barry Meyer was in attendance, and he headlined a closed donor reception, with tickets ranging up to $1,000 per attendee. (Oscar's Bistro, a small restaurant off the theater's main lobby, had been made over into Wayne Manor, complete with "VIP entrance overseen by tuxedo-clad theater employee Tyler Bradley—a dead ringer for Batman's faithful butler Alfred Pennyworth."[72]) Again, proceeds would benefit the Kellogg-Hubbard Library. In fact, perhaps in keeping with Nolan's movement from "escalation" to "epic," Leahy had upped the stakes considerably: the fund-raising around the special premiere would benefit two of Leahy's favorite charities, his childhood library and the Echo Aquarium / Leahy Center for Lake Champlain. Over $120,000 would eventually be raised.

It was an eye-popping display, by Vermont standards, of star power, of philanthropy, of sheer raw influence. And in another moment, it might have been treated as pure divertissement, a windfall for two of the state's deserving causes and nothing more. But the Demand Progress attack on Leahy—simplistic, harsh, and compressed into vivid image—had touched off a flurry of news- and web-based commentary on Leahy's long-standing ties with Hollywood.[73]

It had become, in a word, a meme, the transmission of which was powered by the very same digital medium that Leahy had so faithfully protected and boosted and nurtured in its infancy. It was one more power of the Internet dragons, every bit as unsettling as the ability to raise an army of millions in a matter of hours.

By and large, Leahy let his office handle the spate of questions from the press, but the *Daily Caller* did manage to get a short response outside the Senate chamber a few days after the premiere. Leahy shook his head firmly and "brushed off the suggestion" that there was anything inappropriate in his collaborations with Warner Bros. "No, it's not a gift from the film industry," he maintained. "It's a *huge* gift to the children's library in Montpelier, Vermont."[74]

But there was no denying that if the realities of the issue were complex, the political optics of it were egregious. And for Patrick Leahy, optics— the visual, the framed shot, the supremely focused political image—had been his long suit since his wunderkind days as Chittenden County's youngest state's attorney. The ironies were multiple, and painful.

Although his "Top Cop" performance for Nolan's camera in 2007 had taken Leahy's image-making to a global audience, it was equally clear that the forces in play at that level were titanic in scale and impossible to control. It was no accident that Demand Progress had isolated and repurposed the key still from Leahy's *Dark Knight* performance. As an icon of Leahy's alliance with creative forces of established institutional power, it made an ideal fetish for the invocation of their nemeses.

In a certain way, it was all very Batman: not unlike Harvey Dent, another rising-star prosecutor, Leahy would survive the attack meant to disfigure him, but with his image at least temporarily doubled, two-faced.

But the spotlight moved on, of course. It turned out there was more than enough controversy elsewhere surrounding *The Dark Knight Rises* to feed even the voracious appetites of the twenty-first-century entertainment/media complex. Nolan's final film suddenly seemed to mean everything to everyone everywhere. On July 17, Rush Limbaugh floated the theory that Bane, Nolan's villain, had been so named to hobble GOP presidential nominee Mitt Romney, given that Romney was running in part on his success running Bain Capital. *Rolling Stone*, and many others, wondered aloud whether the behavior of the mercenaries who take over Gotham was a thinly veiled jab at the Occupy Wall Street movement. And on July 20, a deranged shooter named James Eagan Holmes, hair dyed to resemble the Joker, shot and killed twelve people at the midnight sneak preview of the film in Aurora, Colorado. Holmes "was dressed in black and wearing a ballistic helmet and vest, ballistic leggings, throat and groin protector and gas mask and black tactical gloves" and "armed with three weapons." Spenser Sherman, one of those trapped in the theater, later told CBS News, "I thought it was part of the movie, like a fun little prank."[75]

★ ★ ★

It was a strange, turbulent year, and it finished on a strange, turbulent note: the ailing eighty-eight-year-old Hawaiian senator Daniel Inouye died suddenly, owing to respiratory complications. It was the passing of an era. And with that passing, Leahy found himself suddenly the longest-serving senator in the Senate chamber, the only member of the 1974 post-Watergate class still in office.

And so on Tuesday morning, December 18, 2012, Patrick Joseph Leahy slowly walked past Inouye's desk on the Senate floor—covered with a black drape and a dozen white roses, as per tradition—and received the oath as Senate president pro tempore from Vice President Joe Biden.

It was a profoundly emotional moment, involving a lifelong friend and colleague, as well as the sober workings of the institution to which Leahy had devoted his life. It all spoke very deeply to the kid from Montpelier who had shocked his state and himself by leaping into the Senate nearly forty years previously.

"'I can't tell you how much it pains me. . . . Senator Inouye's story is one of great passion for his people,' Leahy said, pausing to hold back tears, before adding, 'Commitment to his calling in public service and dedication to finding a better way forward for all Americans. A true patriot.'"[76]

While powerfully symbolic, the honor had significant real-world implications as well. Leahy had now assumed a position in the line of presidential succession, third in line to the presidency after the vice president and the Speaker of the House. He would chair the powerful Senate Committee on Rules and acquire a twenty-four-hour security detail not unlike that which had guarded him during the days following the anthrax attacks of 2001.

Leahy would also preside over the Senate in the vice president's absence, when he chose not to delegate that responsibility to a freshman colleague in need of parliamentary experience. And the coveted chair of Appropriations, which Inouye had also occupied, was his for the asking (though he would eventually refrain from asking).

It meant something else, as well. When the House and the Senate together passed a bill, the finished text now required Leahy's signature (along with that of Speaker of the House John Boehner) before being passed to the president to sign or veto. Typically the more important of these bills are signed in the president pro tem's palatial office in the Capitol, before a flickering fireplace, at a long antique table polished to a high gloss.

And so Leahy found to his delight that, when he himself had introduced a key bill into the Senate, shepherded it through his own Judiciary Committee, and run interference for it until it finally emerged from both chambers intact, he himself was now expected to sign it as well.[77]

Leahy's Senate website still carries a gorgeous photo of the senator signing his own 2013 Violence Against Women Reauthorization Act, a look of immense satisfaction on his face. He had fought tooth and nail for it against strong opposition in the House, and ultimately succeeded in expanding its provisions to increase protections for victims in the LGBT, Native American, and immigrant communities, over the loud howls of conservatives.[78]

In the photo Leahy is seated, winter sun streaming through the long, ornate, gilt-trimmed windows behind him; the photographer is angling slightly down to capture the image. It's almost exactly the sort of shot Leahy has long been famous for taking himself, standing off to one side of the president's shoulder, focusing intently down on the hand holding the pen, preparing to capture history.

But now, of course, Leahy himself holds a signing pen rather than a camera—possibly the only object in the entirety of the known universe for which he would have been willing to trade.

The Havana Protocol

On Wednesday, December 17, 2014, Leahy's alarm clock went off at 2 a.m. He had gotten a few hours of nervous sleep, but very few. And even those had been extremely difficult to come by. The Senate had been voting until late Tuesday night, and Leahy had had to skip the last vote—a true rarity for a senator with a fifteen-thousand-plus career voting record—in order to find a few moments to shut his eyes. To make matters more unusual, he couldn't so much as hint to anyone why he was leaving.

Now, the sleeplessness and the dark, early hour gave the drive to Andrews Field in Maryland a deliberate and dreamy quality. A dream conceived by le Carré: at a little before 4 a.m., Leahy's car was waved through a series of military gates and finally directed to the Eighty-Ninth Airlift Wing, "the group of military planes that includes Air Force One, and which the White House believes it controls, rather than the Pentagon." In fact, in addition to all the US Senate, most of the Pentagon had been deliberately kept in the dark about Leahy's early morning mission as well.[1]

Defense Secretary Chuck Hagel knew the rough outlines, as did the chairman of the Joint Chiefs, but for the most part the White House had insisted on a tightly held secret.

The clouds overhead had lifted, and the night sky was clear as Leahy's driver was waved around a final large hangar. The plane was one of the president's backup aircraft—Air Force One but for the fact that the president was not currently aboard. This was clearly a flight for which nothing had been left to chance, and after a rapid preflight check, the plane's wheels were up at precisely 5 a.m.

Once in the air, Leahy joined the plane's other select occupants at the president's conference table: Senator Jeff Flake of Arizona, Representative Chris Van Hollen of Maryland, an Obama administration national security official, and Scott Gilbert, a private DC attorney.

And sitting just to Leahy's right was Judy Gross, wife of Alan Gross, a US contractor arrested by the Cuban authorities in 2009 and currently serving a fifteen-year term in a Cuban prison on espionage charges.

With her stylish silver hair and sober glasses, Judy Gross could easily have passed for a college professor plucked from Georgetown. But the truth was that over the last five years she had become more or less a full-time advocate for her husband's release, and her heavy eyes suggested that she had gotten even less sleep than Leahy.

Leahy patted Gross's arm. Over the last few years, he'd had several long, frank conversations with her, about her fears for her husband's life, and the pain that his imprisonment was inflicting on her and the couple's two grown daughters. They looked at some photographs of Alan, and the small group talked about the momentous wheels now turning silently in Havana and back on the American mainland.[2]

Leahy had to chuckle to himself when he thought of the lengths to which the White House and the State Department had gone to conceal the turning of those wheels. The previous night, while Leahy was still voting on the Senate floor, US diplomats in Cuba had thrown "a party at the official residence of Chief of Mission Jeff Delaurentis . . . to keep about 100 journalists, diplomats and other bigwigs—including Rep. Charlie Rangel (D-NY), sporting a white suit—there distracted and drinking late."[3] The plane carrying Leahy and the others was scheduled to touch down in Cuba at 8 a.m. sharp, and the chances of any of those party-goers witnessing the landing—or the events to follow—were slim to none.

As they talked, the jet's bank of windows began to glow with the sunrise. In the distance, Leahy could finally see the big island coming up over the horizon. Go time.

★ ★ ★

If the 2010 midterm elections had been—by President Obama's own rueful admission—a "shellacking," then the November 2014 midterms were undeniably and quantifiably worse. Democrats were stripped of *nine* closely contested Senate seats and overall control of the chamber, and saw their deficit in the House grow alarmingly as well. For Leahy, who had worked overtime fund-raising for endangered Democratic senators, the results were particularly bleak, and the consequences profound: the certain loss of his Judiciary gavel, another humbling return to the minority come January.

When the dust cleared post-election, the media analysis was unstintingly brutal, nowhere more so than at McClatchy News. In a November 4 story titled "President Obama Is Now Truly a Lame Duck," the first paragraph read, in toto, "Now, President Obama limps into his final two years in office."[4]

But somehow Barack Obama never got the lame-duck memo.

Rather than limping, the White house opted instead for the lunge: within two weeks the president revealed a sweeping (if voluntary) climate accord with China, and executive action providing temporary legal status and an "indefinite reprieve from deportation" for more than four million immigrants in the United States illegally.[5] While both actions were long rumored, a disciplined White House had managed a substantial element of surprise in each case, and by late November CNN was carrying an op-ed titled, "The New President Obama," in which the first paragraph read, in toto, "Is there a new President Obama?"[6]

But the nation — and the world — hadn't seen anything yet. A few weeks later, at just after noon on December 17, the president walked into the White House Briefing Room to face a hastily assembled press corps, who had been told only that a major announcement was in the offing.

And Obama didn't disappoint. His fifteen-minute address contained one jaw-dropping surprise after another. Most crucially, the United States would be ending more than a half century of diplomatic and strategic enmity with Cuba. Full diplomatic relations would be restored, and an embassy opened in Havana. Prisoners, including the three remaining members of the "Cuban Five," were to be exchanged for an unnamed American "intelligence asset" (read, spy) being held in Cuba.[7] Perhaps more revealing, though, was a simultaneously televised address to Cubans by Raúl Castro — clearly the White House and Havana had already developed enough trust and back-channel communication to speak by agreement at precisely the same moment to their respective nations.

But there was more. As Obama carefully framed it, "While I have been prepared to take additional steps for some time, a major obstacle stood in our way — the wrongful imprisonment, in Cuba, of a US citizen and USAID subcontractor, Alan Gross, for five years." Gross was undoubtedly the highest-profile prisoner in Cuban custody, and he, along with the US government, had stoutly denied the espionage charges that had landed him in Villa Marista prison in 2011.

Which made the president's bottom line all the sweeter: a carefully selected delegation of US government officials had left US airspace before dawn that morning to rendezvous with Gross's Cuban keepers and whisk him home.

Leading that rescue delegation—and most deeply and proudly enmeshed in the seemingly endless layers of cloak and dagger, layers both revealed and yet to be revealed—was the outgoing Senate Judiciary chairman, Patrick Leahy.

Apparently someone else hadn't gotten the lame-duck memo, either.

Leahy's fascination with Cuba was of long standing. In the early 1990s he had first visited the island on a goodwill mission, with one eye on an eventual market for Vermont dairy products. He had immediately loved the culture, the architecture, the food in particular; and yet there was also a strange, eerie sense of time brought to a standstill by the decades of US embargo, with the streets full of carefully tended prerevolutionary cars. He and Marcelle stayed then in a 1950s-era hotel, and they quickly discovered a favorite Havana haunt: the Meliá Cohiba south from the center of town and right on the Malecón boulevard. You could walk out in the warm evenings and stroll along the water, and it was an enchanting experience.[8]

Castro was a dictator, no doubt about it, and Leahy was clear-eyed about the repressive side of his regime, but he was also determined to forge a connection for the future. And so Leahy had brought along with him what in the early '90s was still something of a secret weapon, globally speaking: Ben & Jerry's ice cream. The pints served as a decent icebreaker, and Leahy and Castro chatted on light topics, ending with the hope to work together at some point in the future.

Once back in the states, Leahy—who was no stranger to the magic Ben & Jerry's could work politically—made sure to send Castro a full case. And a month or two later, "the senator received word back that the ice cream had been well received. Apparently Castro liked the Ben & Jerry's."[9]

His years in the Senate had made Leahy a very patient man, who inevitably took the long view of political change. And so, following that first successful trip to Cuba, he began a low-level, decades-long campaign for normalization of relations. He went back to Cuba, again and again, meeting with Fidel Castro and then his brother Raúl when the regime changed hands. Always he walked the tightrope between friendship and "very direct" criticism of Cuba's human rights record and "repressive

policies." Where and when he could, Leahy pushed for the release of political prisoners, but for the bulk of those years his pleas fell on deaf ears.

And American ears seemed no less deaf. Still, Leahy kept the issue
of normalization alive at the highest levels of US foreign-policy making.
He met with then-President Clinton and his foreign-policy staffers, who
openly feared Cuban American backlash in Florida but who accepted
Leahy's help during the Elián Gonzáles crisis in 1996.

When George W. Bush eventually succeeded Clinton, and Obama
eventually Bush, Leahy was there offering each administration the same
forward-looking message: the embargo was failed policy, and "the Cuban
and American people have a lot more in common than their differences."[10]
Leahy honestly believed that enhanced trade could do for the island what
a half-century of isolation had failed to accomplish—liberalize its politics, and free its people.

And privately, Leahy didn't hesitate to point out the glaring contradictions in America's foreign policy—actively engaging with brutal regimes
like Saudi Arabia, yet insisting that Cuban liberalization be a necessary
precondition to any diplomatic relationship.

It was craziness, Leahy thought, and counterproductive craziness at
that. And the arrest of Alan Gross in 2009 made things all the crazier
—what momentum had been building in the Obama administration
for an eventual change in policy seemed to evaporate overnight. While
the American government had at least one admitted "intelligence asset"
in the Cuban prison system, and had several high-profile Cuban spies
behind bars here at home, the CIA and the State Department continued
to insist that Gross was an innocent contractor caught up in embargo
politics.

For its part the Cuban government felt it had caught Gross red-handed,
distributing prohibited wi-fi equipment as well as sophisticated technology to mask satellite telephone communication. Neither side was willing
to budge on the Gross case, even assuming that common ground could
be found on other issues—a very large assumption indeed.

But Ben & Jerry's ice cream wasn't the only unconventional weapon in
Leahy's arsenal. In this case, he could also fall back on one of his senior
foreign policy staffers, Tim Rieser, who was fluent in Spanish and had a
background in just this sort of back-channel diplomacy, having visited
and advocated for political prisoners like Egyptian activist Saad Eddin
Ibrahim decades earlier.

As Gross's imprisonment stretched from months into years, and the normalization impulse faded, Leahy gave Rieser a very far-ranging brief, to stay in regular contact with Gross, to keep working the crucial officials in the regime of Raúl Castro—in short, to be Leahy's "eyes, ears and legs" on the island.[11] Later, Rieser would marvel at the "running room" Leahy gave him on the Cuba issue. "This was very important to [Leahy]. He wanted to do it. He cared about it personally, and he supported what I was doing. . . . It was like [Leahy's long campaign against] landmines, he raised it at every opportunity."[12]

And what became very clear to Rieser as 2014 came to a close was that Alan Gross would not last much longer in Cuban prison. During his years there, Gross had "lost five teeth, 100 pounds and much of the sight in his right eye."[13] But more crucially, his mental health was rapidly deteriorating. "The biggest concern that we had was his mental health, because he made clear that 2014 was going to be his last year in Cuba," as Rieser delicately framed it.[14]

The truth was that a distraught Gross had launched a hunger strike in recent months, and he had alluded openly to suicide. Rieser reported to Leahy that time had all but run out. And so in May 2014 Leahy took a small delegation of members of Congress to the Oval Office. Both the president and the vice president were present. Leahy and Congressman Jim McGovern of Massachusetts pressed Obama to keep the promise he had made many times on the campaign trail in 2008.[15]

"'You said you were going to do this!' McGovern challenged the president. 'Let's just do it!'" But Obama was defensive; he had back-channel talks of his own under way, had since 2013, and they weren't yet ready to bear fruit. Eventually Leahy, McGovern, and the rest left the White House collectively frustrated.

But by that summer, another major player had suddenly decided to weigh in: Pope Francis. Leahy had written directly to the pontiff earlier in the year—"I sent him some thoughts on this," he would later tell NBC's Andrea Mitchell—and found that "it was not a tough sell with the Pope." And that contact with the Vatican proved highly influential, in more ways than one. Not only did the pope's moral authority push President Obama to honor his original campaign pledge, and not only did his personal intercession provide political cover with Catholic voters—including some of those anti-Castro Cuban émigrés in Florida—but better than that, the pope offered to host a final set of secret talks between the Americans and the Cubans at the Vatican itself.[16]

Which began to look very much like an endgame.

★ ★ ★

Leahy's plane touched down at 8 a.m. in Havana—not at José Martí International, but at a far smaller strip nearby. In the early morning sun, the more obscure airport looked deserted, but for the few Cuban officials there to hand over Gross. Leahy, Flake, and Van Hollen spoke briefly with Cuba's foreign minister, and then were led through the silent airport and finally into a room, and there sat Gross, wearing one rumpled green striped shirt over another blue Hawaiian shirt, faded jeans, and a plain white cap. Even at a glance, he seemed dramatically thinner than when Leahy had seen him last. When Gross looked up and gave a wan smile, only three of his top teeth showed.

Leahy was stunned at the change. He had been briefed on Gross's deterioration, but the reality was sobering. For his part, the former contractor seemed unable to believe that Leahy had actually arrived—that the rescue mission was an actual on-the-ground fact, rather than some elaborate fiction staged by the Cuban government.

The two men hugged, and as they did so, Leahy said softly, "We need to turn right around and get out of here," and the Americans left without more than a few more words to the Cubans. They had hardly reentered the plane's main cabin when the pilot braced the passengers for takeoff, and the plane roared back into the Caribbean sky.

Elapsed time on Cuban soil: thirty-two minutes.[17]

Once aloft, the rescue mission became a welcome-home party. Gross and his wife Judy hugged and cried, Gross unable to stop smiling—a smile rendered more poignant by the five missing teeth. The galley staff had set out a special set of treats: a big bowl of popcorn, a snack Gross had often said he missed, and his favorite sandwich, corned beef on rye with mustard. And too, because it was Hanukkah, latkes with applesauce and sour cream. Leahy watched as Gross moved jubilantly yet gingerly around the cabin—his disbelief in the rescue mission seemed to have been taken to another level by the White House plane and everything it held for him.

At 8:45, when the jet crossed into US airspace, the pilot noted the transition—and a series of loud cheers went up in the cabin. Gross pumped his fists in the air, eyes shut tight. Finally, Leahy went over to him, put a hand on his shoulder, and said, "It's actually real, Alan."

Gross threw his arms around Leahy, saying over and over again, "Patrick, this is wonderful. This is *wonderful.*" As they embraced, Leahy could feel just how much weight Gross had lost, and he was startled to find tears coming to his own eyes. He would later joke about it with reporters — "I thought we were both going to start to cry" " — but Gross's emaciated condition, his gapped smile, his clear inability to believe, even now, in the reality of his good fortune, all of it told Leahy how close they had been to losing him.[18]

Finally, Gross sat at the conference table and placed calls to his two daughters, one in Tel Aviv, one in Oregon, both in their twenties and both overcome by their father's voice and his first words: "I'm free."

Another party waited on the ground at Andrews, including another delegation of US senators and representatives—and after a few more minutes, Secretary of State John Kerry flew in as well, coming into the terminal to wrap Gross in a bear hug.

Leahy was floating on a cloud of adrenaline and exhaustion, almost giddy with success. And when the senators finally reached Capitol Hill, and the inevitable scrum of reporters wanted to know why Flake, Van Hollen, and Leahy had been selected for the delicate diplomatic mission, it was Leahy who broke the short silence. "Well, we had frequent flyer miles," he began, and the barks of laughter from the reporters told him that he had hit just the right note.

In fact, the White House's handling of the affair—not just the secrecy around the Gross release, but the public relations related to the normal-ization announcement—had gone off all but seamlessly. The joy of the Gross family's reunion did a great deal to humanize the delicate exchange of prisoners.

And much the same was true in Havana. Gerardo Hernández, one of the three Cuban spies released by the United States, was given a hero's welcome, and met at the airport by his wife Adriana Pérez. Still, it was im-possible for reporters to ignore the fact that Pérez was heavily pregnant, which seemed puzzling and awkward, given that her husband had been jailed in America since 2001—but only until the reunited couple made it clear that the child was in fact Hernández's. At a concert given in his honor by singer Silvio Rodríguez, Hernández confirmed that the preg-nancy had been achieved through artificial insemination. "I had to do it by remote control," Hernández told the Cuban press a little sheepishly, "but everything turned out well."

And then, in case anyone had missed the practical and symbolic connection to the diplomatic entente under way between America and Cuba, he put his hand on his wife's stomach and added, "One of the first things accomplished by this process was this." Cuban television was delirious over the story.[19]

Just three weeks later, there was more to love: Pérez gave birth to a healthy 7.7-pound baby girl, Gema Hernández Pérez. As McClatchy deftly put it, "The seeds of US-Cuba diplomacy have born fruit." It was *Mission Impossible* timing.[20]

But here was one last secret wrapped in one last mystery, and then nested inside one final tantalizing enigma: how did a high-profile Cuban spy jailed in America manage to impregnate his Cuban wife then living in Panama, given that said spy was held in a maximum-security facility and expressly denied conjugal visits (because his wife was a Cuban intelligence agent too)?

Yet again — and stupefyingly enough this time — the nation's puzzled media quickly realized that all roads led to one Senator Patrick Leahy.

Out of Leahy's handful of trips to Cuba, two had been built specifically around visits to Gross in Villa Marista prison. It was during a February 2013 trip that Cuban officials approached him with a sensitive and confidential request: would Leahy meet personally with the wife of a Cuban spy currently serving a life sentence in the United States? The woman, Adriana Pérez, had a humanitarian request to make of the senator, the officials hinted, a little cryptically.

Leahy's curiosity was piqued, and he was always a sympathetic ear for humanitarian concerns. But beyond that, it was the first time that the Cubans had indicated that there were things *they* needed, things that might — conceivably — be part of an eventual shift in US-Cuban relations, or at least in the treatment Gross was receiving while incarcerated. Leahy's first instinct was to green-light the meeting. Marcelle had come to the island with him, and after talking over the sotto voce request with her, Leahy told the officials that the couple would be glad to meet with Pérez.

Quickly enough, the meeting was arranged in a Havana hotel room, with Tim Rieser rounding out the American side.

It turned out to be a wrenching interview. Pérez wasted no time in making her purpose clear. Her husband would in all likelihood die in a US prison, and she had been trying unsuccessfully to petition the Federal Bureau of Prisons for conjugal visits — now age forty-four, she wanted a child with her husband before it was too late.

Pérez nearly broke down in tears, and over the course of the hour she directed her appeal more and more to Marcelle, who found herself immediately moved. Leahy would later recall the moment for reporters: "It was an emotional meeting. . . . She wanted to have a baby before she got too old. She was deeply in love with her husband."

When Pérez had left the room, Marcelle, Leahy, and Rieser looked at one another, and it was clear that all three had had the same penetrating experience. By the time the three touched down in Washington, Leahy was ready to decide. He and Marcelle both felt that as parents, and as grandparents, they wanted to help, but beyond that Leahy had the sharp, intuitive sense that Pérez's request might somehow be a tipping point in the larger deadlocked diplomatic talks.

He leaned over to Rieser and gave him his marching orders: "Tim, we need to figure out how to do this."[21]

It was enough to give any staffer nightmares; the complications were multiple, each more daunting than the last. Customs was denying Pérez a visa to visit the United States. The Federal Bureau of Prisons typically refuses conjugal visit requests in any event. And in this particular case, American officials were convinced that the jailed spy's wife was *herself* a spy; bringing the two of them together for any reason would be lunacy from their perspective. It was entirely out of the question.

But Leahy had been clear about his intentions, and Rieser had made his bones as a staffer working problems, not allowing himself to be worked *by* them. And so when the FBP rebuffed his inquiries about conjugal visits, Rieser went at it from an entirely different direction: what about artificial insemination?

There was, it turned out, a single precedent.[22] It was a thin reed, and there was strong resistance initially, but with Leahy working the phones at key moments, Rieser eventually got senior officials in both the Justice and State Departments to sign off on the secret arrangement. Cuban officials were allowed to visit Hernández at a federal prison in Victorville, California, and pick up the sample preserved by US medical personnel, with the Cuban government defraying all associated expenses. They in turn flew the sample to Panama, where a first attempt to impregnate Pérez eventually failed.

But the entire process was repeated eight months later, with Gema Pérez Hernández being the improbable, all but miraculous end result.

And Leahy and Rieser saw to it that those months of cooperation on the American side were mirrored in the treatment of Alan Gross. The changes were small things that loomed very large for a man who had recently gone on a hunger strike and threatened suicide over the conditions of his imprisonment.

Suddenly the Cubans were willing to turn off the lights in Gross's cell at night; he was given access to a computer and printer; and he was allowed expanded phone privileges, to talk to his wife, his lawyer, and to Rieser on Leahy's behalf.[23]

Technically there was no quid pro quo, and technically there would be no formal connection between Gross's release and the release by American officials of the three Cuban spies; also, technically, the Cuban spies were exchanged for an unnamed American "intelligence asset" who had spent the last twenty years in Cuban prison, with Gross thrown in as merely a "humanitarian gesture."

But in truth, Leahy's intuition upon hearing Pérez's plea had been spot on — that gesture had seemed to soften Cuban resistance, and it had led to an easier life for Gross, which had in turn helped restart the ponderous machinery of backroom diplomacy, stalled entirely since 2009.

Publicly, Leahy would continue to insist that the cloak-and-dagger conception story had nothing to do with his long-standing belief that the Cuban embargo should be lifted and the two countries opened to one another again. "It was a human thing," Leahy maintained stoutly to reporters. "It had nothing to do with the politics of the two countries." He would add later, "We rejoice this Christmas season that it worked."[24]

Of course, it is possible to do a human thing and a political thing — even a positive political thing — at one and the same instant. But like the White House, Leahy had his public story, and he was sticking to it.

At least technically speaking.

★ ★ ★

On August 14, 2015, after fifty-four years of active enmity, the United States officially reopened its six-story embassy on the Malecón esplanade in Havana. Flags snapped in the breeze, and the blue waters of the Straits of Florida sparkled in the sun. At a key moment, the American flag was carried forward by three of the same military guards who had lowered it in 1961.

Secretary of State John Kerry was present, the highest-ranking US official to visit the island in decades. So too was the Vermont senator who had enjoyed that honor until just a few hours previously.

As the band struck up "The Star-Spangled Banner," the flag was raised slowly into the cloudless sky. Standing with Marcelle at the front of the crowd in the embassy's pavilion, Leahy felt tears suddenly welling. His wife's grip tightened on his arm, and he closed his own hand on hers. It was for this that he had backed Senator Barack Obama from the early days, before Obama had seemed like a political force of nature, long before he had wrested the Democratic nomination from front-runner Hillary Clinton. Back when Obama had said that he would go to America's enemies, not demanding key concessions as the price of talks, but *without* preconditions, as befitted a confident, peace-seeking world power.

As much as anything, as much as Obama's opposition to the war in Iraq, that was the line that had touched him.

It was for this that Leahy had spent decades pushing for Cuban relations behind the scenes, prodding presidents and diplomats. And wasn't it for this, really, that he had considered politics in the first place, back when the political universe was entirely bounded by the sight of the golden dome across the street from his porch in Montpelier? This was what he and his family had talked and argued and dreamed about at their Vermont dinner table, almost every night: a free state, a just nation, a world at peace.

Outside the embassy gates, Cubans who had gathered to watch broke into cheers.

As the applause exploded around him, Leahy found himself looking out past the podium and over the waters of the Gulf of Mexico. He had heard that the reefs here were the best in the Caribbean for snorkeling, and he made a mental note to bring Marcelle back for a quieter vacation sometime over the next few months, just the two of them.[25]

It would be hard to imagine a more exquisitely beautiful sight.

In fact, the entire ceremony felt like the last moments of the last reel of a Hollywood summer blockbuster somehow, all violence and obstacles and trials at an end, the final frames shot through only with pleasant exhaustion and hope. Just the sort of scene Patrick Joseph Leahy had never been one to miss.

And without thinking, he raised the camera hanging from his neck to his one exceptionally good eye and captured the moment forever.

NOTES

PROLOGUE

1. Much of this material regarding intern Grant Leslie's experience comes from two primary sources: Majority Leader Tom Daschle's *Like No Other Time: The Two Years That Changed America* (New York: Crown, 2003), and Leslie's own recollections as recorded in a PBS *Frontline* special aired ten years after the attack (PBS preceded the airing of the October 11 *Anthrax Files* episode with a set of exclusive webisodes, "The Intern Who Opened an Anthrax Letter," October 10, 2011). See especially chapter 7 of Daschle's memoir, "In Cipro We Trust," 143–88. David Willman fills in a few remaining gaps in his outstanding examination of the Amerithrax investigation, *The Mirage Man: Bruce Ivins, the Anthrax Attacks, and America's Rush to War* (New York: Bantam, 2011).

2. *Guardian*, Sunday, October 14, 2001.

3. PBS *Frontline*, "The Intern Who Opened an Anthrax Letter," exclusive footage of Leslie published at PBS.org on October 10, 2011. As the first anthrax letter had instructed, Leslie was prescribed large doses of the antibiotic Cipro, and she never developed anthrax symptoms of any sort. Leslie now works for a consulting firm in Washington, DC.

4. Willman, *Mirage Man*, 100–102.

5. Most of the material about this call comes from Adam Silverman's piece, "Anthrax Letter 'Chilling': Leahy, Staff Determined to Continue Work," *Burlington Free Press*, November 18, 2001.

6. Luke Albee, interview with the author, Burlington, VT, August 23, 2013.

INTRODUCTION

1. Anthony York, "Why Daschle and Leahy?," *Salon*, November 21, 2001.

2. Erin Kelly, "Leahy Office Proves Free of Anthrax," *Burlington Free Press*, November 21, 2001. Ted Kennedy, the Senate's liberal lion and long-standing bête noir of the right wing, was apparently not targeted, although trace spores from either the Leahy or Daschle letters were discovered in Kennedy's Senate offices, along with those of Chris Dodd.

3. *Time*, November 26, 2001.

4. Albee interview.

5. Brent Simon, "What Is Senator Patrick Leahy Doing in 'The Dark Knight'?," *New York*, July 11, 2008.

6. Leahy became the Senate's longest-serving member, and Senate president pro tempore, with the death of Senator Daniel K. Inouye in December 2012. But the pro tem designation is a perquisite of the majority; when Democrats moved into the minority following the 2014 elections, Republican Orrin Hatch moved into the Senate president pro tem's palatial office. Given the seesaw nature of the twenty-first-century Senate majority, Leahy may well assume the title again. Regardless

of the outcome of any particular election, however, Leahy remains the dean of the Senate.

7. *New York Times*, July 12, 2008; *Rutland Herald*, August 11, 2007.

8. Candace Page, interview with the author, Burlington, VT, December 12, 2011.

9. Of course, a case can be made—and a recent biography of former governor Phil Hoff makes it very convincingly—that Hoff is the real heir to Kennedy in Vermont. As the authors of *Philip Hoff: How Red Turned Blue in the Green Mountain State* argue, Hoff's style on the campaign trail in 1962 was modeled explicitly on Kennedy. "As Hoff himself recalled it, 'Jack Kennedy had started a thing called the coffee klatch. And I seized on that. And it was a natural vehicle for Vermont. And it had never been done before.'" My own point above is more specifically that Leahy is the first Vermont politician to use the range of broadcast media as overwhelmingly and successfully as Kennedy did, on the way to constructing a charismatic image that in many ways exceeded his own on-the-stump abilities. See Samuel B. Hand, Anthony Marro, and Stephen C. Terry, *Philip Hoff: How Red Turned Blue in the Green Mountain State* (Hanover, NH: University Press of New England, 2011), 35–37.

10. Garrison Nelson, interview with the author, Burlington, VT, August 28, 2015.

11. For the record, Leahy himself views Justin Smith Morrill as the single most impressive Vermont senator on the national stage. "He not only brought about the creation of the Library of Congress, but also the Land Grant Colleges, and his work with Lincoln was visionary and absolutely essential. He even helped President Lincoln with the construction of the railroads out West. I think in many ways he's the greatest Vermonter ever." From a series of reflections written by Leahy and e-mailed to the author on January 4, 2016.

12. See "AP Calls VT for Obama; Sanders, Welch, Shumlin Re-elected," WCAX.com, November 6, 2012.

13. As our politics have grown more cartoonish over the last two decades, so too has our box office: the combined total for Marvel and DC Comics adaptations now well exceeds $10 billion. See an updated ranking at http://comicbook.com/list/top-100-grossing-comic-book-movies-of-all-time. See also Nick Turner, "Marvel Films Make 47% More at Box Office Than DC Comics," *Bloomberg News*, June 10, 2013.

14. As will become clear to the reader, this biography deals in depth with Leahy's formative years and then shifts deliberately to those years during which he had enough Senate clout to contend at the highest levels of national politics. As such, it largely remains silent on the years 1976–1992. And yet, the 1987 leak of the draft Iran-Contra report is crucial to an understanding of Leahy's trajectory, and so I've covered it here.

15. For the general contours of this flap see Stephen Engelberg, "Iran-Contra Hearings; Senator Leahy Says He Leaked Report of Panel," *New York Times*, July 29, 1987.

16. Rowland Evans and Robert Novak, "Stopping Intelligence Leaks," *Washington Post*, August 5, 1987.

17. Engelberg, "Iran-Contra Hearings."

18. "Sen. Leahy Admits Leaking Report; Vermont Democrat Calls It Careless, Says He Left Committee," United Press International, July 29, 1987.

19. Chris Graff, *Dateline Vermont: Covering and Uncovering the Stories, Big and Small, That Shaped a State—and Influenced a Nation* (North Pomfret, VT: Thistle Hill, 2006), 183–84.

20. Ibid, 184.

21. Rick Perlstein, *Nixonland: The Rise of a President and the Fracturing of America* (Scribner, 2008), 46–47.

22. Daschle, *Like No Other Time*, 84.

23. Jeffords, *My Declaration of Independence* (New York: Simon & Schuster, 2001), 130.

24. For a fine account of Dean's fund-raising innovations see Larry Biddle's informative firsthand narrative, "Fund-Raising: Hitting Home Runs on and off the Internet," collected in Zephyr Teachout, Thomas Streeter, et al., *Mousepads, Shoe Leather, and Hope* (Boulder, CO: Paradigm, 2008).

25. Another way to verify this archetypal opposition between Vermont and Texas is to look at where in the nation the fringe notion of secession has managed to surface as a mainstream political issue. See Christopher Ketcham, "The Secessionist Campaign for the Republic of Vermont," *Time Magazine*, January 31, 2010; and Manny Fernandez, "White House Rejects Petitions to Secede, but Texans Fight On," *New York Times*, January 15, 2013.

26. "Bush Has One State to Go—Vermont," *Washington Times*, December 4, 2008.

27. The Pagano quote comes from an interview with the author, September 6, 2013.

28. "Leahy had never been an administration favorite; after he resisted some provisions of the Patriot Act, White House officials privately nicknamed him Osama Bin Leahy." See Peter Baker, *Days of Fire: Bush and Cheney in the White House* (New York: Anchor Books, 2014), 336.

1. THE ORIGIN STORY

1. Laura Claridge, *Norman Rockwell: A Life* (New York: Random House, 2001), 270. The material on the savage murder of twelve-year-old Peter Levine can be found on 265–68.

2. From an interview of Patrick Leahy by the author, Burlington, VT, July 21, 2014. As luck would have it, Leahy's wife Marcelle would also eventually be hospitalized for toxoplasmosis, although long after she had given birth to the family's three children.

3. Mary Leahy, interview with the author, Montpelier, VT, January 11, 2012.

4. In the service of complete accuracy, I should point out that Leahy's camera fetish actually began with a Hopalong Cassidy box camera his parents gave him in 1951 and continued into his teenage years with a Zeiss Ikon Contaflex Super B. Once he reached adulthood, his preference was for the SLR. See James Estrin, "Senator Leahy's Pictures from Ringside," Lens: Photography, Video and Visual Journalism, *New York Times* website, March 17, 2010.

5. Ibid.

6. Nicole Gaudiano, "Vermont Sen. Leahy Takes Shots Like No One Else," *USA Today*, January 13, 2013.

7. "Truckin': The Pat Leahy Story," *Vermont Business Magazine*, May 2009.

8. Patrick Leahy, introduction to *A Celebration of Vermont Printers, 1904–2004* (Albany, NY: Lane Press, 2004).

9. Ibid.

10. Mary Leahy interview.

11. Ibid.

12. Ibid.

13. Ibid., and the next page is infused with Mary Leahy's recollections from same.

14. Ibid.

15. Patrick Leahy, "The Church We Love Is Being Used," op-ed, *Washington Post*, Sunday, March 8, 1981.

16. Patrick Leahy, "Montpelier Boy Realizes Miss Holbrook Was Right," *Barre Montpelier (VT) Times Argus*, June 13, 1966. When Leahy had this bit of autobiography printed in the *Congressional Record*, he clarified that "Miss Holbrook" had actually been a Mrs.

17. This deep faith in institutions Leahy would immediately transfer to the US Senate, and that love would only strengthen over four decades. For that reason, it was headline news when Leahy—one of the Senate's abiding institutionalists—spoke out in favor of filibuster reform in November 2013. And when Senate president pro tem Pat Leahy presided over the votes that disabled the filibuster for executive and judicial nominees, the irony was palpable. Here was the dean of the Senate himself, a lawmaker who had joined over the years in every ad hoc "gang" to save the filibuster, bringing the gavel down on a tradition that traditionalists no longer recognized. See, for example, Jesse Wegman, "What Is Harry Reid Waiting For?," *Taking Note: The Editorial Page Editor's Blog, New York Times*, November 19, 2013.

18. This quote from Dana Haskins—as well as this overall account of the Leahys' first meeting—is drawn from Dorothy Tod's 1974 Senate campaign film, discussed in much greater detail in chapter 3.

19. "Truckin': The Pat Leahy Story," *Vermont Business Magazine*, May 2009.

20. From the recollections of Costello's son, Paul Costello, in an e-mail to the author, from October 2013. In support of the anecdote, Paul Costello also offered two photographs showing the combined retirement/swearing-in party for the outgoing state's attorney, John Fitzpatrick, and Leahy.

2. THE ACCIDENTAL STATE'S ATTORNEY

1. From the statement Flaherty eventually gave to the Essex police. The following narrative draws upon a series of such official statements, as well as the comprehensive reports filed by the detectives as they drew the strands of the case together in the weeks following July 11, 1966.

2. From Adam's statement to Essex police.

3. From an Essex police report dated August 2, 1966, written by Captain Fortune.

4. And, in what must have seemed like a very strange anomaly in mid-1966, each of those two months had produced a homicide case. A month before Beau Bishop was killed, an Essex Junction air force sergeant named Robert Gold had gunned down his wife and two sons in what the *Free Press* described as "a wild, unexplained

burst of gunfire that erupted during breakfast." One of the two injured boys later died. The Gold incident was technically the first murder that Leahy ever handled, but it presented little challenge from a law enforcement perspective. Gold actually walked up to neighbors in the aftermath of the shooting and told them calmly, "I did it," before climbing into his car to wait for the police to arrive. The Trivento case, some weeks later, would prove far more opaque and disturbing. See "Air Force Man Pleads Insanity in Shooting of Wife, Two Sons," *Burlington Free Press*, June 23, 1966.

5. Patrick Leahy, interview with the author, Burlington, VT, August 12, 2011.

6. Philip Hoff, interview with the author, Burlington, VT, October 12, 2011.

7. The bulk of this exchange comes from "Truckin': The Pat Leahy Story," *Vermont Business Magazine*, May 2009.

8. See Liva Baker's very readable *Miranda: Crime, Law and Politics* (New York: Atheneum, 1983), 177.

9. Ibid., 178–79. More recent legal history has also borne out the conclusion that *Miranda* was never actually the watershed for police practice it was hoped—and feared—to be. See also Lawrence S. Wrightsman and Mary L. Pitman, *The Miranda Ruling: Its Past, Present and Future* (New York: Oxford University Press, 2010), 63.

10. *Burlington Free Press*, July 15, 1966.

11. Leahy interview, August 12, 2011.

12. Again, this material is summarized from Captain Fortune's police report, dated August 2, 1966.

13. Trivento would give various explanations for his discharge over the years. He would tell a childhood friend, Ronald Regimbald, two stories: that he had been discharged "because of liver trouble" and, later, "because he was too slow in learning." But to his first wife, he confessed that "he had been given this type of discharge for fooling around with men." From, respectively, the statements given by Ronald Regimbald, July 16, 1966, and Theresa Cadieux, undated but almost certainly between July 14 and 16, 1966.

14. At this point, Detective Trooper Irvin Maranville took over the official reporting, beginning at the last moments of Trivento's first official statement.

15. Again, working from Maranville's report of July 11, 1966.

16. *Burlington Free Press*, July 13, 1966, 1. The Chicago mass killer was later caught and identified as Richard Speck, a drifter and itinerant sailor. See Speck's obituary for a quick overview of his most infamous crime, "Richard Speck: 49, Chicago Killer of 8 Student Nurses 25 Years Ago," *New York Times*, December 6, 1991.

17. From an article titled "Trivento Pleads Guilty in Slaying of Child, 2," *Burlington Free Press*, Saturday, May 13, 1967.

18. From the lengthy (and initially reluctant but then "quite voluble") statement given by Theresa Cadieux, née LeFebre, to the Essex police on July 14, 1966.

19. From the statement given by Roland Lamore on July 16, 1966.

20. Working again from the statement of Theresa Cadieux, née LeFebre, July 14, 1966.

21. These last two quotes are taken from the statements given by Emma Lamore and by David Bishop, age six, both on July 16, 1966.

22. "Grand Jury Fails to Indict," *Burlington Free Press*, July 26, 1966.

23. This account of the grand jury hearing, and the extreme reaction of one juror, is Leahy's own, given in our second official interview on August 12, 2011. Given the secrecy of grand jury proceedings, corroboration is effectively impossible, but Leahy remembers the incident clearly, and remains proud not only of the outcome of the Trivento case but of his role in fostering the use of color photography itself—understandable, of course, given Leahy's own credentials as a self-taught photographer.

24. "Trivento Pleads Guilty in Slaying of Child, 2," *Burlington Free Press*, May 13, 1967.

25. Brian Harwood and Toby Knox, interview with the author, Waterbury, VT, November 7, 2011; and Chris Graff, interview with the author, Montpelier, VT, January 27, 2012.

26. Marselis Parsons, interview with the author, February 20, 2012. Parsons lost his battle with cancer in May 2015, just a few years after generously allowing me a long conversation over lunch at Isabelle's in Burlington.

27. The search for Chittenden County homicide statistics for the last half of the twentieth century proved remarkably difficult. As a last resort I called the Vermont State Police barracks and spoke with Captain Jean-Paul Sinclair, who seemed puzzled by the lack of historical data. But Sinclair volunteered to cull through the paper case files by hand and compile a comprehensive spreadsheet of homicides from 1950 to the present. That data informs the next several pages, and I can't thank Captain Sinclair enough for taking the trouble.

28. Stuart Perry, "Young Woman Slain, Strangler Is Sought," *Burlington Free Press*, July 21, 1971.

29. Eric Loring, "Lid of Secrecy Clamped on Murder Investigation," *Burlington Free Press*, July 24, 1971.

30. See Ann Rule, *The Stranger beside Me* (New York: W. W. Norton, 1980), though the material on Rita Curran actually comes in an afterword that Rule appended to the text in 1986. Rule's reasons for suspecting Bundy go further: he had a conversation with her in 1971, in which he described traveling to Burlington in 1969 to see the records and the site of his birth. Rule outlines the possibility that the serial killer either deliberately misstated the year of his Burlington trip, or possibly took a second trip that he didn't mention. And it is true that accounts of the Curran murder track precisely with the murders Bundy was committing in the early 1970s. US marshal Dave Demag only shakes his head today when asked about the possibility: "We had assigned a detective to hook up with the Florida Police Department who was interviewing Bundy and had a timeline and so forth, and my best recollection was Bundy was not—they had him somewhere else within the country during [the time of Curran's murder]." From an interview by the author with Dave Demag, now US marshal for the District of Vermont, on October 16, 2011.

31. "More Nudes Swim into Court," *Burlington Free Press*, July 1, 1971.

32. "Leahy Comments on Skinnydipping," *Burlington Free Press*, July 10, 1971.

33. Leahy interview, July 21, 2014.

34. "'My God! They're Killing Us': *Newsweek*'s 1970 Coverage of the Kent State Shooting," *Newsweek*, May 4, 2015. Newsweek's forty-five-year retrospective on

what was sometimes called the Kent State Massacre makes clear that while Ohio Guardsmen might have thought they heard a shot before their own volley, they did not issue a warning of any sort before firing some thirty-five rounds directly into the crowd of students.

35. See "Reaction to Kent Students' Deaths Ranged from Candlelight to Bombs," Associated Press, May 6, 1970.

36. Edward C. Andrews, "Andrews Reports on Student Reaction to Kent State Deaths," *Vermont Cynic*, vol. 88, no. 14, September 5, 1970.

37. See Walter Johnson, "UVM Students Gather to Protest Slayings at Kent State University," *Burlington Free Press*, May 5, 1970.

38. Leahy interview, July 21, 2014.

39. "An Appeal for Reason on the Campus," editorial, *Burlington Free Press*, May 6, 1970.

40. Stephen Carlson, "Draft Sit-In in Burlington Ends Quietly," *Burlington Free Press*, May 7, 1970.

41. Andrews, "Andrews Reports on Student Reaction to Kent State Deaths."

42. The story of that campaign, and Leahy's insistence that it stand effectively apart from his work as a prosecutor, is told in more detail in the following chapter.

43. From Demag interview. Demag makes it clear that Leahy was the driver for the task force: "Leahy had already set up the structure in regards to doing these task force concepts. . . . Pretty much the policy of the Detective Bureau and everything else was kind of done with Pat Leahy's stamp of approval."

44. This material on Lawrence comes from Hamilton E. Davis's fine, book-length account, *Mocking Justice: Vermont's Biggest Drug Scandal* (Crown: New York, 1978), 31.

45. Ibid., 132.

46. Ibid., 134–35.

47. Ibid., 153. Davis reports a phone conversation as well between Beaulieu and Frank Murray, deputy chief state's attorney, in which the captain recounts his suspicions. At the risk of seeming to conflate the conversations, I borrow Beaulieu's phrasing from the Murray conversation and present it here without quotes, as probably the nearest to how the news was actually broken a few days later to Leahy. See Davis, *Mocking Justice*, 149.

48. From an interview with the author on September 5, 2007, originally published on my political blog *Vermont Daily Briefing*, under the title "Tales from the Rusty Scuffer: A Little Light Lunch with Senator Patrick Leahy."

49. Ibid.

50. Over the years there has been some small dispute as to how large a role Leahy played in the Lawrence sting, but Demag makes it clear today that Leahy's office formally initiated the investigation after being approached by Beaulieu: "'And Richard Beaulieu, the captain at the time, had a very close working relationship with Pat Leahy, who was the state's attorney,' Demag related. 'And the State's Attorney's office, along with our agency, initiated the investigation.'" See "Dave Demag Reflects on His Police Career," WCAX.com, August 1, 2007.

51. Ibid., 155.

52. The material from this section comes from Davis, *Mocking Justice*, 158–60, unless otherwise indicated.

53. Davis makes a case for Leahy as slightly more pro-treatment, pro-diversion than was then common, in line with the attitudes of his constituents: "Although there never was a written policy, Chittenden County State's Attorney Patrick Leahy, the local prosecutor, was thought to be the first state's attorney in Vermont to decline to prosecute young people for possession of small amounts of marijuana." Davis, *Mocking Justice*, 22–23.

54. Demag interview.

55. "Lawrence had filed one hundred six drug charges between the time he came to St. Albans in August of 1973 and the time he was arrested in July of 1974. If those arrests were bad, then the community and the state faced a law-enforcement scandal of enormous proportions." Davis, *Mocking Justice*, 163.

56. Mike Donoghue and Carlo Wolf, "Narcotics Agent Is Arrested; Burlington Police Charge Lawrence," *Burlington Free Press*, July 13, 1974. See also Robert D. Kaplan, "Paul Lawrence Faces Charges," *Rutland Herald*, July 13, 1974.

57. Davis, *Mocking Justice*, 164–65.

58. *Free Press* Capital Bureau, "Mallary Announces Plan to Fight Inflation," *Burlington Free Press*, July 13, 1974.

3. THE CHILDREN'S CRUSADE

1. Brian Harwood and Toby Knox, interview with the author, Waterbury, VT, November 7, 2011.

2. Candace Page, interview with the author, Burlington, VT, December 12, 1974.

3. Philip Hoff, interview with the author, Burlington, VT, October 12, 2011.

4. Ibid.

5. "Liberty Unionite Sanders Out to Combat America's 'Socialism of the Rich,'" *Burlington Free Press*, August, 27, 1974.

6. Paul Bruhn, interview with the author, Burlington, VT, October 5, 2011.

7. Harwood and Knox interview.

8. David Schaefer, interview with the author, Shelburne, VT, October 17, 2011.

9. Bruhn interview.

10. Candace Page, "Mallary-Leahy Senate Race Pits 'Incumbent' against Newcomer," *Burlington Free Press*, September 19, 1974.

11. Ibid.

12. *Burlington Free Press*, October 8, 1974.

13. Harwood and Knox interview.

14. Much of the material in these two paragraphs is drawn from Margaret Maurice's highly readable candidate-spouse profile, "Leahy Had Potent Secret Weapon —His Tireless Wife, Marcelle," *Burlington Free Press*, November 7, 1974.

15. Frederick W. Stetson, "Mallary, Not at Ease with Public, Puts in Long Days on Campaign Trail," *Burlington Free Press*, October 25, 1974.

16. Bruhn interview.

17. Schaefer interview.

18. "Leahy Campaigning Marked by Confidence, Openness, and Media Finesse," *Burlington Free Press*, October 28, 1974.

19. Harwood and Knox interview.

20. Schaefer interview.

21. Page interview.

22. For these four headlines see the *Burlington Free Press*, October 10, 19, 31, and 11, respectively.

23. Harwood and Knox interview.

24. *Burlington Free Press*, September 19, 1974.

25. *Burlington Free Press*, September 30, 1974.

26. In the summer of 1974, Bruce Post, then a legislative assistant on Mallary's congressional staff, came to the congressman with concerns about the appropriation—and its potential effects on the Senate election campaign. "This has red flag written all over it," Post warned his boss. Mallary pushed back. "Suppose," he told Post, "you're the member of Congress. You know that chemical weapons are in our stockpile and that accidents in storage could have serious consequences for innocent people. Yet knowing that we have a way of separating these agents so that accidents won't happen, what would you do? How would you vote?" Post agreed, Mallary voted aye on the appropriation, and—before too much time had elapsed—Post's initial fears were borne out. From an e-mail written by Post on December 26, 2011.

27. Harwood and Knox interview.

28. "Mallary Didn't Get Seafarers' Funds," *Burlington Free Press*, October 24, 1974.

29. "Mallary, Leahy Debate Angrily," *Burlington Free Press*, October 15, 1974.

30. "Leahy Attacks Mallary for Ads Which Attack Leahy," *Burlington Free Press*, October 11, 1974.

31. Schaefer interview.

32. Harwood and Knox interview.

33. "Leahy: Mallary Aided by 'Seafarers,'" *Burlington Free Press*, October 23, 1974.

34. To this day, Leahy owns a copy of this particular *Rutland Herald* and takes great delight in telling the story of the Naramore poll, throwing his arms out wide and almost shouting the headline—his own version of the botched Dewey-Truman call.

35. "Naramore Finds Salmon-Jeffords Plurality," *Rutland Herald*, October 30, 1974.

36. "Naramore Says His Conclusions Wrong in Leahy-Mallary Election Poll," *Burlington Free Press*, November 11, 1974.

37. Bruhn interview.

38. Schaefer interview.

39. See Hunter Thompson, *Fear and Loathing on the Campaign Trail '72* (New York: Fawcett Popular Library, 1973), 203–4.

40. "Even in Vermont, Candidates Rely Heavily on Broadcast Advertising," *Burlington Free Press*, October 29, 1974.

41. Dorothy Tod, interview with the author, Vermont Statehouse, December 15,

2011. Much of the material from the next several pages comes from this source, unless otherwise stated.

42. Harwood and Knox interview.

43. "Even in Vermont, Candidates Rely Heavily on Broadcast Advertising," *Burlington Free Press*, October 29, 1974.

44. Harwood and Knox interview.

45. "Truckin': The Pat Leahy Story," *Vermont Business Magazine*, May 2009.

46. "Leahy, Family Get Ovation," *Burlington Free Press*, November 6, 1974.

47. "Mallary Concedes Late," *Burlington Free Press*, November 6, 1974.

48. "Leahy, Family Get Ovation," *Burlington Free Press*, November 6, 1974.

49. Frederick Stetson, "Stunned and Happy, Leahy Credits Number of Factors for Senate Victory," *Burlington Free Press*, November 7, 1974.

50. Ibid.

51. Tod interview.

52. "Leahy Campaigning Marked by Confidence, Openness, and Media Finesse," *Burlington Free Press*, October 28, 1974.

4. NINETY-NINTH OF ONE HUNDRED

1. Paul Bruhn, interview with the author, Burlington, VT, August 14, 2014.

2. See Mark A. Stoler, "What Did He *Really* Say? The 'Aiken Formula' for Vietnam Revisited," *Vermont History*, Spring 1978, 100–108.

3. "Chittenden Politics," *Rutland Herald*, November 1, 1974.

4. Richard E. Meyer, "George Aiken Sticks to Principles, Fulfills Senate Contract," *Burlington Free Press*, January 3, 1975.

5. The official US Senate website carries the story of Durkin's epic nail-biter under the banner, "Closest Election in Senate History." The Democrat finally prevailed, in a repeat election, by twenty-seven thousand votes. See http://www.senate .gov/artandhistory/history/minute/Closest_election_in_Senate_history.htm.

6. "Truckin': The Pat Leahy Story," *Vermont Business Magazine*, May 14, 2009.

7. From a series of reflections written by Leahy and e-mailed to the author on January 4, 2016.

8. The information in these three or four paragraphs comes from an interview with Garrison Nelson on August 28, 2015.

9. Hamilton Davis, "Leahy Stands Good Chance for Agriculture Committee," *Burlington Free Press*, January 3, 1975.

10. "Leahy's Overpaid Staff," *Burlington Free Press*, January 6, 1975.

11. "The Senate: Impressive Freshman Class," *Time*, November 18, 1974.

12. Gary Hart, phone interview with the author, October 9, 2014.

13. See "The Year of Decision: 1975," in P. Edward Haley, *Congress and the Fall of South Vietnam and Cambodia* (Toronto: Associated University Presses, 1982), 47–49.

14. Stanley Karnow, *Vietnam: A History* (New York: Viking, 1991), 675–84.

15. "The Senate: Impressive Freshman Class," *Time* magazine, November 18, 1974.

16. These paragraphs recapitulate historian Mark Stoler's persuasive reading of Aiken's 1966 speech and his sense of the senator's attitudes toward a Vietnam endgame in general. See Stoler, "What Did He *Really* Say?," 100–108.

17. Ibid., 106.

18. "The Senate: Impressive Freshman Class," *Time*, November 18, 1974.

19. Gary Hart, *The Good Fight: The Education of an American Reformer* (New York: Random House, 1993), 165–66.

20. Ibid.

21. Haley, *Congress and the Fall of South Vietnam and Cambodia*, 84. Karnow points out that, in light of their unexpected victories, the Communist leaders in Hanoi had secretly transmitted a new timetable to General Dung on March 23: the new plan was "to 'liberate' the south before the rains began in May." See Karnow, *Vietnam*, 680.

22. On March 15, 1975, Leahy told a group of Jaycees in St. Johnsbury, Vermont, "Our involvement in Cambodia and Vietnam has weakened our country for years to come. There is absolutely no question in my mind that Cambodia will fall whether we continue aid or not. . . . I think it is time we said no. No more money for the southeast Asian military." See "Sen. Leahy Repeats His 'No' to Aid for Cambodia, Thieu," *Burlington Free Press*, March 17, 1975.

23. Details of the Schlesinger meeting come from Bruhn interview, August 14, 2014.

24. Haley, *Congress and the Fall of South Vietnam and Cambodia*, 82.

25. Ibid., 83.

26. Bruhn interview.

27. The accusation was wildly off base for many reasons, not the least of which is that Richard Nixon himself had agreed to a strict cap on military aid just before leaving office. See Karnow, *Vietnam*, 675.

28. Karnow agrees: "Implicit in these pleas was a maneuver to shift the onus to Congress for South Vietnam's almost certain collapse. And indeed, in subsequent years Kissinger, Martin and others did blame the legislature for the catastrophe. Yet the politicians were simply reflecting the opinion of the overwhelming majority of Americans, who favored no further aid to the Saigon government." Ibid., 681.

29. Ibid., 86.

30. As was becoming par for the course, it was Vermont's senior senator Bob Stafford who offered Leahy some much-needed cover. On April 11, Stafford announced his own opposition to the military funding appropriation for Southeast Asia. See "Stafford, Leahy Say No Arms Aid," *Burlington Free Press*, April 11, 1975. Of course, announcing opposition and actually voting against an appropriation are two altogether different matters. Stoler believes that Leahy's present-day characterization of himself as "the only Vermonter to vote against the war in Vietnam" is probably accurate in that sense: "I don't think that Stafford or Aiken, although they spoke out against the war, ever voted against an appropriation." Mark Stoler, phone interview with the author, August 18, 2015.

31. Hart phone interview.

32. The bulk of the information about this particular session of the Senate Armed Services Committee comes from Haley's *Congress and the Fall of South Vietnam and Cambodia*, here 98–99. Haley's central focus is with the House's efforts to shut off funding for the war, but I am indebted to him for the useful information in the

fewer pages he does devote to the Senate. One note for clarification: the votes described here pertain to military funding only. The Foreign Relations Committees in the House and the Senate were moving on a parallel track to provide continuing humanitarian aid, as well as funds specifically earmarked for the evacuations related to the fall of the American-backed governments in Cambodia and Vietnam. Haley's final chapters describe that series of compromises, 125–85.

33. This moment was described with both precision and delight by Leahy in an interview conducted on July 21, 2014. Gary Hart, while acknowledging that "Patrick's recollection is a bit sharper than my own," seconded Leahy's account.

34. David Rosenbaum, "Senate Unit Bars War Aid to Saigon," *New York Times*, April 17, 1975.

35. Ibid.

36. "Leahy and War Politics," *Burlington Free Press*, Wednesday, April 9, 1975.

5. THE SECOND CHILDREN'S CRUSADE

1. Leon V. Sigal, *Negotiating Minefields: The Landmines Ban in American Politics* (New York: Routledge, 2006), 14.

2. See the United Nations' current web page on "demining," at http://www.un .org/en/globalissues/demining/. In 1992, the year Leahy first secured a moratorium on the export of landmines, there were thirty-five countries producing the devices. See also Colman McCarthy, "Land Mines Extend War's Deadly Reach," *Washington Post*, August 11, 1992.

3. Of course, Leahy's underdog bid for the Senate in 1974 would eventually come to be nicknamed "the Children's Crusade," a label that might have begun as an insult but which Leahy adopted as a badge of honor—and which he now looks back on with precisely the sort of sentimental fondness described above.

4. It's worth noting that there is some lingering haziness in the setting of this oft-told story. In 1993, the *Washington Post* placed the boy in a "field hospital in Honduras"; in 2014, the *Boston Globe* cited "a jungle village in Nicaragua." A 1996 account in the *Post* squared the circle by locating the child "in a contra rebel camp on the Honduras-Nicaragua border." See Thomas W. Lippman, "Sen. Leahy Continues Crusade against Export of Land Mines," *Washington Post*, August 8, 1993; Bryan Bender, "Formerly a Leader on Land Mine Ban, Obama Now Balks," *Boston Globe*, June 22, 2014; and Guy Gugliotta, "Caped Crusader and Anti-Mine Crusader Join Forces," *Washington Post*, November 26, 1996.

5. Bobby Muller, phone interview with the author, September 26, 2015. In presenting this pivotal meeting, I'm also drawing on Sigal's interview with Muller, conducted some years earlier and presented in *Negotiating Minefields*, 16.

6. Muller interview, September 26, 2015.

7. See Kenneth B. Lee, *Korea and East Asia: The Story of a Phoenix* (Westport, CT: Praeger, 1997), 235.

8. Bender, "Formerly a Leader on Land Mine Ban." This strategic mind-set persists to the present day. "'I consider them to be an important tool of the arsenal of the armed forces of the United States,' General Martin Dempsey, the Chairman of the Joint Chiefs of Staff, told a Congressional hearing in March [2014], 'especially

on the Korean peninsula, where they are intended to help blunt an invasion by the North Korean army.'"

9. Andrew Cohen, "Leahy Takes on the Pentagon: Unorthodox Senator from Vermont Has Made a Ban on Land Mines a Personal Crusade, Despite Pressure," *Globe and Mail*, September 29, 1997.

10. Muller interview, September 26, 2015.

11. The physics of a ban on US export were far more manageable for reasons easily understood. At that point, while US forces deployed a vast number of the devices, only one manufacturer made them, and their yearly shipment abroad amounted to only ten thousand units. Still, Leahy, Rieser, Muller, Williams, and the rest of the far-flung network of allies were in agreement: the move made a statement, and one that might be substantially expanded in the near term as well as the far. See Sigal, *Negotiating Minefields*, 17.

12. Bobby Muller, phone interview with the author, September 26, 2015.

13. 147 Cong. Rec. S10947 (Wednesday, October 24, 2001).

14. The first quote comes from Evan Lehmann, "Leahy the Storyteller," *Brattleboro Reformer*, June 16, 2007; the second is from my own phone interview with Muller, September 26, 2015.

15. Lehmann, "Leahy the Storyteller."

16. Bender, "Formerly a Leader on Landmine Ban."

17. Jody Williams, *My Name is Jody Williams: A Vermont Girl's Winding Path to the Nobel Peace Prize* (Berkeley: University of California Press, 2013), 158.

18. Sigal, *Negotiating Minefields*, 18.

19. Kenneth R. Rutherford, *Disarming States: The International Movement to Ban Landmines* (Santa Barbara, CA: Praeger Security International, 2011), 74.

20. John Ryle, "City of Words: Princesses of Peace," *Guardian*, June 30, 1997.

21. Rutherford, *Disarming States*, 59.

22. Ibid.

23. 141 Cong. Rec. S10481–84 (Friday, July 21, 1995).

24. Ibid.

25. See Williams, *My Name Is Jody Williams*, 204. It should be noted that my account of the international campaign to ban landmines is focused primarily on Leahy and American domestic politics, although I hope it also gives a flavor of the tireless work done abroad. For comprehensive and blow-by-blow accounts of that international progress, I recommend Williams's autobiography and Sigal's *Negotiating Minefields* in particular. They are both detailed and enlightening histories. I should note that Williams declined several times to be interviewed for this work; I've tried to use her autobiographical account to fill in her side of the story as best I can.

26. Dennis O'Neil, "The Senator Is Golden," COMICM!X, August 28, 2007. The interview is still archived at http://www.comicmix.com/2007/08/28/dennis-o-neil-the-senator-is-golden/.

27. Ibid.

28. "Death of Innocents: The Horror of Landmines," DC Comics, December 1996, p. 1.

29. Gugliotta, "Caped Crusader and Anti-Mine Crusader Join Forces."

30. BBC, January 14, 1997.

31. Details from this Red Cross event have been drawn from Roxanne Roberts's playful write-up, "From London, a Blitz with Glitz," *Washington Post*, June 18, 1997.

32. Ryle, "City of Words, Princesses of Peace."

33. Jayme Deerwester, "How Princess Diana's Death Shook the Media Landscape," *USA Today*, August 31, 2015. See also Craig B. Whitney, "Diana Killed in a Car Accident in Paris," *New York Times*, August 31, 1997.

34. Later Leahy would meet Diana's youngest son at the British Embassy, and Prince Harry would immediately recognize him: "I know who you are," he would tell Leahy, shaking his hand, "and my mother thought the world of you." From recollections contained in a January 4, 2016, e-mail by Senator Leahy. For the quote on the Senate floor see 143 Cong. Rec. S8710 (Wednesday, September 3, 1997).

35. "RIAA News Room — the American Recording Industry Announces Its Artists of the Century — Nov 10, 1999." Recording Industry Association of America website,November 10, 1999.

36. Williams, *My Name Is Jody Williams*, 215–16.

37. Rutherford, *Disarming States*, 109.

38. Williams, *My Name Is Jody Williams*, 221.

39. Cohen, "Leahy Takes on the Pentagon."

40. Williams, *My Name Is Jody Williams*, 224.

41. See Rutherford, *Disarming States*, 119, where the author writes, "However, it was generally agreed that Clinton would not oppose the Pentagon because he believed there was some merit to the Pentagon's point of view that they would be giving up many of their anti-tank mines. Moreover, Clinton needed the Department of Defense to support his policy of extending operations in Bosnia, expanding NATO, and closing military bases." And in 1996, Clinton had told Muller explicitly that he couldn't risk a breach with the Pentagon. Muller interview, September 26, 2015.

42. Sigal, *Negotiating Minefields*, 216.

43. Ibid., 215.

44. As I've noted earlier, Jody Williams declined several requests to be interviewed for this book. It was my hope to have an interview with her to balance my interview with Bobby Muller; given the friction following the Nobel announcement, I wanted to offer each of them equal time and space in these pages. But in lieu of a fresh interview, I have tried to represent Williams and her place in the campaign as best I could with a handful of other sources.

45. Caryle Murphy, "The Nobel Prize Fight; Claims of Jealousy and Betrayal. A Friendship in Ruins. How the World's Most Prestigious Award Turned into a Land Mine," *New York Times*, March 22, 1998. See also Sigal, *Negotiating Landmines*, 218–19, for a similar take on the Nobel frictions.

46. Cohen, "Leahy Takes on the Pentagon." It should be pointed out that in addition to his own independent nomination of Axworthy, Leahy also put his support behind the nomination of Williams and the ICBL. More than anything, he seemed to want recognition of the issue, at that moment, in order to push the ban to conclusion.

47. Muller interview, September 26, 2015.

6. LEAHY VERSUS THE BUSH WHITE HOUSE, MAY–OCTOBER 2001

1. Luke Albee, interview with the author, Burlington, VT, August 23, 2013.

2. Chris Mooney, "The Ashcroft Debate," *American Prospect*, December 19, 2001.

3. Joseph Curl, "Bush Sends Nominees 'in Good Faith'; Leahy Foresees Few Foes to 'Encouraging' Judicial Batch," *Washington Times*, May 10, 2001.

4. Ibid.

5. See Terry Eastland, "Closing Time for the Bar; and Happy Hour for Conservatives," *Weekly Standard*, April 2, 2001. The phrase "early warning missile" comes from Gonzales's biographer. See Bill Minutaglio, *The President's Counselor: The Rise to Power of Alberto Gonzales* (New York: HarperCollins, 2006), 204.

6. Associated Press, "GOP Seeks to Weaken Democrats' Ability to Stop Nominees," April 25, 2001. Under Democratic control, pre-1994, the tradition was to forward a nominee even if only one senator indicated assent with a blue slip; post-1994, Republicans used their majority to require that *both* senators assent, significantly handicapping President Clinton and empowering more hard-line conservatives like Jesse Helms of North Carolina. But in April and May 2001, with a *Republican* president in place, GOP senators were indicating a desire to at least return to the one-slip standard, if not do away with the blue-slip process altogether.

7. For the comment about Gonzales's bearing see Minutaglio, *President's Counselor*, 212; for Supreme Court buzz see ibid., 202.

8. Ibid., 204.

9. James Jeffords, *My Declaration of Independence* (New York: Simon & Schuster, 2001), 93.

10. Ibid., 66.

11. Ibid., 49.

12. Ibid., 90. See also Howard Kurtz, "Daschle on Jeffords's Switch: It's the Demographics," *Washington Post*, May 27, 2001.

13. Nancy Benac, "Emotions Spent as Sun Sets on GOP Control," Associated Press (Washington Dateline), June 6, 2001.

14. See Tom Daschle's *Like No Other Time: The Two Years That Changed America* (New York: Crown, 2003), 65. For Jeffords's take see *My Declaration of Independence*, 119.

15. Transcript of Hearing before the Committee on the Judiciary, United States Senate, 107th Congress, First Session, June 6, 2001, 1–7.

16. Ibid.

17. Jesse J. Holland, "Bush Push for More Conservative Courts in Jeopardy," Associated Press, May 24, 2001.

18. Joan Biskupic, "Bush to Submit New Judicial Choices; Stays Conservative Course on Nominations to Federal Bench," *USA Today*, June 22, 2001.

19. Ibid.

20. Ed Pagano, phone interview with the author, September 6, 2012.

21. Albee interview.

22. "FBI Faces Another Embarrassment," *CNN Live This Morning*, July 18, 2001.

23. Transcript of Hearing before the Committee on the Judiciary, US Senate, 107th Congress, First Session, July 30 and July 31, 2001, 25.

24. Many of the details of Leahy's whereabouts on 9/11 come from Robert O'Harrow Jr.'s long, highly readable magazine piece, "Six Weeks in Autumn." See the *Washington Post Magazine*, Sunday, October 27, 2002. O'Harrow moves back and forth from Leahy to one of John Ashcroft's most trusted assistants, Viet Dinh, to show the genesis and the context of the USA Patriot Act.

25. Donna Leinwand, "Coalition Criticizes Drug Czar Nominee," *USA Today*, September 7, 2001.

26. From Leahy's own recollections of 9/11, from interview with the author, July 21, 2014.

27. O'Harrow, "Six Weeks in Autumn."

28. Steve Twomey, "District Unprepared to Cope with Attack; Police Improvised; No Broadcast Made," *Washington Post*, September 17, 2001.

29. This explosive noise at 10:15 has not been explained, but it was attested to by multiple sources and demonstrates clearly how near panic were the crowds on DC streets. See David Montgomery, "Under a Cloud of Evil; Their Remaining Innocence in Shreds, People Shudder and Carry On," *Washington Post*, September 12, 2001.

30. Sam Hemingway, "Delegation Forced Out of Offices," *Burlington Free Press*, September 12, 2001.

31. Faye Fiore and Greg Miller, "DC Comes to a Crawl," *Burlington Free Press*, September 12, 2001.

32. Marcelle Leahy, interview with the author, Burlington, VT, July 21, 2014.

33. Patrick Leahy interview, July 21, 2014.

34. David Carle, phone interview with the author, October 24, 2013.

35. From C-SPAN's coverage of the September 12, 2001, Senate session. See http://c-spanvideo.org/program/SenateSession2732. All quotes in this section regarding Leahy's 9/12 remarks taken from this source. In his remarks on the floor, Leahy does not mention the name of his friend—that was supplied later by various media outlets. See Erin Kelly, "Vt. Lawmakers Speak of Anger, Anguish, Recovery," Gannett News Service, September 12, 2001.

36. Beryl Howell, phone interview with the author, September 24, 2013.

37. In his memoir *Never Again*, Attorney General Ashcroft describes a tense meeting of the National Security Council on the morning of September 12. FBI director Mueller was uncomfortable with the new line being promulgated for law enforcement, and objected: "Wait a second. If we do some of these things, it may impair our ability to prosecute." Ashcroft interrupted to assert, "This is different. . . . If we lose the ability to prosecute that's fine, but we have to prevent the next attack." Ashcroft points out that he could "see the President nodding slightly," so he continued and carried his point. See Ashcroft, *Never Again: Securing America and Restoring Justice* (New York: Center Street, 2006), 133.

38. O'Harrow, "Six Weeks in Autumn."

39. See C-SPAN video of Leahy's remarks of September 12, 2001, at http://www.c-span.org/video/?165972-1/senate-session.

40. O'Harrow, "Six Weeks in Autumn."

41. Albee interview.

42. See Beryl Howell, "Seven Weeks: The Making of the USA Patriot Act," *George Washington Law Review* 72, no. 6 (August 2004): 1149–51.

43. See 147 Cong. Rec. S9377–78 (September 13, 2001).

44. Federal Document Clearing House Political Transcripts, September 16, 2001, "US Senators Patrick Leahy and Orrin Hatch Hold News Conference at the Department of Justice after Meeting with Attorney General John Ashcroft," 1–2.

45. Ibid., 4.

46. Attorney General John Ashcroft, remarks, Press Briefing with FBI Director Robert Mueller, FBI Headquarters, September 17, 2001.

47. In a profile of Ashcroft, Jeffrey Toobin summed it up as political jujitsu: "Ashcroft's demand was a stunning act of bravado: he implied that anyone who wanted to do anything different, even on a different schedule, was jeopardizing the security of the United States." See Toobin, "Ashcroft's Ascent," *New Yorker*, April 15, 2002.

48. The Leahy quote comes from O'Harrow, "Six Weeks in Autumn"; the Howell quote is from her interview with the author, September 24, 2013.

49. The 9/11 "hardball" strategy was adopted at an October 16 GOP luncheon meeting, and from the first it involved creating and emphasizing a direct linkage between the 9/11 attacks and the slate of conservative judges Bush had nominated several months previously. Republican Party leadership made it clear to reporters that the White House backed the approach, along with a threat to block action on the Senate's foreign aid bill and other must-pass legislation. To the dismay of congressional Democrats, "hardball" seemed to be a trial run for the use of 9/11 as a sharpened spur in other areas, including the upcoming midterm elections. See Donald Lambro, "GOP 'Hardball' Ploy Aims to Fill Benches; Action Demanded on Bush Nominees," *Washington Times*, October 17, 2001. See also Neil Lewis, "Democrats Are Pushed on Judicial Nominees," *New York Times*, October 21, 2001.

50. Lewis, "Democrats Are Pushed on Judicial Nominees."

51. National Public Radio, *Talk of the Nation*, September 19, 2001.

52. In fairness to King Canute (b. 985–d. 1035), the legend has turned his story on its head. According to Henry of Huntingdon's *Historia Anglorum*, Canute ordered that his chair be carried to the shore and did indeed order the waves to cease. But it was a rhetorical move, designed to show that only God had such power. "Let all the world know," Canute decreed, "that the power of kings is empty and worthless and there is no King worthy of the name save Him by whose will heaven and earth and sea obey eternal laws." Rather than infamously proud, Canute was by original accounts actually underlining his own mortal limitations. Leahy here references the legend in its standard, though historically inaccurate, application. See "Is King Canute Misunderstood?" *BBC News Magazine*, May 26, 2011.

53. O'Harrow, "Six Weeks in Autumn."

54. "Pen registers, or 'dialed number recorders,' are instruments that record telephone dial pulses and are used by law enforcement to collect information on the telephone numbers dialed out on a telephone or 'facility' that is targeted in a criminal investigation. . . . Trap and trace is the term for devices and procedures used to collect information on the source of incoming calls to a targeted telephone or facility." Howell, "Seven Weeks," 1150.

55. Ibid., 1154.

56. O'Harrow, "Six Weeks in Autumn."

57. Howell, "Seven Weeks," 1153–54.

58. Ibid., 1155.

59. The preceding three paragraphs all draw from O'Harrow, "Six Weeks in Autumn."

60. Robert O'Harrow Jr., *No Place to Hide* (New York: Free Press, 2005), 24.

61. Howell interview.

62. Ibid.

63. Ibid.

64. Remarks by the president to employees at the Federal Bureau of Investigation, September 25, 2001. See http://georgewbush-whitehouse.archives.gov/news/releases/2001/09/20010925-5.html.

65. O'Harrow, "Six Weeks in Autumn."

66. Howell interview.

67. O'Harrow, "Six Weeks in Autumn."

68. Ibid.

69. John Lancaster, "Anti-Terrorism Bill Hits Snag on the Hill: Dispute between Senate Democrats, White House Threatens Committee Approval," *Washington Post*, October 3, 2001.

70. Ibid.

71. Jane Mayer, "Pat Leahy Recalls a Sting," *New Yorker*, October 15, 2001.

72. "The administration was not interested in congressional deliberation, compromise, or stopping to discuss details and civil liberties concerns. Instead it wanted its legislation passed immediately, and if that entailed pressuring Congress with the uncertain threats of future terrorist attacks and telling the public that congressional delay was handing terrorists an 'advantage,' those were the strategies the administration was prepared to pursue." Howell, "Seven Weeks," 1161.

73. 147 Cong. Rec. S10556, S10559 (October 11, 2001).

74. Pagano interview.

7. OCTOBER AND NOVEMBER 2001

1. The painful irony is that the anthrax powder was rushed directly into the hands of a small group of scientists who would later be recognized as prime suspects, one of whom would ultimately be charged with the crime. The Amerithrax investigation would be severely compromised and effectively sabotaged as a result. See David Willman, *The Mirage Man: Bruce Ivins, the Anthrax Attacks, and America's Rush to War* (New York: Bantam, 2011), 109–11.

2. Ibid., 105–6. See also Willman's appendix, in which he summarizes the case against Bruce Ivins, esp. 343–46.

3. These now-famous characterizations are all from Peter Jahrling. Richard Preston, *The Demon in the Freezer: A True Story* (New York: Random House, 2002), 172. USAMRIID is the US Army Medical Research Institute of Infectious Diseases.

4. For an example of this specious line of analysis see Rick Weiss and Dan Eggen, "Anthrax Additive Helped Spread Spores," *Washington Post*, October 25, 2001.

5. Tom Daschle, *Like No Other Time: The Two Years That Changed America* (New York: Crown, 2003), 171–72.

6. Marilyn W. Thompson, *The Killer Strain: Anthrax and a Government Exposed* (HarperCollins, 2003), 165–66.

7. All quotes from Luke Albee are drawn from an interview with the author in Burlington, VT, August 23, 2013.

8. Thompson, *Killer Strain*, 166.

9. Beryl Howell, phone interview with the author, September 24, 2013.

10. Albee interview.

11. John Lancaster and Susan Schmidt, "31 Exposed to Anthrax on Capitol Hill," *Washington Post*, October 18, 2001.

12. Beryl Howell, phone interview with the author, September 24, 2013.

13. Julie Katzman, phone interview with the author, October 17, 2013.

14. Ibid.

15. Darlene Superville, "Secret Offices a Senate Tradition," *USA Today*, June 4, 2007.

16. Howell interview, September 24, 2013.

17. Albee interview.

18. Robert O'Harrow Jr., "Six Weeks in Autumn," *Washington Post Magazine*, Sunday, October 27, 2002.

19. Ed Pagano, phone interview with the author, September 6, 2012.

20. Daschle, *Like No Other Time*, 136. See also Howell, "Seven Weeks," 1147.

21. With one exception: Daschle would personally press the president to accept the money-laundering provisions agreed upon by the House and Senate, even though the GOP's donor base was not happy with them. Bush, faced with a Daschle ultimatum, would finally agree to the last-minute inclusion. *Like No Other Time*, 136–37.

22. Sonya Ross, "Bush Signs Bill Giving Police Broader Powers," *Burlington Free Press*, October 27, 2001.

23. This quote and much of the background about this trip to Ground Zero come from the Katzman interview.

24. From a series of reflections written by Leahy and e-mailed to the author on January 4, 2016.

25. 147 Cong. Rec. S11005 (October 25, 2001).

26. Albee interview.

27. "Sen. Patrick Leahy, D-VT, Was Struck in the Face," United Press International, May 25, 1983.

28. Dave Gram, "Leahy: We Won't Be Scared Off by Anthrax Threat," Associated Press state and local wire, November 17, 2001.

29. Kevin Johnson, "Authorities Will Use Robot to Open Letter Sent to Sen. Leahy," *USA Today*, November 29, 2001. Within a few days, scientists at Fort Detrick had begun to push back on the story that a robot would be used, and the pictures posted on the FBI website under the heading "Opening the Letter" suggest that it was a more prosaic, though still high-tech operation, with a scientist manipulating the envelope in a sealed box via protective gauntlets. See CNN.com, "Anthrax Cleanup Under Way in Senate Office Building," December 2, 2001. See as well the FBI page, at http://www.fbi.gov/about-us/history/famous-cases/anthrax -amerithrax/the-leahy-letter.

30. Kyra Philips, "Patrick Leahy Holds Press Conference," CNN Event Live/Special 11:42, November 17, 2001.

31. Marselis Parsons, interview with the author, South Burlington, VT, February 20, 2012.

32. "Leahy: Anthrax Letter Could Have Killed 100,000," *USA Today*, November 25, 2001.

33. See Thompson, *Killer Strain*, 172, for the material about the opening of the letter; p. 163 contains the information about the tragic death of Ottilie Lundgren.

34. See, for example, Jennifer A. Dlouhy's piece, "Leahy Pushing Congressional Role in Terrorist Tribunals," *Congressional Quarterly Daily Monitor*, December 6, 2001.

35. Jeffrey Toobin, "Ashcroft's Ascent," *New Yorker*, April 15, 2002.

36. Transcript of Judiciary Committee Hearing, "Department of Justice Oversight: Preserving Our Freedoms While Defending against Terrorism," 107th Congress, First Session, December 6, 2001, J-107-50, pp. 309-10.

37. Ibid.

38. Toobin, "Ashcroft's Ascent."

39. Jerry Seper, "Leahy Challenges Bush on Military Tribunals," *Washington Times*, November 16, 2001.

40. Transcript of Judiciary Committee Hearing, "Department of Justice Oversight: Preserving Our Freedoms While Defending against Terrorism," 107th Congress, First Session, December 6, 2001, J-107-50, p. 311.

41. Toobin, "Ashcroft's Ascent."

42. Surprisingly enough, the sales campaign metaphor actually originated with the White House itself. In early September, then White House chief of staff Andrew Card would point out that the administration had decided to wait out the summer months before rolling out the specifics of its Iraq War resolution. "From a marketing point of view, you don't introduce new products in August," Card noted breezily. See Elisabeth Bumiller, "Traces of Terror: The Strategy; Bush Aides Set Strategy to Sell Policy on Iraq," *New York Times*, September 7, 2002.

43. See David Frum, *The Right Man: The Surprise Presidency of George W. Bush* (New York: Random House, 2003), here 238 for the speech context.

44. Leahy's intuitions were precisely on target. "A secret Justice Department memo written after 9/11 concluded that there were 'no limits' on presidential power when it came to waging the war on terrorism. . . . The president's decisions in a time of war, [John] Yoo wrote, were 'for him alone' and 'unreviewable.'" See Michael Isikoff and David Corn, *Hubris: The Inside Story of Spin, Scandal, and the Selling of the Iraq War* (New York: Crown, 2006), 22-23.

45. These recollections of presidents 41 and 43 are drawn from an interview with the author, July 21, 2014.

46. Frum, *The Right Man*, 29.

47. Steven R. Weisman, "Threats and Responses: Security Council; Powell, in U.N. Speech, Presents Case to Show Iraq Has Not Disarmed," *New York Times*, February 6, 2003.

48. Text available at www.congress.gov/bill/107th-congress/senate-concurrent -resolution/133/text.

49. Warren P. Strobel, "Lawmakers Want Bush to Seek Congressional Approval before Attacking Iraq," Knight Ridder Newspapers, July 31, 2002.

50. See Edward Kennedy, *True Compass: A Memoir* (New York: Hachette, 2009), 494.

51. Leahy interview, July 21, 2014.

52. Isikoff and Corn, *Hubris*, 133–37.

53. Ibid., 137. According to a later biography of Hillary Clinton, she was *not* one of the few who read the NIE, choosing instead to be "briefed on the intelligence." See also "Records: Senators Who Okay'd War Didn't Read Key Report," CNN.com, May 29, 2007.

54. Isikoff and Corn, *Hubris*, 134.

55. Again, from Leahy's recollections in interview, July 21, 2014. Leahy singles out Patty Murray as a particular "profile in courage" for her staunch opposition to the resolution.

56. See http://www.c-span.org/video/?173141-1/senate-session&start=36101 for a C-SPAN video and transcript of this speech.

57. Jeff Zeleny, "Leahy Endorses Obama," *Caucus* blog (*New York Times*), January 17, 2008. The endorsement of Obama would sour relations between Leahy and the Clintons for years. Ed Pagano, Leahy's former chief of staff, describes the reaction of Hillary Clinton's campaign staff as sharp and almost instantaneous: "I remember getting an angry call from Clinton's chief of staff, within an hour of the endorsement, saying, 'What are you *doing*? What are you going to do when you have to work with President Clinton?' And Leahy certainly got the cold shoulder from Bill Clinton for a few years after that." From an interview with Pagano, September 6, 2012.

58. See C-SPAN, "Senator Leahy Iraq War Authorization," at http://www.c-span .org/video/?c4464000/senator-leahy-iraq-war-authorization for video of this speech.

59. Karl Rove, *Courage and Consequence: My Life as a Conservative in the Fight* (New York: Threshold Editions, 2010), 313.

60. All but forgotten, ironically, was the fact that Bush himself had bitterly fought the creation of the Department of Homeland Security in the first place, preferring that it remain the smaller and less all-inclusive Office of Homeland Security. For some typical White House pushback on the idea of a DHS see CNN's transcript of a press conference with Ari Fleischer, CNN Live Event/Special, 12:54, "White House Press Secretary Briefs Reporters," March 19, 2002.

61. Max Cleland, *Heart of a Patriot: How I Found the Courage to Survive Vietnam, Walter Reed, and Karl Rove* (New York: Simon & Schuster, 2010), 193. For the record, Rove insists today that "I did not conceive, create, craft, prepare, or have anything to do with the Chambliss television ad. But I thought it was effective because it was factual." *Courage and Consequence*, 312.

62. Mark Leibovich, "Vermont's Senators, in the Hot Seats," *Washington Post*, November 7, 2002.

63. Ibid.

8. NEMESES AND ARCHENEMIES

1. The level of waste and abuse was titanic in scale. To take one intriguing example, the Pentagon used Air Force C-17 transport planes to ship shrink-wrapped pallets of $100 bills to the new US-supported government in Iraq. The money was drawn from frozen Iraqi accounts in the United States. Billions in cash disappeared, some $1.6 billion of which was later discovered hidden in a rural bunker in Lebanon; Stuart W. Bowen, a special inspector general appointed to look into the missing funds, ultimately couldn't get the US government interested in prosecuting the theft. See James Risen, "Investigation into Missing Iraqi Cash Ended in Lebanon Bunker," *New York Times*, October 12, 2014.

2. Ann Coulter, "Our Move toward Monarchy," *Augusta (GA) Chronicle*, October 21, 2005. See also Evan Lehmann, "Leahy: I Feel Sorry for Miers," *Brattleboro Reformer*, October 26, 2005.

3. Gonzales nomination hearing, January 6, 2005. For an easy-to-access transcript see "Text: The Gonzales Nomination Hearing," *Washington Post*, January 6, 2005.

4. See Bill Minutaglio, *The President's Counselor: The Rise to Power of Alberto Gonzales* (New York: Rayo Books, 2006), 143–45.

5. Patrick Leahy, interview with the author, Burlington, VT, July 21, 2014.

6. Garrett Epps, "Constitutional Myth #3: The 'Unitary Executive' Is a Dictator in War and Peace," *Atlantic*, June 9, 2011.

7. These quotes come from two sources. See David Johnston's "Empowered Democrats Have Questions for Bush; Senators Want to Know about Detainees," *International Herald Tribune*, November 25, 2006. And for the final two quotes see Evan Lehmann, "Leahy Flexes Muscle," *Brattleboro Reformer*, December 14, 2006.

8. This detailed account of the call with Battle is drawn from Iglesias's fascinating memoir, *In Justice: Inside the Scandal That Rocked the Bush Administration*, with Davin Seay (Hoboken, NJ: John Wiley & Sons, 2008), here 1–19.

9. "The U.S. Attorneys fired" on Pearl Harbor Day "were Daniel Bogden, Paul Charlton, Margaret Chiara, David Iglesias, Carol Lam, John McKay, and Kevin Ryan. On January 24, 2006, Todd Graves was told to resign; on June 14, 2006, H. E. 'Bud' Cummins was told to resign." From the Justice Department's September 2008 internal review of the scandal. See the archived report at https://oig.justice.gov/special /s0809a/final.pdf.

10. George W. Bush and other presidents, like Bill Clinton, had asked remaining US attorneys to resign with the beginning of a new administration, as is accepted practice for most other federal appointments. The distinction with the 2006 firings was that they came midterm, on the watch of the same president who had done the hiring, and for no stated reason. See Iglesias's *In Justice*, here 48.

11. Ibid., 64.

12. Ibid., 66.

13. Ibid., 67.

14. Ibid., 132.

15. See "Senators Feinstein, Leahy, Pryor to Fight Administration's Effort to Circumvent Senate Confirmation Process for US Attorneys," archived at www .Feinstein.Senate.Gov/.

16. David Johnston, "Justice Dept. Names New Prosecutors, Forcing Some Out," *New York Times*, January 17, 2007. See also Rachel Van Dongen, "Democrats to Press Gonzales on Dismissals," *Roll Call*, January 18, 2007.

17. David Stout, "Court to Monitor Domestic US Spying; Turnabout Seems to Be Concession by Bush to Critics," *International Herald Tribune*, January 18, 2007.

18. Beth Gorham, "Bush Facing Rough Ride: Democratic Senator Leahy Promises Close Questioning of White House Actions," *Montreal Gazette*, January 20, 2007.

19. Leahy's single line in *The Dark Knight* (2008) is strikingly similar: "We're not intimidated by thugs!" Given that Leahy's shoot for the second film in Nolan's famed trilogy took place in midsummer of 2007, it's conceivable that the script had reached Leahy's hand by the previous January—in which case, his bravado with the Bush administration might have been colored by his upcoming Batman role. Or the distinct echo might be sheer coincidence. The only thing certain is that here, as in many moments of Leahy's long political career, graphic novel and reality finally intermarry.

20. Dan Eggen, "Interim Ark. U.S. Attorney Won't Seek Job; Former Rove Aide Says Senate Democrats Would Block Permanent Nomination," *Washington Post*, February 17, 2007. Also see Adam Cohen's op-ed "Why Have So Many US Attorneys Been Fired? It Looks a Lot Like Politics," *New York Times*, February 26, 2007.

21. For Gonzales's first tentative attempt to denigrate the performance of the nine fired attorneys see Dan Eggen, "US Attorney Firings Set Stage for Congressional Battle," *Washington Post*, February 4, 2007.

22. Iglesias, *In Justice*, 168.

23. All quotes from this March 6, 2007, hearing are drawn from the C-SPAN coverage of the hearing, archived at http://www.c-span.org/video/?196957-1/dismissal-us-attorneys&start=1863.

24. Iglesias, *In Justice*, 181.

25. Readable transcript *Washington Post* archival site, at http://www.washingtonpost.com/wp-srv/politics/documents/senatejudiciary_hearing_030607.htm.

26. See Marisa Taylor and Margaret Talev, "Prosecutors Still Need Senate OK; Legislation in Reaction to Firings Would Bar Attorney General from Naming US Attorneys without Consent," *Contra Costa (CA) Times*, March 9, 2007; James Gordon Meek, "'MISTAKES WERE MADE'; AG Admits Firings Botched; Dem Pressure Grows," *New York Daily News*, March 14, 2007; and Paul Kane and Dan Eggen, "Gonzales Yields on Hiring Interim U.S. Attorneys," *Washington Post*, March 9, 2007. See also C-SPAN's archived footage of the March 13 press conference at http://www.c-span.org/video/?197087-1/us-attorney-dismissals.

27. Dana Milbank, "The Grand Elusion," *Washington Post*, March 14, 2007.

28. Ron Hutcheson, "Bush Defends the Firing of US Attorneys," McClatchy Newspapers, March 14, 2007.

29. Evan Lehmann, "Leahy Puts on Gloves," *Brattleboro Reformer*, April 16, 2007.

30. Ibid.

31. Peter Grier, "Email Trail Shows Power Struggle behind US Attorney's Firings," *Christian Science Monitor*, March 21, 2007; and Dan Eggen and Amy Goldstein, "Emails Show Machinations to Replace Prosecutor," *Washington Post*, March 23, 2007.

32. Sheryl Gay Stolberg, "Bush Criticizes How Dismissals of U.S. Attorneys Were Handled," *New York Times*, March 15, 2007; and also Stolberg's "With Shifting Explanations, White House Adds to Storm," *New York Times*, March 17, 2007.

33. Michael Abramowitz and Paul Kane, "Bush Offers Aides for Hill Interviews; Democrats Probing Firings Chafe at Conditions," *Washington Post*, March 21, 2007.

34. On April 12, Leahy charged in a "tirade" on the Senate floor that the White House had deliberately "lost" a sequence of key e-mails that might have served to demonstrate the complicity of Karl Rove and Harriet Miers. As had become his now-standard practice, Leahy reached immediately for the appropriate Nixon-era analogy. "They say they have not been preserved. I don't believe that! . . . Those emails are there; they just don't want to produce them. It's like the infamous 18-minute gap in the Nixon White House tapes." See Margaret Talev and Marisa Taylor, "Electronic 'Watergate' Alleged; Leahy Says White House Burying Attorney Data," McClatchy Newspapers, April 13, 2007.

35. David G. Savage, "Bush Appointee Saw Justice Lawyers as 'Commies,' 'Crazy Libs,' Report Says," *Los Angles Times*, January 14, 2009.

36. Richard A. Serrano, "Justice Department Reportedly Bent Rules on Voter Fraud Charges," *Los Angeles Times*, June 6, 2007.

37. Leahy's point is simply that the manual directs US attorneys to avoid, if at all possible, bringing prosecutions in the weeks before an election to avoid inadvertently swaying voters—in that narrow sense, the manual advises "timing prosecutions to elections." Text and video available at C-SPAN, "Dismissal of U.S. Attorneys," June 5, 2007, http://www.c-span.org/video/?198474-1/dismissal-us-attorneys.

38. David Stout and Brian Knowlton, "Gonzales Played a Role in Firings, Former Aide Says," *International Herald Tribune*, March 30, 2007; Margaret Talev and Marisa Taylor, "Top Gonzales Aide Quits after Refusing to Testify," *Pittsburgh Post-Gazette*, April 7, 2007; Dan Eggen and Paul Kane, "Gonzales Prepares to Fight for His Job in Testimony," *Washington Post*, April 5, 2007; and Michael A. Fletcher, "Another Top Bush Aide Makes an Exit," *Washington Post*, May 28, 2007.

39. For a transcript of this hearing see the *Washington Post*'s readable copy at http://www.washingtonpost.com/wpsrv/politics/documents/gonzalez_transcript _072407.html. And as always, C-SPAN provides the video, archived at http://www .c-span.org/video/?200082-1/dismissal-us-attorneys.

40. Dana Milbank reports that at the hearing's close, the protesters also "leaped over chairs, getting close enough to Gonzales to make him flinch." See "With Senate and Gonzales, Familiarity Breeds Contempt," *Washington Post*, July 25, 2007.

41. Leahy interview, July 21, 2014.

42. Dana Milbank, "The Caped Crusader from Vermont," *Washington Post*, August 21, 2007.

43. "Tearful Rove Resigns from White House," *Guardian*, August 13, 2007; and Evan Lehmann, "Leahy: Rove Not in Clear," *Brattleboro Reformer*, August 14, 2007.

44. Gonzales would more or less maintain his silence on the scandal until 2010, when an internal investigation by career prosecutor Nora Dannehy found that while the Justice Department's actions under Gonzales were "inappropriately political," there was no basis for criminal charges. Predictably enough, Gonzales chose to

view the findings as entirely exculpatory. "I feel angry that I had to go through this," he told CNN. "That my family had to suffer through and what for?" See "Alberto Gonzales on U.S. Attorney Firing Scandal: 'I Feel Angry That I Had to Go through This,'" *Huffington Post*, July 23, 2010.

45. Iglesias, *In Justice*, 104. See also "Gonzales Calls It Quits," *Brattleboro Reformer*, August 27, 2007.

46. Available at http://www.pbs.org/video/1082073775/.

47. The task force's focus on Ivins would come only after a long, disastrous pursuit of a first suspect—Stephen J. Hatfill, another bioweapons researcher at Fort Detrick. The case against Hatfill never truly materialized, in spite of wisps of evidence, and in February 2008 a federal judge ruled conclusively for Hatfill. The botched investigation would nearly cripple the Amerithrax group, and that damaged credibility would prove its greatest hurdle once it lighted subsequently on Ivins. David Willman, *The Mirage Man: Bruce Ivins, the Anthrax Attacks, and America's Rush to War* (New York: Bantam, 2011), chap. 26, "Not a Scintilla of Evidence," esp. 283–84.

48. Steele "saw that the first three bold-faced characters . . . were TTT. Assuming that TTT represented three consecutive nucleic acids, this sequence would code for a specific amino acid, a building block of DNA called Phenylalanine. The next three boldfaced characters in the New York letter were AAT, which coded for another amino acid, Asparagine. The final three boldfaced characters were TAT, which coded for a third amino acid, Tyrosine. Hence PAT, derived from the first letter of each coded amino acid." Willman, *Mirage Man*, 300–301.

49. Leahy interview: see "Tales from the Rusty Scuffer: A Little Light Lunch with Senator Patrick Leahy," *Vermont Daily Briefing*, September 5, 2007.

50. David Freed, "The Wrong Man," *Atlantic*, May 2010. For additional information about Rosenberg's theories, and Leahy's consideration of them, see Willman, *Mirage Man*, 166–69. It's worth noting that Rosenberg proved correct about the provenance of the anthrax and the professional affiliation of the mailer—the FBI would eventually admit that an American bioweapons researcher working in an American weapons lab was the culprit. Still, Rosenberg's conviction that Hatfill was the perpetrator turned out to be misguided, though again no more misguided than the FBI's own early pursuit of Hatfill.

51. This statement remains true, even though the US government had good reason in the years leading up to 2001 to be on the lookout for the use of the US mail in bioterrorism. See Marilyn W. Thompson, *The Killer Strain* (New York: HarperCollins, 2003), 48–49.

52. Ibid., 169.

53. Tom Daschle, *Like No Other Time: The Two Years That Changed America* (New York: Crown, 2003), 177.

54. Willman, *Mirage Man*, 147–48.

55. Ibid., 350. This paragraph summarizes many of the Amerithrax task force's findings on Ivins, all laid out at length in Willman's text.

56. Ibid., 182–83.

57. Willman very usefully sums up the major tenets of the task force's case in an appendix titled "The Case against Bruce Ivins," ibid., 339–58.

58. Ibid., 310.

59. Dina Temple-Raston, "Anthrax Suspect's Abortion Stance Eyed as Motive," NPR, August 7, 2008. The timing and focus of the article are certainly suggestive: "The Ivins affidavit mentions an article in the September/October 2001 issue of the Right to Life of Greater Cincinnati newsletter that singled out Daschle, Leahy and Sens. Edward Kennedy and Joseph Biden for criticism because of their abortions rights votes."

60. Willman, *Mirage Man*, 80.

61. David Willman, e-mail to the author, June 6, 2015.

62. Daschle continued to voice strong skepticism about the Amerithrax probe even after the FBI's announcement following Ivins's suicide. Ivins, the former majority leader worried publicly, might be "just another false track and a real diversion of where they need to be. We don't know, and they aren't telling us." But within days he had been elaborately briefed on the Ivins dossier and soon voiced his support of the bureau's conclusions, calling them "complete and persuasive." To see the shift, compare CBS News's "Daschle Critical of Anthrax Probe," August 3, 2008, with Mike Nizza's "Daschle Is Persuaded on the Anthrax Case," the *Lede* blog (*New York Times*), August 13, 2008.

63. Willman, *Mirage Man*, 329. Italics in original.

64. "Anthrax Suspicions," editorial, *Washington Post*, September 19, 2008.

65. Laura Fitzpatrick, "Nagging Questions in Anthrax Case," *Time*, August 13, 2008.

66. Chuck Bennett, "'Thrax Man Was a Spore Loser; Homicidal Pat Bared in Shrink's Files," *New York Post*, August 2, 2008; Bennett, "Dr. Anthrax Was Kreepy Kappa Lover," *New York Post*, August 5, 2008; Michael McAuliff, "Anthrax Doc Kills Himself," *New York Daily News*, August 2, 2008; James Gordon Meek, "Feds Unseal Dr. Death's 'Checklist' of Doom," *New York Daily News*, August 8, 2008; "Loon in the Lab," editorial, *New York Daily News*, August 11, 2008.

9. FOR LOVE OF THE BATMAN

1. John Brodie, "D.C. Dreams It Wakes Up Screening," *Variety*, July 10–16, 1995.

2. *Batman Forever* earned $184 million to *Toy Story*'s $191.7 million. *Box Office Mojo*, 1995 Domestic Grosses.

3. The Glover quote is drawn from *Shadows of the Bat: The Cinematic Saga of the Dark Knight Part 6 — Batman Unbound*, 2005, Warner Home Video; for Clooney's quote see Mac Daniel, "Batman and Robin," *Boston Globe*, May 17, 2006; see also Nate Jones, "A Brief History of George Clooney Apologizing for Being a Bad Batman," Vulture.com, October 14, 2014.

4. "Bat Senator, the Sequel," *Roll Call*, June 28, 2007.

5. Leahy described one such night in his impromptu eulogy for Valenti, on May 9, 2007: "On a personal basis, with he and Mary Margaret, we would sit sometimes having a quiet meal at their house or on one occasion at a favorite restaurant of theirs, on a soft summer evening, sitting outdoors and talking about kids and, in that case, their pending grandchild" (153 Cong. Rec. S11730). Of course, not all of Valenti's events were so placid in nature. When he was not in Washington, Valenti

was living a life of old-school Hollywood luxury at the Beverly Hills Hotel. There he all but owned the booth facing the entrance in the Polo Lounge, and as he wrote in 2007, "I conducted my meetings in regal, and visible, splendor." Jack Valenti, *This Time, This Place* (New York: Harmony Books, 2007), 299–300.

6. Ibid.

7. Roxanne Roberts, "Out and About," *Washington Post*, December 20, 1999.

8. Amy Argetsinger and Roxanne Roberts, "Stars and Pols See Jack Valenti Off to 'Holy-World,'" *Washington Post*, May 2, 2007.

9. Ibid., 317. Leahy's remarks for the *Congressional Record*, on the day of Valenti's funeral, include the information about the memoir's place in his Senate desk.

10. See Warner Bros. extensive and atmospheric online production notes for *Batman Begins* at http://www2.warnerbros.com/batmanbegins/productionnotes/. Much of the material in these few paragraphs derives from this source.

11. Information from *The Worldwide Guide to Movie Locations*, "*The Dark Knight* film locations." See www.movie-locations.com.

12. This characterization of the relationship is Senator Leahy's, from interview with the author, July 21, 2014.

13. "Christopher Nolan Talks about Escalating the Batman Saga," Film School Rejects, July 14, 2008.

14. The anecdotes that follow, including both quoted and unquoted material, are drawn primarily from the Leahy interview of July 21, 2014.

15. From a contemporaneous CNN report: "Hydrocodone and oxycodone are painkillers. Diazepam is an anti-anxiety drug commonly sold under the brand name Valium; alprazolam is also an anti-anxiety drug sold under such names as Xanax. Temazepam, sold under such names as Restoril and Euhypnos, is a sleeping agent. Doxylamine, an antihistamine, can be obtained over the counter as a sleep aid." "Ledger's Death Caused by Accidental Overdose," CNN, February 6, 2008, http://www.cnn.com/2008/SHOWBIZ/Movies/02/06/heath.ledger/.

16. Jody Duncan Jesser and Janine Pourroy, *The Art and Making of the Dark Knight Trilogy* (New York: Harry N. Abrams, 2012), 169.

17. Pam Belluck, "A Bigger Stage for a Senator," *New York Times*, July 12, 2008.

18. Ibid.

19. From the first, the character created for Leahy in the *Dark Knight* films drew much more from DA Harvey Dent than playboy Bruce Wayne. Dent, as his introductory panels in August 1942 would describe him, was "Gotham City's youngest District Attorney—a man on the rise" (Detective Comics no. 66). Both are the youngest prosecutors ever in their respective worlds, and each begins his career prosecuting crime at the tender age of twenty-six. Nolan's script itself seems only to forward the parallel. To take one prime example, when Heath Ledger—in the bravura performance of his short life—comes rampaging into Bruce Wayne's birthday party, knife in hand, calling loudly for Harvey Dent, it's actually Senator Patrick Leahy of Vermont that he finds.

20. Leahy has donated all his Hollywood royalties to the Kellogg-Hubbard, in addition to the much larger amounts generated by fund-raisers associated with the premieres of *The Dark Knight* and *The Dark Knight Rises*. A wing of the grateful

Kellogg-Hubbard now bears Leahy's name. Paul Heintz, "Holy Cash, Batman!," *Seven Days*, July 11, 2012.

21. Jane Lindholm, "Leahy Says New Batman Film Won't Disappoint Fans," Vermont Public Radio, July 17, 2008.

22. Barry Meyer, chairman and CEO, Warner Bros., MPAA Symposium: "The Business of Show Business," February 6, 2007.

23. Ibid.

24. "What Is Senator Patrick Leahy Doing in 'The Dark Knight'?," Vulture.com, July 11, 2008.

25. Tim Arango, "Time Warner Focuses on the Big Picture; New Chief Bets on TV and Film as the Company Cuts Back Elsewhere," *International Herald Tribune*, August 11, 2008.

26. The writing of Dennis O'Neil and the art of Neal Adams refashioned the Joker more along sociopathic lines, starting in 1973. See *Batman* no. 251. This emphasis on the Joker as serial killer continued throughout the 1980s and served as the dark backdrop for many of the contemporary film adaptations.

27. Jesser and Pourroy, *Art and Making of the Dark Knight Trilogy*, 169.

28. "Christopher Nolan Talks about Escalating the Batman Saga," Film School Rejects, July 14, 2008.

29. Wrote Manohla Dargis of the *New York Times*, "His death might have cast a paralyzing pall over the film if the performance were not so alive. But his Joker is a creature of such ghastly life, and the performance is so visceral, creepy and insistently present that the characterization pulls you in almost at once." From "Showdown in Gotham Town," *New York Times*, July 18, 2008.

30. Ibid.

31. Dana Milbank, "But Enough about Her," *Washington Post*, June 3, 2009.

32. The material on this July 2000 Judiciary Committee hearing comes from Philip Shenon's "Cybersenator Defends the Net, Despite Some Sour Notes," *New York Times*, July 17, 2000.

33. Valenti, *This Time, This Place*, 301–2.

34. Barry Meyer, chairman and CEO, Warner Bros., MPAA Symposium: "The Business of Show Business," February 6, 2007

35. From a November 18, 2000, Leahy press release titled "Senate Judiciary Committee Advances Bipartisan Bill to Combat Copyright Infringement and Counterfeits." Archived at Leahy.senate.gov.

36. As critics pointed out, the 1998 Digital Millennium Copyright Act had given copyright owners the narrow power to have their copyrighted material removed from an infringing website, and only that material. But COICA would allow entire sites to be taken offline, effectively disappearing all noncontested material along with the infringed. See Peter Eckersley, "The Case against COICA," from the website for the Electronic Frontier Foundation, November 18, 2010. See www.eff.org.

37. Edward Lee, *The Fight for the Future: How People Defeated Hollywood and Saved the Internet—for Now* (Creative Commons Attribution Non-Commercial-ShareAlike 3.0 United States License), 11–12.

38. Ibid.

39. During the 1998 election cycle, the Leahy campaign had actually run a sixty-second television ad entitled "Cyber-Senator," designed not just to show Leahy's technological savvy but also the Internet's direct implications for economic development. The ad itself is still available on Leahyforvermont.com. For an early instance of the media's use of the alliterative nickname see Philip Shenon's "Cybersenator Defends the Net."

40. Shenon, "Cybersenator Defends the Net."

41. Chris Pratt, "Leahy's Law (COICA) and Free Speech on the Internet," *Brattleboro Reformer*, November 5, 2010.

42. Nate Anderson, "Senator: Web Censorship Bill a 'Bunker-Busting Cluster Bomb,'" *Wired Magazine*, November 20, 2010.

43. Net neutrality is the concept that Internet service providers should enable access to all content regardless of the source, and without favoring or impeding particular products or websites. Like free speech, Net neutrality is a foundational principle for most online activists, and Franken connected early with this constituency. In another way, however, Franken's support for both COICA and PIPA (like Leahy's) was complicated by the fact that he himself was a copyright holder, as a best-selling author and *SNL* cast member. And in that way, critics might dismiss the support as essentially self-interested. See Zach Carter, "SOPA: Washington vs. the Web," *Huffington Post*, August 12, 2014.

44. Ben Sisario, "Internet Providers to Help Thwart Online Piracy," Media Decoder, *New York Times*, July 7, 2011.

45. Mike Masnick, "Full Text of the Protect IP Act Released: The Good, the Bad, and the Horribly Ugly," *TechDirt*, May 11, 2011. See www.techdirt.com. For another typical reaction to the first draft of PIPA see Larry Downes, "Leahy's Protect IP Bill Even Worse Than COICA," *CNET Magazine*, May 12, 2011.

46. Google's willingness to self-censor in order to penetrate China's lucrative market represents a kind of original censorship sin for online free speech advocates. Linking any new development with it is a very charged rhetorical move. For background see "Google Censors Itself for China," BBC News, January 25, 2006.

47. "Wyden Places Hold on Protect IP Act; Overreaching Legislation Still Poses a Significant Threat to Internet Commerce, Innovation and Free Speech," press release posted on Wyden's congressional website, May 26, 2011. See www.Wyden.senate.gov.

48. Report from the Senate Judiciary Committee, to Accompany S. 968, Preventing Real Online Threats to Economic Creativity and Theft of Intellectual Property Act of 2011, issued July 22, 2011, 4–5.

49. A good amount of the information for this segment is drawn from an interview Leahy did in the run-up to the film's premiere. See "Senator Leahy Talks 'The Dark Knight Rises,'" Movies in the Morning, WCAX Channel 3, July 12, 2012.

50. Jesser and Pourroy, *Art and Making of the Dark Knight Trilogy*, 51.

51. Much of the information about the November 9 meeting, as well as the push against SOPA/PIPA in general, comes from Edward Lee's *Fight for the Future*, here 39–40.

52. Ibid., 30.

53. Beth Marlowe, "SOPA (Stop Online Piracy Act) Debate: Why Are Google and Facebook against It?," *Washington Post*, November 17, 2011. The *Post* referred to SOPA as "buzzy," and from the end of October forward SOPA generated significantly more negative attention and opposition than Leahy's PIPA, although quite often the two were simply lumped together as SOPA/PIPA and treated as a single entity to be contested.

54. Lee, *Fight for the Future*, 40.

55. Ibid., 40–41.

56. Ibid., 44–46.

57. The White House automatically responds to any We the People petition that garners over one hundred thousand signatures in thirty days; in this case, the two anti-SOPA/PIPA petitions taken together crossed that threshold. View the successful petitions at https://petitions.whitehouse.gov/response/combating-online -piracy-while-protecting-open-and-innovative-internet.

58. *Vermont Edition* with Jane Lindholm, Vermont Public Radio, January 12, 2012.

59. Ibid.

60. As the *New York Times* read it, the White House statement was in fact a mortal blow: "The Obama administration said Saturday that it strongly opposed central elements of two Congressional efforts to enforce copyrights on the Internet, all but killing the current versions of legislation that has divided both political parties and pitted Hollywood against Silicon Valley." See Edward Wyatt, "White House Says It Opposes Parts of Two Anti-Piracy Bills," *New York Times*, January 14, 2012.

61. Lee, *Fight for the Future*, 96.

62. Ibid., 96–98. For more information on real-world protests see Jenna Wortham, "Protests against Antipiracy Bills Take to the Streets," *New York Times*, January 18, 2012; for the Wyden quote see Jonathan Weisman, "After an Online Firestorm, Congress Shelves Antipiracy Bills," *New York Times*, January 20, 2012.

63. Lee, *Fight for the Future*, 99–101.

64. Weisman, "After an Online Firestorm."

65. Mitch Wertlieb, "Leahy Says PIPA Concerns Unfounded," Vermont Public Radio, January 19, 2012.

66. See LazyTechGuys, "3 out of 4 Presidential Debate Candidates Oppose SOPA at Charleston Debate," http://lazytechguys.com/news/3-out-of-4-gop-presidential -candidates-oppose-sopa-at-charleston-debate-video.

67. Weisman, "After an Online Firestorm."

68. Ibid.

69. Video of the January 23 speech is available at http://www.c-span.org/video /?303818-1/us-senate.

70. See Zach Carter, "Patrick Leahy, Democratic Senator, Mocked by Progressive Group for Batman Appearance," *Huffington Post*, July 18, 2012; and also Andy Bromage, "Holy Slamming-Leahy's-Ties-to-Hollywood-and-Batman, Batman!," *Seven Days*, July 19, 2012.

71. "During the six-year election cycle leading up to Leahy's 2010 reelection, Time Warner was the second-biggest donor to his campaign and political action committee, according to OpenSecrets.org. The company and its employees ponied

up more than $84,000 to the senator—more than to any other politician." Heintz, "Holy Cash, Batman!" Surprisingly, given the sharpness of his column's implications, Heintz repeatedly declined to be interviewed for this project.

72. Luke Baynes, "'Dark Knight' Descends on Williston," *Williston (VT) Observer*, July 19, 2012.

73. Even long-standing and very small-bore congressional perks related to Hollywood suddenly came under withering critique. The *Nation* breathlessly reported that a group of congressional staffers had been invited to a screening of *The Dark Knight Rises*—with a portion of "issue education" before the film to satisfy rules governing even small gifts to those with ties to public officials. Lee Fang, "Lobbyists Bribed Congress with a Free Screening of 'The Dark Knight Rises,'" *Nation*, July 23, 2012.

74. Alex Pappas, "Democratic Sen. Pat Leahy Draws Criticism for Cameos in Batman Movies," *Daily Caller*, July 18, 2012.

75. See "Limbaugh's Dark Knight Rises / Romney Conspiracy," Media Matters, July 17, 2012; "Christopher Nolan: 'The Dark Knight Rises' Isn't Political," *Rolling Stone*, July 20, 2012; for the material on Aurora see Sara Burnett and Jessica Fender, "Aurora Shooting Suspect Left Apartment 'Booby-Trapped,' Music Blaring," *Denver Post*, July 20, 2012, and "Aurora Witnesses Describe Shooter's Entrance, Chaos," CBS News, July 20, 2012.

76. Emma Brown, "Daniel K. Inouye, U.S. Senator, Dies at 88," *Washington Post*, December 18, 2012.

77. "The only thing that gave me pause," Leahy said of his sudden promotion to president pro tempore, "is that they sat me down at one of those briefings to get the password I need to get the nuclear codes if all hell broke loose." Given the military's often hysterical approach to his proposed landmine ban, Leahy's potential access to America's most powerful weapons could only be seen as deeply ironic. See Howard Weiss-Tisman, "Vermont's Sen. Leahy Reflects on Life, Career in Washington," *Brattleboro Reformer*, March 16, 2013.

78. Catalina Camia, "Congress Sends Violence against Women Act to Obama," *USA Today*, February 28, 2013.

10. THE HAVANA PROTOCOL

1. In general, the reporting on Leahy's Cuba mission was detailed, sharp, and immediate. Within twenty-four hours, several revealing ticktock accounts had appeared, and this section draws on a few of the best. See Jake Tapper, Eric Bradner, and Deirdre Walsh, "Gross Release: How It Happened," CNN, December 17, 2014; Adam White, "Leahy Recounts 'Surreal' Cuba Trip to Bring Back Gross," *Burlington Free Press*, December 17, 2014; and Nicole Gaudiano, "Leahy Brings Gross Home from Cuba," *USA Today*, December 17, 2014.

2. In fact, Leahy's connection to Raúl Castro's regime had also been strengthened over time by sharing pictures of his grandchildren with Castro, who responded with pictures of his own. See Robert Audette, "Leahy's Multi-Year Mission to Normalize Relations with Cuba," *Brattleboro Reformer*, December 18, 2014.

3. Tapper, Bradner, and Walsh, "Gross Release."

4. Lesley Clark and Anita Kumar, "President Obama Is Now Truly a Lame Duck," *McClatchy Washington Bureau*, November 4, 2014.

5. Max Ehrenfreund, "Your Complete Guide to Obama's Immigration Executive Action," *Wonkblog* (*Washington Post*), November 20, 2014.

6. Julian Zelizer, "The New President Obama," CNN, November 24, 2014.

7. The Cuban Five were arrested in Miami in 1998; they were subsequently convicted of a range of espionage-related crimes. "One of them, Gerardo Hernández, was convicted in 2001 of conspiracy to commit murder in connection with the 1996 shoot-down of two private airplanes dropping anti-regime leaflets." See Michael Crowley's "We Have to Talk: How Obama and Castro Came Together," *Politico*, December 17, 2014.

8. From a series of recollections written by Senator Leahy in response to e-mailed questions from the author, January 4, 2016.

9. Robert Audette, "Leahy's Multi-Year Mission to Normalize Relations with Cuba," *Brattleboro Reformer*, December 18, 2014.

10. Ibid.

11. Ibid.

12. David Rogers, "The Senate's Back-Channel in Cuba Deal," *Politico*, December 18, 2014.

13. Krishnadev Calamur, "Alan Gross' Release: How It Went Down," the Two-Way, NPR.org, December 17, 2014.

14. Erin Lee, "Tim Rieser '76 Helped Shape Cuba Policy Changes," *Dartmouth*, February 27, 2015.

15. On August 12, 2007, Obama was the star attraction at a fund-raiser held in Norwich, Vermont, at the home of Jane and Bill Stetson. Leahy squired the younger senator at that event and stood approvingly by as Obama spoke about the need to negotiate with even hostile regimes like Cuba. It's difficult to recapture the impact of Obama's words, coming as they did on the heels of the Bush administration's outright hostility to the very idea of negotiation itself. But it became a signature feature of his campaign's evolving message of change. "Now, they have been making a big fuss out of the fact that I said I would meet not just with our friends, but with our enemies. And I would do so without preconditions. But you know, they're confusing preparation with preconditions. Of course, I will prepare for these meetings, and I won't pull any punches in the meetings. But that's different from setting preconditions. It doesn't do any good to say, we'll talk to you, but only after you accede to all of our demands. We can't demand that our enemies come to us first as vassal-states. Now, I'll tell you—I'm not worried about losing a PR battle with Kim Jong-il. Because for one thing, I've got a better haircut [laughter]. And for another, I'm not starving my own people. So I think we can handle that PR initiative." From an essay posted August 14, 2007, on my political blog, *Vermont Daily Briefing*.

16. Leahy's quote about writing the pope comes from an interview on MSNBC with Andrea Mitchell, "Senators Leahy, Flake and Van Hollen on the Release of Alan Gross," December 17, 2014. The quote about the pope being an easy sell is taken from Bob Audette's piece, "Leahy's Multi-Year Mission to Normalize Relations with Cuba," *Brattleboro Reformer*, December 18, 2014. And for the fact of the pope's offer

of talks, and delivery of same, see Michael Crowley's "We Have to Talk: How Obama and Castro Came Together," *Politico*, December 17, 2014.

17. Adam White, "Leahy Recounts 'Surreal' Cuba Trip to Bring Back Gross," *Burlington Free Press*, December 17, 2014. I am also working here from Leahy's own reflections, e-mailed to me on January 4, 2016.

18. Gaudiano, "Leahy Brings Gross Home from Cuba."

19. Jill Reilly, "Revealed: How Freed Cuban Spy Got His Wife Pregnant While He Was Still in US Prison," *Daily Mail*, December 22, 2014.

20. Tim Johnson, "Wife of Freed Cuban Spy Gives Birth after Artificial Insemination," McClatchy News, January 7, 2015.

21. The details of this meeting come from Ernesto Londoño's fine *New York Times* piece, "How a Cuban Spy and His Wife Came to Be Expectant Parents," December 22, 2014.

22. See Reilly, "Revealed: How Freed Cuban Spy Got His Wife Pregnant."

23. Londoño, "How a Cuban Spy and His Wife Came to Be Expectant Parents."

24. Tracy Connor and Kate Snow, "'A Human Thing': Senator Says No Politics in Cuban Sperm Deal," NBC News, December 23, 2014.

25. Paris Achen, "Leahy on US Embassy in Cuba: 'Remarkable,'" *Burlington Free Press*, August 17, 2015.

INDEX

Note: Page numbers with *n* indicate endnotes.

blacklist provision, in COICA, 234, 235–36, 238

"blue slip" practices, 126, 130–31, 287n6

Boehner, John, 258

Bogden, Daniel, 294n9

Boston Globe, 284n4

Bowen, Stuart W., 294n1

Boyle, Terrence, 131

Bradley, Kevin, 44

Brown, Jane, 55

Bruhn, Paul, xxiii, xxvi, 50, 53–56, 59, 80, 81–82, 84–85, 91–92, 114

bumper stickers, 129

Bundy, Ted, 37, 278n30

Burlington Free Press: on Aiken and Leahy, 82; on antiwar protests, 42–43; "Children's Crusade," 56; on Gold tragedy, 276–77n20; on Lawrence case, 50; on Leahy, 22, 37, 84–85, 96–97; on *Miranda* procedure meetings, 22; on Sanders, 53, 64; on Senate campaign (1974), 58, 62, 63, 64, 68, 74, 77; Trivento story in, 29, 32; on venereal disease and nude swimming, 38; on Watergate, 61

Bush, George H. W., 108, 174–75

Bush, George W., and Bush administration: on anthrax attacks, 157–58; at bill-signing ceremonies, 6; critics of, xxix; Cuba and, 264; existential characteristic of, 128; on Homeland Security Department, 293n60; Judiciary Committee and, 132; midterm elections (2002), 180–81; Patriot Act and, xx, 143–53; Senate, relations with, 198; US attorney firings by, 197, 294n10; Vermont, antipathy toward, xxx; on War on Terror, 173–74. *See also* Iraq; Leahy, Patrick Joseph, as Bush antagonist

Byrd, Harry, Jr., 94–95

Byrd, Robert, xx, 177

Cadieux, Theresa, 30–31

Caine, Michael, 226, 230

Cambodia, in Vietnam War, 87, 283n22, 284n32

Canada, support for landmine ban treaty, 111

"Candle in the Wind" (John), 118

Canute, King, 145, 289n52

Card, Andrew, 292n42

Carle, David, 138

Carrey, Jim, 218

Cassell, Paul, 131

Castro, Fidel, 263

Castro, Raúl, 262, 263, 265, 303n2

CDC (Centers for Disease Control), xiii, 168

censorship, COICA as, 234, 236

Center for Copyright Information, 237

Centers for Disease Control (CDC), xiii, 168

Central Intelligence Agency (CIA), on Gross, 264

CFSA (Commercial Felony Streaming Act), 244

Chalabi, Ahmed, 178

Chambliss, Saxby, 180

Charlton, Paul, 294n9

Cheney, Dick, xxx–xxxi, 126, 128, 175, 177, 207

Cheney, Kim, 49

Chertoff, Michael, 151, 172

Chiara, Margaret, 294n9

Chicago, in *Batman Begins*, 221–22

"Children's Crusade." *See* Senate campaign (1974)

China, aid to Viet Cong, 92

Chittenden Magazine staff, 55

Christiangallery (web site), xv

Church, Frank, 83

CIA (Central Intelligence Agency), on Gross, 264

Cipro (drug), 157, 160, 162, 273n3

CJS Appropriations Bill (2001), 141

Claridge, Laura, 3

Clark, Oscar, 35

Cleland, Max, 180–81

Clinton, Bill: antilandmine campaign and, 108, 109, 110, 120, 286n41; and congressional rules changes for moving nominees forward, 287n6; Cuban embargo, 264; failed congressional race (1961), 61; former nominees renominated by George W. Bush, 125; nerve-gas factories in Arkansas issue, 62; souring of relations with, after Obama endorsement, 293n57

Clinton, Hillary Rodham, 116, 178, 179, 271, 293n53, 293n57

Clooney, George, 218–19

CNN, 251–52, 262

Cohen, Bruce, 149, 160, 165

color photography, 32, 278n23

Combating Online Infringement and Counterfeits Act (S. 3804, COICA), 232–36

"Combating Terrorism Act" (Hatch/ Feinstein bill), 142–43, 148

Commerce Department, appropriations for, 141

Commercial Felony Streaming Act (CFSA), 244

Communications Decency Act (1996), 235

Concurrent Resolution 133, 176

congenital toxoplasmosis, Leahy's, 4

Congressional Internet Caucus, 234

Congressional Management Foundation, 234

Constitution, Ashcroft on interpretation of, 140

"Contract with America," 109

Coolidge, Calvin, 40

copyright theft. *See* intellectual property rights

Costello, Paul, 276n20

Craigslist, 249

credit card companies, COICA and, 233

Cuban Five, 262, 304n7

Cuba, US and Leahy's relations with, 261–71

Culver, John, 88, 91, 94

Cummins, H. E. "Bud," 190, 194, 198, 294n9

Curran, Rita, 36–38

cybersenator, Leahy as, 235

Daily Caller (newspaper), on Leahy, 256

Dalai Lama, 17

Daly, Robert, 218

Dannehy, Nora, 296n44

Dargis, Manohla, 300n29

The Dark Knight Returns (Miller), 112

Dark Knight trilogy (Nolan), xxi, xxii–xxiii, xxvi, 112, 216–31, 230, 241–44, 253–57, 295n19

Daschle, Tom: anthrax attacks against, xi–xiv, xvi, xvii, xix–xxi, 157–58, 160–61, 169, 208, 209, 210, 213, 215, 298n59, 298n62; Feingold and, 154; Jeffords and, xxix, 127, 129; Patriot Act negotiations, 162, 164, 291n21

Dateline Vermont (Graff), xxvii

Davis, Deane, 41, 279n47, 280n53

DC Comics, xxii, xxvi, xxxi, 12, 112–14, 167, 217, 274n13

Dean, Howard, xxix–xxx

"Death of Innocents: The Horror of Landmines" (O'Neil), 113–14

Defense Department, 114, 212

Demag, Dave, 44, 48, 278n30, 279n43, 279n50

Demand Progress, 254–55, 256

Democratic Steering Committee (Senate), 83, 87, 88

Dempsey, Martin, 284–85n8

Dent, Harvey, 257

Dent, Harvey (fictional character), 257, 299n19

detention powers (attorney general), 146–47, 148

dialed number recorders (pen registers), 146, 289n54

Diana, Princess of Wales, 115–18

Digital Millennium Copyright Act (1998), 300n36

McGovern, Jim, 265

McKay, John, 194, 294n9

media industry, xii, xxii, xxiv, xxvi–xxviii, 54, 59–61, 70–74

Meyer, Barry, 227–29, 231, 232, 255

Miers, Harriet, 186, 296n34

Milbank, Dana, 196, 205–6, 296n40

Milens, Sandy, 55, 76–77

Miles, Harry, 44

military: appropriations process, 90; army's use of landmines, 104; tribunals for enemy combatants, 170, 172; waste and abuse in procurement programs, 294n1. *See also* anti-landmine campaign

Miller, Sam, 63

The Mirage Man (Willman), 214

Miranda v. Arizona, 21, 23–29, 277n9

Montreal Gazette, on Gonzales and Leahy, 193

Moral Majority, 11

Morrill, Justin Smith, 274n11

Motion Picture Association of America (MPAA), 220, 227, 232

movie industry. *See* Hollywood

Mozilla company, 244–46

Mueller, Robert, xiv–xvi, 133, 144, 215, 288n37

Muller, Bobby, 101, 103–11, 119–20, 121

murders, in Vermont, 34, 35–38

Murray, Frank, 46, 48, 279n47

Murray, Patty, 178, 293n55

My Declaration of Independence (Jeffords), xxix, 129

Naramore, Vincent, and Naramore poll, 68–70, 77–78, 281n34

National Intelligence Estimate (NIE), 177–78, 179, 293n53

National Security Council, UN, 288n37

Nation magazine, 303n73

Nelson, Garrison, xxv, 84

nerve-gas strategy, 62–63, 67, 74

net neutrality, 232–36, 238–41, 244–53, 301n43, 302n53

Never Again (Ashcroft), 288n37

New Mexico, claims of voter fraud, 191

Newsom, Eric, 119–20

Newsweek, 278–79n34

New York, anthrax outbreaks in, xii

New York Daily News, 216

New Yorker, 152–53

New York magazine, xxi

New York Post, 162, 216

New York Times, 120–21, 179, 194, 235, 250

NIE (National Intelligence Estimate), 177–78, 179, 293n53

Nixonland, xxix, xxxi

Nixonland (Perlstein), xxviii

Nixon, Richard, xxviii, 33, 53, 61–62, 92, 283n27

Nobel Peace Prize, 120

Nolan, Christopher, 112, 216–17, 219, 228, 230, 253

Northeast Kingdom, Vermont: Leahy's Senate campaign in, 58, 75

North Korea, as axis of evil constituent, 174

nude swimming, 38–40

Obama, Barack: at bill-signing ceremonies, 6; Cuba and, 264, 265, 267, 271, 304n15; final two years as president, 262; on Internet copyright enforcement, 302n60; Leahy's endorsement of, 179, 293n57; We the People petitions and, 246

O'Connor, Sandra Day, 186

O'Neil, Dennis, 112–13

O'Neil, John, 139, 300n26

online piracy. *See* intellectual property rights

Oslo conference (on landmines), 118–20

Ottawa Conference on Anti-Personnel Landmines, 111, 117

Pagano, Ed, xxx, 132, 154, 163, 293n57

Page, Candace, xxiv, 52, 60

Parsons, Marselis "Div," 34–35, 48–49, 169–70, 278n26

Senate campaign (1974), 51–79; announcement of, xxi; campaign film, xxiii, 70–74; Election Day, 74–77; final debate in, 63–68; impact of, 77–79; Leahyites, origins of, 54–59; Leahy's handicaps in, 51–53; media, relationship with, 54; Naramore poll, 68–70; Nixon's impact on, 61–63; success of campaign message, 44; technology and media in, 59–61

senatorial career, 80–97; anthrax attack against, xiv–xvi, xix–xxi, 167–70, 208–16; anti–copyright theft legislation, 231–41, 244–53; antilandmine campaign, 101–22; Armed Services Committee, service on, 88–97; filibuster reform, 276n17; security surrounding, 134; as Senate president pro tempore, 257–59, 273–74n6, 303n77; seniority, xx, 81–87, 273–74n6; USA Patriot Act and, 161–65. *See also* Leahy, Patrick Joseph, as Bush antagonist

Sensenbrenner, Jim, 163

September 11 terrorist attacks: Ashcroft's references to, 170–71; description of, 133–38; impact on Senate deliberations, 142–43; Justice Department's response to, 171; Leahy's visits to sites of, 165–67; negotiations in response to, 143–53; responses to, 138–42. *See also* USA Patriot Act

Seven Days (Vermont arts weekly), on Leahy, 255

sexual psychopaths, 29–30, 32–33

Sherman, Spenser, 257

The Shield (college yearbook), 5

Sigal, Leon V., 101, 108

Simon, Brent, 228–29

Sinclair, Jean-Paul, 278n27

skinny-dipping, 38–40

social media, 246, 249, 250

social networks, origins of Leahyites, 54–59

Sotomayor, Sonia, 231

Soviet Union, in Vietnam War, 87, 92

Speck, Richard, 277n16

Specter, Arlen, 195, 201, 202–3, 206, 215–16

Stafford, Robert, 52, 83, 84, 283n30

State Department, 109, 114, 119, 141, 264, 269

state's attorney of Chittenden County, Leahy as, 16–50; appointment, 13, 19–20; Curran case, 36–38; death threats against, xv; drug task force and Lawrence investigation, 44–50; early work, 20–21; importance of role, xxiii; *Miranda* ruling, implementation of, 22, 132; murder investigations, frequency of, 34–36; public image of, 38, 43; skinny-dipping issue and, 38–40; swearing in ceremony, 15; Trivento case, 17–18, 22–33, 132; Vietnam war protests and, 40–44

Steele, Darin, 208

Stennis, John, 94–96

Stoler, Mark, 89, 282n16, 283n30

Stop Online Piracy Act (SOPA), 244–47, 249–50, 252, 254–55, 302n53

sunset provisions, for USA Patriot Act, 148–49, 155, 163–64

Supreme Court. *See* US Supreme Court

tabloids, use in Leahy's Senate campaign, 57

TechDirt, on PIPA, 238

technology, 59–60, 72, 81, 232, 234–35

television, in Senate campaign (1974), 63–64, 70–74

terrorists, lack of civil rights, 172–73

Texas, comparison with Vermont, xxx, 275n25

This Time, This Place (Valenti), 221

Thomas, Emma, 241

Thurmond, Strom, 116

Tibet, Leahy in, 16–17

Time magazine, xx, 40, 86, 87–88

Time Warner, 254–55, 302–3n71